# CHALLENGE TO THE NATION-STATE

UNIVERSITY OF
**WOLVERHAMPTON**
KNOWLEDGE • INNOVATION • ENTERPRISE

Harrison Learning Centre
City Campus
University of Wolverhampton
St Peter's Square
Wolverhampton WV1 1RH
Telephone: 0845 408 1631
Online Renewals:
www.wlv.ac.uk/lib/myaccount

# Challenge to the Nation-State

## Immigration in Western Europe and the United States

Edited by

# CHRISTIAN JOPPKE

OXFORD UNIVERSITY PRESS

1998

Oxford University Press, Great Clarendon Street, Oxford OX2 6DP
Oxford New York
Athens Auckland Bangkok Bogota Bombay
Buenos Aires Calcutta Cape Town Dar es Salaam
Delhi Florence Hong Kong Istanbul Karachi
Kuala Lumpur Madras Madrid Melbourne
Mexico City Nairobi Paris Singapore
Taipei Tokyo Toronto Warsaw
and associated companies in
Berlin Ibadan

Oxford is a trade mark of Oxford University Press

Published in the United States
by Oxford University Press Inc., New York

British Library Cataloguing in Publication Data
Data available

Library of Congress Cataloging in Publication Data
Challenge to the Nation-State : immigration in Western Europe and the
United States / edited by Christian Joppke.
Includes bibliographical references.
1. United States—Emigration and immigration—Government policy.
2. Europe, Western—Emigration and immigration—Government policy.
3. Citizenship—United States.   4. Citizenship—Europe, Western.
5. Sovereignty.   I. Joppke, Christian.
JV6483.C45   1997   325'.1'09049—dc21   97–31038
ISBN 0–19–829229–5

1 3 5 7 9 10 8 6 4 2

Typeset by Graphicraft Typesetters Ltd., Hong Kong
Printed in Great Britain
on acid-free paper by
Biddles Ltd, Guildford and King's Lynn

*Pour Catherine*

# PREFACE

With the exception of Gary Freeman's contribution (which was commissioned last and arrived first!), all chapters to this volume were originally presented at two workshops on the politics of immigration which took place in December 1995 and January 1996 at the European University Institute in Florence. The road to the meetings, and from the meetings to the book, has been a long one. To get it done, the help of three people was indispensable. Marie-Ange Catotti (not just an alphabetical and lady first) organized the meetings, with a smile and on top of her regular secretarial duties. It is no flattery to say that she gave the best performance of all of us. On the academic side, an anonymous reviewer wrote an acid-sharp report that should have been reprinted here in full splendour. Finally, Yves Mény, Director of the Institute's Robert Schuman Centre, had the idea, provided the funds, and established the contact with Oxford University Press. With such help there was little to add on my part.

Christian Joppke

*San Domenico di Fiesole*
*April 1997*

# CONTENTS

# NOTES ON THE CONTRIBUTORS

**Adrian Favell**, European Research Centre on Migration and Ethnic Relations, University of Utrecht.

**Miriam Feldblum**, California Institute of Technology, Pasadena, and University of San Francisco.

**Gary P. Freeman**, Department of Government, University of Texas at Austin.

**Virginie Guiraudon**, Center for European Studies, Harvard University.

**Christian Joppke**, Department of Political and Social Sciences, European University Institute, Florence.

**Rey Koslowski**, Department of Political Science, Rutgers University at Newark, NJ.

**Saskia Sassen**, Graduate School of Architecture, Columbia University, New York.

**Peter H. Schuck**, Yale Law School.

# Introduction

## CHRISTIAN JOPPKE

Long confined to the specialist discourses of demography, jurisprudence, or public policy analysis, the study of immigration is increasingly related to macro-processes of social change and the transformation of nation-states. This volume assembles some leading scholars of this 'second wave' of macro-orientated immigration studies. It concentrates on two aspects of the nation-state challenged by recent migrations: the sovereignty over entry and expulsion, and unitary membership as citizenship. Separate clusters of scholarship have evolved around both of these aspects. This book attempts to bring them together. Not just an attempt at synthesis, this book also contrasts opposite viewpoints on the state-migration problem. Regarding sovereignty, contrary positions are presented on the impact of globalization on immigration control, and on the kind of constraints (domestic or external) that states face in this policy domain. Regarding citizenship, some authors in this volume take up the recent debate about post-national membership, presenting opposing positions on the question whether post-national membership is a stable alternative to, or temporary deviation from, national citizenship.

My chapter 'Immigration Challenges the Nation-State' is perhaps an unorthodox opening, because it does not just lay out the basic concepts of this volume—sovereignty and citizenship; it also gives a partisan (if, it is to be hoped, not random) interpretation of their resilience in the face of immigration.

Saskia Sassen's 'The *de facto* Transnationalizing of Immigration Policy' (Chapter 2) starts the discussion about challenged sovereignty with a strong claim that economic globalization and the rise of an international human rights regime have fundamentally altered the parameters of immigration control. She argues that the coexistence of diametrically opposed regimes for the circulation of capital and immigrants, the former open and 'denationalized', the latter closed and 'renationalized', cannot be stable. She assembles evidence that the pressures of a globalized economy and international human rights norms and discourses have reduced the autonomy of the state in immigration policy.

Not so, respond Gary Freeman and Christian Joppke. Freeman's 'The Decline of Sovereignty?' (Chapter 3) scrutinizes two hypotheses that often appear jointly in the writings of globalists: the thesis of declining sovereignty, and the thesis of pervasive restrictionism. Freeman argues that there is little empirical evidence for both. Joppke's 'Asylum and State Sovereignty' (Chapter 4) argues similarly that in this most contested field of recent migration pressures there is no evidence that (properly understood) sovereignty is in decline. Moreover, the constraints that states face in asylum policy arise more from domestic than from international legal norms.

Rey Koslowski's 'EU Migration Regimes, Established and Emergent' (Chapter 5) tackles the most prominent example of states trying to find transnational solutions to globalized migration pressures. He points at the paradoxical coexistence of two opposite migration regimes at the level of the European Union: an established regime enabling the free movement of EU nationals within the Union states; and an emergent regime restricting the access of non-nationals to Union territory. For those who stubbornly insist on the principle of state sovereignty (as does the 'neo-realist' mainstream of international relations theory), the development of transnational regimes on that most sensitive and jealously guarded of all state functions—the control over entry and exit—should not have happened at all. But the 'inter-governmental' nature of the emergent European immigration and asylum regime, which leaves the member states in charge, betrays an unwillingness of states to abandon traditional sovereignty.

Peter Schuck's 'The Re-Evaluation of American Citizenship' (Chapter 6) leads us into the second half of this volume, which deals with challenged citizenship. Correcting his own earlier diagnosis of increasingly 'devalued' citizenship, Schuck adduces evidence for a reverse process of 're-evaluation'. Distinguishing between three domains of 'citizenship talk', Schuck traces the roots of the foundational debate on citizenship that is taking place in the United States today. Internationally, global pressures let citizenship appear as an 'anchor' in a disordered world. Domestically, today's citizenship talk reacts to its own past devaluation, which has carried the rights of aliens too far. At the subnational level, Schuck diagnoses a devolution of authority to the states. This opens up an opportunity for 'state citizenship', not as harbinger of a post-national order of things, but as a devious wedge between 'citizens' and 'aliens'.

Discussing recent citizenship policies and debates in western Europe, Miriam Feldblum's 'Reconfiguring Citizenship in Western Europe' (Chapter 7) observes that 'post-national' membership is not the only contender to traditional national membership: there is 'neo-national' citizenship also, in which the quest for closure is transposed to new political entities such as the European Union. Feldblum makes an additional observation: France has recently moved towards restricting its immigrant-friendly *jus soli* citizenship regime, whereas Germany is increasingly liberalizing its blood-based *jus sanguinis* regime, moving towards territorial citizenship. Remember Rogers Brubaker's famous argument, in his *Citizenship and Nationhood in France and Germany* (1992), that national citizenship laws and policies are overdetermined by 'cultural idioms' of nationhood? Not quite so, Feldblum says.

Virginie Guiraudon's 'Citizenship Rights for Non-Citizens' (Chapter 8) injects political science into the analysis of post-national membership (a bit as Gary Freeman has done on the part of challenged sovereignty). Granted the trend towards more rights and benefits for foreign migrants, she asks, how are such rights and benefits actually achieved and implemented, and why are some states more receptive than others to grant such non-citizenship privileges? Post-nationalists have simply stated the existence of a global human rights discourse, and ignored the concrete practices and actors by which they become effective at the domestic level. Comparing the cases of France, Germany, and the Netherlands, Guiraudon suggests a 'policy process' model to explain the domestic expansion of migrant rights. She reaches a disturbing conclusion: containing debate behind the closed doors of government bureaucracy is necessary for securing more rights for immigrants. This is the best-kept secret of post-national citizenship: democracy is not its friend but its enemy.

Adrian Favell's 'Multicultural Race Relations in Britain' (Chapter 9) rounds off this volume with a subtle demystification of 'multiculturalism' in the one European country where it was practised *avant la lettre*, Great Britain. He thus leads us into a discussion of citizenship as an identity rather than as a legal category. Favell points out that the politicization of British Muslims, far from epitomizing multiculturalism-gone-astray, has actually been an exception to the way multiculturalism has normally functioned in Britain. Built around the category of 'race', the British framework of anti-discriminatory policies and recognition of cultural difference has ignored claims based on 'religion'—Muslims *qua* Muslims do not even exist for the British race relations industry. This has been the major cause of Muslim rage in Britain. Favell concludes that British 'multiculturalism in one nation', attuned to integrating its post-colonial immigrants after the Second World War, may have run out of steam. New supranational solutions are needed to integrate refugees, new economic migrants, and non-nationals in general. Alas, no such solution is as yet in sight.

# 1

# Immigration Challenges the Nation-State

## CHRISTIAN JOPPKE

That immigration is a challenge to the nation-state seems to be obvious. If the whole world could move the established configuration of political space, the division of the world into nation-states as 'bordered power-containers' (Giddens 1985: 120) would be washed away. The notion of challenge conceives of immigration as an externally motivated event, with states as passive receivers who are forced to respond. This is a convenient optic, because it justifies the restrictionist rhetoric and policies of border control that currently predominate in the Western world. But it is a distorting optic, because it obscures that the modern state and system of states have helped produce what they seek to contain: international migration. This is, first, a definitional production. Only in a world divided into states is there immigration, which by definition involves a 'transfer of jurisdiction' (Zolberg 1981: 5).[1] But the state has also factually helped produce immigration. In a counterpoint to erecting new linear boundaries, the modern state's principle of territorial rule has liberated the individual from personalistic dependencies of the master–servant type and from the inertia of local community, opening up new spaces of mobility. In addition, states in the plural, locked into a system of similarly constituted units, have created an encompassing communicative grid and regularized interchange of information, resources, and people: there are no more white spots on the landmap. Whereas traditional empires were alone in the world, shielded by border zones beyond which communication was haphazard and erratic, the modern state system has made the world one, and with it immigration as a permanent, structural option.[2] Finally, states have intentionally created migration flows, as labour-recruiting states in the past colonial or more recent guestworker eras. Conversely, most of today's migration of refugees and asylum-seekers stems from the turbulence of nation-state-building on the south-eastern periphery of the modern state system. There seems to be no significant migration episode, past or present, in which states have not had an active, rather than reactive, hand.

Some of the best and most influential social science scholarship on immigration has in fact sought to disturb the north-western complacency of unsolicited south-eastern immigration, identifying the active part of receiving states and societies in the production of immigration flows.[3] However, the notion of challenge to the nation-state is more than convenient rhetoric. As much as modern states have been actively involved in producing immigration, they are also dependent on containing immigration. Sedentariness, not mobility, is their constitutive principle. Fixed to territory, and segmentarily rather than functionally differentiated, states are an archaic anomaly within the organization of modern society, which is based on the principle of non-territorial, functional differentiation (see Bommes and Halfmann 1994). This functional order integrates individuals only in specific respects (e.g. as workers, consumers, or churchgoers), but never in their totality, thus requiring them to be multiply orientated and allied, and in this sense perpetually flexible and mobile. States are an exception to this. They include the individual as a whole and involuntarily by ascription at birth, further expecting her to be attached to just one state among a plurality of similarly conceived states, and not to change this attachment over a lifetime.

This peculiarity is partially rooted in the territorial organization of states. Once the emergence of states switched the reference-point of rule from the personalistic master–servant dyad to the anonymous control of territory, individuals were set free and mobilized to a degree that conflicted with the very exigencies of rule. Once internal feudal barriers to mobility had fallen, the external boundaries of territory had to be controlled more thoroughly. More than that, a form of membership had to be introduced that was more demanding than mere residence. Unlike Schumpeter's classes, states cannot afford to be like buses, always full, but always filled by different people (see Schumpeter 1927/1953: 171). As service institutions, states as buses would be a free-for-all and quickly depleted; as institutions of rule, they would have to communicate orders every day anew, without the guarantee of being heard and understood, and thus they would probably be reduced to brute force. Accordingly, fusing both service and rule aspects, the early modern states within the incipient system of states instituted a predemocratic form of membership in order to distribute responsibility for 'difficult' categories of people, most notably the migrant poor, thus containing the propensity for 'dumping' the undesirables on the other side of the border.[4]

The principle of sedentariness is not only grounded in the stateness, but also in the nationness of modern nation-states. Nations, in their modern form invented by the French Revolution, revalued the membership of modern states as democratic citizenship, while providing a potent justification for the exclusiveness of states. If states were like buses, they could not be nations, historical 'communities of character' (Walzer 1983: 62) with a distinct identity and legitimacy. But their nationness is not just a legitimatory prop for states. As T. H. Marshall (1992: 24) pointed out, the development of citizenship rights was contingent upon 'a direct sense of community membership based on loyalty to a civilization which is a common possession'. The underlying reasoning is straightforward. In a world of scarce resources, rights are costly, and they can never be for the whole world. Spreading rights more evenly requires slashing existing privilege. Historically, the nation was the vehicle to make this possible. This does not mean that no other vehicle could further citizenship, but some communal vehicle probably will have to be, if the costly redistribution of rights and resources is to be justified. This is precisely why immigration is even more jealously rejected by developed welfare states, which would go bankrupt overnight if literally everyone could reap its benefits. Logical but irritating for democratically minded social scientists, the calls for rejecting immigration in nation-states are inherently popular calls, confounding the established left-vs.-right perspective, and unlikely to be silenced by the standard intellectual recipes of more civil society or public participation.

The notion of immigration as a 'challenge' to the nation-state has two possible meanings. It may be taken conservatively as a challenge to be incorporated within the existing framework of nation-states, if only in the absence of an alternative political organizing principle. Or it may be taken progressively as a challenge that points to a fundamental transformation of nation-states. The (analytically) 'conservative' line is pursued in the work of Rogers Brubaker. In his path-breaking reconceptualization of the state as membership association, Brubaker (1992) takes nation-states as independent variable, whose historical legacies explain national variations of incorporating immigrants. This design prevents Brubaker from even considering a reconfiguration of nation-states in response to immigration. Where he takes immigration as independent variable impacting on nation-states, Brubaker (1989) considers the new forms of denizenship or partial state membership as 'deviation' from the 'normal' model of national citizenship, and urges particularly the European immigrant-receiving states to 'transform . . . long-settled immigrants into citizens' (p. 27). The nation-state model is not enthusiastically embraced, but factually accepted in the absence of a viable alternative. 'We lack a developed political theory of partial or limited state-membership,' says Brubaker (p. 5).

To deliver at least empirical rudiments for such a theory is the merit of Yasemin Soysal's (1994) agenda-setting work on post-national membership in Europe, which delivers an (analytically) 'progressive' interpretation of immigration as transforming, rather than reaffirming, the nation-state model. If Brubaker took partial state membership as 'deviation' subject to correction, Soysal takes it as a new form of membership in its own right. Extrapolating from the experience of European guestworkers, who attained a relatively safe permanent resident status without becoming citizens, Soysal argues that rights and identities, formerly fused in the concept of national citizenship, have become decoupled. Legitimized by an international discourse on human rights, the rights component of citizenship is reconfigured as universal rights of personhood, independent of nationality: the rights of Turks in Germany are not contingent on their nationality. In turn, the identity component of citizenship is still territorialized, while immigrant identities are undergoing diasporic transformation and creolization (see Soysal 1996). Somewhat clipping the wings of her post-national utopia, Soysal concedes that nation-states remain the organizational form to implement universal rights of personhood (e.g. guestworker rights): 'The exercise of universalistic rights is tied to specific states and their institutions' (p. 157). Accordingly, she sees the global system characterized by the 'institutional duality' of national sovereignty and universal human rights.

Brubaker's nation-state-defending and Soysal's nation-state-bashing are the extreme poles in a lively debate on immigration and citizenship, which is taken up by some authors in this volume. However, there is a second dimension of nation-states challenged by immigration, which is largely ignored by Brubaker and Soysal but receives equal attention here: sovereignty. The nation-state is a dual concept. *Qua* states, nation-states are territorial organizations characterized by the monopolization of legitimate violence; *qua* nations, nation-states are membership associations with a collective identity and a democratic pretension to rule. The two concepts have different origins, stateness being rooted in the geopolitical transformation of Europe after the Peace of Westphalia and receiving its apotheosis under absolutism, nationness being rooted in the cultural transformation brought about by Protestantism, the rise of vernaculars, and the Enlightenment. Since the two components were fused in the French Revolution, the nation-state has become the universal political organizing principle of the modern world.

Interestingly, the state-related component of nation-states, sovereignty, has not received the same macro-sociological attention in recent immigration scholarship as their nation-related component, citizenship.[5] One of the purposes of this volume is to remedy this shortcoming, and to pay equal attention to the reconfiguration of sovereignty in response to immigration. Before distinguishing in the following between the immigration-based challenges to sovereignty and to citizenship, I wish to concede that this distinction is to a certain degree artificial. Before it was democratically and nationally revaluated, the concept of one uniform membership—subjectship as proto-citizenship—had been carved out by the emergent territorial state, which did away with the multiple and unequal membership forms of the feudal order and made all individuals equal subjects of the monarch.[6] When citizenship had reached its national-democratic form, thus instituting the state-legitimizing formula of national sovereignty, the restrictionist immigration policies of states were everywhere presented as 'national interest' policies, and crafted to protect the social and cultural integrity of the national citizenry.[7] While the citizenship and sovereignty aspects of nation-states are evidently fused and mutually implicated in manifold ways, it is still useful to hold them apart analytically. Indeed, separate lines of immigration scholarship have evolved around each of these two aspects of the nation-state, with little cross-fertilizing attention. International relations specialists and legal scholars have automatically addressed the immigration problem from the vantage-point of challenged state sovereignty.[8] Sociologists and some political scientists have equally automatically tackled immigration from the perspective of challenged citizenship. As Tomas Hammar (1985) suggested in his influential distinction between 'immigration' and 'immigrant' policy, questions of immigration control are indeed separate from questions of immigrant integration. But this volume seeks to foster communication between divided camps and perspectives, and sharpen an awareness that underneath these divisions there is a common object that defies disciplinary pigeon-holing and is best tackled through a pooling of perspectives: the nation-state and its reconfiguration in a world of migration.

## THE CHALLENGE TO SOVEREIGNTY

Illegal immigration, mass asylum-seeking, and, particularly in Europe, the increasing number of legal (family) immigrants despite explicit zero-immigration policies, point to a crisis of immigration control in Western states. In this vein, Cornelius, Martin, and Hollifield (1994*b*) have diagnosed a 'gap' between restrictive policy intention and an expansionist immigration reality. In the following, I call this the 'challenge to sovereignty'. Sovereignty, understood as ultimate control over a bounded territory and populace, has a domestic and international dimension. The true domain of sovereignty is the international state system, in which states are definitionally invested with final authority over 'their' space and people. But note that, in so far as the sovereignty of a state is dependent on the recognition by other states, it is not absolute, even in its home domain of international relations.[9] Domestically, sovereignty is best captured by Max Weber's definition of the state as an institution invested with the monopoly of legitimate violence in a given place and time. However, political sociologists have interestingly preferred to address the domestic state under the labels of state strength, capacity, or autonomy—not sovereignty (see Evans *et al.* 1985). This indicates that, internally, the sovereignty of states is more a matter of degree than of kind. Certainly, only the state can make and enforce collectively binding decisions. But from a domestic angle the state rarely appears as a monolithic actor. Instead, the domestic state is multiply fractured into executive, legislature, and legal system, not to mention party-political or corporatist arrangements between polity and society; federal states are even territorially fractured. In addition, the domestic state coexists with other societal actors and spheres, economic, cultural, and religious, which follow their own logics and imperatives, and over which state authority is structurally limited. Whereas the international state, at least according to classic international law, meets only its own kind, and this as undivided legal persons, the domestic state is enmeshed in exchanges with multiple spheres and actors, and this in internally specified aspects only, rarely as a whole. And whereas the international state is judicially sovereign, equal, and protected by the doctrine of non-intervention, the domestic state is empirically most unevenly developed in various societies, and its capacity to formulate and implement policy and law vary accordingly.[10]

Regarding immigration, which is located precisely at the boundary between domestic and international state, sovereignty is by definition in place as the discretion of states to admit or expel aliens. Again, this discretion is not absolute, even in its international dimension. It is limited, first, by the exigencies of state interdependence, where hostility towards aliens might be taken as an act of inter-state hostility, and, secondly and more recently, by a nascent international law of human rights, which invests individuals with elementary rights that states have to respect. In at least two areas, such rights constraints have matured into customary international law that is binding on states: the principle of non-refoulement, which prohibits states from sending refugees back to states where they would risk torture or death, and the principle of non-discrimination, which prohibits states from not admitting or expelling aliens for blatantly discriminatory reasons, most notably race (see Goodwin-Gill 1978, ch. 5). As Richard Plender (1988: 477) concludes his survey on migration law in the international state system: 'Formerly characterized as aspects of the State's absolute discretion, these powers [over the entry and residence of aliens] are regulated and controlled . . . by a system of rules now sufficiently advanced and cohesive to be described as the international law of migration.'

However, surveying the major statements on international migration law by Goodwin-Gill or Plender, even the non-lawyer is puzzled by their hopeful vagueness and manifold qualifications and concessions. Refugee law is a notorious example, because in this area the degree of codification and bindingness is most advanced. But, as it is codified in the United Nations Universal Declaration of Human Rights, the right of asylum is the right of sovereign states to grant asylum, not the right of the individual to be granted asylum. 'No state', Plender concedes (1988: 415), 'is obliged by current international law to admit to its territory a person who establishes that he is a refugee.' In fact, it couldn't be otherwise, because the state system is 'open at the top' (Poggi 1978: 88), and ultimate enforcement and sanction powers rest with the individual states. This starkly relativizes the stipulated 'international law of migration' (Plender 1988), and it is questionable if a law that is not enforcable is law at all. International migration law is essentially a function of actual state practice, not vice versa, and its constraint on states is the 'soft' constraint not to stray from the norms of 'civilized' conduct in the community of states (see Martin 1989).

What then is the origin of the current 'migration crisis' (Hollifield 1994), which consists of the fact that Western states end up admitting more (*de facto*) immigrants than their restrictive policies would have it? There are two opposite answers to this question, one that stresses external and a second that stresses internal constraints on state sovereignty. In the following, I discuss them as 'globally limited sovereignty' and 'self-limited sovereignty'.

## Globally Limited Sovereignty

It is always a risk in social science discourse to use categories that have been overstretched in public discourse. This is certainly the case with 'globalization', a public term to capture the diffuse *Zeitgeist* of a world becoming one and uncontrollable at the same time.[11] 'Globalization' is a paradoxical term, because it is a spatial term to indicate the increasing irrelevance of space in contemporary social life.[12] If space becomes irrelevant for the flow of capital or information, the territorial state becomes irrelevant too. This is the meaning of globalization in relation to the state: the state, immobile and fixed to a territory, is incapacitated to control hypermobile, deterritorialized economic and cultural flows. The underlying assumption is that in the past economic and cultural transactions had been territorially fixed, and thus controlled by the state. This is a most problematic assumption, because capitalist markets are inherently globalizing and decoupled from territory, while cultural innovations, from the cognitive invention of advanced mathematics in ancient Egypt to the moral invention of universal human rights in the European Enlightenment, had never been limited to their place of birth. Markets and culture in principle do not respect the gravity of territory.

Empirically, Janice Thomson and Stephen Krasner (1989: 198) have shown that there never was a 'golden age of state control', which is the (always implicit) premiss of globalists. Regarding economic transactions, world trade in goods and foreign capital investment only recaptured in the 1970s and 1980s the prominence they had had in mid-nineteenth-century liberal capitalism, but which was interrupted by a century of wars. Regarding the flow of information and people, international travel, mail, and telephone calls have all increased—but so have domestic travel and communication. The technological advances that have reduced international transaction costs have also reduced domestic transaction costs, increasing the 'infrastructural power' (Mann 1986) of the state. Even if one concedes that in economic regard states have lost some of their previous power, particularly regarding the control of financial markets and macro-economic steering due to high capital mobility, globalists overlook that in other dimensions state capacity has increased, particularly regarding the elimination of non-state violence in the international system (Thomson 1994).

Regarding immigration, globalists draw a conflicting picture of diminished state sovereignty. On the one hand, people, especially poor people and refugees, are obviously excepted from the increasingly deregulated flows of capital and information. States are thus depicted as, almost vengefully, controlling even more what is still under their control: people. In this context, Saskia Sassen (1996, ch. 3; and Chapter 2 in this volume) juxtaposes a 'renationalizing' of immigration policies and a 'denationalizing' of economies in the age of globalization, clearly suggesting that restrictionist immigration policies are more rhetorical and symbolic than driven by substantive concerns. On the other hand, globalists depict the symbolic politics of immigration control as undermined by external economic and human rights constraints. Accordingly, Saskia Sassen points out, and not without good evidence, that the co-existence of two contradictory regimes—an open one for capital, and a closed one for immigrants—is inherently unstable, suggesting that the latter will succumb to the exigencies of the former—an example being the strangely invisible liberal immigration regime that is already in place for the élite personnel of the global economy.[13] In addition, Sassen finds state discretion over immigrants curtailed by an emergent international human rights regime. This is a typical argument of globalists, who reduce the nation-state to its sovereignty dimension, and externalize its individual rights dimension to the supranational plane.[14]

Is the diagnosis of externally diminished state sovereignty in immigration control correct? Consider the two examples of illegal immigration in the United States and the failure of European states to halt immigration after the guestworker era. Both examples receive prominent treatment in David Jacobson's globalist treatise *Rights across Borders* (1996, chs. 2, 3). Regarding the US failure to control illegal immigration from Mexico, Jacobson shares the popular perception, sanctioned by the influential Select Commission on Immigration and Refugee Policy, that the United States has 'lost control of its border'. This is a most questionable assumption, because the United States had never controlled its southern land border. The end of the *Bracero* guestworker programme in 1964 and the introduction of a numerical cap on Western hemisphere immigration in the 1965 Immigration Act pushed an established migration network into the shadow of illegality. Illegal immigration is a by-product of the attempt to build a unified, national system of immigration control, not a relapse from a once-successful control (that never was). Trying to explain why the United States cannot control illegal immigration, Jacobson rightly identifies ethnic and economic interest group pressure on immigration policy and a culture of non-discrimination that has discredited the very concept of bounded nationhood.[15] But these long-entrenched domestic causes are peculiarly rejuvenated and externalized as 'transnational ties . . . constrain[ing] the autonomy of the state' (ibid. 71). That ethnic groups and employers have had an expansionist impact on immigration policy is a long-established fact in the United States, no novelty in the age of globalization. The culture of non-discrimination is not rooted in the fact that the United States is no longer 'primarily [an] Anglo society'. Instead, its roots are the civil rights achievements of American blacks, which by means of isomorphism and piracy have become extended to the new, non-European immigrant groups. The rightly diagnosed difficulty of legitimizing bounded nationhood in the contemporary United States is not due to proliferating 'transnational ties', but grounded in America's paradoxical self-description as a non-ethnic 'nation of immigrants', which delegitimizes the necessarily discriminatory nature of effective immigration control. To say that 'the state has lost control of international migration [because of] the transnational ties that have developed . . . between the aliens and their associations and groups in the host society' (ibid.) is tautological. If 'transnational ties' is another word for the presence of immigrants in the host society, it amounts to saying that states accept immigrants because they accept immigrants.

Regarding guestworkers in Europe, Jacobson identifies a similar 'regulatory failure', this time because states were 'unable to induce the . . . "guest workers" to return to their home countries' (p. 27). As in the US case, the questionable yardstick is a 'strong' sovereignty that never was. France and Germany, Europe's major guestworker-receiving countries, had never seriously entertained rotating or repatriating its guestworkers. There was a diffuse, only half-articulated, expectation that the labour migrants would not stay, but never an explicit policy that had 'failed'.[16] Wilhelmine Germany's strict rotation and violent expulsion of Polish migrant workers in the late 1880s and 1890s was due to a unique historical context of imperialist state competition and frantic, belated nation-building (see Brubaker 1992: 128–34). Such measures were never on the cards in the Bonn Republic, or anywhere else in western Europe, where the consequences of war had fundamentally reshuffled inter-state relations and delegitimized nationalism. But the question how and why sojourners became settlers to spin forward new immigration through family ties is still relevant. And again, Jacobson strangely reinterpretes domestic as 'transnational' causes. Domestic pressure by unions, churches, and welfare organizations on behalf of migrants is repackaged as 'transnational ties' between these groups and foreign workers that 'overcame the traditional national pact between state and nation' (Jacobson 1996: 38). If the emphasis is on 'transnational', the argument is again tautological: states accept immigrants because they accept immigrants. If the emphasis is on domestic group pressure, state sovereignty is internally, not externally, diminished. To the degree that a transnational resource helping migrants is identified, Jacobson points to international human rights norms and treaties (ibid., ch. 4). But the residence and family rights of French and German guestworkers had a much more profane basis: domestic constitutions protecting elementary human rights, independent of citizenship. [17]

As this brief discussion suggests, the diagnosis of globally limited sovereignty suffers from two problems. First, it rests upon a questionable premiss of 'strong' sovereignty that never was, or that existed only in brief moments in the development of modern states. Secondly, it fails to identify concrete 'transnational' causes of diminished sovereignty. If 'transnational' is another word for the presence of foreigners in the receiving society, the argument is circular. If 'transnational' refers to international human rights norms, conventions, and treaties, the onus is to show their empirical impact. Globalists have failed to do so. They correctly point to judicial–constitutional constraints of state sovereignty regarding immigration control.[18] But, as I suggest in the following, these constraints are domestic, not inter- or transnational constraints.

## Self-Limited Sovereignty

Globalists have not answered the question why Western states end up admitting more immigrants than their restrictionist rhetoric would predict. Globalists are strongest in identifying the factors that mobilize would-be immigrants at the periphery of the world system: the presence of multinational corporations in the remotest parts of the world, information and cultural images of first-world riches more widely diffused, and the availability of cheap and fast mass transport technologies (see Sassen 1988). If a more ambitious argument is made about the constraints on states by universal human rights norms, globalists face the problem that these constraints are most unevenly distributed across the state system. A comparison with the immigrant-receiving states of the Middle East, which prohibit labour migrants from acquiring property and settling down, and which practise routine mass expulsions, would show—shocklike—the specificity of Western states in accepting immigrants (see Weiner 1995: 80–3). This specificity of the West by definition cannot be grasped within the space-indifferent logic of globalization.

An alternative explanation of the generosity and expansiveness of Western states towards immigrants turns to domestic factors. In the following, I discuss two of them: a political process under the sign of 'client politics' (Freeman 1995*a*), and a judiciary invoking constitutional norms to protect immigrants.

## Client Politics

A deficit of much scholarship on immigration policy is the absence of explanatory political science. There have been few attempts to clarify the logic of immigration policy within the political process of liberal democracies, and how this logic might differ across states.[19] A giant step in this direction has been made by Gary Freeman (1995*a*), who has interpreted the logic of immigration policy as 'client politics'. Freeman starts from the premiss that, contrary to the widespread rhetoric and stereotype of 'restrictionism', the politics of immigration in liberal democracies is in fact 'broadly expansionist and inclusive' (p. 881). To explain this, he identifies two features of immigration that condition its processing in liberal democracies: the costs of immigration are highly diffused and invisible, whereas its benefits are concentrated and tangible. This is a constellation in which—according to J. Q. Wilson's (1980) original notion of client politics—the exigencies of collective action favour the organized recipients of concentrated benefits over the non-organized bearers of diffuse costs. Not the uninformed, non-mobilized, and tendentially restrictionist public, but the expansionist 'organized public' of employers, ethnic groups, and civil rights advocates comes to shape immigration policy in liberal states: 'The typical mode of immigration politics . . . is client politics, a form of bilateral influence in which small and well-organized groups intensely interested in a policy develop close working relationships with officials responsible for it. Their interactions take place largely out of public view and with little outside interference. Client politics is strongly oriented toward expansive immigration policies' (p. 886). Freeman adds that the expansionist thrust of immigrant policy in liberal states is further backed by a 'strong antipopulist norm', which prohibits political élites from addressing the ethnic or racial complexion of immigrants. Finally, except cross-national variations due to the timing and institutionalization of immigration, the same basic logic of anti-populist client politics is said to be in place in the English-speaking settler societies, European states with post-colonial and guestworker immigration, and the new immigrant-receiving states of southern Europe.

This simple model states a paradox. The immigration policies of liberal states, while notionally 'national interest' policies and emphatic expressions of national self-determination, are in reality 'special interest' policies, crafted in remote bureaucratic arenas. But is the model correct? It has instantly provoked a lively discussion. Rogers Brubaker (1995) responded that the generosity and expansiveness of immigration policy in Western states cannot be derived from generic features of liberal democracy, but requires a more period-specific and contextual explanation. Pointing out that immigration politics in western Europe has become 'chronically populist' recently, Brubaker suggests that anti-populist 'constraints on legitimate discourse are conjunctural features of particular discursive fields', and not grounded in liberal democracy as such (pp. 908, 906). To which Freeman (1995*b*) replied, with some suggestive force, that in his Tocquevillian view democracy is not just a structure but an ethos—once the values of equality and individualism have taken hold, as they unmistakably have in the post-nationalist democracies after the Second World War, they are most difficult to reverse. Striking a similar chord to Brubaker's, Ted Perlmutter (1996) remarked that the stipulated 'depoliticization' of immigration is less pervasive than Freeman would have it. Only if strong party leaders control the political agenda in relatively unitary polities will immigration be taken off the political agenda and proceed according to the logic of client politics. Pointing to the examples of Germany and Italy, Perlmutter argues that in multiple party and federalist polities there is a chronic incentive to politicize immigration, in often inflammatory and blatantly populist ways.

Freeman's model of immigration policy as client politics is an excellent starting-point for theoretically driven comparisons across Western states. The model works best in settler societies like the United States, where immigration coincided with nation-building and is deeply entrenched as a recurrent, infinite process. In western Europe, where immigration post-dated nation-building, it is less well entrenched and looked at as a historically unique, non-recurrent event. In Great Britain, where immigration policy was from the start a restrictive policy to shut down unsolicited post-colonial immigration, immigration policy never was client politics. In France and Germany, immigration policy was client politics only temporarily, during the classic guestworker recruitment period from the late 1950s to the early 1970s. This period ended with the recruitment stop imposed during the first oil crisis, which signalled the end of the post-war economic boom. After 1973 immigration policy in Germany and France was no longer expansive 'client' but (notionally) restrictionist 'national interest' politics.

The interesting question, which cannot be answered within Freeman's political process model, is why and how notionally restrictionist policies were undermined by an expansionist reality, with the immigrant populations in western Europe not only not diminishing but increasing. A major reason for post oil crisis expansionism is the emergence of an activist judiciary invoking constitutional norms to curtail the restrictionist policy intentions of the executive.

### Constitutional Politics

Martin Shapiro and Alec Stone (1994) observed that constitutional judicial review, long considered a North American speciality, has struck deep roots in post-war Europe, particularly regarding human rights protection. Immigration is a prime, yet severely under-studied, example of the rise of constitutional politics. All Western constitutions, epitomized by the French Declaration of the Rights of Man and Citizens (in that order!), contain a catalogue of elementary human rights, independent of citizenship, which are to be protected by the state and thus limit its discretionary power. Universal human rights are an invention not of the United Nations in 1945, but of liberal nation-states in the late eighteenth century. Certainly, such rights were originally meant to protect the members of a state from a despotic executive, reflecting their historical origins in the intra-state revolution against absolutism. That they could also protect foreigners against a state now acting on behalf of a democratic nation was not foreseen. International migrations have driven a wedge between the two principles of nation-states: popular sovereignty and human rights. Insisting on these rights is not 'democratic', but 'humanitarian'.[20] The legal system, not civil society, is the key protective institution for immigrants.

The legal system is also the true domain of self-limited sovereignty. As stated most succinctly by the German legal scholar Josef Isensee

(1974), self-limited sovereignty means that states have discretion in allowing or rejecting the entry of aliens; but, once admitted, an alien enjoys the equal protection of the law, and the state has 'self-limited' its capacity to dispose of her at will. It is important to see that on-entry sovereignty and subsequent self-limitation are differently developed in different states. In the United States, on-entry sovereignty is solemnly enshrined in the plenary power doctrine, which stipulates that the regulation of entry and exit of aliens is the domain of the political branches of government, and unreviewable by courts. In Germany, until the asylum reform of 1993, even on-entry sovereignty had been self-limited by a constitution that guaranteed a subjective right of asylum. The self-limitation after entry is most developed in states with written constitutions, where independent courts control the executive by means of judicial review. In Britain, with no written constitution and deferential courts, there is very little self-limitation of the state, which explains its exceptionally effective immigration control policies.

Germany is an extreme example of self-limited sovereignty. Not the political process, as Freeman (1995*a*) would predict, but the legal process is key to Germany's expansiveness towards immigrants. The Foreigner Law of 1965 originally endowed the executive with nearly total discretion over granting residence permits to guestworkers, while not regulating at all crucial areas such as family reunification. In the face of decades of legislative inattention to remedy these shortcomings, administrative and constitutional courts stepped in to stabilize the precarious status of guestworkers. Invoking the human rights catalogue of the Basic Law, a series of landmark decisions by the Constitutional Court established, first, that the executive could not deport aliens at will, because they had 'liberty rights' protected by Article 2(1) of the Basic Law; secondly, that the previous routine granting of temporary residence permits created a constitutionally protected 'reliance interest' on the part of the alien in permanent residence; and, thirdly, that following Article 6 of the Basic Law aliens had (conditional) rights of family reunification (see Neuman 1990). As the legal scholar Gunther Schwerdtfeger (1980) postulated, even the Basic Law distinction between citizen rights and human rights was moot. With the alien's increasing length of residence, the rights originally reserved to Germans (such as the rights of association, free movement and residence, and choice of occupation) must also be opened up to the alien, because she now had nowhere else to go (*Rechtsschicksal der Unentrinnbarkeit*). The message of these legal opinions and court rules is clear: contrary to the

official policy that Germany was 'not a country of immigration', she
had become a country of immigration for constitutional reasons alone.

Domestic client and constitutional politics better explain the generosity and expansiveness of Western states towards immigrants than
the vague reference to a global economy and an international human
rights regime. The sovereignty of states regarding immigration control
is more internally than externally restricted. This does not mean that
global processes are irrelevant. After the war, epitomized by the Tokyo
and Nuremberg war crime tribunals that persecuted 'crimes against humanity' and by the UN Universal Declaration of Human Rights, human
rights advanced as a powerful moral constraint on judicial sovereignty
in the inter-state system, which for the first time had to recognize individuals, and not just states, as carriers of rights and duties (see Henkin
1990). But this meant externalizing a principle that liberal nation-states
had long adhered to, human rights. While some of the legitimatory
discourse of human rights has thus been relocated to the international
plane, the concrete mechanisms of realizing and enforcing them rests
with nation-states. A fully satisfying explanation of limited sovereignty in a world of migration would have to consider the interplay of
domestic and global processes, where the ceremonial concessions of
sovereign states create path-dependent 'soft' constraints that limit their
discretion in the next round.[21]

## The European Union and Sovereignty

What started as a modest regional trade regime, the European Coal
and Steel Community, has taken on features that strikingly resemble
the dialectic of nineteenth-century European state formation: internal
barriers to the movement of persons, capital, and goods are removed,
while new external frontiers—the fabled 'Fortress Europe'—are being
erected. Accordingly, there are two opposite migration regimes in the
European Union, an open one for intra-European migration, and a closed
one for inter-European migration (see Koslowski, Chapter 5 in this
volume). But the configuration of these migration regimes deviates from
the classic model of sovereignty, and epitomizes the emergence of a
post-nation-state 'system of overlapping authority and multiple loyalty'
(Bull 1977: 245). The intra-European migration regime is entrusted to
the supranational key institutions of the European Union, the European
Commission and the European Court of Justice, and thus removed from
the control of member states. The nation-states constituting the European

Union are no longer free to admit or reject foreigners from other member states. This is a remarkable novelty in the history of the international state system. However, regarding the entry and exit of third-state nationals, the sovereignty of European nation-states is uncurtailed. The fledgling inter-European migration regime is only a so-called 'intergovernmental' arrangement, in which the heads of national governments are in the driver's seat.

Both European migration regimes are dominated by opposite philosophies and epistemic communities. The intra-European regime stands under the sign of universal human rights. In its comfortable view from Brussels the secretive Trevi, Dublin, and Schengen efforts of external border fortification appear as a disgusting relapse into a bygone era of sovereign states. Indeed, the inter-European regime stands under the opposite sign of internal security. This is epitomized by including immigration control into the so-called 'Third Pillar' of the Maastricht Treaty, in which the member states are called upon to co-operate more closely in the combat against illegal immigration, drug-trafficking, and international terrorism. From the less comfortable view of national interior ministries, who are in charge of Third Pillar co-operation, this is still a Hobbesian world with borders that have to be policed properly.

There have always been two types of state border: the perfunctorily controlled borders between similarly developed 'friendly' states, say Germany and Switzerland, and the problematic borders that separate the First from the Third World, say the United States and Mexico. The European Union, which comprises the developed core of Europe, has swallowed all of its harmless borders and is left with exclusively problematic external borders that separate developed from significantly less-developed regions, say an enlarged European Union from Russia. It is hard to see how such borders can be anything less than the heavily policed borders of a fortress. The inter-European migration regime is national immigration control writ large. Since no European state has been actively recruiting immigrants in the past twenty-five years, the inter-European regime cannot but be a negative, control-orientated, zero-immigration regime. The critique of Fortress Europe is a mirage, based on the false expectation that with the crumbling of boundaries in Europe state boundaries would crumble everywhere.

From our perspective of nation-state challenges, the human-rights-orientated intra-European migration regime is of considerably more interest. Even outside the EU nexus, human rights codification and implementation has reached a level that is unparalleled in the world.

The (non-EU) European Convention of Human Rights, set up in the rubble of a continent destroyed by war and genocide, is the only human rights treaty with its own jurisdiction whose decisions are binding on signatory states. This has carried the winds of constitutional human rights protection even into countries without such principles, most notably Britain. Britain, where archaically undivided sovereignty rests in a parliament that grants or withdraws rights as it sees fit, has repeatedly been forced to adjust 'racially' or 'sexually' discriminatory immigration policies to European standards (see Storey 1994). The mellowing impact of EU law on Britain's strict immigration control was first felt in the European Court's *Surinder Singh* decision of 1992, which exposed that under EU law British (naturalized immigrant) citizens have more family rights than under British law. Here we seem to have a prime example of an inter- or transnational human rights regime putting brakes on nasty, little nation-states.

This poses the double question how typical or exceptional both Britain and the European Union are. Regarding the first, Britain is the only country in Europe without a written bill of rights, which is a superb irony considering England's invention of modern constitutionalism (see Poggi 1990: 54–7). European pressure seems to be the trick to give Britain what all modern states have, a written constitution.[22] The second question of European exceptionalism is more difficult to answer. There is an academic turf war raging between 'intergovernmentalists' and 'neo-functionalists' over the nature of the European Union, overblown regional trade regime or supranational state, and opinions differ if the Union strengthens or weakens the nation-state.[23] An emergent consensus suggests that the truth is in between. The peculiarity of Europe is still best captured by Hedley Bull's (1977: 245–6) metaphor of 'new medievalism', which denotes a multi-tiered polity with multiply fractured and divided sovereignty and allegiances. In some areas, most notably the economy, EU states have lost authority, only to gain strength in other areas, such as welfare provisions.[24] Regarding immigration, EU states seem to have won and lost authority at the same time.

Is the European Union showing the world the image of its future? Those high on globalization answer with a loud Yes. In this optic, Europe's 'multiperspectival polity' foreshadows the rise of other 'multiperspectival institutional forms' that are better suited to cope with the deterritorialized transactions and spillovers in a global world (Ruggie 1993: 174). Philippe Schmitter (1991: 16) argued similarly that the modern state is 'being undermined and overreached' everywhere, and that in an emergent Post-Hobbesian Order similar 'intermediate forms of domination', combining elements of markets and states in a sort of neo-corporatism writ large, would mushroom around the world. If one looks at Europe's own south-eastern backyard, such reasoning appears wishful (see Brubaker 1996a). As Michael Mann (1993) pointed out, in the global picture the nation-state is 'still maturing', not dying. Europe's new political institutions of divided, confused sovereignty are better seen as a 'response to a particular regional situation' (p. 137), not a blueprint for the world. If Europe is exceptional, its supranational human rights monitoring of nation-states is exceptional as well, calling for a regionally specific, rather than globalist, explanation.

## THE CHALLENGE TO CITIZENSHIP

The multiplication of membership categories, which goes along with the rise of post-national membership, and the resistance of immigrants to assimilate, which is expressed in multicultural identity politics, point to a crisis of citizenship in Western states. In the classical model, citizenship is both a legal status and an identity, fusing the divergent legacies of territorial stateness and republicanism.[25] From the subjectship of the absolutist state, citizenship inherited the features of immediacy—no estate or corporate allegiance should stand between the individual and the state; personality—the state was a membership association whose complex, reciprocal infrastructure was too demanding to rely on mere birth on territory or residence; continuity and exclusivity—the relationship between individual and state was so intense as not to be changed over a lifetime, and not to be divided between several states at the same time; and effectiveness—the state rewarded such demanding commitment on the part of the individual with her physical and social protection (see Grawert 1973: 213–46). In the French Revolution, this statist legacy was fused with the republican legacy of a self-governing political community of free and equal citizens. Citizenship now took on the identitarian dimensions of being sacred, national, and democratic (see Brubaker 1989: 3–4).

It is easy to see that contemporary immigration with its dual implications of post-national membership and multicultural identity politics must be a profound challenge to every component of the classical model of citizenship. The component of immediacy is undermined by reinserting ascriptive, intermediary allegiances between individual and state, as in models of 'differentiated citizenship' (Young 1990) or 'multicultural citizenship' (Kymlicka 1995). If mere residence qualifies for membership, the idea of the citizenry as a non-random, personal membership association is relativized. The very fact of immigrating, often with the effect of acquiring double membership, defies the expectation that state membership should be continuous and exclusive. If effective physical and social security is available already to resident aliens, citizenship is being devalued.[26] Regarding citizenship as an identity, the investment of one's emotive allegiances and loyalties in the subnational, deterritorialized categories of ethnicity and race revoke the abstractions from one's communal and natural ties that have historically underpinned 'civic' life, thus cutting off the ties that bind the members of a state.[27]

In the following, I distinguish between the challenge to citizenship as a legal status, which is associated with the rise of post-national membership, and the challenge to citizenship as an identity, which is associated with multicultural identity politics. Regarding post-national membership, the central question is if such denizenship is an irregularity subject to correction, or a new membership form in its own right.[28] Contrary to Soysal (1994), I suggest that the former is the case. Regarding multiculturalism, whose popularity as a political fighting term is not matched by its clarity as a concept, I limit myself to a delineation of its origins and meanings, while comparing its different incarnations in western Europe and the United States.

### *Post-national Membership*

Political sociology has traditionally taken citizenship in its Marshallian sense as a progressing, if contested, set of rights that saved the individual from the vagaries of capitalism. Brubaker's blow to this 'progressive' view of citizenship was to rediscover the 'conservative' function of citizenship as a mechanism of closure, which is the legacy of the pre-democratic, absolutist state. This closure function of citizenship had to escape Marshall, who was writing in an era of frozen nationalisms and domestic welfare state expansion, and could come to view only for a contemporary of welfare state retrenchment and renewed international migration. However, as an emergent school of post-Brubakerian citizenship analysts points out (Soysal 1994; Jacobson 1996), citizenship proved to be a most imperfect mechanism of closure, considering that many of the new immigrants settled for the lesser status of permanent resident alien or denizen, which still allowed them to reap most of citizenship's fruits—most notably civic and welfare rights.[29] These post-Brubakerians thus return to Marshall's focus on citizenship as an evolving set of rights, while stripping them of the formal status of citizenship. Migrant rights are rights of 'personhood', argues Yasemin Soysal (1994, ch. 8), still implemented by states, but legitimized by a supranational discourse of universal human rights.

A striking feature of post-national membership analysts is their combination of explanation and (implicit) advocacy. As implicit advocates, they carry the torch of internationalism in a post-socialist era. More concretely baffling is their positive reinterpretation of the guestworker experience, transforming the vice of second-class membership into a virtue. As Michael Walzer (1983: 62) objected to a frozen guestworker status, 'no community can be half-metic, half-citizen and claim that its admissions policies are acts of self-determination or that its politics is democratic'. Post-national membership advocates slight the exclusion of denizens from the political community of the nation-state, because the latter is deemed irrelevant in an age of globalization. 'We are Berlin', the multicultural slogan promoted by Berlin's Foreigner Office, epitomizes Soysal's vision of a post-national world, in which the local and the global have swallowed the national: 'The trajectory of "being part of Berlin" precludes national fixities and allows for shifting categories and fluid confines, and thus can traverse multiple borders' (Soysal 1994: 166). This is as evocative as it is vague. It depicts the world as a neighborhood, with fluid and self-chosen attachments. But, as Michael Walzer (1983: 39) objected, 'neighborhoods can be open only if countries are at least potentially closed'. The exclusion from this larger unit, still the nation-state, leaves denizens as vulnerable second-class members, which is hard to reconcile with the democratic principle of equal rights.

The analysis and implicit advocacy of post-national membership can be criticized along at least four lines. First, it elevates the fringe into the core experience. Immigration touches only the margins of society. It does not stir up the national order of things. Most people do not migrate. For the majority national citizenship remains a meaningful, even ever more relevant, anchor in a disorderly world (see Schuck, Chapter 6 in this volume). This is trivial, but bears repeating. Post-national membership advocates suffer from professional myopia— they fail to see their subject in proportion. Perhaps they even write

their own experience large. As courted young sociologists and political scientists, they belong to a small élite of global academics who
move comfortably between continents and conferences. Citizenship is
neither empowering nor excluding them. They are truly 'post-national
members' of a global circuit. But most people do not live like this.
Even the guestworkers in Europe, the academic élite's post-national
fellows at the bottom, are only a small fraction of the populace,
rarely exceeding the 10 per cent mark (if EU nationals are subtracted,
they are even less).[30] And they are a dying species, because no
European country seems poised for a second wave of guestworker
immigration.

Secondly, and more substantially, post-national membership analysts
draw a wrong dualism between nation-states and individual rights. The
protection of individual rights is an inherent feature of nation-states
*qua* liberal-constitutional states. It does not meet them as an external
imperative. The 'discourse' of global human rights principles is a most
feeble substitute for enforceable municipal rights, which were and are
the main resource for guestworkers-turned-settlers. It is true that there
are international rules and norms that integrate the 'society of states'
(Bull 1977). But they have been around since the inception of the
modern state system; they are no novelty of a world undergoing globalization. Only during brief periods of 'official nationalism' (Anderson
1991, ch. 6), and in extreme situations like war, were they undercut
by hypertrophied sovereignty. Soysal (1994: 132–3) rightly juxtaposes
the harsh repatriation and expulsion measures of Wilhelmine Germany
with the more mellow integration of guestworkers in post-war democratic Germany. Why this difference? Certainly, universal human rights
was the background noise that helped install strikingly similar denizenship provisions across European states (ibid., ch. 7). But more immediately, nation-building concerns and nationalism no longer stood in
the way of unfolding the individual rights component of uniformly
liberal-constitutional states. In the German case, the extended human
rights guarantees in the Basic Law were a very concrete response to
the Nazist past, which more than any 'global' constraint compelled
Germany to act differently this time around. In essence, the civic and
social rights of post-national members are grounded, first, in the
modern rule of law, which allows no distinctions on the basis of race,
ethnicity, and (in certain respects) nationality; and, secondly, in the
residence- rather than nationality-based inclusion principle of the welfare state, whose boundaries are in important respects drawn differ-

ently from those of the nation-state (see Bommes and Halfmann 1994). If the pressure of human rights meets nation-states from the outside, post-national membership analysts face the problem that this pressure is more urgently felt in the West than elsewhere. Soysal (1994: 156) sees the problem that an allegedly global process is regionally concentrated, but sidesteps the logical conclusion that domestic factors must be more prominent to a generous guestworker reception than her post-national scheme would have it.

This points to the third weakness of the post-national membership model, its lack of a spatial marker. This is inherent in its globalist and generalizing thrust. But it is no accident that this model is mostly about western Europe. These are ethnic nation-states that have readily embraced and incorporated international human rights norms and treaties, not least because this allowed them to leave their culturally demanding, exclusive citizenship schemes intact. Germany has elevated the dualism of guestworker inclusion and national exclusion into an artform. In her comparison of 'national models' of immigrant integration, Dominique Schnapper (1994: 136–7) observed that the delegitimization of nationhood in post-war Germany conditioned a non-national, socioeconomic form of integration. From this optic, post-national membership is Germany's 'national model' of integrating immigrants. This allowed the (West) German state to concentrate its explicitly national aspirations to the subjugated German diaspora in the communist East, as whose homeland the pre-unity Bonn Republic defined itself. Such a spatially concrete perspective could be prolonged, and modified, to each west European country, in which nationhood was fundamentally shaken up and reconfigured as a political organizing principle after the caesura of war and Nazism. By the same token, post-national membership must be a very awkward concept for American ears. The low entry thresholds into a non-ethnic, politically constituted immigrant nation obliterated the creation of second-tier membership. There are no 'post-national members' in the United States, only permanent resident aliens who have not yet naturalized. Hispanics, especially Mexican Americans, are an exception to the routine disposition to naturalize, and their hesitation requires a specific explanation—the contiguity of territory, which allows multiple returns and feeds the illusion (or reality) of only temporary migration; the colonial legacy in the American South-West; a restrictive Mexican property law; etc.[31] Most importantly, a *jus soli* birthright citizenship guarantees that there will never be post-national members in the second generation. In sum, post-national membership analysts

have failed to look at spatial variations that would force them to rela-
tivize their globalist, generalizing claims.

Fourthly, the post-national membership model lacks a temporal
marker. While it has a clear beginning—the post-war period—post-
national membership is conceived of as having no end. The temporary
turmoil caused by a historically finite immigration episode, and the
historically specific adjustment of states to this challenge, are over-
drawn into a fundamental transformation of nation-states. Certainly,
all historical ruptures come in concrete episodes, whose significance
is often realized only after the fact. But it is unlikely that the guestworker migrations after the Second World War mark such a rupture
in the evolution of nation-states. They occurred against a backdrop of
weakened nationhood as a political ordering principle in post-war
Europe, but did not open the door into a post-national beyond. It is
important to point out that, independent of the academic stance taken,
the actual immigrant-receiving societies have treated post-national membership as an intolerable anomaly. In Germany, there is no political
actor today, including the *de facto* immigrants themselves, who do not
consider the permanent exclusion of second- and third-generation foreigners from the citizenry via *jus sanguinis* as a serious deficit. For
post-national membership advocates, the current movement, overwhelmingly supported by the moderate conservative to left-liberal spectrum,
in favour of lowered naturalization hurdles and *jus soli* citizenship for
third-generation immigrants must be utterly incomprehensible. Denizenship is not celebrated; it is detested. Similarly, in the United States, the
recent Congressional movement for restrictive immigration policies,
which includes cutting welfare benefits even for legal immigrants, has
demonstrated the inherent political vulnerabilities of non-citizens. The
current rush for US citizenship may be instrumentally motivated, but
it points to the unbroken vitality of traditional national citizenship. Only
if post-national membership advocates could show that such membership is a recurrent, transmittable, and positively valued status with its
own institutional apparatus would it be a viable alternative to national
citizenship. As long as there is no supranational or even world polity,
there is no alternative to national citizenship.

Post-national membership is parasitical on nation-states, because it
requires them for the provision of rights and benefits, without doing
much to regenerate them. As Raymond Aron (1974: 642) pointed out
in his rejection of the idea of multinational citizenship, 'one person's
right . . . implies a duty on the part of somebody else'. This duty must

be both legitimized and enforced. The nation-state did both, *qua* nation legitimizing costly rights and redistribution for disadvantaged fellow citizens, and *qua* state enforcing them if necessary. Short of an alternative apparatus of providing and implementing rights and benefits, the legitimacy of rights and benefits for non-citizens is chronically precarious. Non-citizenship is tolerable in the interim, but not in principle.

Hedley Bull (1977, ch. 4) pointed out that order and justice are incompatible principles in world politics. The state system is built on the principle of order, not justice. Justice is possible only within, not between, states. Justice in the sense of human rights must be an element of disorder in the state system: 'for if men have rights, which other states or international authorities may champion, there are limits to [the state's] authority; and if men have duties, to causes or movements beyond the state of which they are citizens, the state cannot count on their loyalty' (p. 80). Post-national membership advocates champion a cosmopolitan sense of justice that conflicts with the way the world is set up. Hedley Bull dryly concluded that order was more important than justice, because it was the 'condition of the realisation of other values' (p. 93). Unless it solves the problem of order, post-national membership must remain either utopian or an anomaly within a world of nation-states.

### Is European Citizenship Post-National Membership?

Yasemin Soysal (1994: 148) has argued that European citizenship is 'postnational membership in its most elaborate legal form'. Is she right? Prima facie yes, because in the absence of a Euro-nation, membership of the European Union does not signify nation membership. It derives its legitimacy from supranational norms and discourses (like free movement and non-discrimination), while its implementation is assigned to the member states. However, European citizenship is subsidiary and complementary to, not substitutive of, national membership. Created in the 1991 (Maastricht) Treaty on European Union, the purpose of European citizenship is to 'strengthen the protection of the rights and interests of the nationals of its member states' (quoted in Soysal 1994: 148). If Turks could acquire a safe resident status in Germany, this was not premissed on and indifferent to their Turkish nationality. In this sense, their status as settled guestworkers *is* post-national membership. If the French have become citizens of the European Union after Maastricht, this is because of their French nationality.

This is a decisive difference, because it shows that European citizenship is not decoupled from but premissed on a person's nationality. Only the nationals of member states are Euro-citizens. As Marco Martiniello (1994: 35) notices in dismay (because at heart a post-nationalist no less than Soysal), 'Citizenship of the European Union does not break the association between citizenship and nationality but renews it in a slightly different way.'

In Ulrich Preuss's (1996: 28) nice analogy to the US Supreme Court's characterization of US citizenship, European citizenship serves the goal to remove 'from the citizens of each state the disabilities of alienage in the other states'. But whereas US citizenship helped to fuse a collection of independent states into a nation, the trajectory of European citizenship is much less clear. A classic spillover from the economic core of the European project, the notion of Euro-citizen was launched just when the legitimacy of the emergent European polity was at its nadir, as remedy to the latter's notorious 'democratic deficit'. Assigning the insignia of nation-states, along with a flag and a hymn, to the fledgling European Union only attests to the tyranny of the old state model, and deflects from the inherent novelty of the former. As Ulrich Preuss concludes, European citizenship is 'as novel, unprecedented, imperfect, and evolving as this very European Union itself' (p. 26). It certainly defies a neat categorization into a grander scheme of things, national or post-national.

European citizenship would become post-national membership if the non-citizen immigrants residing in the member states would get it too. But currently the right of free movement, settlement, and work in other member states—the substantial core of European citizenship—is reserved to the nationals of member states. The 'anti-racist' and 'internationalist' impetus of the European project focuses precisely on these immigrant outcasts, whose cause is carried by a plethora of Union institutions and non-governmental organizations, like the European Migrants' Forum. The prospects for endowing non-citizen immigrants with European citizenship are at present difficult to gauge. It could in principle happen. But if it happens, it will touch only the fringe, not the core of the European project.

## *Multiculturalism*

As T. H. Marshall (1992: 25) pointed out, the development of citizenship rights both depended on and reinforced the development of 'modern national consciousness'. In this sense, citizenship is not only a legal, but also a cultural concept. As a cultural concept, citizenship refers to identities and practices in which citizens constitute and reconstitute themselves as a nation. Historically, immigrants were expected to become part of the nation, i.e. to 'assimilate' into the common culture of the host society. Throughout the West, this expectation is challenged by 'multiculturalism'. The umbrella of multiculturalism unites a bewildering variety of claims and actors. Regarding immigrants, its common denominator is the demand that the cultural difference of immigrant groups is to be maintained, rather than abandoned, in the host society. Multiculturalism is the rejection of assimilation.

Multiculturalism challenges a fundamental principle of the nation-state: the congruence of political and cultural boundaries.[32] Before entering into the origins and reasons of this challenge, it is important to realize the magnitude of it. One culture shared by all members of a society has been an evolutionary achievement of modern society. As Ernest Gellner (1983) has argued, one high literate culture diffused through all strata of society was a prerequisite of modern industrialism, enabling mobility and communication across large spaces. In the language of institutional economics, monoculture lowered the transaction costs of a society. Beyond Gellner, monoculture may be looked at as not only a cognitive, but also a moral, achievement. For John Stuart Mill (1991: 310), democracy was not possible without a commonly shared culture: 'Free institutions are next to impossible in a country made up of different nationalities. Among a people without fellow-feeling, especially if they read and speak different languages, the united public opinion, necessary to the working of representative government cannot exist.' Borrowing from cultural anthropology, Talcott Parsons (1951) stipulated more generally that commonly shared norms and values were the glue that kept even functionally differentiated societies together.

A tool of integration from an intra-societal perspective, culture has also been a tool of resistance from an inter-societal perspective. Nineteenth-century German nationalists were the first to mobilize an endogenous and particularistic *Kultur* against the exogenous encroachment by a universalistic Anglo-French *Zivilisation*. This impulse was taken up by modern anti-colonialism, which denounced the allegedly civilizatory intent of the colonizing nations as a subtle tool of domination. As Frantz Fanon famously argued, the liberation of the colonies had to be in the first place a cultural liberation, and to be based on a

changed self-conception, that is, 'identity'.[33] For Westerners, the affront
to dignity that is implied in colonialism's claim to cultural superiority
is not easy to grasp. W. E. B. Du Bois characterized the effect on part
of the colonized as 'double consciousness', 'this sense of always looking at one's self through the eyes of others, of measuring one's soul
by the tape of a world that looks on in amused contempt and pity'
(quoted in Young 1990: 60).[34] The trick of anti-colonialism was to
revalue the stigma as the positive fixed point of one's identity. Anti-
colonialism was the first modern politics of identity. Since it responded
to an external encroachment that had to be repudiated, anti-colonialism's
thrust was separation, not integration. The focus on identity and difference was picked up by multiculturalism, which may be understood as
a generalized form of anti-colonialism. After all, the novelty of post-
war immigration is its predominant origins in the former colonies and
Third World countries. This immigration may be seen as colonialism
in reverse, carrying the politics of cultural difference from the periphery
into the core of the modern world system.[35]

If anti-colonialism revalued cultural difference, the politics of Western
states in the post-war era devalued cultural difference. In this incongruity
multiculturalism could prosper. The experience of Nazism delegitimized
nationalism, not to mention racism, as a form of politics and identity
in Western states. After the war, Western states became truly liberal
states. Liberal states are culturally neutral. They hesitate to impose particular cultural ways on their members, because this would violate the
dignity and autonomy of the individual. This is expressed in a new
tolerance to homosexuality and other forms of cultural otherness no
less than in a uniform rejection of 'assimilating' immigrants. Assimilation, which means to make alike, made sense in a world of mutually
hostile, nationalizing states and Fordist mass production, requiring dis-
ciplined, carbon-copy individuals.[36] All that liberal states expect today,
in an era of post-nationalism and flexible specialization, is commitment to the same civic rules. Consensus in liberal states is procedural, not substantive.[37] One could even boldly argue that—like religion
once—today nationality as a cultural form is becoming separate from
the state—an expression of this being the approximation of citizenship
and resident alien status diagnosed by post-national membership analysts.[38] However, this is the point at which the universalist thrust of
liberalism is clipped by the insurmountable boundedness of states. In
addition to the unfolding of liberalism in a post-nationalist era, some
liberal states are also post-imperial states, and not without guilt about

their colonialist past. As in the case of Britain, this has been an additional incentive not to assimilate their post-colonial immigrants.

Multiculturalism originates from a combination of push and pull factors. On the pull side, liberal states do not require immigrants to assimilate. On the push side, immigrants do not want to assimilate. Anti-colonialism alone is not responsible for this. Today's migrations occur in a developed nation-state system, in which there is a strong resistance on the part of migrants to abandon entrenched national loyalties. Modern transport and communication technologies have enabled the maintenance and cultivation of old identifications in the host society. Immigration is no longer a one-way trip, with a clear and irrevocable dividing-line between past and present, place of origin and place of destination. The diaspora, which fuses old and new allegiances into a transnational network of circular relations and exchanges, has become a permanent option for migrants. In this regard, international is being transformed into transnational migration. John Lie (1995: 304) has outlined this new perspective well: 'The sojourn itself is neither unidirectional nor final. Multiple, circular, and return migrations, rather than a singular great journey from one sedentary space to another, occur across transnational spaces.'

Underneath these communalities, multiculturalism has taken different forms in different societies. One of the most common yet questionable uses of comparisons is to hypostasize positive or negative foreign models for purposes of domestic consumption. In such pidgin comparisons, the United States serves variously as a balkanized Sodom or model of multicultural tolerance, to be emulated or avoided by one's own society. In the following sketch of the different origins and logics of multiculturalism in the United States and western Europe, I suggest that the experiences on each side of the Atlantic are incommensurable. There is very little the Old and New Worlds can learn from one another.

*Multiculturalism in the United States*

Michael Lind (1995) has got it right. American multiculturalism is 'an aftershock of the black-power radicalism of the sixties' (p. 13). Its origin is the intractable race problem. Its logic is the retributive treatment for an expanding circle of discriminated, domestic minorities—paradoxically, even those that are immigration-based. In consequence, the United States would have multiculturalism even without immigration. Michael Lind established two more important messages. First, multiculturalism is no longer the oppositional, anti-establishment doctrine it likes to think. It is the established principle of the Third American Republic: after Anglo- and Euro-America, there is now Multicultural America. Secondly, multiculturalism may be on the way out, not just because of white backlash politics, but because of its own paradoxes and contradictions.

Multiculturalism both radicalizes and subverts the American concept of non-ethnic, politically constituted nationhood. In a universal nation of immigrants, there is place for all ethnicities and races. But in its roots-orientated public exaltation of ethnic and racial identity, multiculturalism tears apart the future-orientated, civic layer that had kept the fragile fabric of an essentially 'new' nation together.[39] There are two paradoxes nibbling at American multiculturalism today. First, the official minority (or 'victim') categories are artificial and random, carved out more for administrative convenience than for life-world reasons. 'Asians' and 'Hispanics', to name the most obvious, did not exist before the set-up of an elaborate affirmative action industry. One may interpret multiculturalism, which is in the first place an educational philosophy incorporated in a plethora of ethnic studies programmes and high-school and college curricula, as *ex post facto* legitimizations of administrative categories, as attempts to breathe life into just that: abstractions without life-world implications. Where should the line of victimhood be drawn? Who counts as minority? These are not academic, but eminently practical, questions. Take the current movement for 'mixed race' as a new census category (see Wright 1994). The latest offshoot of multicultural identity politics, and presumably intent on clamouring for similar minority privileges, the 'mixed race' quest threatens to bring down the whole edifice of race-based policies and politics. Understandably, it is fiercely opposed by ethnic and racial leaders, because it depletes their constituencies. More importantly, it exposes the questionable constitution of the established race categories. 'One drop of blood' made you black, according to racist Jim Crow law; but it also makes you black for the purposes of affirmative action, and is now strangely defended by the victims of racism. The contradiction is obvious. The reality of a multi-ethnic society is mixing and creolization, as in a painting of Kokoschka. But the affirmative action regime forces ethnic leaders to draw clear rectangular lines between separate groups, as in a painting of Modigliani.[40]

There is a second paradox inherent in American multiculturalism. Immigrant groups without historical connection to American society also qualify for special affirmative action privileges. To put it drastically,

they came voluntarily, but they qualify as victims. So there is preferential access to college, employment, or the political system for the
children of Cuban or Philippine immigrants, even though these groupings can't look back to a history of discrimination comparable to that
of American blacks. This oddity feeds the combined anti-immigrant
and affirmative action backlash in the United States today.

The group that epitomizes the ambivalences of American multiculturalism are the Hispanics, particularly those of Mexican origins.
Mexican Americans are, as Peter Skerry (1993) has called them in a
provocative study, an 'ambivalent minority', torn between the conflicting conceptions of traditional ethnic immigrant group and oppressed
racial minority. It is important to notice that there is a disjunction
between what Hispanic immigrants actually do and what their political
and intellectual leaders say about them.[41] What they do is to assimilate
not unlike the immigrant groups before them, the best indicator being
that one in three Hispanics marry outside their ethno-racial group. What
their leaders say about them is that Hispanics are an oppressed minority group, systematically excluded from white majority society, and in
need of resurrecting their indigenous culture (such as through schemes
of bilingual, bicultural education that are increasingly criticized as retard-
ing second- and third-generation integration[42]). However, against the
normative tone of Skerry and Chavez's (1991) analyses, it must be seen
that Hispanic leaders (shrewd political animals no less than the Irish
bosses of Tammany Hall) only respond to the political opportunity
structure of affirmative action, which happens to be the game with
the biggest benefits in town. And in adopting the idiom of civil rights
(rather than of patronage and spoils, as in classic machine politics),
they are only adopting the universal political idiom in the United States
today.[43] Scare scenarios of the impending balkanization of America do
not sufficiently take into account that multiculturalism is fed not by
immigration *per se*, but by a peculiar opportunity structure and élite
culture.

The critique of the public uses of ethnicity should not deflect from
its pivotal importance for the integration of immigrants. As William
I. Thomas and Florian Znaniecki (1984: 289) put it with reference to
the Polish peasant in America, ethnicity and ethnic self-help was the
cushion that stood between the uprooted immigrant and 'complete
wildness'. This is no less true today than it was seventy years ago. In
an important study, Alejandro Portes (1995) has found out that urban
second-generation immigrants assimilate very well—alas, they assimilate

into the culture of the crime- and drug-infested American underclass. To prevent this from happening is perhaps the strongest case to be made for the maintenance of ethnicity. Whether 'multiculturalism' as currently in place is any help in this is another question.

### Multiculturalism in Western Europe

Whereas the United States would have multiculturalism even without immigration, western Europe has multiculturalism as a result of immigration. As Nathan Glazer (1996) has sharply observed, American multiculturalism turns to 'citizens'; by contrast, multiculturalism in western Europe turns to 'foreigners'. As a result, west European multiculturalism is limited to the public recognition and tolerance of the ethnic difference imported by immigration. It does not entail retribution for past discrimination; it is not 'affirmative action'.

To compare the United States with an undifferentiated western Europe does not go without question. French authors in particular have emphasized the existence of different national 'models' of integrating immigrants, such as the Republican French, the explicitly multicultural British, and the post-national German (Schnapper 1994). But these differences at the level of public philosophy often hide very similar problems and actual modes of immigrant incorporation.[44] Western Europe as a whole differs from the United States in two crucial respects. First, while prominently involved in the transatlantic slave-trade, western Europe either has not known imported slavery, or—like Britain—has abandoned it early on. Thus there was no domestic race question to turn multiculturalism into the retributive direction of affirmative action. Secondly, European nationhood has inherently ethnic connotations. Nowhere has immigration become a nation-founding myth. Even France, which has periodically been engaged in the large-scale recruitment of immigrants for demographic reasons, has forgotten its immigrant past.[45] This makes the integration of immigrants a much more difficult problem in Europe than in the United States, where there is no ethno-national culture to become socialized into.[46] And multiculturalism, despite its many national variations, limits itself to a more modest call for inter-ethnic understanding and tolerance. In sum, multiculturalism in Europe originates from the shock of ethnically and racially homogeneous societies being confronted, for the first time, with ethnic and racial diversity, in a sudden reversal of centuries of out-migration and world-conquering colonization.

The crucial group for European multiculturalism are Muslim immigrants, who are everywhere considered as difficult to integrate—not unlike Hispanics in the United States. Here it is interesting to note that Muslims have become equally assertive in European countries with elaborate multicultural policies (e.g. Britain) and in those without such policies (e.g. France). By contrast, the United States has had neither a Foulard nor a Rushdie affair. Muslims are simply no issue in the United States, even after the bombing of the World Trade Center. Why?

There are several possible explanations. First, the majority of Muslim immigrants to the United States came through the individualized quota channels of high-level occupation and education, such as Iranians who arrived in larger numbers after the Mullah take-over in 1979 (see Waldinger and Bozorgmehr 1996, ch. 12). Such upper-class Muslims tend to lack religious instincts. By contrast, the post-colonial Muslim immigrants to France or Great Britain, and also to Germany, had over-whelmingly rural and less-educated backgrounds. Combined with the experience of insulation and discrimination, this is a more fertile ground for religious mobilization. Secondly, religion and state are less perfectly separated in Europe than in the United States. European nations have remained essentially Christian nations, in which religious toleration does not come as easily as in the United States.[47] Thirdly, and perhaps decisively, European nations do not offer their immigrants alternative identifications. There is no French or British Dream. But there is an American Dream. Everyone can be a member of the American nation, which has no ethnic connotations. There are few more moving scenes than an American naturalization ceremony, in which brown, yellow, red, and white faces from all corners of the globe are magically transformed into the faces of American citizens. In Europe, Islam is the identity to fall back on for the outcast second- or third-generation immigrants, who have no job, no education, no legitimate membership in the national community.

Multiculturalism, whether explicit as a policy of symbolic recognition or implicit as a liberal *laissez-faire*, does not help much in this regard, because nation-defining myths are not changed by fiat and overnight. One could even argue that multiculturalism dodges the crucial challenge of a civic redefinition of nationhood in Europe, which would allow Muslim immigrants to be included. On the contrary, multiculturalism reinforces the ethnic tilt of European nations, in pledging for tolerance towards members of other ethnic nations on their soil. European multiculturalism thus keeps the majority and minority tribes neatly separated. In fact, multiculturalism has already been pirated by the majority tribe. As Miriam Feldblum points out in Chapter 7 of this

volume, the new racism of Le Pen emulates the multicultural right to
be different; this racism no longer argues in terms of biological superiority but of cultural difference. European multiculturalism has borne
strange fruits indeed.

In the end, the problem of immigrant integration in Europe is not
all that dramatic. This is because, unlike to the United States, where
immigration is a recurrent phenomenon, post-war immigration to Europe
has been a unique event that has come to a close now. Europe is now
facing the second- and third-generation aftermath of historically unprecedented (and in this sense, anomalous) post-colonial and guestworker
immigration. It does not want any further immigration, and it is quite
firm about implementing this. The source of family immigration is
gradually ceasing, and the bulk of the new migrations occurs through
the asylum valve. The great source country diversity and low sense of
obligation on the part of asylum-granting states will probably prevent
today's asylum claimants from becoming tomorrow's multicultural
claimants. Accordingly, the European problem of immigrant integration
boils down to very specific groups: Turks in Germany, Pakistanis and
Bangladeshis in Britain, Moroccans and Algerians in France. Muslims
they are all indeed, indicating that this is the nut that Europe has to
crack. The multicultural recognition of difference will be indispensable
for this; but so will something more mundane: jobs, education, and
full membership in the national communities of the receiving states.

## NOTES

My thanks to Adrian Favell, who gave this text a close and witty reading.
Yasemin Soysal did not like the section on post-national membership, and
convinced me to make some corrections.
1. See also Zolberg (1989: 405): 'it is precisely the control which states exercise over borders that defines international migration as a distinctive social
   process'.
2. See Kratochwil's (1986) interesting comparison of imperial frontier zones
   and the linear boundaries of nation-states.
3. Some (e.g. Zolberg 1981) identify states, others (e.g. Sassen 1988; Piore
   1979) the capitalist economy as major pull factors.
4. The paradigmatic case is the Prussian *Staatsangehörigkeit* (see Brubaker
   1992: 64–72, who builds on Grawert 1973: 133–45).
5. See Cornelius *et al.* (1994*a*), which may be considered the state-of-the-art
   volume on immigration control. Despite its many excellent contributions, the
   volume does not engage in a more sustained argument on the transformation (or maintenance) of stateness in a world of migration, and remains

limited to a descriptive comparison of immigration policies in various parts of the world.

6. This is, of course, the story of Tocqueville's *The Old Regime and the French Revolution* (1856/1955).

7. Even the liberal US Select Commission on Immigration and Refugee Policy, which laid the ground for the US immigration and refugee legislation in the 1980s and early 1990s, entitled its final report *U.S. Immigration Policy in the National Interest* (1981).

8. From an international relations perspective, see Weiner (1992–3); from an international law perspective, see Goodwin-Gill (1978) and Plender (1988).

9. As Wendt (1992: 412–13) put it, 'it is only in virtue of mutual recognition that states have "territorial property rights" '.

10. See Jackson and Rosberg's (1982) distinction between 'empirical' and 'judicial' statehood, and their interesting argument that the empirically weak states of post-colonial Africa are kept alive only by their recognition within the international state system.

11. The quality of the burgeoning literature on 'globalization' is inversely related to its quantity. Among the few usable general discussions is Giddens (1990, ch. 2). The economic aspect of globalization is best captured by Reich (1992); the spatial aspect by Sassen (1991); and the cultural aspect by Hannerz (1992).

12. But see the qualifying observations by Sassen (1991) on the spatial concentration of global processes in a few world cities. Global finance and service transactions are nevertheless processed through electronic 'cyberspace', which defies territorial state controls.

13. This global élite constitutes about 25 per cent of the non-EU citizens legally resident in the Union. As Böhning (1991: 446) observes, 'Few Western Europeans view them as immigrants or workers; indeed, they hardly notice them, as though they were invisible'.

14. See also Soysal (1994, ch. 8) and Jacobson (1996, chs. 4, 5). In contrast, Habermas (1994) has pointed out that popular sovereignty and human rights are dual constitutive principles of liberal nation-states.

15. The two best accounts of US immigration policy in the 1980s, stressing interest group pressure and cultural constraints, are Schuck (1992) and Tichonor (1994).

16. Brubaker (1994: 228–9) makes the same point.

17. For France, see Guendelsberger (1988); for Germany, see Neuman (1990).

18. Especially Jacobson (1996, chs. 4 and 5).

19. Notable exceptions are Freeman (1979); Hammar (1985); and Messina (1989).

20. Brubaker (1994: 230) has sharply observed this difference.

21. Such a comprehensive domestic–global analysis of limited sovereignty in immigration control does not exist. An excellent approximation is Martin (1989).

22. If only to shed the bad image as Europe's notorious human rights offender, there is now a large groundswell for constitutional reform in Britain. See *The Economist* (1995).

23. For intergovernmentalism and traditional nation-statism, see Hoffmann (1982), Moravcsik (1991), and Milward (1992). Naïve neo-functionalism and supra-statism, formulated in the post-war euphoria about a post-national, federalist Europe (Haas 1964), is not defended by anyone today. Cautious reappraisals of neo-functionalism are Weiler (1991) and, most recently, Pierson (1996).

24. This is the argument of Milward's seminal *European Rescue of the Nation-State* (1992).

25. I am building on Preuss (1996), Kymlicka and Norman (1994), Grawert (1973), and Brubaker (1989).

26. On the devaluation of citizenship, see Schuck (1989).

27. Preuss (1995: 275) has evocatively characterized citizenship as enabling 'a kind of community in which aliens can become associates'. This associational capacity of citizenship is undermined by primordial programmes of multiculturalism.

28. See Soysal (1994: 139), who is very clear about this alternative.

29. Of course, Brubaker (1989) himself has diagnosed the emergence of 'dual membership' in the immigrant-receiving West, but taken it as an anomaly subject to correction. This is the view I want to defend in the following.

30. In 1992–3, the only countries with a bigger than 10 per cent foreign population share were Switzerland (18 per cent) and the tax havens Luxembourg (29.1 per cent) and Liechtenstein (37.5 per cent) (see Münz 1995: 23). Of the 14.2 million foreigners residing in the European Union in 1991, slightly over 9 million were from non-EU countries (see Koslowski 1994: 377).

31. Note, however, that in response to the current anti-immigrant backlash in the United States even Mexican immigrants are naturalizing in historically unprecedented numbers (see *New York Times* 1995).

32. This is a normative, not a factual, congruence. Few nation-states have ever achieved a congruence of political and cultural boundaries. But there is no nation-state that has not at least tried to achieve it (for a particularly successful case, see Weber 1976). Where this ended in a 'truce', as in multinational Canada or Switzerland, a special explanation is required. As precarious exceptions, they reaffirm the rule.

33. 'In the colonial context the settler only ends his work of breaking in the native when the latter admits loudly and intelligibly the supremacy of the white man's values. In the period of decolonization, the colonized masses mock at these very values, insult them, and vomit them up' (Fanon 1963: 43).

34. See also Fanon's classic essay *Black Skin, White Masks* (1986).

35. The separatist, anti-colonial impulse of multiculturalism is overlooked in Kymlicka's (1995) liberal defence of multiculturalism. From a normative point of view, Kymlicka distinguishes between national minorities entitled to 'self-government rights' and immigrant minorities entitled to 'polyethnic rights'. These polyethnic rights are 'usually intended to promote integration into the larger society, not self-government' (p. 31). Kymlicka thus obscures the differentialist, identitarian thrust of immigrant multiculturalism. But, in Kymlicka's defence, his analysis is primarily normative, not empirical.

36. As an explicit policy, assimilation was imposed especially in periods of impending war. In the United States, it reached its apex during the First World War. Before that, especially German immigrants pursued a politics of difference that would make latter-day multiculturalists blush (see Higham 1954, ch. 8).

37. This is the liberal position of Rawls, Habermas, and Dworkin. They are of course challenged by communitarians like Walzer.

38. Accordingly, there has been a debate among German constitutional lawyers whether the non-discrimination article in the Basic Law included actual nationality (as different from national origins). See Zuleeg (1973: 363–4), who argued that it did, and Isensee (1974: 75), who argued to the contrary. In the United States, the Supreme Court declared in *Graham* v. *Richardson* (1971) that at the level of state law 'alienage' was a 'suspect classification', like race or gender, on the basis of which state governments were generally not allowed to discriminate.

39. The notion of new nation (see Lipset 1979) is a paradox, because nations (whose root word is the Latin *nasci*, to be born) are usually defined by their past. But it catches very well the peculiarity of a non-ethnic nation of immigrants, whose spring is not birth and ancestry but the fresh start and perpetual unfinishedness.

40. I owe this nice analogy to Brubaker (1996*b*: 13–14), who picked it up from Gellner (1983: 139–40).

41. This is the claim made by Chavez (1991) and Skerry (1993, ch. 10).

42. For a credible critique of bilingual education, see Porter (1990).

43. A good analysis of immigrant integration through urban machine politics is Erie (1988).

44. The paradigmatic study is Noiriel (1996), who actually showed that France was a 'melting-pot' no less than the United States, despite its very different public philosophy (France repressing ethnicity, the United States celebrating it). From an American perspective, an excellent study of French *de facto*, local-level multiculturalism is Schain (1996).

45. At least until its rediscovery, in the mid- to late 1980s, for purposes of reinvigorating Republican integration. On the period of forgetting, see Noiriel (1996, ch. 1).

46. The Englishman Peter Brimelow's (1995) flamboyant critique of 'America's immigration disaster' falsely projects European ethnic nationhood to the United States. Even Lind's (1995) more moderate case for civic nationalism suffers from an 'ethnocultural' misreading of American nationhood (esp. p. 285).

47. An example is the Bavarian crucifix affair in 1995. The Federal Constitutional Court had ruled that the Bavarian state government could not order its schools to have a crucifix in every classroom; according to the constitutional separation of state and church, the hanging of a crucifix had to be voluntary. In response, the pious people of Bavaria let themselves be carried away in public outrage and mass protest—led by the Minister President, calling for 'civil disobedience' against the 'rule from Karlsruhe'. This neglect of a Constitutional Court rule has been unprecedented in the history of the Federal Republic. See Wesel (1996: 61–5).

# REFERENCES

Anderson, Benedict (1991), *Imagined Communities* (London: Verso).

Aron, Raymond (1974), 'Is Multinational Citizenship Possible?', *Social Research*, 41: 638–56.

Böhning, W. R. (1991), 'Integration and Immigration Pressures in Western Europe', *International Labour Review*, 130/4: 445–9.

Bommes, Michael, and Jost Halfmann (1994), 'Migration und Inklusion', *Kölner Zeitschrift für Soziologie und Sozialpsychologie*, 46/3: 406–24.

Brimelow, Peter (1995), *Alien Nation* (New York: Random House).

Brubaker, Rogers (1989), 'Introduction', in R. Brubaker (ed.), *Immigration and the Politics of Citizenship in Europe and North America* (Lanham, Md.: University Press of America).

—— (1992), *Citizenship and Nationhood in France and Germany* (Cambridge, Mass.: Harvard University Press).

—— (1994), 'Commentary', in Cornelius *et al.* (1994*a*).

—— (1995), 'Comments on "Modes of Immigration Politics in Liberal Democratic States"', *International Migration Review*, 29/4: 903–8.

—— (1996*a*), *Nationalism Reframed* (New York: Cambridge University Press).

—— (1996*b*), 'Myths and Misconceptions in the Study of East European Nationalism', paper presented at the European Forum Conference on Multiculturalism, Minorities, and Citizenship at the European University Institute, Florence, 18–23 Apr.

Bull, Hedley (1977), *The Anarchical Society* (London: Macmillan).

Chavez, Linda (1991), *Out of the Barrio* (New York: Basic Books).

Cornelius, Wayne, Philip Martin, and James Hollifield (eds.) (1994*a*), *Controlling Immigration* (Stanford, Calif.: Stanford University Press).

—— —— —— (1994*b*), 'Introduction: The Ambivalent Quest for Immigration Control', in Cornelius *et al.* (1994*a*).

*Economist, The* (1995), 'Why Britain Needs a Bill of Rights', 21 Oct., 44–6.

Erie, Steven P. (1988), *Rainbow's End: Irish-Americans and the Dilemmas of Urban Machine Politics 1840–1985* (Berkeley: University of California Press).

Evans, Peter, Dietrich Rüschemeyer, and Theda Skocpol (eds.) (1985), *Bringing the State back In* (New York: Cambridge University Press).

Fanon, Frantz (1963), *The Wretched of the Earth* (New York: Grove Press).

—— (1986), *Black Skin, White Masks* (London: Pluto Press).

Freeman, Gary (1979), *Immigrant Labor and Racial Conflict in Industrial Societies* (Princeton: Princeton University Press).

—— (1995*a*), 'Modes of Immigration Politics in Liberal Democratic States', *International Migration Review*, 29/4: 881–902.

—— (1995*b*), 'Rejoinder to Brubaker', *International Migration Review*, 29/4: 909–13.

Gellner, Ernest (1983), *Nations and Nationalism* (Ithaca, NY: Cornell University Press).

Giddens, Anthony (1985), *The Nation-State and Violence* (Oxford: Polity Press).

—— (1990), *The Consequences of Modernity* (Stanford, Calif.: Stanford University Press).

Glazer, Nathan (1996), 'Multiculturalism and American Exceptionalism', paper presented at the European Forum Conference on Multiculturalism, Minorities, and Citizenship at the European University Institute, Florence, 18–23 Apr.

Goodwin-Gill, Guy (1978), *International Law and the Movement of Persons between States* (Oxford: Clarendon Press).

Grawert, Rolf (1973), *Staat und Staatsangehörigkeit* (Berlin: Duncker & Humblot).

Guendelsberger, John (1988), 'The Right to Family Unification in French and United States Immigration Law', *Cornell International Law Journal*, 21/1: 1–102.

Haas, Ernst B. (1964), *Beyond the Nation-State* (Stanford, Calif.: Stanford University Press).

Habermas, Jürgen (1994), 'Human Rights and Popular Sovereignty', *Ratio Juris*, 7/1: 1–13.

Hammar, Tomas (1985), 'Introduction', in T. Hammar (ed.), *European Immigration Policy* (New York: Cambridge University Press).

Hannerz, Ulf (1992), *Cultural Complexity* (New York: Columbia University Press).

Henkin, Louis (1990), *The Age of Rights* (New York: Columbia University Press).

Higham, John (1954), *Strangers in the Land* (New Brunswick, NJ: Rutgers University Press).

Hoffmann, Stanley (1982), 'Reflections on the Nation-State in Western Europe Today', *Journal of Common Market Studies*, 21/1–2: 21–37.

Hollifield, James (1994), 'The Migration Crisis in Western Europe: The Search for a National Model', paper presented at the Annual Meeting of the American Political Science Association, New York, 1–4 Sept.

Isensee, Josef (1974), 'Die staatsrechtliche Stellung der Ausländer in der Bundesrepublik Deutschland', in *Veröffentlichungen der Vereinigung der Deutschen Staatsrechtslehrer*, xxxii (Berlin: de Gruyter).

Jackson, Robert, and Carl Rosberg (1982), 'Why Africa's Weak States Persist', *World Politics*, 34: 1–24.

Jacobson, David (1996), *Rights across Borders* (Baltimore: Johns Hopkins University Press).

Koslowski, Rey (1994), 'Intra-EU Migration, Citizenship and Political Union', *Journal of Common Market Studies*, 32/3: 369–402.

Kratochwil, Friedrich (1986), 'Of Systems, Boundaries, and Territoriality', *World Politics*, 39: 27–52.

Kymlicka, Will (1995), *Multicultural Citizenship* (Oxford: Clarendon Press).

—— and W. J. Norman (1994), 'Return of the Citizen', *Ethics*, 104/2: 352–81.

Lie, John (1995), 'From International Migration to Transnational Diaspora', *Contemporary Sociology*, 24: 303–6.

Lind, Michael (1995), *The Next American Nation* (New York: Free Press).

Lipset, Seymour Martin (1979), *The First New Nation* (New York: Norton).

Mann, Michael (1986), *The Sources of Social Power*, vol. 1 (Cambridge: Cambridge University Press).

—— (1993), 'Nation-States in Europe and Other Continents: Diversifying, Developing, not Dying', *Daedalus*, 122/3: 115–40.

Marshall, T. S. (1992), *Citizenship and Social Class* (London: Pluto Press).

Martin, David (1989), 'Effects of International Law on Migration Policy and Practice: The Uses of Hypocrisy', *International Migration Review*, 33/3: 547–78.

Martiniello, Marco (1994), 'Citizenship of the European Union: A Critical View', in Rainer Bauböck (ed.), *From Aliens to Citizens* (Aldershot: Avebury).

Messina, Anthony (1989), *Race and Party Competition in Britain* (Oxford: Clarendon Press).

Mill, John Stuart (1991), *Considerations on Representative Government* (Buffalo, NY: Prometheus Books).

Milward, Alan (1992), *The European Rescue of the Nation-State* (London: Routledge).

Moravcsik, Andrew (1991), 'Negotiating the Single European Act', *International Organization*, 45/1: 19–56.

Münz, Rainer (1995), *Where did they all Come From? Typology and Geography of European Mass Migration in the Twentieth Century*, Demographie aktuell Working Paper no. 7 (Berlin: Humboldt University).

Neuman, Gerald L. (1990), 'Immigration and Judicial Review in the Federal Republic of Germany', *New York University Journal of International Law*, 23: 35–85.

*New York Times* (1995), 'Legal Immigrants in Record Numbers Want Citizenship', 2 Apr.

Noiriel, Gérard (1996), *The French Melting Pot* (Minneapolis: University of Minnesota Press).

Parsons, Talcott (1951), *The Social System* (New York: Free Press).

Perlmutter, Ted (1996), 'Bringing Parties back In: Comments on "Modes of Immigration Politics in Liberal Democratic Societies"', *International Migration Review*, 30/1: 375–88.

Pierson, Paul (1996), 'The Path to European Integration', *Comparative Political Studies*, 29/2: 123–63.

Piore, Michael (1979), *Birds of Passage* (New York: Cambridge University Press).

Plender, Richard (1988), *International Migration Law* (Dordrecht: Martinus Nijhoff).

Poggi, Gianfranco (1978), *The Development of the Modern State* (Stanford, Calif.: Stanford University Press).

—— (1990), *The State* (Stanford, Calif.: Stanford University Press).

Porter, Rosalie Pedalino (1990), *Forked Tongue: The Politics of Bilingual Education* (New York: Basic Books).

Portes, Alejandro (1995), 'Children of Immigrants: Segmented Assimilation and its Determinants', in A. Portes (ed.), *The Economic Sociology of Immigration* (New York: Russell Sage).

Preuss, Ulrich (1995), 'Problems of a Concept of European Citizenship', *European Law Journal*, 1/3: 267–81.

—— (1996), 'Two Challenges to Modern Citizenship', MS, University of Bremen.

Reich, Robert (1992), *The Work of Nations* (New York: Vintage).

Ruggie, John (1993), 'Territoriality and Beyond', *International Organization*, 47/1: 139–74.

Sassen, Saskia (1988), *The Mobility of Labor and Capital* (New York: Cambridge University Press).

—— (1991), *The Global City* (Princeton: Princeton University Press).

—— (1996), *Losing Control?* (New York: Columbia University Press).

Schain, Martin (1996), 'Minorities and Immigrant Incorporation in France: The State and the Dynamics of Multiculturalism', paper presented at the European Forum Conference on Multiculturalism, Minorities, and Citizenship at the European University Institute, Florence, 18–23 Apr.

Schmitter, Philippe (1991), *The European Community as an Emergent and Novel Form of Political Domination*, Working Paper no. 26 (Madrid: Juan March Institute).

Schnapper, Dominique (1994), 'The Debate on Immigration and the Crisis of National Identity', *West European Politics*, 17/2: 127–39.

Schuck, Peter (1989), 'Membership in the Liberal Polity: The Devaluation of American Citizenship', in R. Brubaker (ed.), *Immigration and the Politics of Citizenship in Europe and North America* (Lanham, Md.: University Press of America).

—— (1992), 'The Politics of Rapid Legal Change: Immigration Policy in the 1980s', *Studies in American Political Development*, 6: 37–92.

Schumpeter, Josef (1927/1953), 'Die sozialen Klassen im ethnisch homogenen Milieu', in J. Schumpeter, *Aufsätze zur Soziologie* (Tübingen: Mohr).

Schwerdtfeger, Gunther (1980), *Welche rechtlichen Vorkehrungen empfehlen sich, um die Rechtsstellung von Ausländern in der Bundesrepublik Deutschland angemessen zu gestalten?*, Gutachten A zum 53. Deutschen Juristentag Berlin 1980 (Munich: C. H. Beck).

Shapiro, Martin, and Alec Stone (1994), 'The New Constitutional Politics of Europe', *Comparative Political Studies*, 26/4: 397–420.

Skerry, Peter (1993), *Mexican Americans: The Ambivalent Minority* (New York: Free Press).

Soysal, Yasemin (1994), *Limits to Citizenship* (Chicago: University of Chicago Press).

Soysal, Yasemin (1996), *Boundaries and Identity: Immigrants in Europe*, EUF Working Paper no. 96/3 (Florence: EUI).

Storey, Hugo (1994), 'International Law and Human Rights Obligations', in Sarah Spencer (ed.), *Strangers and Citizens* (London: Rivers Oram Press).

Thomas, William I., and Florian Znaniecki (1984), *The Polish Peasant in Europe and America*, ed. and abridged by Eli Zaretsky (Urbana: University of Illinois Press).

Thomson, Janice (1994), *Mercenaries, Pirates, and Sovereigns* (Princeton: Princeton University Press).

—— and Stephen Krasner (1989), 'Global Transactions and the Consolidation of Sovereignty', in Ernst-Otto Czempiel and James Rosenau (eds.), *Global Changes and Theoretical Challenges* (Lexington, Mass.: Lexington Books).

Tichonor, Daniel (1994), 'The Politics of Immigration Reform in the United States 1981–1990', *Polity*, 26/3: 333–62.

Tocqueville, Alexis de (1856/1955), *The Old Regime and the French Revolution* (New York: Doubleday).

United States Select Commission on Immigration and Refugee Policy (1981), *U.S. Immigration Policy and the National Interest* (Washington: Government Printing Office).

Waldinger, Robert, and Mehdi Bozorgmehr (eds.) (1996), *Ethnic Los Angeles* (New York: Russell Sage).

Walzer, Michael (1983), *Spheres of Justice* (New York: Basic Books).

Weber, Eugen (1976), *Peasants into Frenchmen* (Stanford, Calif.: Stanford University Press).

Weiler, J. H. H. (1991), 'The Transformation of Europe', *Yale Law Journal*, 100: 2403–83.

Weiner, Myron (1992–3), 'Security, Stability, and International Migration', *International Security*, 17/3: 91–126.

—— (1995), *The Global Migration Crisis* (New York: HarperCollins).

Wendt, Alexander (1992), 'Anarchy is what States Make of It: The Social Construction of Power Politics', *International Organization* 46/2: 391–425.

Wesel, Uwe (1996), *Die Hüter der Verfassung* (Frankfurt am Main: Eichborn).

Wilson, J. Q. W. (ed.) (1980), *The Politics of Regulation* (New York: Basic Books).

Wright, Lawrence (1994), 'One Drop of Blood', *New Yorker*, 25 July.

Young, Iris Marion (1990), *Justice and the Politics of Difference* (Princeton: Princeton University Press).

Zolberg, Aristide (1981), 'International Migrations in Political Perspective', in M. Kritz, C. Keely, and S. Tomasi (eds.), *Global Trends in Migration* (New York: Center for Migration Studies).

—— (1989), 'The Next Waves: Migration Theory for a Changing World', *International Migration Review*, 23: 403–30.

Zuleeg, Manfred (1973), 'Zur staatsrechtlichen Stellung der Ausländer in der Bundesrepublik Deutschland', *Die öffentliche Verwaltung*, 26/11–12: 361–70.

# PART I

# The Challenge to Sovereignty

# 2

# The *de facto* Transnationalizing of Immigration Policy

## SASKIA SASSEN

While the state continues to play the most important role in immigration policy-making and implementation, it has been transformed by the growth of a global economic system and other transnational processes. These changes have brought on conditions that bear on the state's regulatory role and capacity. Two particular aspects of this development are of significance to immigration policy-making and implementation. One is the relocation of various components of state authority to supranational organizations such as the institutions of the European Union, the newly formed World Trade Organization, or international human rights codes. A second is the emergence of a new privatized transnational legal regime for cross-border business transactions which now also includes certain components of cross-border labour mobility, notably professional workers.

The major implication for immigration policy is that these developments have had an impact on the sovereignty and territoriality of the state and that in so far as the state has participated in the implementation of many of these new arrangements, the state itself has been transformed and so has the inter-state system. Thus, in so far as immigration policy is deeply embedded in the question of state sovereignty and the inter-state system, it is no longer sufficient simply to assert the sovereign role of the state in immigration policy design and implementation. It is also necessary to examine the transformation of the state itself and what that can entail for migration policy and the regulation of migration flows and settlement. For the purposes of immigration policy analyses it is becoming important to factor in these transformations of the state and the inter-state system precisely because the state is a major actor in immigration policy and regulation.

Nor is it sufficient simply to assert that globalization has brought with it a declining significance of the state in economic regulation. The state has been a participant in this process, and is the strategic institution for the legislative changes and innovations necessary for economic globalization as we know it today (e.g. Panitch 1996; Cox 1987). Some of these issues may seem far removed from the question of immigration policy. But we need to expand the analytic terrain within which we examine the options in immigration policy-making in the highly developed countries.

This chapter focuses on how this reconfiguration has brought with it a *de facto* transnationalism in the handling of a growing number of immigration issues. This can take many forms: the shift of certain elements of immigration policy onto supranational institutions in the European Union; the sharp increase in the extent and content of collaboration in the United States–Mexico Binational Immigration Commission; the rapid increase in the use of international human rights instruments by judges adjudicating on immigration and refugee questions in both Europe and the United States; the formation of a privatized regime for the circulation of service workers in the major free trade agreements as part of the liberalization of international trade and investment in services.

I consider these and other developments as *de facto* transnationalism because they are fragmented and incipient, and have not been fully captured at the most formal levels of international public law and conventions, nor in national representations of the sovereign state. My argument is, then, that there is more transnationalism than meets the formal eye.

In order to develop this particular way of framing the evidence it is important first to bring some precision to concepts such as economic globalization and transnationalism and their impact on the sovereignty and exclusive territoriality of national states. This is the subject of a first section confined largely to states operating under the rule of law. The second section briefly examines two of the corner-stones of current immigration policy in highly developed countries: the border and the individual as sites for regulatory enforcement. The third and fourth sections focus on the constraints faced by the state in highly developed countries in the making of immigration policy today.

## THE STATE AND THE NEW ECONOMIC REGIME

Two notions underlie much of the discussion about globalization. One is the proposition that what the global economy gains, the national state loses and vice versa. The other is the proposition that if an event (from business transactions to judiciary decisions) takes place in a national territory it is a national event. In other words, dualism and geography (in a narrow territorial sense) are the hallmarks of this type of understanding.

But there is by now a considerable body of scholarship that has shown us that the spatiality of the global economy does not simply lie somewhere in the interstices between states (e.g. various chapters in Mittelman 1996, and in Knox and Taylor 1995). To a good extent global processes and institutional arrangements materialize in national territories; even the most digitalized global financial market is grounded in a set of very material resources and spaces largely embedded in national territories.

As a consequence, one of the key features of the role of the state *vis-à-vis* economic globalization (unlike earlier forms of the global economy) has been to negotiate the intersection of national law and foreign actors—whether firms, markets, or individuals (e.g. Drache and Gertler 1991). We generally use the term 'deregulation' to describe the outcome of this negotiation. The problem with this term is that it only captures the withdrawal of the state from regulating its economy. It does not register all the ways in which the state participates in setting up the new frameworks through which globalization is furthered; nor does it capture the associated transformations inside the state (see Sassen 1996*a*).

Coding everything that involves the national state as an instance of the national is simply inadequate. The theoretical and methodological challenge presented by the current phase of globalization is that it entails a transcending of exclusive national territoriality and of the inter-state system yet is implanted in national territories and institutions. Hence globalization directly engages two marking features of the nation state: exclusive territoriality and sovereignty.

Similarly, the emergent international human rights regime engages territoriality and sovereignty. What matters here is not so much the moral force of the idea, but the far more practical fact of a rapid multiplication of instruments available to judges and the build-up of case-law where this applies, as in the United States, for example (e.g. Jacobson 1996). The key issue here is the fact that international regimes or codes, such as human rights, largely become operative in national courts. One could of course simply assert that in such cases we are dealing with what is ultimately a national institution. To do so means discounting even the possibility that the ascendance of such international regimes engages the sovereignty and territoriality of the national state. And since the multiplication of instruments and their growing use by national courts is a very recent development—unlike the concept of human rights—we must at least allow for the possibility that there are new processes afoot also in this realm.

As has been frequently noted, much social science rests on the explicit or implicit assumption of the nation-state as the container of social processes. There is, it seems to me, a second common assumption underlying much social science: that national territoriality is the same as national territory (Sassen 1996*a*, ch. 1). Both these assumptions describe conditions that have held for a long time, i.e. the history of the modern state, but are now being unbundled. One of the features of the current phase of globalization is that the fact that a process happens within the territory of a sovereign state does not necessarily mean it is national. This transgression of borders does violence to many of the methods and conceptual frameworks prevalent in social science. Developing the theoretical and empirical specifications that can accommodate this transgression of borders is difficult and will be time-consuming. But it has started (see, for instance, the effort in this direction by Mazlish and Buultjens 1993; Knox and Taylor 1995; Sassen 1996*a*).

These assumptions about the nation-state as container and territoriality as synomymous with territory are also present among experts of the global economy. This has meant that they have typically confined themselves to cross-border processes, notably international trade and investment, and have produced a rather empirically and theoretically thin account that raises more questions than it answers.

In terms of sovereignty, the emergent consensus in the community of states to further globalization has created a set of specific obligations on participating states. The state remains as the ultimate guarantor of the 'rights' of global capital, i.e. the protection of contracts and property rights. Thus the state has incorporated the global project of its own shrinking role in regulating economic transactions (Cox 1987; Mittelman 1996). Firms operating transnationally want to ensure the functions traditionally exercised by the state in the national realm of the economy, notably guaranteeing property rights and contracts. The state here can be conceived of as representing a technical administrative capacity which cannot be replicated at this time by any other institutional arrangement; furthermore, this is a capacity backed by military power, with global power in the case of some states.

But this guarantee of the rights of capital is embedded in a certain type of state, a certain conception of the rights of capital, and a certain type of international legal regime: it is largely embedded in the state of the most developed and most powerful countries in the world, in Western notions of contract and property rights, and in a new legal regime aimed at furthering economic globalization (Trubek *et al.* 1993; Coombe 1993).[1] The state continues to play a crucial, though no longer exclusive, role in the production of legality around new forms of economic activity (Sassen 1996*a*).

Transnational economic processes inevitably interact with systems for the governance of national economies. There are few industries where deregulation and transnationalization have been as important to growth as in international finance and advanced corporate services. What matters for my purposes here is one particular way of conceiving of deregulation, one not usually emphasized in the specialized literature: deregulation in finance has had the effect of partly denationalizing national territory (Sassen 1996*a*, ch. 1). For example, the so-called International Banking Facilities in the United States implemented in 1981 can be seen as an instance of a partial denationalizing of US territory for the purposes of international financial transactions for both national and foreign firms. New York City, and particularly Manhattan, which concentrates a disproportionate share of these facilities, is the equivalent of a free trade zone for finance. Yet another, more familiar instance can be found in various forms through which manufacturing production has been internationalized, e.g. export-processing zones which fall under special regimes that reduce the obligations of firms to both the capital-receiving and the capital-sending state, notably regarding taxes, and, in the case of the receiving state, labour and environmental legislation (see e.g. Bonacich *et al.* 1994; Morales 1994; Mittelman 1996). In brief, in so far as global processes materialize in concrete places, they continue to operate under sovereign regulatory umbrellas, but they do so under new emergent transnational regimes and, often, under conditions of a denationalizing of national territory.

It is through the formation of such transnational regimes and the denationalizing of national territory that the state guarantees a far broader range of rights of national and foreign capital. These rights are often in addition to those guaranteed through strictly national regimes. In this regard, deregulation and other policies furthering economic globalization cannot simply be considered as an instance of a declining significance of the state. Deregulation is a vehicle through which a growing number of states are furthering economic globalization and guaranteeing the rights of global capital, an essential ingredient of the former. Deregulation and kindred policies constitute the elements of a new legal regime dependent on consensus among states to further globalization. This manner of conceptualizing deregulation suggests that the duality national–global as mutually exclusive is problematic in that it does not adequately represent what economic globalization has actually entailed for national states.

While central, the role of the state in producing the legal encasements for economic globalization is no longer as exclusive as it was ten years ago. Economic globalization has also been accompanied by the creation of new, privatized legal regimes and legal practices and the expansion and renovation of some older forms that bypass national legal systems. Among the most important ones are international commercial arbitration and the variety of institutions which fulfil rating and advisory functions that have become essential for the operation of the global economy (Dezalay and Garth 1995; Salacuse 1991; Sinclair 1994).

Over the past twenty years international commercial arbitration has been transformed and institutionalized as the leading contractual method for the resolution of cross-border commercial disputes.[2] In a major study on international commercial arbitration, Dezalay and Garth (1995) conclude that it is a delocalized and decentralized market for the administration of international commercial disputes, connected by more or less powerful institutions and individuals who are both competitive and complementary (see also Salacuse 1991; *Journal of Global Business and Political Economy* 1995). Another instance of a private regulatory system is represented by debt security or bond-rating agencies, which have come to play an increasingly important role in the global economy.[3] Ten years ago Moody's and Standard & Poor had no analysts outside the United States; by 1993 they each had about 100 in Europe, Japan, and Australia.

These and other such transnational institutions and regimes do raise questions about the relation between state sovereignty and the governance of global economic processes. International commercial arbitration is basically a private justice system and credit-rating agencies are private gatekeeping systems. Along with other such institutions they have emerged as important governance mechanisms whose authority is not centred in the state. They contribute to maintain order at the top, one could say.

All of this has had an impact on sovereignty and on the mutually exclusive territoriality that has marked the history of the modern state. This is an extremely complex and highly differentiated history that cannot be adequately described here. There is an enormously rich scholarship on this subject.[4]

There are two points I would want to emphasize about this history here because they are relevant to the subject of this chapter, particularly the notion that we may need considerable innovation in immigration policy given today's major transformations. One of these points is that at various periods of major transitions there was a coexistence of multiple systems of rule. This was the case, for instance, in the transition from the medieval system of rule to the modern state.[5] And it may well be the case today in this period of transition to a global economy. There were and continue to be other forms of concentration of power and other systems of rule, for instance non-territorial or non-exclusive systems such as the Catholic Church and the so-called Arab nation, to mention just two of the better known. As I will argue later, supranational organizations today and regimes such as the General Agreement on Tariffs and Trade (GATT) and the North American Free Trade Agreement (NAFTA) may well signal the strengthening of other non-exclusive systems of rule today.

A second element in the history of the modern state that matters here is the enormous opposition to the formation of and claims by central states (see Tilly 1975). Again I see this as relevant to the contemporary period in that today strong resistance, in this case from national governments, still does not preclude the possibility of regimes that go beyond state sovereignty or that involve far more developed instances of multilateralism notwithstanding strong resistance from national governments, among policy-makers, and analysts to even the idea of such a possibility.

While these new conditions for transnational economies are being produced and implemented by governments and economic actors in highly developed countries, immigration policy in those same countries remains centred in older conceptions about control and regulation.[6] But can the state escape its own transformation and the pressures towards transnationalism when it comes to immigration policy design and implementation? Before getting into these questions, I very briefly examine a few key aspects about immigration policy in highly developed countries that capture the contrast with the new economic regime. The ensuing sections examine the extent to which the state in highly developed receiving countries is in fact experiencing institutional transformation and *de facto* transnationalization when it comes to immigration policy design and implementation.


## THE BORDER AND THE INDIVIDUAL AS REGULATORY SITES

In my reading there is a fundamental framework that roots all the country-specific immigration policies of the developed world in a common set of conceptions about the role of the state and of national borders. The purpose here is not to minimize the many differences in national policies, but to underline the growing convergence in various aspects of immigration policy and practice.[7]

First, the sovereignty of the state and border control, whether land borders, airports, or consulates in sending countries, lie at the heart of the regulatory effort. Secondly, immigration policy is shaped by an understanding of immigration as the consequence of the individual actions of emigrants; the receiving country is taken as a passive agent, one not implicated in the process of emigration. In refugee policy, in contrast, there is a recognition of other factors, beyond the control of individuals, as leading to outflows.[8] A fundamental trait of immigration policy is, then, that it singles out the border and the individual as the sites for regulatory enforcement.

The sovereignty of the state when it comes to power over entry is well established by treaty law and constitutionally. The Convention of The Hague of 1930 asserted the right of the state to grant citizenship; the 1952 Convention on Refugees, which asserted that the right to leave is a universal right, remained silent on the right to entry— better silence than evident contradiction. (As is well known, the status of refugees and their right not to be forcibly returned are established in international law, but there is no corresponding right of asylum; such right is at the discretion of a receiving state.) There are various human rights declarations and conventions that urge states to grant asylum on humanitarian grounds, but they all recognize the absolute discretion of states in this matter.[9] A few states, notably Austria and Germany, until recently gave those formally recognized as refugees a legal right to asylum. The various agreements towards the formation of the European

Union keep asserting the right of the state to control who can enter. This is quite a contrast with the assertions in the GATT, NAFTA, and the European Union about the need to lift state controls over borders when it comes to the flow of capital, information, services, and state controls over the domestic financial markets.

Secondly, on the matter of the individual as a site for enforcement, two different operational logics are becoming evident. One of these logics—the one embedded in immigration policy—places exclusive responsibility for the immigration process on the individual, and hence makes of the individual the site for the exercise of the state's authority. There is a strong tendency in immigration policy in developed countries to reduce the process to the actions of individuals. The individual is the site for accountability and for enforcement. Yet it is now increasingly being recognized that international migrations are embedded in larger geopolitical and transnational economic dynamics. The world-wide evidence shows rather clearly that there is considerable patterning in the geography of migrations, and that the major receiving countries tend to get immigrants from their zones of influence. This holds for countries as diverse as the United States, France, and Japan. Immigration is at least partly an outcome of the overseas actions of the governments and major private economic actors in receiving countries. Economic internationalization and the geopolitics resulting from older colonial patterns suggest that the responsibility for immigration may not be exclusively the immigrant's. Analytically these conditions can only enter into theorizations about the state and immigration when we suspend the proposition implicit in much immigration analysis, that immigration is the result of individual action.

In the other logic, that embedded in human rights agreements, the individual emerges as a site for contesting the authority (sovereignty) of the state because s/he is the site for human rights.

## BEYOND SOVEREIGNTY: CONSTRAINTS ON STATES' POLICY-MAKING

When it comes to immigration policy, states under the rule of law increasingly confront a range of rights and obligations, pressures from both inside and outside, from universal human rights to not-so-universal ethnic lobbies. The overall effect is to constrain the sovereignty of the state and to undermine old notions about immigration control.

First, we see emerging a *de facto* regime, centred in international agreements and conventions as well as in various rights gained by immigrants, that limits the state's role in controlling immigration. (See e.g. Hollifield 1992; Bauböck 1994; Sassen 1996*a*, part 3). An example of such an agreement is the International Convention adopted by the General Assembly of the United Nations on 18 December 1990 on the protection of the rights of all migrant workers and members of their families (Resolution 45/158). Further, there is a set of rights of resident immigrants widely upheld by legal authorities. We have also seen the gradual expansion over the last three decades of civil and social rights to marginal populations, whether women, ethnic minorities, or immigrants and refugees.

The extension of rights, which has taken place mostly through the judiciary, has confronted states with a number of constraints in the area of immigration and refugee policy. For instance, attempts by the legislature in France and Germany to limit family reunification were blocked by administrative and constitutional courts on the grounds that such restrictions would violate international agreements. The courts have also regularly supported a combination of rights of resident immigrants which have the effect of limiting the government's power over resident immigrants. Similarly, such courts have limited the ability of governments to restrict or stop asylum-seekers from entering the country.[10]

Finally, the numbers and kinds of political actors involved in immigration policy debates and policy-making in western Europe, North America, and Japan are far greater than they were two decades ago: the European Union, anti-immigrant parties, vast networks of organizations in both Europe and North America that often represent immigrants, or claim to do so, and fight for immigrant rights, immigrant associations and immigrant politicians, mostly in the second generation, and, especially in the United States, so-called ethnic lobbies.[11] The policy process for immigration is no longer confined to a narrow governmental arena of ministerial and administrative interaction (Jacobson 1996; Hollifield 1992).[12] Whole parties position themselves politically in terms of their stand on immigration, especially in some of the European countries.

These developments are particularly evident in the case of the European Union. Europe's single market programme has had a powerful impact in raising the prominence of various issues associated with free circulation of people as an essential element in creating a frontier-free community; the institutions of the European Community lacked the legal competence to deal with many of these issues but had to begin to address them. Gradually these institutions have wound up more deeply involved with visa policy, family reunification, and migration policy— all formerly exclusively in the domain of the individual national states. National governments resisted EC involvement in these once exclusively national domains. But now both legal and practical issues have made such involvement acceptable and inevitable, notwithstanding many public pronouncements to the contrary.

It is becoming evident that many aspects of immigration and refugee policy intersect with EC legal competence. A key nexus here is the free movement of persons and attendant social rights as part of the formation of a single market. In practice the European Union is assuming an increasingly important role and the fact that these are immigration countries is slowly being acknowledged. Monetary and economic union would require greater flexibility in movement of workers and their families and thereby pose increasing problems for national immigration laws regarding non-EU nationals in EU member states.

There is now growing recognition of the need for an EU-wide immigration policy, something denied for a long time by individual states, though very slowly the general direction has been towards a closer union of immigration policies. The formulation of such a unified policy has become even more urgent with the collapse of the socialist bloc, and the rapid increase in refugees.

In the case of the United States, the combination of forces at the governmental level is quite different, yet has similar general implications about the state's constraints in immigration policy-making. Immigration policy in the United States today is largely debated and shaped by Congress, and hence is highly public and subject to pressure from a vast multiplicity of local interests, notably ethnic lobbies.[13] This has made it a very public process, quite different from other processes of policy-making.[14] Indeed, immigration has become part of a broader renationalizing of politics in the United States—a process that can be seen as partly a reaction to economic globalization and in that regard not unlike the ascendance of regionalisms in western Europe in the context of a strengthened European Union.

Thus, after two decades of rights-based liberalism, Congress and public opinion are now pushing for pronounced curtailments of the rights and entitlements of legal immigrants, not to mention undocumented immigrants. Immigration policy and other types of legislation have expanded the rights of immigrants, including those of undocumented immigrants.[15] Even as the 1990 Act was passed, in a great hurry and without much public debate, public opinion was already turning against immigration. And the recently approved immigration reform of 1996 tightens the rules regulating legal entries and sets stricter limits on the ability of US citizens and permanent residents to bring in other family members into the United States. These developments are happening in a broader context of a drive to fiscal cost-cutting, significant levels of unemployment and wage stagnation, and radical devolution to the states.[16]

The fact that immigration in the United States has historically been the preserve of the federal government assumes new meaning in today's context of radical devolution—the return of powers to the states.[17] Aman (1995) has noted that although political and constitutional arguments for reallocating federal power to the states are not new, the recent re-emergence of the Tenth Amendment as a politically viable and popular guideline is the major political shift since the New Deal in the relations between the federal government and the states. There is now an emerging conflict between several state governments and the federal government around the particular issue of federal mandates that lack mandatory federal funding, such as access to public health care and schools. Thus states with disproportionate shares of immigrants are asserting that they are disproportionately burdened by the putative costs of immigration. In the United States the costs of immigration are an area of great debate and wide-ranging estimates.[18]

At the heart of this conflict is the fact that the federal government sets policy but does not assume responsibility, financial or otherwise, for the implementation of many key aspects of immigration policy. The radical devolution under way now is going to accentuate some of these divisions further. States are beginning to request reimbursement from the federal government for the costs of benefits and services that they are required to provide, especially to undocumented immigrants (Clark *et al.* 1994; GAO 1994, 1995). In 1994 six states (Arizona, California, Florida, New Jersey, New York, and Texas) filed separate suits in federal district courts to recover costs they claim to have sustained because of the federal government's failure to enforce US immigration policy, protect the nation's borders, and provide adequate resources for immigration emergencies (Dunlap and Morse 1995).[19] The amounts range from $50.5 million in New Jersey for 1992/3 costs of imprisoning 500 undocumented criminal felons and construction of future facilities, to $33.6 billion in New York for all state and county costs associated with undocumented immigration between 1988 to 1993. US District Court judges have dismissed all six lawsuits; some of the states are appealing the decision.

One of the questions raised by these developments concerns the nature of the control by national states in regulating immigration. The question here is not so much how effective is a state's control over its borders?—we know it is never absolute. The question concerns rather the substantive nature of state control over immigration given international human rights agreements, the extension of various social and political rights to resident immigrants over the last twenty years, and the multiplication of political actors involved with the immigration question.

There is, first, the matter of the unintended consequences of policies, whether immigration policies as such or other kinds of policy which have an impact on immigration. For instance, the 1965 US Immigration Act had consequences not intended or foreseen by its framers (Reimers 1983; Briggs 1992); given its emphasis on family reunion, there was a general expectation it would bring in more of the nationalities already present in the country, e.g. Europeans. Other kinds of unintended consequence are related to the internationalization of production and foreign aid (Sassen 1988; *Journal für Entwicklungspolitik* 1995; Bonacich *et al.* 1994). These often turned out to have unexpected impacts on emigration. Similar unintended consequences have been associated with military aid and subsequent refugee flows, e.g. El Salvador in the decade of the 1980s (Mahler 1995). Although immigration policy has rarely been an explicit, formal component of foreign policy in the United States, the latter has had significant impacts on immigration besides the well-established fact of refugee flows from Indo-China. If one were to be discreet, one would say that foreign aid has rarely deterred emigration.[20]

It is also a fact that domestic US policies with an overseas impact have contributed to promote emigration to the United States. There is the notorious sugar price support provision of the early 1980s, according to which taxpayers paid $3 billion annually to support the price of sugar for US producers. This kept Caribbean Basin countries out of the competition and resulted in a loss of 400,000 jobs there between 1982 and 1988; for example, the Dominican Republic lost three-quarters of its sugar export quota in less than a decade. The 1980s was also an era of large increases in emigration from that region.

A second type of condition that illuminates the issue of the substantive nature of the control by states over immigration is a twist on the zero-sum argument. If a government closes one kind of entry category, recent history shows that another one will have a rise in numbers. A variant on this dynamic is that if a government has, for instance, a very liberal policy on asylum, public opinion may turn against all asylum-seekers and close up the country totally; this in turn is likely to promote an increase in irregular entries.[21]

There is a third set of conditions that can be seen as reducing the autonomy of the state in controlling immigration. Large-scale international migrations are embedded in rather complex economic, social, and ethnic networks. They are highly conditioned and structured flows. States may insist on treating immigration as the aggregate outcome of individual actions and as distinct and autonomous from other major geopolitical and transnational processes. But they cannot escape the consequences of those larger dynamics and of their insistence on isolating immigration policy from those larger dynamics.

These constraints on the state's capacity to control immigration should not be seen as a control crisis. This type of analysis opens up the immigration policy question beyond the familiar range of the border and the individual as the sites for regulatory enforcement. It signals that international migrations are partly embedded in conditions produced by economic internationalization both in sending and in receiving areas. While a national state may have the power to write the text of an immigration policy, it is likely to be dealing with a complex, deeply embedded, and transnational process that it can only partly address or regulate through immigration policy as conventionally understood.[22]

## WHEN DIFFERENT REGIMES INTERSECT

Immigration policy continues to be characterized by its formal isolation from other major processes, as if it were possible to handle migration as a bounded, closed event. There are, one could say, two major epistemic communities—one concerning the flow of capital and information; the other, immigration. Both of these epistemic communities are international, and both enjoy widespread consensus in the community of states.

The coexistence of such different regimes for capital and for immigrants has not been seen as an issue in the United States. The case of the

European Union is of interest here because it represents an advanced stage of formalization in the capital mobility regime, and in this effort European states are discovering the difficulties if not impossibility of maintaining a different labour mobility regime. The European Community and the national governments of member states have found the juxtaposition of the divergent regimes for immigration flows and for other types of flows rather difficult to handle. The discussion, design, and implementation of policy aimed at forming a European Union make it evident that immigration policy has to factor in rapid economic internationalization. The European Union shows us with great clarity the moment when states need to confront this contradiction in their design of formal policy frameworks. The other major regional systems in the world are far from that moment and may never reach it. Yet they contain less-formalized versions of the juxtaposition between border-free economies and border controls to keep immigrants out. NAFTA is one such instance, as are, in a more diffuse way, various initiatives for greater economic integration in the Western hemisphere.

Though less clearly than in western Europe and in free-trade zones, these issues are also present in other regions with cross-border migrations. These are regional systems constituted partly as zones of influence of major economic or geopolitical powers, e.g. the long-term dominance of the United States over the Caribbean Basin. What matters here is that to a good extent major international migration flows have been embedded in one or another variant of these regional systems. The quasi-transnational economic integration characterizing such regional systems produces its own variety of contradictions between drives for border-free economic spaces and border control to keep immigrants and refugees out.

There are strategic sites where it becomes clear that the existence of different regimes for the circulation of capital and the circulation of immigrants poses problems that cannot be solved through the old rules of the game, where the facts of transnationalization weigh in on the state's decisions regarding immigration. For instance, the need to create special regimes for the circulation of service workers within both GATT and NAFTA as part of the further internationalization of trade and investment in services (see Sassen, forthcoming). This regime for the circulation of service workers has been uncoupled from any notion of migration; but it represents in fact a version of temporary labour migration. It is a regime for labour mobility which is in good part under the oversight of entities that are quite autonomous from the government. This points to an institutional reshuffling of some of the components of sovereign power over entry and can be seen as an extension of the general set of processes whereby state sovereignty is partly being decentred onto other non- or quasi-governmental entities for the governance of the global economy.[23]

NAFTA's chapters on services, financial services, telecommunications, and 'business persons', for example, contain considerable detail on the various aspects relating to people operating in a country that is not their country of citizenship. For instance, chapter 12, 'Cross-Border Trade in Services', of the Agreement (White House document, 29 September 1993) includes among its five types of measures those covering 'the presence in its territory of a service provider of another Party' under Article 1201, including provisions both for firms and for individual workers. Under that same article there are also clear affirmations that nothing in the agreement on cross-border trade in services imposes any obligation regarding a non-national seeking access to the employment market of the other country, or any right on the part of that non-national to expect employment. Article 1202 contains explicit conditions of treatment of non-national service-providers, as do Articles 1203, 1205, 1210 (especially Annex 1210.5), and 1213.2a and b. Similarly, chapter 13, on telecommunications, and chapter 14, on financial services, contain specific provisions for service-providers, including detailed regulations applying to workers. Chapter 16, 'Temporary Entry for Business Persons', covers provisions for those 'engaged in trade in goods, the provision of services or the conduct of investment activities' (Article 1608).

The development of provisions for workers and business persons signals the difficulty of *not* dealing with the circulation of people in the implementation of free trade and investment frameworks. In their own specific ways each of these efforts—NAFTA, GATT, and the European Union—has had to address cross-border labour circulation.

One instantiation of the impact of globalization on governmental policy-making can be seen in Japan's new immigration law passed in 1990. While this is quite different from how the issue plays in the context of free trade agreements, it none the less illustrates one way of handling the need for cross-border circulation of professional workers in a context of resistance to the notion of open borders (Sassen 1993). This legislation opened the country to several categories of highly specialized professionals with a Western background (e.g. experts in international finance, in Western-style accounting, in Western medicine, etc.) in recognition of the growing internationalization of the professional world in Japan; it made the entry of what is referred to as 'simple labor' illegal. This can be read as importing 'Western human capital' and closing borders to immigrants.

Further, the need to address cross-border circulation of people has also become evident in free trade agreements in the less-developed world, notably in Latin America. There has been a sharp increase in activity around the international circulation of people in each of the major regional trading-blocks: Mercosur, the Grupo Andino, and the Mercado Común de Centroamérica. Each one launched a variety of initiatives in the early 1990s on international labour migration among their member countries. This is in many ways a new development. Some of the founding treaties long preceded the recent flurry of meetings on labour migrations and the circulation of people. When one examines what actually happened it becomes evident that the common markets for investment and commerce in each of these regions had themselves become activated in the 1990s under the impact of globalization, deregulation, and privatization. It was the increased circulation of capital, goods, and information under these impacts that forced the question of the circulation of people on the agenda.

In the case of the Pacto Andino, an agreement on labour migration, the Simón Bolívar Agreement on Social and Labour Integration, was set up in the early stages of the trade agreement, in 1973. It resulted in an operational agreement, the 1977 Andean Labour Migration Statement. Parallel administrative agencies were created in each country's Ministry of Labour to implement and enforce it, but, along with the general agreement on the Andean common market, it became in practice inactive. It was not until the agreement of an Andean Strategy was signed by the presidents of the member countries in 1989 that they became reactivated. Furthermore, the outlook of the Grupo Andino itself has changed from its earlier period, reflecting the sharp changes in the overall global and regional context.[24] (For more detailed accounts, including the original treaty documents, see Acuerdo de Cartagena 1991*a,b*; Acuerdo de Cartagena and OIM 1991; Banco interamericano de desarrollo and JUNAC 1993; JUNAC and OIM 1993; Leon and Kratochwil 1993.)

Mercosur represents a new generation of regional agreements (Kratochwil 1995). The founding treaty was signed by the presidents of Argentina, Brazil, Paraguay, and Uruguay in Asunción only in 1991; but this agreement actually absorbed earlier cross-border agreements in the region that had been semi- (or fully) dormant for years (Torales 1993). It acquired legal status in international law with the 1994 Ouro Preto Protocol, which put the Customs Union into effect. Not long after the founding, migration and labour officials of member countries set up two working groups, one of which included a Commission on Migration Control and Border Control Simplification. Various additional committees and working groups have been set up concerned with general border and social and labour questions. Labour migration is on several agendas and is the subject of various agreements (for detailed accounts, see OIM 1991*b*; CEPAL 1994; Torales 1993; Marmora 1994).

The Organization of Central American States (ODECA) was created in 1951 and the Central American Common Market in the mid-1960s. It was not until 1991 that the Central American Migration Organization (OCAM) was set up. In the same year the Central American Parliament (PARLACEN) was established and also the new System for Regional Integration (SICA); neither of these institutions has the full participation of all the countries of the region, although this is their aim. OCAM has been very active over the last few years, but it must be emphasized that conditions in this region are radically different from those in the other two Latin American regional blocks: the devastating civil war has created large refugee flows all over the region, while the cessation of many of the worst military conflicts has brought with it complicated return flows. But though this is the dominating factor, it is also the case that the 1990s has seen enormous interest in regional economic integration and a framework for the circulation of persons linked to it. This is an effort that lies outside the region's refugee and return migration crisis and is clearly linked to the new economics of the 1990s (for more detailed accounts, see Directores generales de migraciones 1992; CEPAL 1992; Stein 1993; OIM 1991*a,d*; see also Fagen and Eldridge 1991).

In the case of the United States and its major immigration source country, Mexico, it appears that the signing of NAFTA has also had the effect of activating a series of new initiatives regarding migration— a sort of *de facto* bilateralism which represents a radically new phase in the handling of migration between these two countries. It is worth providing some detail on these.

Not unlike the case of Latin America, we are seeing a reactivation of older instruments and a flurry of new activity around the question of international migration. Twenty years ago Presidents Carter and Lopez Portillo established the US–Mexico Consultative Mechanism to provide better co-ordination between the two countries. This eventually led to the formation of the US–Mexico Binational Commission in 1981 to serve as a forum for meetings between Cabinet-level officials from both countries. It was conceived as a flexible mechanism that would meet once or twice a year. One of the early working groups was the Border Relations Action Group, formed in 1981.

What is different over the last two years is the frequency, focus, and actual work that is getting done in the meetings of the working groups, and NAFTA has further contributed to strengthen the contacts and collaboration between the groups. Particularly active is the Working Group on Migration and Consular Affairs, which has become an effective means of resolving serious border problems of mutual interest.[25] In its joint communiqué of 16 May 1995 it discussed progress made on the agreements reached at its most recent meeting, in Zacatecas in February. Its particular concern was to ensure the safe operation of borders as border areas have become increasingly dynamic with the growing interactions between the two countries, and to prevent and eliminate criminality and violence affecting both migrants in transit and border communities. It also reaffirmed its commitment to protect the human and civil rights of all Mexican migrants in the United States regardless of their legal status. Many of the members of the working group for both countries seem convinced that this is a new and unprecedented phase of communication and collaboration. It is also the first time the Mexican government has become so involved with international migration issues, to which in the past, it is generally acknowledged it had a *laissez-faire* position and no developed policies.

There are also disagreements between the two delegations, which are discussed openly. Notably, the Mexican delegation is deeply concerned about the growing anti-immigrant feeling and measures in the United States (and most recently with the new 1996 immigration law). The US delegation has agreed to work together to combat these developments. The Mexican delegation also expressed concern at the US proposal to expand and strengthen border fences to improve security in various locations, emphasizing the negative effects of such a measure on the border communities and Mexican efforts to resolve the problems in the most troubled locations. Notwithstanding these serious disagreements, or perhaps precisely because of them, both delegations appear convinced of the importance of continuing the communication and collaboration that has developed over the last two years.

The February 1995 meeting in Zacatecas was extremely important in advancing the effort towards closer collaboration and open communications.[26] Apart from the agreements arrived at during the meeting that the Mexican government should create groups to combat violence in border locations, one effort has been to expand the activities of the human rights non-governmental organization called Beta. On the US side, there is now a Citizens' Advisory Panel, which has as one of its primary purposes the review of procedures dealing with reports of abuse at the border. The border liaison mechanisms have turned out to be a very effective way of handling border problems and new ones are being set up at additional border locations.

Another major effort to come out of the Zacatecas meeting was the facilitation of documented migration and the return of undocumented migrants in full compliance with human rights codes. Acting upon this agreement, the US delegation affirmed in the joint communiqué of 16 May that the backlog in processing border crossing card applications had been eliminated at major ports of entry by 1 April. Finally, both delegations are developing criteria, procedures, and legal conditions consistent with international practices for the safe and orderly repatriation of undocumented Mexican migrants to ports of entry within Mexico without intermediate stops, with full respect for their human rights.

Both delegations recognize that having access to the necessary information about migration is essential, and they continue to support the ongoing Binational Study on Migration. The expectation is that this will facilitate the development of new and constructive long-term policies to deal with bilateral migration flows.

There are also non-official indications of a move towards *de facto* bilateralism regarding international migration. For instance, the enormous expansion and strong government support received by the Colegio de la Frontera Norte, whose headquarters is outside Tijuana but which has units along the whole border. The goal of this university is to develop a body of research and a cadre of professionals who understand the border as a region that involves both the United States and Mexico. A second example is the formation of the US–Mexico Consultative Group sponsored by the Carnegie Endowment for International Peace in Washington. It seeks to facilitate cooperation in US–Mexican relations on migration and attendant labour issues by engaging senior policy-makers and non-governmental experts from the two countries in an ongoing off-the-record, non-official dialogue. The first meeting was held in June 1995. Among the top government representatives were the ambassadors of the two countries. All of these developments have the effect of reducing the autonomy of the state in immigration policy-making; and of multiplying the sectors within the state that are addressing immigration policy and thereby increasing the room for conflicts within the state. The assertion that the state is in full charge of immigration policy is less and less helpful. Not only has the state itself been transformed by its participation in the global economy, but policy-making regarding international issues can engage very different parts of the government. The state has, of course, never been a homogeneous actor, being constituted of multiple agencies and social forces. Indeed it could be said (cf. Mitchell 1989) that although the state has central control over immigration policy, the work of exercising that claimed power often begins with a limited contest between the state and outside social forces. These interest groups include agribusiness, manufacturing, humanitarian groups, unions, ethnic organizations, and zero-population-growth efforts. Today we need to add to this the fact that the hierarchies of power and influence within the state are being reconfigured by the furthering of economic globalization.[27]

The conditions within which immigration policy is being made and implemented today range from the pressures of economic globalization and its implications for the role of the state to international agreements on human rights. And the institutional setting within which immigration policy is being made and implemented ranges from national states and local states to supranational organizations.

Why does this transformation of the state and the interstate system matter for immigration? The displacement of governance functions away from the state to non-state entities affects the state's capacity to control its borders. New systems of governance are being created. Increasingly they may create conflicts with the state's capacity to keep on regulating immigration in the same ways. Further, the transformation of the state itself through its role in the implementation of global processes may well contribute to new constraints, options, and vested interests. The ascendance of agencies linked to furthering globalization and the decline of those linked to domestic equity questions is quite likely to have an eventual effect on the immigration agenda.

## HUMAN RIGHTS AND IMMIGRATION POLICY

Beyond the new conditions brought about by economic globalization, immigration policy and practice is also increasingly affected by the new international human rights regime.[28] The invocation of international covenants to make national policy signals yet another type of displacement of government functions: a displacement in the legitimization process. This is a move away from statism—the absolute right of states to represent their people in international law and international relations—towards a conceptual and operational opening for the emergence of other subjects and actors in international law. The international human rights regime has been a key mechanism for making subjects out of those hitherto invisible in international law—first-nation people, immigrants and refugees, women (Sassen 1996*a*, 1996*c*). This has brought about a growing number of instances where one sector of the state is in disagreement with another. It is perhaps most evident in the strategic role that the judiciary has assumed in the highly developed countries when it comes to defending the rights of immigrants, refugees, and asylum-seekers.

Human rights are not dependent on nationality, unlike political, social, and civil rights, which are predicated on the distinction between national and alien. Human rights override such distinctions. Even where rooted in the founding documents of nation-states, as is the case with the United States and France, we need to understand the specific development of these rights over the last few years. Human rights today are a force that can undermine the exclusive authority of the state over its nationals and thereby contribute to transform the interstate system and international legal order.[29] Membership in territorially exclusive nation-states ceases to be the only ground for the realization of rights. All residents, whether citizens or not, can claim their human rights (Jacobson 1996; Henkin 1990). Human rights begin to impinge on the principle of nation-based citizenship and the boundaries of the nation. They contribute to strengthen concepts of personhood. Human rights codes can erode some of the legitimacy of the state if it fails to respect such human rights—it is no longer just a question of national self-determination (see Franck 1992). This is a very significant shift.

The growing influence of human rights law is particularly evident in Europe. It was not until the 1980s that such influence started to be felt in the United States and it still lags behind.[30] This has been seen to be partly a result of American definitions of personhood, which have led courts in some cases to address the matter of undocumented immigrants within American constitutionalism, notably the idea of inalienable and natural rights of people and persons, without territorial confines. The emphasis on persons makes possible interpretations about undocumented immigrants, in a way it would not if the emphasis were on citizens. It was not until the mid-1970s and the early 1980s that domestic courts began to consider human rights codes as normative instruments in their own right. The rapid growth of undocumented immigration and the sense of the state's incapacity to control the flow and to regulate the various categories in its population were factors leading courts to consider the international human rights regime, which allows courts to rule on basic protections of individuals not formally accounted in the national territory and legal system, notably undocumented aliens and unauthorized refugees.[31]

The growing accountability of states under the rule of law to international human rights codes and institutions, together with the fact that individuals and non-state actors can make claims on those states in terms of those codes, signal a development that, according to some (e.g. Jacobson 1996), goes beyond the expansion of human rights within the framework of nation-states; it contributes to redefining the bases of legitimacy of states under the rule of law and the notion of nationality.

Under human rights regimes states must increasingly take account of persons *qua* persons, rather than *qua* citizens. The individual is now an object of law and a site for rights, regardless of whether a citizen or an alien.[32]

Immigrants, in accumulating social and civic rights and even some political rights in countries of residence, have diluted the meaning of citizenship and the specialness of the claims citizens can make on the state. When it comes to social services (education, health insurance, welfare, unemployment benefits) citizenship status is of minor importance in western Europe and, until the 1996 law, in the United States. What matters is residence and legal alien status. And most of these countries will pay retirement benefits even if recipients no longer reside there. Some countries have also granted local voting rights, e.g. Sweden and the Netherlands. Aliens are guaranteed full civil rights either constitutionally or by statute. Given the little difference between the claims that citizens and immigrants can make, there is also a low propensity to naturalize.

Even unauthorized immigrants can make some of these claims. Schuck has noted that new 'social contracts' are being negotiated in the United States every day between undocumented aliens and US society, contracts that cannot be nullified through claims about nationality and sovereignty. Courts have had to accept the fact of undocumented aliens and to extend to these aliens some form of legal recognition and guarantees of basic rights (see Bosniak 1992; Isbister 1996). Various decisions have conferred important benefits of citizenship to undocumented aliens. This clearly undermines older notions of sovereignty.

## CONCLUSION

The developments described here point to a number of trends that may become increasingly important for sound immigration policy-making. First, where the effort towards the formation of transnational economic spaces has gone the furthest and been most formalized it has become very clear that existing frameworks for immigration policy are problematic. It is not the case that the coexistence of very different regimes for the circulation of capital and for that of people is free of tension and contention. This is most evident in the legislative work necessary for the formation of the European Union.

Secondly, we see the beginning of a displacement of government functions on to non-governmental or quasi-governmental institutions. This is most evident in the new transnational legal and regulatory regimes created in the context of economic globalization. But it is also intersecting with questions of migration, specifically temporary labour migration, as is evident in the creation of special regimes for the circulation of professional workers and business persons both within GATT and NAFTA as part of the further internationalization of trade and investment in services. This regime for the circulation of service workers has been separated from any notion of migration; but it represents in fact a version of temporary labour migration. It is a regime for labour mobility which is in good part under the oversight of entities that are quite autonomous from the government. We can see in this displacement the elements of a privatization of certain aspects of the regulation of cross-border labour mobility.

Thirdly, the legitimization process for states under the rule of law calls for respect and enforcement of international human rights codes, regardless of the nationality and legal status of an individual. While enforcement is precarious, it none the less signals a major shift in the legitimization process. This is perhaps most evident in the strategic role that the judiciary has assumed in the highly developed countries when it comes to the rights of immigrants, refugees, and asylum-seekers.

Finally, the state itself has been transformed by this combination of developments. This is so partly because the state under the rule of law is one of the key institutional arenas for the implementation of these new transnational regimes—whether the global rights of capital or the human rights of all individuals regardless of nationality. And it is partly because the state has incorporated the objective of furthering a global economy, as is evident in the ascendance of certain government agencies, e.g. the treasury, and the decline of others, such as those linked to the social fund.

Because so many processes are transnational, governments are increasingly not competent to address some of today's major issues unilaterally or even from the exclusive confines of the interstate system narrowly defined. It is not that this is the end of state sovereignty, but rather that the 'exclusivity and scope of their competence' (see Rosenau 1992) has altered, that there is a narrowing range within which the state's authority and legitimacy are operative.

There is no doubt that some of the intellectual administrative technology that governments have and that allow them control, i.e. Foucault's governmentality, has now shifted to non-state institutions. This is dramatically illustrated in the new privatized transnational regimes for cross-border business and the growing power of the logic of the global capital market over national economic policy.

These are transformations in the making as we speak. My reading is that they matter. It is easy to argue the opposite: that the state is still absolute and nothing much has changed. But it may well be the case that these developments signal the beginning of a new era. Scholarship on mentalities has shown how difficult it is for people to recognize systemic change in their contemporary conditions. Seeing continuity is much simpler and often reassuring.

Official immigration policy today is not part of the explicated rules of the new game. Is this helpful in seeking to have a more effective long-term immigration policy in today's globalizing world?

## NOTES

This chapter is based on *Immigration Policy in a Global Economy: From National Crisis to Multilateral Management*, a book being prepared for the Twentieth Century Fund. I thank the Fund for its support. It also draws on Sassen (1996a).

1. This dominance assumes many forms and does not affect only poorer and weaker countries. For instance, France, which ranks among the top providers of information services and industrial engineering services in Europe and has a strong, though not outstanding, position in financial and insurance services, has found itself at an increasing disadvantage in legal and accounting services. French law firms are at a particular disadvantage because Anglo-American law governs international transactions. US and UK firms with offices in Paris dominate the servicing of the legal needs of firms, whether

French or foreign, operating out of France (Carrez 1991). Similarly, Anglo-American law is increasingly dominant in international commercial arbitration, an institution grounded in continental traditions of jurisprudence, particularly French and Swiss (Dezalay and Garth 1995).

2. Today international business contracts for example, for the sale of goods, joint ventures, construction projects, or distributorships typically call for arbitration in the event of a dispute arising from the contractual arrangement. The main reason given today for this choice is that it allows each party to avoid being forced to submit to the courts of the other. Also important is the secrecy of the process. Such arbitration can be 'institutional' and follow the rules of institutions such as the International Chamber of Commerce in Paris, the American Arbitration Association, the London Court of International Commercial Arbitration, or many others. Or it can be *ad hoc*, often following the rules of the United Nations Commission on International Trade Law (UNCITRAL). The arbitrators are private individuals selected by the parties; usually there are three. They act as private judges, holding hearings and issuing judgments.

3. There are two agencies that dominate the market in ratings, with listings of $US3 trillion each. They are Moody's Investors' Service, usually referred to as Moody's, and Standard & Poor's Ratings Group, usually referred to as Standard & Poor. There are several rating agencies in other countries, but they are orientated to the domestic markets. The possibility of a European-based rating agency has been discussed, particularly with the merger of a London-based agency (IBCA) with a French one (Euronotation).

4. This is a scholarship with a diversity of intellectual lineages, e.g. Ruggie (1993); Wallerstein (1974); Arrighi (1994); Jessop (1990); Leftwich (1994); Rosenau (1992). See Sassen (1996a) for a discussion of this literature as it concerns the particular question under discussion here.

5. Thus, there were centralizing monarchies in western Europe, city-states in Italy, and city-leagues in Germany (see Arrighi 1994; Wallerstein 1974). Further, even at a time when we see the emergence of nation-states with exclusive territoriality and sovereignty, it can be argued that other forms might have become effective alternatives.

6. One of the key obstacles to even beginning to think along totally different lines about immigration policy is the widespread conviction that any other approach than border control would lead to massive invasions from the Third World. Much general commentary and policy-making, wittingly or not, tends to proceed as if most people in less-developed countries want to go to a rich country, as if all immigrants want to become permanent settlers, as if the problem of current immigration policy has to do basically with gaps or failures in enforcement, as if raising the levels of border control is an effective way of regulating immigration. This type of understanding of immigration clearly leads to a certain type of immigration policy, one centred on the fear of being invaded by people from less-developed countries everywhere and hence on border control as the only answer. The evidence on immigration shows that most people do not want to leave their countries, that overall levels of permanent immigration are not very large, that there is considerable circulation and return migration, that most migration

flows eventually stabilize if not decline (see Sassen, forthcoming, for a review of the evidence on these issues). Making these the central facts about the reality of immigration should allow for a broader set of options when it comes to immigration policy than would be the case with mass emigration and invasion. See also Isbister (1996).

7. There is a vast and rich scholarly literature that documents and interprets the specificity and distinctiveness of immigration policy in highly developed countries, e.g. Weil (1991); Cornelius *et al.* (1994); Weiner (1995); Soysal (1994); Thränhardt (1992); Bade (1992), to mention just a few. As a body this literature allows us to see the many differences among these countries.

8. Refugee policy in some countries does lift the burden of immigration from the immigrant's shoulders. US refugee policy, particularly for the case of Indo-Chinese refugees, does acknowledge partial responsibility on the part of the government. Clearly, in the case of economic migrations, such responsibility is far more difficult to establish, and by its nature far more indirect.

9. One important exception is the 1969 Convention on Refugee Problems in Africa adopted by the Organization of African Unity, which includes the right to entry.

10. These efforts that mix the conventions on universal human rights and national judiciaries assume many different forms. Some of the instances in the United States are the sanctuary movement in the 1980s, which sought to establish protected areas, typically in churches, for refugees from Central America; judicial battles, such as those around the status of El Salvadoreans granted indefinite stay though formally defined as illegal; the fight for the rights of detained Haitians in an earlier wave of boat lifts. It is clear that, notwithstanding the lack of an enforcement apparatus, human rights limit the discretion of states in how they treat non-nationals on their territory. It is also worth noting in this regard that the United Nations High Commission for Refugees is the only UN agency with a universally conceded right of access to a country when there is a recognized crisis.

11. While these developments are well known for the cases of Europe and North America, there is not much general awareness of the fact that we are seeing incipient forms in Japan as well (see e.g. Shank 1994). For instance, in Japan today we see a strong group of human rights advocates for immigrants; efforts by non-official unions to organize undocumented immigrant workers; organizations working on behalf of immigrants which receive funding from individuals or government institutions in sending countries (e.g. the Thai ambassador to Japan announced in Oct. 1995 that his government will give a total of 2.5 million baht, about $100,000, to five civic groups that assist Thai migrant workers, especially undocumented ones; see *Japan Times*, 18 Oct. 1995).

12. Further, the growth of immigration, refugee flows, ethnicity, and regionalism raise questions about the accepted notion of citizenship in contemporary nation-states and hence about the formal structures for accountability. My research on the international circulation of capital and labour has raised questions for me on the meaning of such concepts as national economy and national workforce under conditions of growing internationalization of capital and the growing presence of immigrant workers in major industrial

countries. Furthermore, the rise of ethnicity in the United States and in Europe among a mobile workforce raises questions about the content of the concept of nation-based citizenship. The portability of national *identity* raises questions about the bonds with other countries, or localities within them; and the resurgence of ethnic regionalism creates barriers to the political incorporation of new immigrants (see e.g. Soysal 1994; Bauböck 1994; Sassen 1996*a*).

13. Jurisdiction over immigration matters in the US Congress lies with the Judiciary Committee, not with the Foreign Affairs Committee as might have been the case. Congressional intent on immigration is often at odds with the foreign affairs priorities of the executive. There is a certain policy-making tug of war (Mitchell 1989). It has not always been this way. In the late 1940s and 1950s there was great concern with how immigration policy could be used to advance foreign policy objectives. The history of what government agency was responsible for immigration is rather interesting. When the Department of Labor (DOL) was created in 1914 it was given responsibility for immigration policy. In June 1933 President Roosevelt combined functions into the Immigration and Naturalization Service (INS) within the DOL. The advent of the Second World War brought a shift in the administrative responsibility for the country's immigration policy: in 1940 President Roosevelt recommended it be moved to the Department of Justice, because of the supposed political threat represented by immigrants from enemy countries. This was meant to last for the duration of war and then the INS was to be returned to the DOL. But it never was. It also meant that immigration wound up in Congress in committees traditionally reserved for lawyers, as are the Senate and House Judiciary Committees. It has been said that this is why immigration law is so complicated (and, I would add, so centred on the legalities of entry and so unconcerned with broader issues).

14. There are diverse social forces shaping the role of the state, depending on the matter at hand. Thus in the early 1980s bank crisis, for instance, the players were few and well coordinated; the state basically relinquished the organizing capacity to the banks, the International Monetary Fund, and a few other actors. All very discreet; indeed so discreet that if you look closely the government was hardly a player in that crisis. This is quite a contrast with the deliberations around the passing of the 1986 Immigration and Reform Control Act—which was a sort of national brawl. In trade liberalization discussions there are often multiple players, and the executive may or may not relinquish powers to Congress.

15. This is illustrated by the now-famous 1982 US Supreme Court *Plyler* v. *Doe* guaranteeing undocumented immigrant children the right to a K-12 public school education, deportation hearings, and use of appeal rights for apprehended undocumented immigrants and political asylum applicants.

16. A major new piece of legislation where many of these attempts come together is in the welfare reform as they affect immigrants. Under previous law naturalized US citizens had full eligibility on the same terms as native-born individuals, and so did lawful permanent residents (with the exception of deeming provisions). But the sharp changes recently

approved by Congress will have the effect of curtailing or eliminating completely the eligibility of legal immigrants for most federal means-tested programmes.

17. In this light it is worth noting that in Nov. 1995 a federal judge ruled large sections of Proposition 187 unconstitutional, citing individual rights and the fact that 'the state [of California] is powerless to enact its own scheme to regulate immigration'.

18. The latest study by the Washington-based Urban Institute found that immigrants contribute $30 billion more in taxes than they take in services.

19. President Clinton's 1994 crime bill earmarked $1.8 billion in disbursements over six years to help reimburse states for these incarceration costs.

20. Take El Salvador in the 1980s: billions of dollars in aid poured in, and hundreds of thousands of Salvadoreans poured out as US aid raised the effectiveness of El Salvador's military control and aggression against its own people. Or the case of the Philippines, a country that received massive aid and has had high emigration. In both cases it was foreign aid dictated by security issues. Emigration resulting from US economic and political interventions is evident in the Dominican emigration in the 1960s and in the emigration from India and Pakistan to the United States—the latter two associated as well with security aid from the United States. (I have long argued as a scholar that policy-makers should have migration impact statements attached to various policies.)

21. Increasingly, unilateral policy by a major immigration country is problematic. One of the dramatic examples was that of Germany, which began to receive massive numbers of entrants as the other European states gradually tightened their policies and Germany kept its very liberal asylum policy. Another case is the importance for the European Community today that the Mediterranean countries—Italy, Spain, and Portugal—control their borders regarding non-EC entrants.

22. On a somewhat related matter, it seems to me that the sense of an immigration control crisis that prevails today in many of the highly developed countries is in some ways unwarranted, even though states have less control than they would like because immigration is caught in a web of other dynamics. When we look at the characteristics of immigrations over time and across the world, it is clear that these are highly patterned flows, embedded in other dynamics which contain equilibrating mechanisms; that they have a finite duration (many immigrations have lasted for fifty years and then come to an end); that there is more return migration than we generally realize (e.g. Soviet engineers and intellectuals who went back to Moscow from Israel; Mexicans who returned after becoming legal residents through the Immigration Reform and Control Act amnesty programme, feeling that now they could circulate between the two countries); we also know from earlier historical periods when there were no controls that most people did not leave poorer areas to go to richer ones, even though there were plenty of such differences in Europe within somewhat reasonable travel distances (Sassen 1996*b*).

23. Elsewhere (Sassen 1996*a*; forthcoming) I have argued that in some ways this can be seen as yet another instance of privatization of that which

is profitable and manageable. We are seeing the privatizing of what was once government policy in several emergent cross-border legal and regulatory regimes for international business, notably the rapid growth of international commercial arbitration and the growing importance of credit-rating agencies discussed in the preceding section. In this case it would be a privatizing of immigration policy through NAFTA of components that are characterized by 'high-value-added' (i.e. persons with high levels of education and/or capital), manageability (they are likely to be temporary and working in leading sectors of the economy and hence are visible migrants, subject to effective regulation), and benefits (given the new ideology of free trade and investment). Governments are left with the supervision of the 'difficult' and 'low-value-added' components of immigration—poor, low-wage workers, refugees, dependants, and potentially controversial brain-drain flows. This can clearly have a strong impact on what comes to be seen as the category 'immigrant', with policy and broader political implications.

24. An Andean Social Charter was created with the active participation of trade unions and the Andean parliament, as was a basic regulatory framework for regional international migration. In 1992 the member countries set up the Committee of Migration Officials of the Grupo Andino, which includes migration officials of the member countries, to advise the Junta del Acuerdo de Cartagena, the technical and administrative body of the Cartagena Agreement.

25. The US delegation for this group is chaired by the Assistant Secretary of State for Consular Affairs and the INS Commissioner.

26. The meeting of the Working Group on Migration and Consular Affairs in Zacatecas followed the three meetings held in 1994. The Mexican delegation was headed by the Under-Secretary for Bilateral Affairs from the Secretariat of Foreign Affairs, the Under-Secretary of Population and Migration Services of the Secretariat of the Interior, and the Commissioner of the National Migration Institute. The US delegation was headed by the INS Commissioner, the US ambassador to Mexico, and the Deputy Assistant Secretary for Inter-American Affairs of the Department of State. These are, then, fairly high-level government delegations; they are not simply technical personnel.

27. For instance, an item on internal changes in the state which may have impacts on immigration policy is the ascendance of so-called soft security issues. According to some observers, recent government reorganization in the departments of State, Defense, and the CIA reflects an implicit redefinition of national security.

28. This is a complex subject that cannot be developed here, but it is important to mention some of its impact. For fuller treatments about the impact on immigration policy in particular, see Jacobson (1996); Heisler (1986); see also Soysal (1994); Bauböck (1994); Sassen (1996a: ch. 3; forthcoming).

29. Already in the early 20th century there were several legal instruments that promoted human rights and made the individual an object of international law. But it was not until after the Second World War that we see an elaboration and formalization of such rights; the covenants and

conventions that guarantee human rights today are derived from the Universal Declaration of Human Rights adopted by the United Nations in 1948. And it is not until the late 1970s and 1980s that there is a sufficiently large array of instruments and agreements that judiciaries, particularly in Europe, can use in their decisions. In the case of the Americas, the system for the protection of human rights is the Inter-American Commission on Human Rights. It is grounded on two distinct legal documents. They are the Charter of the Organization of American States (OAS) and the American Convention on Human Rights, adopted in 1969 and entered into force in 1978. The human rights regime of the OAS was markedly strengthened in a 1967 protocol that came into force in 1970.

30. And its weight in many of the Latin American countries is dubious. For a very detailed (and harrowing) account of the situation in Mexico, see Reding (1996). See also generally Sikkink (1993).

31. For instance, the Universal Declaration was cited in 76 federal cases from 1948 to 1994; over 90 per cent of those cases took place after 1980 and, of those, 49 per cent involved immigration issues—54 per cent if we add refugees (Jacobson 1996: 97). Jacobson also found that the term 'human rights' was referred to in 19 federal cases before the 20th century, 34 times from 1900 to 1944, 191 from 1945 to 1969, 803 cases in the 1970s, over 2,000 in the 1980s, and *c*.4,000 cases through the 1990s.

32. There is a whole debate about the notion of citizenship and what it means in the current context (see Soysal 1994; Bauböck 1994). One trend in this debate is a return to notions of cities and citizenship, particularly in so-called global cities, which are partly denationalized territories and have high concentrations of non-nationals from many different parts of the world (e.g. Holston 1996; Knox and Taylor 1995; *Social Justice* 1993). The ascendance of human rights codes strengthens these tendencies to move away from nationality and national territory as absolute categories.

# REFERENCES

Acuerdo de Cartagena, Junta del (1991*a*), *Acta final de la 1ra. reunión de autoridades migratorias del Grupo Andino* (Lima: JUNAC).

—— (1991*b*), *Bases de propuesta para la integración fronteriza Andina* (Lima: JUNAC).

—— and OIM (Organización internacional de migraciones) (1991), *La migración internacional en los procesos regionales de integración en America del Sur* (Lima: JUNAC).

Aman, Alfred C., Jr. (1995), 'A Global Perspective on Current Regulatory Reform: Rejection, Relocation, or Reinvention?', *Indiana Journal of Global Legal Studies*, 2: 429–64.

Arrighi, Giovanni (1994), *The Long Twentieth Century: Money, Power, and the Origins of our Times* (London: Verso).

Bade, Klaus J. (ed.) (1992), *Ausländer, Aussiedler, Asyl in der Bundesrepublik Deutschland*, 2nd edn. (Hanover: Niedersächsische Landeszentrale für politische Bildung).

Banco Interamericano de Desarrollo and JUNAC (Junta del Acuerdo de Cartagena) (1993), *Política de integración fronteriza de los paises miembros del Grupo Andino: Cooperación técnica* (Lima: JUNAC).

Basch, Linda, Nina Glick Schiller, and Cristina Szanton-Blanc (1994), *Nations Unbound: Transnationalized Projects and the Deterritorialized Nation-State* (New York: Gordon & Breach).

Bauböck, Rainer (1994), *Transnational Citizenship: Membership and Rights in International Migration* (Aldershot: Edward Elgar).

Berner, Erhard, and Rüdiger Korff (1995), 'Globalization and Local Resistance: The Creation of Localities in Manila and Bangkok', *International Journal of Urban and Regional Research*, 19/2: 208–22.

Böhning, W. R., and M.-L. Schlöter-Paredes (eds.) (1994), *Aid in Place of Migration* (Geneva: ILO).

Bonacich, Edna, Lucie Cheng, Norma Chinchilla, Nora Hamilton, and Paul Ong (eds.) (1994), *Global Production: The Apparel Industry in the Pacific Rim* (Philadelphia: Temple University Press).

Bose, Christine E., and Edna Acosta-Belen (eds.) (1995), *Women in the Latin American Development Process* (Philadelphia: Temple University Press).

Bosniak, Linda S. (1992), 'Human Rights, State Sovereignty and the Protection of Undocumented Migrants under the International Migrant Workers' Convention', *International Migration Review*, 25/4: 737–70.

Briggs, Vernon M., Jr. (1992), *Mass Immigration and the National Interest* (Armonk, NY: M. E. Sharpe).

Carbonneau, Thomas (ed.) (1990), *Lex Mercatoria and Arbitration* (Dobbs Ferry, NY: Transnational Juris Publications).

Carrez, Jean-Francois (1991), *Le Développement des fonctions tertiares internationales à Paris et dans les métropoles régionales*, Rapport au premier ministre (Paris: La Documentation française).

CEPAL (Comisión Economica para Latino America) (1992), 'Consideraciones sobre la formación de recursos humanos en Centroamerica', CEPAL, Mexico City, mimeo.

—— (1994), *Desarrollo reciente de los procesos de integración en America Latina y el Caribe* (Santiago: CEPAL).

Clark, Rebecca L., Jeffrey Passel, Wendy Zimmermann, and Michael Fix (1994), *Fiscal Impacts of Undocumented Aliens: Selected Estimates for Seven States*, Report to the Office of Management and Budget and the Department of Justice, Sept. (Washington: Urban Institute).

Coombe, Rosemary J. (1993), 'The Properties of Culture and the Politics of Possessing Identity: Native Claims in the Cultural Appropriation Controversy', *Canadian Journal of Law and Jurisprudence*, 6/2 (July), 249–85.

Cornelius, Wayne A., Philip L. Martin, and James F. Hollifield (eds.) (1994), *Controlling Immigration: A Global Perspective* (Stanford: Stanford University Press).

Cox, Robert (1987), *Production, Power, and World Order: Social Forces in the Making of History* (New York: Columbia University Press).

Dezalay, Yves, and Bryant Garth (1995), 'Merchants of Law as Moral Entrepreneurs: Constructing International Justice from the Competition for Transnational Business Disputes', *Law and Society Review*, 29/1: 27–64.

Directores generales de migraciones (Centroamerica) (1992), 'Politicas de control sobre las corrientes migratorias en Centroamerica', in *La migración internacional: Su impacto en Centroamerica* (San José, Costa Rica: DGMC).

Drache, D., and M. Gertler (eds.) (1991), *The New Era of Global Competition: State Policy and Market Power* (Montreal: McGill-Queen's University Press).

Dunlap, Jonathan C., and Ann Morse (1995), 'States Sue Feds to Recover Immigration Costs', *Legisbrief* (National Conference of State Legislatures), 3 Jan., 1.

Espenshade, Thomas J., and Vanessa E. King (1994), 'State and Local Fiscal Impacts of US Immigrants: Evidence from New Jersey', *Population Research and Policy Review*, 13: 225–56.

Fagen, Patricia Weiss, and Joseph Eldridge (1991), 'Salvadorean Repatriation from Honduras', in Mary Ann Larkin (ed.), *Repatriation under Conflict: The Central American Case* (Washington: HMP, CIPRA, Georgetown University).

Franck, Thomas M. (1992), 'The Emerging Right to Democratic Governance', *American Journal of International Law*, 86/1: 46–91.

GAO (General Accounting Office) (1994), *Illegal Aliens: Assessing Estimates of Financial Burden on California*, GAO/HEHS-95-22 (Washington: GAO, Nov.).

—— (1995), *Illegal Aliens: National Net Cost Estimates vary Widely*, GAO/HEHS-95-133 (Washington: GAO, July).

Goodwin-Gill, G. S. (1989), 'Nonrefoulement and the New Asylum Seekers', in D. A. Martin (ed.), *The New Asylum Seekers: Refugee Policy in the 1980s* (Dordrecht: Martinus Nijhoff).

Gulbenkian Foundation (1996), *Report on the Status of the Social Sciences* (Lisbon).

Haus, Leah (1995), 'Openings in the Wall: Transnational Migrants, Labor Unions, and U.S. Immigration Policy', *International Organization*, 49/2 (Spring), 285–313.

Heisler, Martin (1986), 'Transnational Migration as a Small Window on the Diminished Autonomy of the Modern Democratic State', *Annals of the American Academy of Political and Social Science*, 485 (May), 153–66.

Henkin, Louis (1990), *The Age of Rights* (New York: Columbia University Press).

Hollifield, James F. (1992), *Immigrants, Markets, and States* (Cambridge, Mass.: Harvard University Press).

Holston, James (ed.) (1996), *Public Culture*, 8/2 (Winter), Special Issue: *Cities and Citizenship*.

Hugo, Graeme (1995), 'Indonesia's Migration Transition', *Journal für Entwicklungspolitik*, 11/3: 285–309.

Isbister, John (1996), *The Immigration Debate: Remaking America* (West Hartford, Conn.: Kumarian Books).

Jacobson, David (1996), *Rights across Borders* (Baltimore: Johns Hopkins University Press).

Jessop, Robert (1990), *State Theory: Putting Capitalist States in their Place* (University Park: Pennsylvania State University Press).

*Journal of Global Business and Political Economy*, 1/1, Special Issue: *Competition and Change*.

*Journal für Entwicklungspolitik* (1995), 11/3, Special Issue: *Migration*.

JUNAC (Junta del Acuerdo de Cartagena) and OIM (Organización internacional de migraciones) (1993), *Integración, migración y desarrollo sostenible en el Grupo Andino* (Lima: JUNAC and OIM).

Knox, Paul L., and Peter J. Taylor (eds.) (1995), *World Cities in a World-System* (Cambridge: Cambridge University Press).

Kratochwil, K. Hermann (1995), 'Movilidad transfronteriza de personas y procesos de integración regional en America Latina', *Revista de la OIM sobre migraciones en America Latina*, 13/2: 3–12.

Leftwich, A. (1994), 'Governance, the State, and the Politics of Development', *Development and Change*, 24/4: 363–86.

Leon, Ramon, and K. Hermann Kratochwil (1993), 'Integración, migraciones y desarrollo sostenido en el Grupo Andino', *Revista de la OIM sobre migraciones en America Latina*, 11/1 (Apr.), 5–28.

Mahler, Sarah (1995), *American Dreaming: Immigrant Life on the Margins* (Princeton: Princeton University Press).

Marmora, L. (1985a), *Las migraciones laborales en Colombia* (Washington: OEA).

—— (1985b), *Las migraciones laborales en Venezuela* (Washington: OEA).

—— (1994), 'Desarrollo sostenido y politicas migratorias: Su tratamiento en los espacios latinoamericanos de integración', *Revista de la OIM sobre migraciones en America Latina*, 12/1–3 (Apr.–Dec.), 5–50.

Martin, Philip L. (1993), *Trade and Migration: NAFTA and Agriculture* (Washington: Institute for International Economics, Oct.).

Massey, Douglas S., Joaquin Arango, Graeme Hugo, Ali Kouaouci, Adela Pellegrino, and J. Edward Taylor (1993), 'Theories of International Migration: A Review and Appraisal', *Population and Development Review*, 19/3: 431–66.

Mazlish, Bruce, and Ralph Buultjens (eds.) (1993), *Conceptualizing Global History* (Boulder, Colo.: Westview Press).

Mitchell, Christopher (1989), 'International Migration, International Relations and Foreign Policy', *International Migration Review* (Fall) 3: 681–708.

Mittelman, James (ed.) (1996), *Globalization: Critical Reflections. International Political Economy Yearbook*, ix (Boulder, Colo.: Lynne Rienner Publishers).

Morales, Rebecca (1994), *Flexible Production: Restructuring of the International Automobile Industry* (Cambridge: Polity Press).

OIM (Organización internacional de migraciones) (1991*a*), *Proyecto regional de la Organización centroamericana de migración, políticas e instrumentos migratorios para la integración de América Central* (San José, Costa Rica: PROCAM/OIM).

—— (1991*b*), *Programa de integración y migraciones para el Cono Sur* (Buenos Aires: PRIMCOS/OIM).

—— (1991*c*), *Aspectos juridicos e institucionales de las migraciones: Perú, Colombia, Bolivia, Venezuela* (Geneva: OIM).

—— (1991*d*), *Aspectos juridicos e institucionales de las migraciones: Costa Rica, El Salvador, Honduras, Nicaragua y Panamá* (Geneva: OIM).

Panitch, Leo (1996), 'Rethinking the Role of the State in an Era of Globalization', in Mittelman (1996).

Plender, R. (1988), *International Migration Law* (Dordrecht: Martinus Nijhoff).

Reding, Andrew A. (1995), *Democracy and Human Rights in Mexico*, World Policy Papers (New York: World Policy Institute).

Reimers, David M. (1983), 'An Unintended Reform: The 1965 Immigration Act and Third World Immigration to the U.S.', *Journal of American Ethnic History*, 3 (Fall), 9–28.

Rosen, Fred, and Deidre McFadyen (eds.) (1995), *Free Trade and Economic Restructuring in Latin America*, NACLA Reader (New York: Monthly Review Press).

Rosenau, J. N. (1992), 'Governance, Order, and Change in World Politics', in J. N. Rosenau and E. O. Czempiel (eds.), *Governance without Government: Order and Change in World Politics* (Cambridge: Cambridge University Press).

Ruggie, John Gerard (1993), 'Territoriality and Beyond: Problematizing Modernity in International Relations', *International Organization* 47/1 (Winter), 139–74.

Salacuse, Jeswald (1991), *Making Global Deals: Negotiating in the International Marketplace* (Boston: Houghton Mifflin).

Sassen, Saskia (1988), *The Mobility of Labor and Capital: A Study of International Investment and Labor Flow* (London: Cambridge University Press).

—— (1993), 'The Impact of Economic Internationalization on Immigration: Comparing the U.S. and Japan', *International Migration*, 31/1: 73–99.

—— (1995), 'Immigration and Local Labor Markets', in A. Portes (ed.), *The Economic Sociology of Immigration* (New York: Russell Sage).

Sassen, Saskia (1996*a*), *Losing Control? Sovereignty in an Age of Globalization*, 1995 Columbia University Leonard Hastings Schoff Memorial Lectures (New York: Columbia University Press).

—— (1996*b*), *Migranten, Siedler, Flüchtlinge. Von der Massenauswanderung zur Festung Europa* (Frankfurt: Fischer Verlag).

—— (1996*c*), 'Toward a Feminist Analytics of the Global Economy', *Indiana Journal of Global Legal Studies*, 4/1 (Fall), 7–41.

—— (forthcoming), *Immigration Policy in a Global Economy: From National Crisis to Multilateral Management* (New York: 20th Century Fund).

Shank, G. (ed.) (1994), *Social Justice*, 21/2 (Summer), Special Issue: *Japan Enters the Twenty-First Century*.

SIECA (SISTEMA de Integración Economica de Centro América) (1991*a*), *III reunión de la Organización Centroamericana de Migración* (Managua: SIECA).

—— (1991*b*), *Antecedentes y acuerdos de la Comisión centroamericana de migración* (OCAM).

Sikkink, Kathryn (1993), 'Human Rights, Principled Issue-Networks, and Sovereignty in Latin America', *International Organization*, 47 (Summer), 411–41.

Sinclair, Timothy J. (1994), 'Passing Judgement: Credit Rating Processes as Regulatory Mechanisms of Governance in the Emerging World Order', *Review of International Political Economy*, 1/1 (Spring), 133–59.

*Social Justice* (1993), 20/3–4 (Fall–Winter), Special Issue: *Global Crisis, Local Struggles*.

Soysal, Yasmin (1994), *Limits of Citizenship* (Chicago: University of Chicago Press).

Stein, Eduardo (1993), 'Las dinámicas migratorias en el Istmo centroamericano en la perspectiva de la integración y el imperativo de la sostenibilidad', *Revista de la OIM sobre migraciones en America Latina*, 11/2 (Aug.), 5–51.

Thränhardt, Dietrich (ed.) (1992), *Europe: A New Immigration Continent* (Hamburg: Lit Verlag).

Tilly, Charles (ed.) (1975), *The Formation of National States in Western Europe* (Princeton: Princeton University Press).

Torales, Ponciano (1993), *Migración e integración en el Cono Sur: La experiencia del Mercosur* (Buenos Aires: OIM).

Trubek, David M., Yves Dezalay, Ruth Buchanan, and John R. Davis (1993), *Global Restructuring and the Law: The Internationalization of Legal Fields and Creation of Transnational Arenas*, Working Paper on the Political Economy of Legal Change no. 1 (Madison, Wis.: Global Studies Research Program, University of Wisconsin).

United Nations (1996), *World Population Monitoring 1993: With a Special Report on Refugees* (New York: Population Division, UN Department for Economic and Social Information and Pol icy Analysis).

Wallerstein, Immanuel (1974), *The Modern World System*, i (New York: Academic Press).

Weil, Patrick (1991), *La France et ses étrangers* (Paris: Calmann-Lévy).

Weiner, Myron (1995), *The Global Migration Crisis* (New York: HarperCollins).

Zolberg, Aristide R. (1990), 'The Roots of US Refugee Policy', in R. Tucker, Charles B. Keely, and Linda Wrigley (eds.), *Immigration and U.S. Foreign Policy* (Boulder, Colo.: Westview Press).

# 3

# The Decline of Sovereignty? Politics and Immigration Restriction in Liberal States

## GARY P. FREEMAN

As immigration has emerged over the last two decades as a topic of urgent public interest and belated fascination for political science two propositions have arguably attained the status of conventional wisdom. The first is that under present circumstances the forces propelling individuals and groups to move across national boundaries are so strong, ineluctable, and pervasive, and the constraints on states so confining, that traditional efforts to control national borders and determine the numbers and types of people who enter and remain in their territory are no longer effective. We might call this the 'thesis of declining sovereignty'.[1] A second proposition, often advanced by the same writers, holds that popular reaction within the rich states against large-scale migration, legal and illegal, has resulted in a systematic backlash reflected in the rise of extremist parties, episodic outbreaks of violence, and the adoption of harshly restrictive official immigration policies. This might be labelled the 'restrictionist thesis'.[2]

Neither of these conventionally held theses is valid in my view. On empirical grounds, I will argue that the evidence is far from conclusive for either proposition. Liberal democracies have much more capacity to control immigration than most commentators seem to believe. The vitality of state sovereignty depends on the particular state, the type of immigration, and the aspect of immigration policy one is considering. Contrary to the view that they have taken overwhelmingly strict stands against immigration in all its forms, democratic states often display a tendency towards expansionist and liberal immigration policies because of the way the costs and benefits of migration are distributed and because of the organizational and resource advantages of those interests supportive of migration. By strictly empirical criteria, therefore, neither the thesis of declining sovereignty nor that of pervasive restrictionism can be sustained.

The two propositions also pose theoretical issues. On the surface, the thesis of declining sovereignty appears to be inconsistent with the restrictionist thesis, however often they are presented together. How can migration be overrunning the capacities of national states, how can the meaning of national boundaries be contested, and most of the rights and benefits of citizenship be extended to non-citizens, at the same time as national electorates are strongly mobilized against immigration and governments, with extremist parties snapping at their heels, are busily enacting more and more heavy-handed measures to keep foreigners out? Advocates of the two positions would probably answer that the apparent inconsistency in fact highlights a profound contradiction that is precisely the point. They believe that no matter how hard they try, states will fail in their attempts to control immigration. In the process of trying, migrants and refugees will be harmed, the standards of public discourse debased, and partisans of control will become more and more frustrated. Restrictionism is the policy preferred by the voters and pursued by states, in other words, but it is not a realistic goal, at least not within the framework of a free economy and polity.

It is evident that proponents of this view at least implicitly adopt a theoretical posture holding that with respect to international migration political processes are subordinate to the stronger forces of economic inequality, market pressures, or long-term cultural transformations. Restrictionist sentiments and the government measures taken in response to them are seen, in this perspective, as futile and unfortunate epiphenomena reflecting the more fundamental structural characteristics of a globalizing world-order.

My argument turns this conventional wisdom on its head. Its logic is that states could mount immigration policies that are as effective as most of the others they attempt, but that domestic politics, rather than constituting a powerful and uniform stimulus for restrictionism, is a much more complex force that actually undermines such efforts. Domestic political considerations, rather than the external pressures buffeting Western states, cause immigration policy to fail as often as it does. The external pressures are real enough, but my account gives primacy to political factors both in shaping the migration problematic and in responding to it.

This chapter assesses the theses of declining sovereignty and pervasive restrictionism in the context of the politics of immigration in Western nations. I argue that despite numerous obstacles to immigration control, the situation is not nearly as grim as some observers suggest. On the contrary, state control of migration is undeniably increasing over time, not decreasing. Moreover, certain states are considerably more effective in their efforts at migration regulation than others. Finally, it is necessary to disaggregate what is a highly complex policy arena and develop particularized generalizations about each component of overall immigration policy.

Nevertheless, it would be foolish to deny that the migration regimes of most liberal democracies are under intense pressure and are in some cases in disarray. Without doubt, state sovereignty is besieged by international migration, itself an aspect of the more general internationalizing forces in the world economy. The question is, why? The answer, I believe, lies in the political dynamics of immigration in the receiving states. The chief obstacles to immigration control are political, not economic, demographic, or technical. Furthermore, contrary to the implications of the restrictionist thesis, the predominant drift of immigration politics across the Western world is at least modestly expansionist. The most striking feature of immigration politics in democratic states is the persistent gap between the policies of governments and the preferences of mass publics. This disparity and the obstacles to immigration control that lead to it reflect difficulties in developing political will, building support for policies that promise to be effective, and overcoming the direct opposition to immigration restrictions by powerful domestic policy interests.

## SOVEREIGNTY IN DECLINE?

An ancient philosophical concept that implies the prerogative and authority to rule (de Jouvenel 1957), sovereignty, when attached to the modern nation-state, entails a claim to the exclusive use of legitimate force within a defined territory (Gerth and Mills 1958: 78; Hendrickson 1992). For present purposes, the most pertinent aspect of sovereignty is that which holds that national states may exercise broad powers to decide who may enter the national territory and enjoy the privileges of citizenship, powers that follow logically from the contractual basis of state legitimacy (Berns 1972: 380–2).

Sovereignty is a broad concept rich with meaning and ambiguity. Although I follow customary practice in using the term in this discussion of migration, I operationalize sovereignty in a more limited way to make it suitable for empirical analysis. I take the thesis that the contemporary migration crisis is indicative of declining sovereignty within Western nations to involve two separate claims: (1) that the locus of decision-making over migration policy is shifting from the plane of national states to extra- or subnational actors, and (2) that national states are encountering such problems trying to master population flows across their borders that we are justified in concluding that they cannot do so. Both of these can be addressed as empirical issues, although limitations of data, and reasonable disagreements about their meaning, suggest that a good measure of interpretation is still required to reach conclusions. This chapter lays out only the broad outlines of the empirical case that is actually required.

## The Locus of Decision-Making

The notion that immigration policy-making is slipping out of the hands of national authorities and being taken over by international institutions or subnational interlopers is obviously rooted in real developments. Immigration policy arenas are probably more complex today than they have been at any time since the inter-war era, when many of the modern accoutrements of migration regulation were put into place (Torpey 1996; Collinson 1993). A variety of actors—transnational, subnational, quasi-governmental, and private—have a hand in influencing, if not actually making, migration and refugee policy. Nevertheless, it is important not to overstate the extent to which this relative messiness contrasts with an earlier period when states presumably held a much clearer and unchallenged sway over immigration. National governments only gradually and belatedly established their claims to make policy without the interference of subnational governments in the mid- and late nineteenth century. No sooner had that been imperfectly accomplished than transnational institutions emerged to constrain unilateral state action. The golden age of state control of population movements, if it existed at all, was short-lived, perhaps extending from 1918 to 1951, when the United Nations Convention on the Status of Refugees was adopted.

That multilateral institutions and collaborative decision-making are of growing significance in the migration field is undeniable. The real questions are to what extent they are supplanting traditional state claims with regard to border control and citizenship and what the sources of such a transformation might be. I will consider several important cases:

the international refugee regime, provisions regulating migration within and into the European Union, the North American Free Trade Agreement (NAFTA), and the Closer Economic Relations (CER) pact between Australia and New Zealand.

The only truly international regime for migration involves that for refugees organized principally around the United Nations High Commissioner for Refugees (UNHCR). Although it is an admirable example of inter-state co-operation, the UNHCR is a troubled agency with limited purposes and weak enforcement mechanisms. The regime deals, first of all, only with a specific sort of migrant, the refugee. Very narrowly construed initially, the definition of refugee has broadened considerably over the years (Skran 1992; Deng 1993: 8). Nevertheless, there remains strong resistance to the elimination of the critical distinction between economic and political migrants, which would be necessary to generalize the UN refugee system to all migrants. All national states treat refugees separately in their own immigration law (Adelman 1991; Jenks 1992). As great a part of the migration crisis as refugees constitute, a refugee regime is not capable of organizing state policies towards the much larger question of economic migration.

Even with respect to refugees, the UN system has serious problems enforcing its sanctions. Signatories of the UN Convention and Protocol have a treaty obligation to comply with their stipulations, but there is no effective enforcement mechanism, and national refugee policies are often blatantly tied to foreign policy objectives (Zolberg *et al.* 1989; Mitchell 1992; Loescher 1993). Worse still, the incentives of leading Western nations to support the UN refugee system may be disappearing today, because it can be depicted as a product of Great Power competition during the Cold War. In the wake of the collapse of the Soviet Empire, old assumptions are being challenged and the future role of the UNHCR is unclear. On the one hand, the scope of its activities has widened, especially after the Gulf War, to include unprecedented intervention inside the territories of states to protect endangered groups (Weiner 1995: 155–7; Meissner *et al.* 1993: 74–88). On the other hand, absent the ideological imperatives of the East–West conflict, states may become more reluctant to fund programmes or to accept large numbers of refugees.

Most work on international co-operation on migration issues has focused, reasonably enough, on the European Union. The EU is the most impressive instance of the internationalization of immigration policy, the largest and most comprehensive regional labour regime in the world.[3] In so far as internal movement of EU nationals is concerned, free circulation has been achieved (Koslowski 1994). More interesting for our purposes are regulations regarding the entry of non-EU nationals into the community. This is an exceedingly complex subject that need only be touched on here as Koslowski provides a detailed summary in Chapter 5 in this volume (cf. Hollifield 1992*a*; Freeman 1992; Kessler 1996; Collinson 1993; Niessen 1992; Callovi 1992; Phillip 1994). There has been significant progress towards the harmonization of member state policies with regard to visas, external border crossings, and asylum policy. This rapid movement was prompted by the accelerated pace of economic integration after 1985 and the sudden rise of asylum claims after 1989. Depending on how impressed one is by these developments, they may appear to refute realist theory on the circumstances under which international co-operation will take place. If so, EU developments relating to immigration would be a stunning case of voluntarily relinquished sovereignty.

There have been major snags along the path to harmonization, however. Some member states have balked at signing on to key agreements; most EU decision-making on migration is still carried out at the intergovernmental rather than at the community level; and the co-operation that has been achieved has been motivated by a desire to enact restrictive measures. Co-operation, in other words, has been the means of enhancing traditional state attempts to bar entry to unwanted migrants and to limit state obligations to asylum-seekers. That France suspended the implementation of Schengen in 1995 due to national security concerns illustrates the fact that member states will still defend their national interest when they believe it is at risk, whatever the general trend in international agreements and collaboration.

Moreover, the states that have pushed hardest for a European approach to the asylum crisis are precisely those (like Germany) which have been in the weakest position to control their borders. Germany has been called a semi-sovereign state because of its unique situation after defeat in the Second World War (Katzenstein 1987). It was in a particularly vulnerable position *vis-à-vis* the massive asylum claims after 1989 and turned to its European partners for help (Freeman 1992: 1158). This, however, only strengthens the case that co-operation has so far reinforced rather than replaced state sovereignty.

The other experiments with regional labour regimes may be dispensed with quickly. The NAFTA does not mention labour migration except for a minor provision for the temporary movement of business persons. Indeed, the agreement was partly motivated by the belief that increased trade between Mexico and the United States would diminish migration pressures (Weintraub 1992). The NAFTA illustrates one of the reasons even regional labour regimes are scarce. The migration interests of the United States and Mexico conflict. Whereas trade concessions involve reciprocity and mutual gain, at least in theory, Mexico has little to gain and much to lose by co-operating with the United States in reducing illegal migration. Hundreds of thousands of Americans are not trying to slip into Mexico undetected.

Australia and New Zealand have always permitted free movement between themselves. The Trans-Tasman Travel Arrangement has been in place since the 1920s (Poot 1993: 396; Nana and Poot 1996). The Australian–New Zealand Closer Economic Relations Trade Agreement, adopted in 1983 and strengthened in 1988, goes much farther than NAFTA by virtually eliminating all barriers to trade in goods between the two countries, making real progress on services, and mandating free movement of persons. This arrangement puts pressure on both countries, in practice most particularly on New Zealand, to monitor their external entries closely as anyone arriving in either country is free to move on to the other. This has not caused serious problems, but it opens the possibility that Australia could exert pressure on New Zealand's immigration policy because if it became concerned it might shut off free movement (Holmes 1990). The Trans-Tasman regime has not resolved migration problems between Australia and New Zealand. It works precisely because there are few if any migration issues to be resolved between the two partners.

Evidence from the UN refugee regime, the EU, NAFTA, and CER supports the view that there is a tendency for states to seek co-operation on migration issues, especially as they relate to asylum and usually within the context of intensifying trading relations. These efforts, however, leave migration policy essentially in the hands of national states.

A number of commentators have recently observed that control over migration policy is not only being challenged from above, by international institutions and actors, but also from below, by subnational governments. These arguments typically deal with the United States (Schuck, Chapter 6 in this volume; Skerry 1995), but the dynamics they identify might apply elsewhere. Subnational migration policy-making, which may involve much more than attempts to influence intake decisions, is a potentially significant subject that has been heretofore overlooked. Nevertheless, we need to establish whether these trends represent a challenge to state sovereignty. In federal systems such as those in Canada, the United States, and Australia, devolving authority over some aspects of immigration policy may be an appropriate and deliberate decision.[4] Even if changes in the locus of decision-making are unintended and the result of political struggle, it is not obvious that this represents a breakdown in the immigration control process or a challenge to sovereignty since state and local governments are administrative components of sovereign national entities.

## A Decline in State Capacity?

To sum up the discussion thus far, the thesis of the decline of sovereignty, in so far as it is operationalized in terms of the locus of decision-making authority over migration, is only modestly and inconsistently supported by the evidence discussed here. The thesis must also be tested by the measure of whether states can control immigration. In other words, while they may still nominally enjoy sovereign powers over migration, are they incapable of exercising them effectively? To answer this question requires a more extensive discussion than is possible here. Moreover, the conclusions one draws in this context depend on interpretation of the facts as much as on different versions of what the facts are. Here I offer a few generalizations that bear on a properly documented assessment of the issue:

1. liberal states generally have more capacity to control migration than is typically recognized;
2. capacity is growing over time, not declining;
3. its extensiveness varies across nations, across types of migration flows, and across different aspects of migration policy.

To address adequately the question of state capacity to control unwanted migration one needs to disaggregate the concepts migration and migration policy and consider particular states, as point 3 implies. As a general proposition, I simply note that liberal states regulate movement across their borders every day, that the effectiveness of policies is imperfect, but that there is little justification for declaring that migration regulatory regimes are on the verge of catastrophic breakdown or that they have little meaning these days. Anyone who thinks differently should try landing at Sydney airport without an entry visa or go to France and apply for a job without a work permit. Reality is less dramatic but still problematic; namely, that states face continuing challenges in managing unwanted migration, their policies are often inefficient and even counter-productive, and the tasks they are asked to perform are more and more complicated, difficult, and expensive.

One should recognize immediately that although immigration is a general phenomenon within the industrial world, the nature of the policy problems it entails and the ability of states to deal with them vary enormously from country to country. This is not the place for a detailed excursion into this subject, but extensive research supports the contention that Great Britain, Australia, and the Scandinavian countries are more effective in their regulation of population flows than the United States, Greece, Spain, Italy, or Portugal. Canada, Switzerland, Austria, and Germany would fall somewhere in the middle on a continuum running from strong to weak controls. Explanations for these variations include geopolitical, historical, and institutional factors that cause some countries to be more vulnerable to inflows than others. The point is simply that for all the commonalities among the democracies with respect to migration, there are substantial differences that are clearly pertinent to a discussion of state capacities (Cornelius *et al.* 1994; Miller, 1994*a,b*; Adelman *et al.* 1994; Hammar 1985; Thränhardt 1992; Fassman and Münz 1994; Richmond 1994; and Kubat 1993).

Not every form of migration presents the same task for state regulators. Generally speaking, states do an acceptable job of overseeing and controlling the flow of migrants, permanent or temporary, through legal migration and refugee settlement schemes. Among the traditional countries of settlement, Australia and Canada, which employ points systems for the selection of potential migrants, are more effective in attracting migrants with skills and meeting annual numerical goals than the Americans with their larger and more chaotic preference system (Borjas 1988). In all three countries, however, family-related entries tend to push aside the claims of skill migration (Freeman, forthcoming, *b*). The settler societies have much longer experience of selecting and incorporating migrants than do the west European states, most of whom have become recipients of significant permanent immigration unwittingly and unwillingly in the last several decades. The law in most European states makes only limited provision for new legal migration for settlement. Since the mid-1970s these countries have been concerned primarily with family reunification claims deriving from earlier supposedly temporary labour migration and asylum applications. Otherwise, their principal concern is illegal migration.

On-site asylum-seekers pose serious problems for governments as they have less control over the asylum process than they do over the normal refugee selection processes. Officials have less discretion in the distribution of asylum claims, obviously, because the individuals are already inside the national territory or at the border. The rapid rise in the number of asylum applications in the aftermath of the fall of the Berlin Wall in 1989 spawned a kind of panic that liberal democracies would be overrun by desperate migrants seeking to use the only available legal route into the West. Seven years later the picture is much clearer and the panic has subsided. The European Union has developed a co-ordinated asylum procedure that deters multiple applications and that establishes a common list of safe countries. Recognition rates of claims have fallen across Europe. Germany, which had been the centre of the asylum crisis and had received the largest number of claims among European states between 1990 and 1993, saw claims decline dramatically after revising Article 16 of the Basic Law. Total numbers in OECD countries are down as well (SOPEMI 1995: 195). In 1993 claims fell in Sweden, Germany, Canada, Austria, the United Kingdom, France, and Finland, but they went up in Switzerland, Denmark, Norway, Belgium, the Netherlands, and the United States. Preliminary data for 1994 indicate that claims rose only in the United Kingdom and the Netherlands (ibid.: 18–19). Recent changes in asylum law in Britain appear to have produced a reduction in claims in 1996 (FCO 1996: 269–70). Although asylum still constitutes a problem of considerable magnitude, it is increasingly manageable (Joppke, Chapter 4 in this volume). Oddly enough, one of the principal outcomes of the asylum crisis has been the comprehensive strengthening of immigration control mechanisms throughout Europe and the West more generally.

States exercise least mastery over people who try to enter the country outside the legal framework, stay beyond the terms of their visas, or work without authorization. It stands to reason that persons actively seeking to avoid detection pose a more intractable challenge than those who present themselves at immigration control in airports. Illegal or unauthorized migration is highly complex, being composed of a variety of forms and activities. The failure to cope with illegal migration is typically cited as evidence of a more general collapse of state sovereignty. Does the scale and character of illegal movements justify doubts about the viability of sovereign national states?

No reliable estimate can be made of the scale of illegal migration into the Western democracies. Nor can it be asserted with any confidence that the problem is worsening or improving. Only the roughest guesses can be given as to probable trends. Around the mid-1970s it was estimated that about 10 per cent of the foreign populations of western Europe were illegal (Castles and Miller 1993: 91). We know that at about the same time there were at least 3 million illegal aliens in the United States since that many came forward to benefit from amnesty under legislation passed in 1968. Since that time, all the Western states have undertaken measures to stem the flow of unwanted migrants. At the same time, certain events, such as the collapse of the Soviet Union after 1989 and the crisis of the Mexican peso in January 1995, have contributed to expanding the pool of potential migrants. The International Labour Office estimated that in 1991 there were 2.6 million illegal residents in western Europe, about 14 per cent of the total non-citizen population (Böhning 1991). Given the tumultuous events and radically changed policy framework, does a 4 per cent increase in the relative size of the illegal population from the early 1970s to the early 1990s represent a failure or a limited success?

The process by which persons find their way into countries illegally appears to be increasingly organized, commercialized, and criminalized. In some places, as in the United States, the smuggling of persons is progressively entangled with drug smuggling, and conditions at the border are more dangerous even as the area is more heavily policed. The production of false documents is now a major industry, especially in the United States, where a wide variety of easily obtained credentials may be used to show authorization to work.

But state controls are also increasingly sophisticated. Border patrols, which are still the first line of defence, have been enhanced, especially in those states in the European Union with external borders. Several of these—Italy, Spain, Portugal, and Greece—are relative newcomers to the problems of immigration and have been rapidly establishing new instruments of control. The United States, a country with uniquely vexing border challenges, has also beefed up its capacity. The effectiveness of these efforts is yet to be proven, but preliminary evidence is encouraging (Bean *et al.* 1994; USCIR 1994; Miller 1987, 1994*a*; Cornelius *et al.* 1994).

The most promising strategy for deterring unwanted migration, employer sanctions, is perhaps the chief target of those critics who believe the search for immigration control is futile. Business opposes sanctions as an undue interference in the market, civil libertarians as an intrusion into personal freedoms, and minorities as a mode of discrimination based on national origin or appearance. For all this, sanctions are now in place in every major west European state except the United Kingdom. Many of the negative perceptions of sanctions need to be discounted by the length of time they have been in effect. Most states have had them for two decades or less and they have frequently altered procedures and penalties in light of experience. It is obvious that sanctions will be more pervasive and more fully enforced in the future, not less. As they become more institutionalized, they should also become more effective (Miller 1994*b*). It is already evident, despite the absence of concrete data, that those states with strongly organized labour and business federations (what have been labelled neo-corporatist institutions) enjoy significant advantages of self-regulation and consequently greater effectiveness of sanctions.

Taking into consideration both the locus of decision-making and the effectiveness of immigration policy, one must conclude that, although liberal states are struggling to establish control of their borders, they are at least struggling and they appear to be making some appreciable headway. It is not my purpose to paint a rosy picture of the situation; quite the contrary. The failures of government migration policies in the last two decades have been striking, are markedly out of step with the wishes of Western electorates, and are arguably a prime source of rising public cynicism and disaffection more generally. I only want to argue that worries about the disappearance of state sovereignty over population movements are premature.

## PERVASIVE RESTRICTIONISM?

The restrictionist thesis is not so much wrong as it is incomplete, misleading, and under-theorized. There is certainly a broad pattern of restrictionist legislation either proposed or adopted across the Western world, legislation backed up by anti-immigration opinion, groups, and political parties. In this respect, Western politics today differs markedly from that of the 1960s and 1970s. Proponents of the restrictionist thesis err, however, by overstating the pervasiveness and intensity of restrictive policies and sentiment, by ignoring the ineffectiveness of much legislation, and by failing to account properly for the patterns they describe.

It is useful, first of all, to put the current wave of restrictionist politics into perspective. It is not as if there had been a well-established regime of more or less open immigration within the Western world, or between the poorer countries and the richer countries, which has been lately overturned by a conservative backlash. Migratory movements into western Europe in the 1960s and 1970s were deviations from the more typical experience of the region. The policies that permitted those migrations never rested on an explicit political consensus, moreover, and they produced substantial unanticipated consequences in the form of secondary migrations and permanent settlement. Those policies and their unintended consequences became the focus of political attack. The relatively hostile response of Europeans to the recent asylum crisis must be understood within this more general framework. The contemporary politics of immigration in western Europe is not a reversal of an open, liberal, popular policy. It is an attempt to limit the effects of a major transformation of the demographics of the region.

Within the broad pattern of reaction against the rapid increase in the scale of migration and changes in its composition, there is considerable variation across at least three sets of countries. Events in the major societies of immigration for permanent settlement—the United States, Canada, and Australia—fit uneasily under the rubric of restrictionism. Canada has been relatively immune to calls for serious changes in its large immigration and refugee programme. Indeed, the refugee selection and settlement scheme has been liberalized in recent years and the annual immigration intake has been increased. Reforms have been undertaken to make the programme more efficient and to tie it more closely to economic policy goals, but these were, along with population growth, the basis for the programme all along (Adelman 1991; Adelman *et al.* 1994; SOPEMI 1995: 72–6; Ruddick and Burstein 1993; Freeman 1992: 1152–4).

The story of Australia is slightly more complicated. In general, Australia remains open with respect to legal immigration for settlement and refugees selected from abroad. More restrictive measures have been adopted to deal with on-site asylum-seekers and illegal migration. The Labour government raised immigration levels in both 1994/5 and 1995/6 (86,000 and 96,000, respectively) (Birrell 1995). The election in the spring of 1996 brought to office a coalition government led by the Liberal Party that cut the annual intake target for 1996/7 by 11 per cent to 76,000 and pledged to focus more narrowly on the recruitment of needed skills (*Australian Financial Review*, 4 July 1996). Reasons given for the new policy included the high rates of unemployment among recent migrants and the tendency in previous years to overshoot targets. The changes are a response to market conditions and do not represent a fundamental reversal of direction.

The climate in the United States is more complicated still. Many observers apparently would lump the United States into the category of countries that have succumbed to anti-immigrant hysteria. There is certainly evidence to cite: the overwhelming passage of Proposition 187 in California in 1994 (a voter initiative to restrict most publicly funded benefits to persons who are legally in the country). After the Republican sweep of both houses of Congress in 1994 major bills were introduced to revamp the legal immigration programme and clamp down on illegal flows. A number of new measures have been implemented at the border, as noted above, and stricter treatment of asylum-seekers on the high seas and persons fleeing Cuba has been adopted. Most of the legislative proposals with respect to legal immigration would have had the effect of merely moving policy back to where it was in the mid-1960s when the first of a number of strongly expansive laws were enacted. They would have simply reinstated the status quo ante, in other words (Freeman 1996). Even these measures, most of them endorsed by a high-level national commission (USCIR 1994, 1995), were too controversial and failed to pass the Congress. In sum, the temperature of immigration politics in the United States is higher than it has been in years, but even in this atmosphere no about-face in basic policy is discernible. Indeed, what may turn out in retrospect to have been the most significant effect of the attention given to the issue is the massive wave of naturalizations to citizenship taking place among the nation's vast population of permanent resident aliens. The naturalizations seem largely a reaction to fears generated among permanent residents over loss of public benefits. Over a million potential new voters applied for citizenship in both 1995 and 1996.

The restrictionist thesis finds little support in the outcomes, if not the forms, of immigration politics in the settler societies. The situation in western Europe is different. The general tone of discussion of immigration in Europe since at least 1974, and especially in the immediate aftermath of the epochal events in the Soviet Union after 1989, has been decidedly restrictionist. Moreover, immigration has had a substantial impact on the character of European politics more broadly, fostering the rise of third parties and new political figures, and reshaping the traditional positions of the major parties.

Discussions of European immigration politics need to distinguish those countries that mounted guestworker programmes in the 1960s and 1970s or experienced significant migrations of ex-colonials from those countries that have very recently undergone the migration transition from sending to receiving states. The countries with guestworker legacies or post-colonial migrations are the centrepieces of anti-immigrant politics in the West. These countries—Germany, Switzerland, France, Britain, Belgium, the Netherlands, and Sweden, foremost—experienced mass immigration for the most part after they were fully developed national states.[5] Contemporary immigration politics is haunted by the legacy of the guestworker era. Although circumstances differ in each case, one can summarize that legacy as follows.

The policies that tolerated or stimulated the post-war guestworker and post-colonial migrations were rarely debated in public and did not enjoy the support of political majorities. The creation of substantial permanent population settlements of non-European origin was not predicted by governments, which either did not foresee them or deliberately misled their electorates. The same may be said of the continuing stream of secondary migration for family reunion, asylum, and illegal entry which transpired after labour recruitment was halted in the early 1970s. The guestworker programmes undoubtedly contributed significantly to post-war growth (Kindleberger 1967; Böhning 1974; Hollifield 1992b). This may make opponents of immigration today appear churlish or hypocritical. Nevertheless, restrictionism in western Europe is not a radical enterprise, at least if one looks at how it is embodied in the positions of the major parties and government policies rather than the proposals of the extreme right. It consists of (1) ending active labour recruitment, (2) more rigorously monitoring secondary migration to limit fraud and discourage potential applicants, and (3) combating illegal migration.

While it is undeniable that some of the tactics employed, not to mention the heated rhetoric aired, have been on the margins of legality and fairness, the basic point remains: these measures have done little more than end a set of policies that were of recent vintage, were uncharacteristic and devoid of popular support, produced undesired outcomes, and by most indicators were no longer economically wise. Policies directed at asylum-seekers cannot be disentangled from this more general political climate and the continuing effort to limit illegal migration. It is interesting to imagine how much more generous the response of west Europeans to the asylum crisis might have been if the guestworker era had never transpired.

The third distinctive grouping of countries that merits discussion includes those south European states (Portugal, Spain, Italy, and Greece) that have recently started receiving more migrants than the The politics of immigration in these states diverges from the European cases just discussed because it is new and because they are in the process of building for the first time the institutional capacity to regulate migration. The trajectory of these states is likely to be different as well because they are undergoing their migration transition in the context of intensifying pressures for harmonization of migration policies within the European Union. Although it is premature to draw definitive conclusions, a good deal of early evidence suggests that these countries are inclined to take a moderate, if not inclusive, approach to migration (Cornelius *et al.* 1994; King and Rybaczuk 1993). As these states have struggled to piece together administrative machinery to regulate migration, they have employed a mix of restrictive and expansive techniques. With respect to illegal migration, the dominant policy thus far has been legalization.[6] Reaction to the asylum crisis has been mixed, but a hardening of formal policies over time has apparently reduced the number of claims in Italy and Greece though not in Spain or Portugal (SOPEMI 1995: 92, 98, 115, 117). Governments, especially in Spain, seem tolerant of illegal entrants, or those denied asylum who choose to stay on in the informal economy (Cornelius 1994; Calavita 1994).

To recapitulate, the tendency towards restrictionist policies is not at all uniform across Western democracies. The settler societies continue to be genuinely open to mass immigration. The European states that ran guestworker programmes during the post-war boom are dealing with their long-term fall-out and have the most contentious politics and exclusive migration and asylum policies. The new countries of immigration in southern Europe have yet to establish institutionalized policies; at present they exhibit contradictory impulses.

## TOWARDS A POLITICAL EXPLANATION OF MIGRATION POLICY

The sovereign powers of states to regulate their borders and the terms of membership in their societies remain substantial. In important respects states show signs of actually increasing their capacity to manage migration and a stubborn reluctance to cede control over such important matters to external institutions. Nevertheless, Western democracies seem at times to enjoy only weak sovereignty. National immigration policies have a disconcerting tendency to misfire or to be fecklessly implemented.

The idea that there is a common tendency across the Western world to slam the gates closed and exclude would-be migrants and refugees, to create a privileged Western fortress, is also inconsistent with the facts as I understand them. A more accurate statement is that there is considerable variation within the democratic world. Some states continue to exercise impressive sway over migration issues; others exercise much less. Some pursue fundamentally restrictionist goals; others not at all.

How can this motley pattern of outcomes be explained? Most analysts who have written on the topic hold that weak sovereignty is the result of important structural changes in the external environment of states, especially changes in the organization and dynamics of the global political economy. These changes generate pressures that overwhelm the efforts of national polities to resist. Among these pressures are international movements of population in the form of economic migrants and refugees, economic or political. Changes that may be broadly understood as economic in origin are taken to supersede the political activities of increasingly outmoded national states.

The most popular explanation of the restrictionist stance of Western states, on the other hand, is to be found in the xenophobia among sectors of Western publics, feelings rooted in confusion, resentment, and hopelessness in the face of macro-structural changes in the global economy. These changes produce, among other things, rising unemployment and economic vulnerability for that portion of the society without access to the knowledge essential to success in post-industrial, service-based economies.[7] Restrictionism is a political phenomenon, obviously, but it is treated as epiphenomenal because it derives from underlying economic changes. Furthermore, however much voters may rail against foreigners, they have little power to stop the transformation of their world. Restrictionists, in this view, may at best win temporary victories as the dynamic forces of multicultural, post-industrial change work their will on the old industrial order in which the national state once thrived.

Without denying the importance of long-term structural changes in the global economy or the genuine obstacles states confront in seeking to manage international migration today, I believe political factors should be at the centre of the explanation of comparative immigration policy. An important reason why states don't do a better job of controlling migration, and why they have not adopted a more consistently restrictionist stance in the face of migration pressures, is that they are prevented from doing so by domestic politics.[8] The politics of immigration in democratic states, despite widespread perceptions to the contrary, have a number of features that tend to be supportive of immigration and that undermine a strict regime of immigration control. Although most students have been motivated by a concern to explain the rise of anti-immigrant opinion, groups, and parties, an equally compelling subject is the chronic gap between the immigration policy preferences of mass publics and the policies and outcomes produced by states. The most puzzling aspect of immigration politics is not that host populations are upset by immigration, but that their preferences are so frequently ignored by governments.

Powerful economic interests press for ready access to cheap and plentiful labour and support policies that fuel population expansion, real estate development, and consumer growth. The ethnic kin of previous immigrants constitute a natural constituency to agitate for maintenance or liberalization of immigration programmes. The legal establishment—trial lawyers, civil libertarians, and the courts—work to protect immigrant and refugee rights and portray immigration controls as harsh, unfeeling, and illiberal. Intellectuals, broadly construed, tend to support immigrant causes and discredit opposition views as based on fear, ignorance, and race prejudice. Anti-racist movements put these ideas into practice in the streets. When push comes to shove, sensational media accounts of hapless migrants threatened with deportation erode the will of enforcement-orientated ministers.

These are only a few of the possible protagonists in a political struggle over control of immigration policy in Western nations. The shape of pro-immigration coalitions varies over time and across nations. Their relative clout *vis-à-vis* anti-immigrant parties waxes and wanes, depending on the phase of particular migration cycles, economic conditions, and unpredictable events such as the end of the Cold War. My point is that politics, rather than being exclusively a force for restriction, is an active impediment to it in many cases. Rather than a sideshow in the larger story of socio-economic change, politics is itself a cause of weak sovereignty and ineffective immigration policy.

The analysis of immigration politics, for all the attention it has attracted from the academic community, is largely unfinished business. We need to develop theoretically informed analyses that account for the leading aspects of immigration politics and policy in the democracies.[9] We need to give considerably more attention to those interests that are supportive of migration and that actively resist efforts to curtail it. When these are fully accounted for, we will be in a better position to assess the strength of sovereign powers and explain the direction of state policy.

## NOTES

1. Although this view is widely held, it is surprisingly rare to see it carefully or systematically argued. The literature on immigration policy and politics tends to be largely descriptive and the arguments that are made are too often expressed as much by tone and normative posture as by logical analysis. One often encounters the implication of declining sovereignty in throw-away lines about the futility of immigration control measures and the wrong-headedness of anti-immigration parties and groups. Among the systematic arguments that fit more or less comfortably into this camp are Soysal (1994), Cornelius et al. (1994), Richmond (1994: 216–17), Sassen (Chapter 2 in this volume).
2. The literature espousing this view is huge. See e.g. Cornelius et al. (1994), Papademetriou and Hamilton (1996), Wrench and Solomos (1993), Thränhardt (1992), Miles and Thränhardt (1995), Richmond (1994), Baldwin-Edwards and Schain (1994), Costa-Lascoux and Weil (1992).
3. No international regime for the migration of labour exists, but in 1990 the United Nations adopted an International Convention on the protection of the rights of all migrant workers and their families (Resolution 45/158).
4. Canada permits Quebec to exercise substantial control over immigration to the province in an attempt to recruit francophones (Employment and Immigration Canada 1991). The other provinces have the option to manage their own policies if they wish to exercise it. American states have traditionally been more important to immigration policy-making than is commonly understood (Klebaner 1958; Spiro 1994).
5. For a more extensive discussion of this argument that permits greater qualification and documentation, see Freeman (1995).
6. Italy enacted amnesties in 1981, 1986, and 1990; Spain in 1985 and 1991 (Rellini 1992: 184–6).
7. I develop this analysis more completely in Freeman (forthcoming, a). For a leading example of the genre, see Betz (1994).
8. In no way do I mean to imply that domestic political processes are unaffected by external developments. On the contrary, some of the most interesting work being done on immigration politics and policy seeks to predict domestic coalitions through theorems derived from the theory of international trade. See Kessler (1996).
9. I offer the beginnings of such a model in Freeman (1995; forthcoming, a). It develops predictions of the coalitions that will form around immigration issues based on perceptions of the distribution of the costs and benefits of migration and the resources of those groups benefiting or losing.

## REFERENCES

Adelman, H. (ed.) (1991), *Refugee Policy: Canada and the United States* (Toronto: York Lanes Press).

—— A. Borowski, M. Burstein, and L. Foster (1994), *Immigration and Refugee Policy: Australia and Canada Compared*, 2 vols. (Toronto: University of Toronto Press).

Baldwin-Edwards, M., and M. Schain (1994), *The Politics of Immigration in Western Europe* (London: Frank Cass).

Bean, F., *et al.* (1994), *Illegal Mexican Migration and the United States/ Mexico Border: The Effects of Operation Hold-the-Line on El Paso–Juarez* (Washington: USCIR).

Berns, L. (1972), 'Thomas Hobbes', in L. Strauss and J. Cropsey (eds.), *History of Political Philosophy*, 2nd edn. (Chicago: University of Chicago Press).

Betz, H.-G. (1994), *Radical Right-Wing Populism in Western Europe* (New York: St Martin's Press).

Birrell, B. (1995), 'The 1995–1996 Migration Program', *People and Place*, 3/2: 30–8.

Böhning, W. (1974), *Les Consequences économiques de l'emploi des travailleurs étrangers, concernant en particulier les marches du travail de l'Europe occidentale* (Paris: OECD).

—— (1991), 'Integration and Immigration Pressures in Western Europe', *International Labour Review*, 130/4.

Borjas, G. (1988), *International Differences in the Labor Market Performance of Immigrants* (Kalamazoo, Mich.: UpJohn Institute).

Calavita, K. (1994), 'Italy and the New Immigration', in Cornelius *et al.* (1994).

Callovi, G. (1992), 'Regulation of Immigration in 1993: Pieces of the European Community Jig-Saw Puzzle', *International Migration Review*, 26/2: 353–72.

Castles, S., and M. Miller (1993), *The Age of Migration* (New York: Guilford).

Collinson, S. (1993), *Europe and International Migration* (London: Pinter Publishers).

Cornelius, W. (1994), 'Spain: The Uneasy Transition from Labor Exporter to Labor Importer', in Cornelius *et al.* (1994).

—— P. Martin, and J. Hollifield (eds.) (1994), *Controlling Immigration: A Global Perspective* (Stanford, Calif.: Stanford University Press).

Costa-Lascoux, J., and P. Weil (eds.) (1992), *Logiques d'états et immigrations* (Paris: Éditions Kime).

de Jouvenel, B. (1957), *Sovereignty: An Inquiry into the Political Good* (Chicago: University of Chicago Press).

Deng, F. (1993), *Protecting the Dispossessed: A Challenge for the International Community* (Washington: Brookings Institution).

Employment and Immigration Canada (1991), *Canada–Quebec Accord relating to Immigration and Temporary Admission of Aliens* (Ottawa: Supply and Services Canada).

Fassman, H., and R. Münz (eds.) (1994), *European Migration in the Late Twentieth Century* (London: Edward Elgar).

FCO (Foreign and Commonwealth Office) (1996), *Survey of Current Affairs*, 26/7 (July), 269–70.

Freeman, G. (1992), 'Migration Policy and Politics in the Receiving States', *International Migration Review*, 26/4: 1144–67.

—— (1994), 'Can Liberal States Control Unwanted Migration?', *Annals of the American Academy of Political and Social Science*, 534 (July), 17–30.

—— (1995), 'Modes of Immigration Politics in Liberal Democratic States', *International Migration Review*, 29/112 (Winter), 881–902.

—— (1996), 'Continuity or Change in American Immigration Policy?', *People and Place*, 4/1: 1–7.

—— (forthcoming, *a*), 'Mass Politics and the Immigration Agenda in Liberal Democracies', *International Political Science Review*.

—— (forthcoming, *b*), 'The Quest for Skill: A Comparative Analysis', in M. Weiner (ed.), *Migration and Refugee Policies: The International Experience and its Relevance to South Africa* (London: Cassell Academic Publishers).

Gerth, H., and C. Mills (eds.) (1958), *From Max Weber: Essays in Sociology* (New York: Oxford University Press).

Hammar, T. (ed.) (1985), *European Immigration Policy: A Comparative Study* (Cambridge: Cambridge University Press).

Hendrickson, D. (1992), 'Migration in Law and Ethics: A Realist Perspective', in B. Barry and R. Goodin (eds.), *Free Movement: Ethical Issues in the Transnational Migration of People and of Money* (University Park: Pennsylvania State University Press).

Hollifield, J. (1992*a*), 'Migration and International Relations: Cooperation and Control in the European Community', *International Migration Review*, 26/2: 568–95.

—— (1992*b*), *Immigrants, Markets, and States: The Political Economy of Postwar Europe* (Cambridge, Mass.: Harvard University Press).

Holmes, F. (1990), 'CER, the Free Movement of People and Immigration Policies', paper presented at the National Immigration Outlook Conference, Melbourne, 14–16 Nov.

Jenks, R. (ed.) (1992), *Immigration and Nationality Policies of Leading Migration Nations* (Washington: Center for Immigration Studies).

Katzenstein, P. (1987), *Policy and Politics in West Germany* (Philadelphia: Temple University Press).

Kessler, A. (1996), 'International Migration, Cooperation, and Policymaking in Postwar Europe', paper prepared for the Annual Meeting of the International Studies Association, San Diego, 1996.

Kindleberger, Charles (1967), *Europe's Postwar Growth: The Role of Labor Supply* (Cambridge, Mass.: Harvard University Press).

King, R., and K. Rybaczuk (1993), 'Southern Europe and the International Division of Labour: From Emigration to Immigration', in R. King (ed.), *The New Geography of European Migrations* (London: Belhaven Press).

Klebaner, B. (1958), 'States and Local Immigration Regulation in the United States before 1882', *International Review of the Social Sciences*, 3: 269–81.

Koslowski, R. (1994), 'Intra-EU Migration, Citizenship and Political Union', *Journal of Common Market Studies*, 32/3: 369–402.

Kubat, D. (1993), *The Politics of Migration Policies* (Staten Island, NY: Center for Migration Studies).

Loescher, G. (1993), *Beyond Charity: International Cooperation and the Global Refugee Crisis* (Oxford: Oxford University Press).

Meissner, D., R. Hormats, A. Walker, and S. Ogata (eds.) (1993), *International Migration Challenges in a New Era* (New York: Trilateral Commission).

Miles, R., and D. Thränhardt (eds.) (1995), *Migration and European Integration: The Dynamics of Inclusion and Exclusion* (London: Pinter Publishers).

Miller, M. (1987), *Employer Sanctions in Europe* (Staten Island, NY: Center for Migration Studies).

—— (ed.) (1994), *Annals*, 534 (July), Special Issue: *Strategies for Immigration Control: An International Comparison*.

—— (1994), 'Towards Understanding State Capacity to Prevent Unwanted Migrations', in Baldwin-Edwards and Schain (1994).

Mitchell, C. (ed.) (1992), *Western Hemisphere Immigration and United States Foreign Policy* (University Park: Pennsylvania State University Press).

Nana, G., and J. Poot (1996), 'Trans-Tasman Migration and Closer Economic Relations', in P. Lloyd and L. Williams (eds.), *International Trade and Migration in the APEC Region* (Melbourne: Oxford University Press).

Niessen, J. (1992), 'European Community Legislation and Intergovernmental Cooperation on Migration', *International Migration Review*, 26/2: 675–84.

Papademetriou, D., and K. Hamilton (1996), *Converging Paths to Restriction: French, Italian, and British Responses to Immigration* (Washington: Carnegie Endowment for International Peace).

Phillip, A. (1994), 'European Union Immigration Policy: Phantom, Fantasy or Fact?', in Baldwin-Edwards and Schain (1994).

Poot, J. (1993), 'The Role of Trans-Tasman Migration in Forecasting the New Zealand Population', *Asian and Pacific Migration Journal*, 2/4: 395–416.

Rellini, G. (1992), 'Les Étrangers en Italie: Une politique a l'épreuve des faits', in Costa-Lascoux and Weil (1992).

Richmond, A. (1994), *Global Apartheid: Refugees, Racism, and the New World Order* (New York: Oxford University Press).

Ruddick, E., and M. Burstein (1993), 'New Directions for the Management of the Canadian Immigration Program', *People and Place*, 1/4: 24–9.

Skerry, P. (1995), 'Many Borders to Cross: Is Immigration the Exclusive Responsibility of the Federal Government?', *Publius*, 25/3: 71–85.

Skran, C. (1992), 'The International Refugee Regime: The Historical and Contemporary Context of International Responses to Asylum Problems', in G. Loescher (ed.), *Refugees and the Asylum Dilemma in the West* (University Park: Pennsylvania State University Press).

SOPEMI (Continuous Reporting System on Migration) (1995), *Trends in International Migration* (Paris: OECD).

Soysal, Y. (1994), *Limits to Citizenship: Migrants and Postnational Membership in Europe* (Chicago: University of Chicago Press).

Spiro, P. (1994), 'The States and Immigration in an Era of Demi-Sovereignties', *Virginia Journal of International Law*, 35: 121–77.

Thränhardt, D. (ed.) (1992), *Europe: A New Immigration Continent* (Münster: Lit Verlag).

Torpey, J. (1996), 'The Surest Thermometer of Freedom: The Evolution of Passport Controls in Europe', paper presented at the Tenth International Conference of Europeanists, Chicago, 14–16 Mar.

USCIR (United States Commission on Immigration Reform) (1994), *US Immigration Policy: Restoring Credibility* (Washington: USGPO).

—— (1995), *Legal Immigration: Setting Priorities* (Washington: USGPO).

Weiner, M. (1995), *The Global Migration Crisis* (New York: HarperCollins).

Weintraub, S. (1992), 'North American Free Trade and the European Situation Compared', *International Migration Review*, 26/2: 506–24.

Wrench, J., and J. Solomos (eds.) (1993), *Racism and Migration in Western Europe* (Oxford: Berg).

Zolberg, A., A. Suhrke, and S. Aguayo (1989), *Escape from Violence: Conflict and the Refugee Crisis in the Developing World* (Oxford: Oxford University Press).

# 4

# Asylum and State Sovereignty: A Comparison of the United States, Germany, and Britain

## CHRISTIAN JOPPKE

This chapter takes issue with two, related claims regarding the capacity of states to control immigration: first, that this capacity is declining;[1] and second, that such decline of control capacity is related to the rise of an international human rights regime, which restricts the ability of states to determine entry and exit of migrants as they see fit.[2] Both claims are especially raised in view of unwanted migrations, which have predominated in western Europe since the first oil crisis and have become a subject of perennial concern also in the United States. Next to illegal immigration and the acceptance of family members of already settled migrants, the acceptance of asylum-seekers represents the third source of unwanted, i.e. non-solicited, immigration, one that has grown dramatically since the early 1980s.[3]

As I shall demonstrate, an analysis of asylum policy in three major asylum-granting Western societies does not validate the claim that the capacity of states to control immigration is declining. On the contrary, one can observe an increasing willingness and insistence of states to maintain their sovereignty over the determination of entry and expulsion in this contested area,[4] often at the cost of confounding genuine refugees with *de facto* economic migrants. Mass asylum-seeking from the Third World represented a fundamentally new phenomenon, which overburdened an individual-centred process of determining genuine refugee status, attuned to the trickle of (politically convenient) refugee flows in the Cold War era. This exacted great adaptation costs by states, but adaptation was eventually made.

The second claim of an international human rights regime constraining state sovereignty is questionable in at least two regards. First, it is too pessimistic about nation-states drained of internal human rights principles; second, it is too optimistic about the effectiveness of the international human rights regime. Regarding the first, recent analyses (and advocacies) of human rights internationalism have drawn a misleading dualism between nation-states and an external human rights regime. The protection of human rights is a constitutive principle of, not an external imposition on, liberal nation-states. The international human rights regime set up after the Second World War is, after all, the externalization of principles which liberal states have internally long adhered to. Jürgen Habermas (1994: 1) has argued correctly that liberal states are equally obliged to the principles of human rights and popular sovereignty: 'The two ideas of popular sovereignty and human rights have shaped the normative self-understanding of constitutional states up to the present day. With the first idea we postulate that members of a democratic community are governed by themselves collectively; with the second, that they are governed by law and not by man.' Immigration and asylum-seeking have activated the contradiction between the universalistic rights dimension and the particularistic identity dimension of nation-states. The opposite stances in the field of immigration control seek to vindicate one nation-state principle at the cost of the other. Immigrant and asylum advocates stress the human rights principle, while being notoriously silent about the popular groundswell for tight immigration control. Restrictionists insist on the principle of sovereignty, and (often noisily and with an eye on their electoral advantage) boast to act on popular mandate. As the following comparison will show, conflicts over asylum policy are in the first domestic conflicts over the dual mandate of liberal nation-states to respect human rights while protecting the integrity of the people from which their sovereignty derives.

Complementary to the false depletion of nation-states of their liberal rights component, human rights internationalists have inflated the effectiveness of international norms and regimes. Certainly, the principle of non-refoulement, codified in the 1951 Geneva Convention on Refugees and prohibiting receiving states from expelling bona-fide refugees to states in which they face persecution and torture, has since matured into customary international law that is binding on states. But consonant with the principles of international law, the right of asylum is the right of states to grant asylum, not the right of individuals to be granted asylum. This is enshrined in Article 14(1) of the United Nations Universal Declaration of Human Rights, which proclaims that 'everyone has the right to seek and *to enjoy* in other countries asylum from persecution'. The alternative version 'and *to be granted*' was rejected by some participating states, including the United Kingdom, because this would have violated state sovereignty (see Plender 1988: 346–7). The duty corresponding to the sovereign right of states to grant asylum is the respect for that asylum decision by other states, which are not to presume an 'unfriendly act' by the asylum-granting state. As David Martin (1988*a*: 13) summarized the restrictive practices of states since the onset of mass asylum-seeking in the early 1980s, 'imposing visa requirements, or interdicting boats on the high seas—and perhaps arranging for a quick and dirty screening of asylum claims at a designated border post or on the airplane—are technically consistent with international refugee law'. States are not just free to grant, but also to prescribe, the conditions under which asylum is to be enjoyed. This implies discretion relating to the length of asylum, and, in the pre-asylum stage, discretion to deny work permission, confinement to certain areas or even strict detention, and in-kind rather than money provisions—all measures that states have widely resorted to since the early 1980s to make themselves less attractive for asylum-seekers.

Regarding the discretion of states in asylum-granting, Goodwin-Gill (1983: 107) concludes that 'the humanitarian practice exists, but the sense of obligation is missing'. The humanitarian practice and its institutionalization in an international human rights regime arose out of the experience of Nazism and the Second World War, when the Western world had remained largely impassive to the fate of Jewish and other refugees trying to escape persecution and genocide (see Henkin 1990; Sikkink 1993). If the human rights regime established by the League of Nations after the First World War only applied to national minority groups (especially in the new nation-states of south-eastern Europe), the UN refugee regime gives refugee status to individuals rather than groups, thus heralding the transition from an era of national rights to an era of universal human rights. In this regard, Richard Plender (1988: 398) is certainly right to say that the spirit, while not the word, of the right of asylum suggests a right of the individual, to be held against states. At least, this is the way states treated asylum-seekers in the immediate post-war period. Asylum-seekers were then in a 'position of privilege' (Martin 1988*a*: 9), often summarily recognized as UN convention refugees without much individual screening, and endowed with protection and assistance that went far beyond the international obligations imposed on receiving states. Generosity was partially guilt-driven compensation for past negligence, partially a political decoy in the Cold War confrontation with communism, from which most refugees originated, always enabled by the relatively small number of individuals claiming refugee status in western Europe and North America during this period.

This changed dramatically in the early 1980s. In Europe, North America, and Australia, applications for asylum rose more than nine-fold, from 90,444 in 1983 to 825,000 in 1992 (Keely and Stanton Russell 1994). 'Jet-age asylum seeking' (Martin 1988*a*), particularly from the crisis zones of post-colonial Africa and Asia, represented a fundamentally new phenomenon that forced the receiving states to reconsider their previous generosity. A new, insidious distinction had to be drawn between the small circle of genuine refugees and the large majority of those who obviously pursued the 'asylum strategy of immigration' (Teitelbaum 1984: 77).[5] In western Europe, the linkage between asylum and immigration was especially clear, because after the oil crisis of 1973 and the wide imposition of zero-immigration regimes, asylum remained 'the only significant remaining legal avenue' for new entrants (Freeman 1992: 1155). But also in the United States, where legal immigration did not just continue but increased, the asylum option was rational in several respects, such as legalizing clandestinity or bypassing the rigid quotas and long line-ups for regular immigration. In all cases, the erosion of the old distinction between political refugee and economic migrant has been the main casualty of the new era of mass asylum-seeking.

While there is convergence in states' restrictionist and deterrent responses to the new asylum-seekers, the domestic paths along which they arrived at this outcome differ significantly. The three cases considered here—the United States, Germany and Britain—lend themselves to comparison because they exhibit various combinations of communalities and differences along at least two axes of comparison. On a first axis, the United States is distinguished from Germany and Britain in possessing a separate system of legal immigration. This allows us to compare different patterns of fusing or separating the two policy areas. The quick confounding of 'refugees' with 'economic migrants' in the United States asylum debate, despite the clear institutional separation of the two policy areas there, casts doubt on the claim of German asylum advocates, raised with increasing urgency since the late 1980s, that a separate system of legal immigration could solve the problem of mass asylum-seeking. On a second axis of comparison, Germany and the United States are distinguished from Britain in possessing strong domestic constitutional provisions to be invoked by asylum-seekers: in the United States, an expansive Constitution, which protects the procedural and substantive rights of aliens, not just of citizens; in Germany, a unique constitutional right of political refugees to be granted (not just: to enjoy) asylum. These favourable domestic resources have helped make Germany and the United States the world's biggest magnets for asylum-seeking. By contrast, the lack of a written constitution and of domestically incorporated international human rights treaties and conventions has helped Britain to maintain its zero-sum immigration regime on the asylum front, and to prevent asylum flows from becoming more than a trickle.

In all three cases, asylum policy is conditioned by the dual, and increasingly opposite, nation-state principles of human rights protection and popular sovereignty, the strength of both varying across time and place. In the United States, the trajectory of asylum policy may be reconstructed as a zigzag of, first, liberating a 'humanitarian' asylum policy from foreign policy tutelage, and, second, closing this sudden opening for mass asylum-seeking, west European style. In Germany, asylum policy became a major stake in the grand national debate over special 'German' responsibilities to be derived from the Nazi past. In a curious reversal of the stipulated international regime versus state sovereignty dichotomy, German state sovereignty in asylum-granting was recovered through invoking the need for a European 'harmonization' of asylum policy, which allowed to cut beyond recognition the subjective right of asylum enshrined in the Basic Law. In Britain, finally, the trajectory of asylum policy lacks such epic twists and turns. Due to the domestic weakness of human rights provisions and actors and a zealous and instant equation of asylum-seeking with immigration, state sovereignty prevailed easily, without a major challenge.

Britain is the 'odd case out',[6] because this is a liberal state that failed to institute strong legal protections for aliens. This reflects Britain's lack of experience with non-nationals on its territory—the New Commonwealth immigrants of the post-war era had arrived, after all, as British nationals with full political and social rights. But most importantly, the principle of parliamentary sovereignty and concomitant absence of legal–constitutional constraints on the executive is responsible for this outcome. The British case thus underlines, *ex negativo*, the importance of judicial–constitutional resources for the protection of migrant interests, and it suggests—rather uncomfortably—limits to democracy in a world of migration.

## LIBERATING ASYLUM FROM FOREIGN POLICY TUTELAGE: THE US CASE

Until the late 1980s US asylum and refugee policy had remained a bastion of state sovereignty within an immigration regime where strong sovereignty had long been in retreat. In summarily granting refugee status to individuals fleeing communist regimes while denying asylum claims of individuals fleeing dictatorial yet 'friendly' regimes, asylum and refugee policy represented a curious anomaly within an immigration regime that had abandoned national discriminations in favour of source country universalism. The trajectory of asylum and refugee policy was thus to a large degree a catching-up with the non-discriminatory principles of immigration law and policy. Rescuing asylum and refugee policy from foreign policy tutelage, which was not completed before the end of the Cold War and the fall of communism, appeared itself as the curiously anomalous liberalization of a policy area that in western Europe had by then fallen to the sway of illiberal restrictionism. Yet no international legal rules and norms were responsible for this outcome. As the Supreme Court famously ruled in the *Paquete Habana* case of 1900, international law is US law only interstitially, in the absence of a 'controlling executive or legislative act' (quoted in Henkin 1987: 873). This cautious line was reaffirmed in *Garcia-Mir* v. *Meese* (1986), where a federal court held that the prolonged and arbitrary detention of asylum-seekers, even though in clear violation of international law, was still lawful if ordered by the Attorney-General (Helton 1991: 2339). Accordingly, any asylum liberalization had to have exclusively domestic roots.

A core domestic resource of asylum liberalization has been the 'communitarian' transformation of American immigration law (Schuck 1984), which extended broad constitutional protection and privileges from citizens to aliens. In classic immigration law, aliens were utter strangers without legal claims upon the government other than those the latter had consented to, not unlike the private law relationship between landowner and trespasser. Its premiss of strong state sovereignty was expressed in a Supreme Court rule of 1892, which consolidated the 'plenary power' doctrine established in the famous *Chinese Exclusion* case a few years earlier: 'It is an accepted maxim of international law, that every sovereign nation has the power, as inherent in sovereignty, and essential to self-preservation, to forbid the entrance of foreigners within its dominions, or to admit them only in such cases and upon such conditions as it may see fit to prescribe' (quoted ibid. 1). In the new 'communitarian' legal order, according to which legal obligation is not consent-based but reflective of the social and moral embeddedness of individuals, government owes legal duties to all individuals on US territory, even to strangers to whose presence it has not explicitly consented—such as illegal immigrants and asylum-seekers. The hallmark of communitarian immigration law is the blurring between the categories of citizen and alien, vindicating for aliens the broad 'due process' and 'equal protection' privileges provided by the Constitution. Applied to the law of asylum, this has amounted to court-imposed limitations on the government's discretion to detain and exclude asylum-seekers, or—in the case of illegal aliens awaiting deportation —guaranteeing the right to be notified of the possibility to apply for asylum. To be sure, these rights only concern the pre-asylum stage, and leave state discretion of granting asylum fully intact. But in creating evasion, delay, and administrative overload, they often entail a *de facto* right to stay, independently of a positive asylum decision. 'These rights', writes Peter Schuck (1984: 71) about the 'emergent law of asylum', 'may as a practical matter amount to the right to work and live in the United States indefinitely. To enjoy them, all the aliens need to do is reach our shores.'

US asylum policy proper is the result of a double differentiation: first, of refugee from immigration policy; and second, of asylum from refugee policy. In the 1965 Immigration Act, refugee policy was still a subordinate part of immigration policy. The 'seventh preference' category of the Act reserved 6 per cent of Eastern hemisphere immigrant visas to refugees from 'communist-dominated countries' or the Middle East—thus inaugurating the ideological, discriminatory bias of US refugee policy after the Second World War (see Loescher and Scanlan 1986: 73). In addition, the Attorney-General, acting on behalf of the President, had discretionary 'parole' power to admit refugees outside the normal immigration process—a power first used by Eisenhower to 'parole in' 40,000 Hungarian refugees after the Soviet crack-down in 1956. Only the Refugee Act of 1980 clearly separated refugee from immigration policy. It first established the regular legal status of refugee and— consonant with the principles of an immigrant nation—the subsequent expectation of refugees to acquire permanent citizenship, along with generous resettlement benefits to ease the transition. In incorporating the 1951 UN refugee definition and non-refoulement obligation, the Act's purpose was to overcome the ideological bias of US refugee policy, and to achieve more congressional control over the executive's erratic parole authority—still by the early 1990s largely 'unrealized goals' (Schuck 1991: 7). Finally, in a more subterranean yet momentous change for asylum-seekers, the Refugee Act levelled the so-called entry doctrine's sharp distinction between 'excludable' aliens at the borders, with no statutory and constitutional rights, and 'deportable' aliens on US territory, endowed with constitutional due process protection (Dinh 1994). Compliant with the non-refoulement obligation, the exclusion process was henceforth framed by extensive statutory and due process rights for aliens, including access to federal courts.

While the 1980 Refugee Act formally introduced the right to apply for political asylum on US territory or at the borders, this remained essentially 'an afterthought' (Meissner 1988: 60). For the United States, refugees have traditionally been an overseas phenomenon, relevant only if it touched upon foreign policy interests or obligations. As in the Indo-Chinese refugee crisis that followed the American withdrawal from Cambodia and Vietnam in the mid-1970s, refugee policy meant the screening and selection of refugees in camps overseas, with at best loose application of UN convention refugee criteria, and their resettlement in the United States. Such refugee policy was not antithetical to, but a direct outgrowth of, state sovereignty, because it reflected unforced state action towards non-nationals to which the United States, as one of the world's two superpowers after the Second World War, felt special obligations and responsibilities.

Mass asylum-seeking, and with it the differentiation of asylum from refugee policy, first became an issue with the so-called Mariel Boat Lift, a few weeks after the passing of the Refugee Act in March 1980. As Doris Meissner (1988: 61) put it, 'asylum, the sleeper of the new legislation, emerged as the dragon lady, center stage'. In an obvious attempt to embarrass the US government, Castro allowed some 124,000 Cubans to sail freely, on rigged-up rafts and boats, to the shores of Florida, among them a good portion of criminals and mentally disturbed. While met with considerable ambivalence, most Marielitos were allowed to enter without individual screening for refugee status, privileged by the Cuban Adjustment Act of 1966, which allowed Cubans to apply for permanent resident status after a short period on US territory. No such privileged reception was granted to a parallel flotilla of about 60,000 Haitian refugees who arrived in Florida at about the same time, but whose departure from the notoriously ruthless yet 'friendly' Duvalier regime led the government to label them 'illegal immigrants' without legitimate asylum claims. This opened up the debate about a discriminatory 'double standard' in US asylum policy, which operated on the simple principle of 'Cuba, yes, Haiti, no' (*New York Times* 1993*d*). The double standard was further exposed by the general denial of refugee status to new land-based arrivals from civil-war-torn Central America, whom the government likewise labelled 'illegal immigrants' subject to deportation.

Strictly speaking, the anomaly of US asylum policy was not the generally restrictionist response to mass asylum-seeking at the country's land and sea borders, which was in line with the practice of other Western states, but the preferential treatment for Cubans and other refugees from communist regimes. In rejecting pleas to grant 'extended voluntary departure' (temporary safe haven) status to about 100,000 El Salvadoreans in the United States, a government official could credibly point at the bad-precedence effect of such a measure for 'all other migrants from poor, violent societies to our south' (Abrams 1983). But why had this status been granted to 5,000 Poles during martial law? This imbalance created a double dynamic of asylum advocates trying to 'lift up' the general asylum practice to the generosity displayed to refugees from communism, and of a government cautiously but steadily abandoning its preferential treatment for some categories of asylum-seekers. Already the Marielitos were not unequivocally welcome, and one of the uglier asylum battles of the early 1980s was to detain and deport thousands of them whose criminal or medical records did not make them eligible for entry in the first, or whose 'parole' status had been forfeited by crimes committed while in the United States. Curiously, a Cuban advocate wondered aloud whether it was 'just' if Cuban hijackers were no longer welcomed as heroes but sent back to Havana, complaining that 'today's Cubans must file their requests for asylum with the rest of the world' (Fuentes 1983). In fact, the Marielitos' privileged transition from temporary parole ('Cuban–Haitian entrant') status to permanent residence, by means of the Cuban Adjustment Act, which so blatantly left out the Haitians, was forced by a federal court rule upon a government that would have preferred to settle jointly the legal status of both groups within an omnibus immigration bill (*New York Times* 1984).[7]

Throughout the 1980s hard-nosed government measures of mass detention, deportation, and high-sea interception were undercut by increasingly activist courts which no longer deferred to the traditional 'plenary power' of Congress and the President over immigration, and brought to bear the communitarian impetus of immigration law on the new field of asylum. In this respect, the decade is marked by a string of legal victories for asylum-seekers. Here one may distinguish between court rules limiting the deportation and detention power of the executive, and court rules easing the burden of proof and enlarging the grounds of standing for asylum applicants. With regard to the first, it is safe to say that few events since the black civil rights struggles have equally 'seared the judicial conscience' (Schuck 1984: 68). A variety of lower-court rules invoked constitutional due process and equal protection principles to correct allegedly 'discriminatory' race or national-origin-based decisions of the Immigration and Naturalization Service (INS) against certain classes of asylum-seekers. In *Haitian Refugee Center* v. *Civiletti* (1980), a class action suit of 4,000 Haitians challenging their deportation by the INS, a federal district judge found this policy 'offensive to every notion of constitutional due process and equal protection', ordering the INS to discontinue the deportation until all asylum applications were orderly processed (Loescher and Scanlan 1986: 176–7; Potelicki 1981: 415–18). In *Rodriguez-Fernandez* v. *Wilkinson* (1980), a convicted Marielito was released from detention, because the court deemed indefinite detention cruel 'punishment' in violation of Fifth and Eighth Amendment principles (Motomura 1990: 593). To be sure, the explicit invocation of constitutional principles to protect first entrants, which openly challenged the dominant plenary power doctrine in immigration, remained essentially a lower-court phenomenon.[8] In a review of a detention case, *Jean* v. *Nelson* (1985), the Supreme Court upheld the lower-court verdict of discriminatory agency behaviour on sub-constitutional grounds only.[9]

In addition, court rules eased the burden of proof in asylum determination, for instance, in no longer using false documentation or witness as automatic grounds for dismissal of a case (see Anker and Blum 1989). More importantly still, in *INS* v. *Cardoza-Fonseca* (1987), the Supreme Court ruled that the Reagan administration's demanding 'clear probability' of persecution standard for deciding asylum claims had to be replaced by the looser 'reasonable possibility' of persecution standard, pointing out that a one-in-ten chance of persecution would qualify as a legitimate asylum claim (Porter 1992: 234–5). Finally, there has been a tendency towards broadening the grounds on which individuals can raise asylum claims. For instance, in *Bolanos-Hernandez* v. *INS* (1984), a court stipulated that 'political neutrality' also constituted a 'political opinion' subject to persecution.[10] A 'gender-conscious' judiciary has even been willing to grant asylum to homosexuals who claim to be persecuted for their sexual orientation.[11]

The court-driven liberalization of asylum culminated in new asylum rules given out by the Justice Department in 1990. They replaced the uneven, politically driven 'interim rules' that had guided the administrative asylum process since 1980.[12] In addition, a corps of professional asylum officers trained in international relations and human rights law was established, with the mandate to make politically neutral asylum decisions, unimpaired by State Department prerogatives. According to the new rules, work permits and the help of lawyers were to be granted routinely to asylum-seekers. Most importantly, the new rules gave asylum-seekers the benefit of the doubt. Claimants no longer needed to prove that they were individually singled out for persecution; it was enough to show 'a pattern or practice of persecuting the groups of persons similarly situated' (quoted in *New York Times* 1990*b*)—a refugee definition considerably looser than the UN convention refugee definition. Moreover, aliens now qualified for asylum on the basis of their own statements, without objective corroboration, if the testimony was 'credible in light of general conditions' in the home country (to be ascertained by means of a newly established documentation centre). In David Martin's (1988*a*: 14) terms, this new policy moved back from the (preferred) state option of 'deterrence' to 'fair adjudication', and as such it stood out in the Western world.

The double standard was officially put to rest in a subsequent court settlement, in which the government agreed to stop detaining and deporting illegal aliens from El Salvador and Guatemala, granting new asylum hearings for all 150,000 applicants denied since 1980 and for 350,000 illegal aliens who had never applied previously. The settlement averted a trial on the government's 'discriminatory' denial of asylum to El Salvadoreans and Guatemalans, who claimed violation of their constitutional rights to free speech, equal protection, and due process (*New York Times* 1990*c*).[13] The government now explicitly obliged itself to rule out foreign policy, border control, and the applicant's country of origin as criteria of asylum determination. This was a major victory for the 'sanctuary movement' of Church leaders, social workers, and human rights lawyers, who had filed the suit in May 1985. This movement, which included not just 200 churches and synagogues but entire cities like Los Angeles and Sacramento declaring themselves 'sanctuaries' for Central American refugees, epitomizes the normative cloth out of which US asylum liberalization was made: not abstract human rights principles hovering above nation-states, but—as a Church leader put it—'the deepest values of our United States traditions of being a place of refuge, a place to where persecuted people can come' (*New York Times* 1985).

Just when western Europe erected its fabled 'fortress' against the turmoils in the post-communist East, America's doors for refugees had swung wide open. A Harvard Law School report found that by late 1992 the approval rate for Central American and Haitian asylum-seekers was approaching or even surpassing the 30 per cent mark—a dramatic increase from the old 3 per cent mark, and a curious outlier if compared with western Europe, where by now over 90 per cent of asylum applications were denied (*New York Times* 1992).

But the high-minded return to America's founding myth of an 'asylum of nations' could not last. The bombing of the World Trade Center in March 1993, one of whose suspects had entered the United States on the asylum ticket, the uncovery of professional smuggling-rings for Chinese refugees, and the general anti-immigrant groundswell moving eastwards from California, forced the pendulum back towards restrictionism. In fact, the liberalized asylum policy amounted to 'a world-wide siren's call to foreigners'.[14] In 1993 the number of new asylum claims was up to 150,000, which is a 300 per cent increase since 1990, while the backlog of pending cases grew to 300,000, even 425,000 in 1994—no small thing for a fledgling corps of 150 asylum officers. Even immigrant advocates admitted that fraudulent claimants were now 'shopping for airports' with a reputation of leniency, such as New York's JFK.[15] So wide had the asylum door swung open that all an immigrant had to do was arrive at an airport, destroy his travel documents to eradicate disqualifying third-country stops, plead for asylum, and leave with only a tentative court date in the distant future.

Ironically, it was left to the Democratic Clinton administration to curtail the liberal asylum legacy of its Republican predecessor, and to reinvigorate state sovereignty in asylum policy. In December 1994 the INS announced new regulations to reduce the 'abuse' of the asylum system, which included an expedited review process with an enlarged body of asylum officers, on-the-spot interviewing at the port of entry, increasing detention and swift deportation of those denied asylum, and restrictions on work permits (*New York Times* 1994*b*).[16]

More dramatically, the Clinton administration resumed the highly contested Bush administration practice of intercepting Haitian refugees on the high seas, and sending them back without an interview (see

Motomura 1993). After candidate Clinton had condemned the 'cruel policy of returning Haitian refugees to a brutal dictatorship without an asylum hearing', the newly inaugurated President was forced to do just that, when facing an armada of some 150,000 Haitians on 1,000 hastily built boats to cash in on his promise of 'temporary asylum' (*New York Times* 1993a). This practice of extraterritorializing asylum flows was upheld by an important Supreme Court rule, *Sale* v. *Haitian Centers Council* (1993), which argued that exclusion protection under the Refugee Act and non-refoulement obligations existed only *within* US territory (*New York Times* 1993e). This was one of the few court rules since the onset of mass asylum-seeking that limited, rather than enlarged, the reach of constitutional protection for aliens. But it did not diminish the domestic dilemma of asylum in a liberal state, particularly in a state both open to interest group pressure and paralysed by the spectre of race. Haitians, after all, are black, and tough action against them is not well received by black American citizens. Moved by a widely publicized hunger strike by the leader of the Transafrica Forum, a black civil rights group, Clinton temporarily stepped back from strict interception and granted Haitian exiles asylum hearings at sea (*New York Times* 1994a). The mass exodus of Haitians promptly resumed, with some 10,000 Haitians picked up at sea in less than a month. Emboldened by the favourable Supreme Court rule in the meantime, Clinton abruptly shifted policy again towards renewed high-seas interception, but now deflecting the US-bound asylum flow to 'safe havens' in Panama and other Caribbean countries (see Aleinikoff 1994). The second Haitian boat people episode was eventually put to an end by the US-backed reinstatement of the ousted President Aristide. In the post-communist era US asylum policy has evidently not shed its close linkage with foreign policy.

But an equally tough response to a parallel exodus of Cubans—the biggest since the Mariel Boat Lift of 1980—confirms that the old embarrassment of the asylum–foreign policy linkage—the discriminatory 'double standard'—is not up for a renewal. In a reversal of the US's thirty-year open-door policy for Cubans, US coastguards redirected a Florida-bound flotilla of over 30,000 Cubans to 'safe haven' detention camps in Panama and Guantánamo Bay, the US naval base on Cuba. Here the disappointed would-be exiles, who had counted on a continuation of America's special welcome for the victims of communism, were told to queue up for a legal immigrant visa, and that from Cuba. A government official's declaration that Cuba must not 'control the immigration policy of the United States' reveals a new determination not to lose out on the asylum front (*The Economist* 1994).

## EUROPE TO THE RESCUE: THE GERMAN CASE

If the overall trajectory of US asylum policy is one of increasingly restricted state sovereignty, the trajectory of German asylum policy is the opposite one of recovering state sovereignty from a unique constraint. Alone in the world, the German Constitution provides a subjective right for political refugees to be granted asylum. Article 16 of the Basic Law stipulates: 'Politically persecuted enjoy the right of asylum'. In Germany, the right of asylum is not the right of the state to grant asylum, to be held against the persecuting state, but the right of the persecuted individual to be held against the receiving state. This is a unique limit on state sovereignty, with unique implications. It invalidates the sovereign right of the state to deny access to its territory: every individual claiming, however spuriously, to be politically persecuted enjoys the right of entry and the full arsenal of legal–constitutional protection, including access to the Federal Constitutional Court.[17] The 'quick and dirty' border screening, practised by all other states in the age of mass asylum-seeking, has not been an option in Germany. The constitutional right of asylum made Germany Europe's, if not the world's, prime target for the asylum strategy of immigration. Germany's asylum debate thus revolves around protecting, or abolishing, this vestige of German exceptionalism. Ironically, only European integration would eventually allow Germany to recover its sovereignty in asylum policy.

As in the United States, human rights constraints on German state sovereignty are home-grown, based on an expansive constitution protecting the rights of non-citizens. However, not a positive founding myth of an 'asylum of nations', but the negative reference to the Nazi past, is the origin of Germany's unique asylum law. The fathers of the Basic Law, many of them exiled during the Nazi regime, conceived of an asylum law that went far beyond existing international law as a conscious act of redemption and atonement. As Carlo Schmid famously defended the Article 16 in 1948, 'the granting of asylum is always a question of generosity and if you want to be generous, you must take the risk of being mistaken in a particular case' (quoted in Wolken

1988: 24). As a 'confessional right', the constitutional right of asylum depended on 'the continued presence of the [Nazi] experience' (Rottmann 1984: 344). Accordingly, asylum advocates elevated Article 16 into a quasi-sacred taboo: 'The promise of the constitutional right of Article 16 . . . must remain untouched.'[18] Conversely, one of the earliest advocates of abolishing Article 16 considered himself 'part of a generation that is free of personal guilt', pointing out the mundane need for the state to get out of the self-made asylum trap: 'We can't have our asylum law dictated by our guilt of the past.'[19] Because it was tied up with deeply divided views about national identity, the German asylum debate was more polarized and emotionally led than elsewhere. And only the time-bound weakening of the Nazi presence ('normalization', some would say) allowed the touching of the tabooed 'confessional right' at all.

The right of asylum is only the most visible part of a constitutional law strongly protective of the rights of non-citizens. In an often ignored counterpoint to a restrictive, and widely criticized, citizenship and naturalization regime based on blood affiliation (*jus sanguinis*) and thus derivative of *völkisch* nationalism, Germany's constitutional, administrative, and judicial systems are 'among the most protective of non-citizens' rights in the world' (Kanstroom 1993*a*: 160). In fact, just because of the persistent legacy of closed ethnic nationhood that severely restricts access to citizenship, the status of aliens is also exceptionally well protected in Germany. In sharp contrast to the United States and Britain, Germany has quickly and unreservedly incorporated into municipal law all major United Nations and European human rights and refugee conventions.[20] Constitutional law itself, 'a reaction against the ideology of Nazism' (ibid. 166), enshrines fundamental human rights, independently of citizenship, to be aggressively and expansively protected by independent constitutional courts.[21] While the Aliens Law of 1965, set up to regulate the status of guestworkers in (West) Germany, conceived of foreigners as economic commodities at the discretion of 'German state interests',[22] assertive federal courts have construed aliens' rights analogous to the rights of Germans, arguing that acquired social and economic ties entailed the right of permanent stay (Neuman 1990). Entitled also to wide-ranging social benefits according to the constitutional *Sozialstaatsprinzip*, aliens are in crucial respects equal to German citizens (see Hailbronner 1992). As Kanstroom (1993*a*: 184–5) concludes, 'citizenship is . . . not nearly as important to the day-to-day life of a foreigner in Germany as it might be elsewhere'. In combination with the automatic right to territorial access, these socio-legal features made Germany an obvious destination of mass asylum-seeking.

German asylum policy has revolved around two separate axes of conflict, a territorial local-vs.-federal axis and an ideological left-vs.-right axis. The territorial axis has been dominant during a first round of conflict, from the late 1970s to the mid-1980s, in which the constitutional right of asylum remained largely unquestioned. In this phase, municipalities and *Länder* governments, which are legally responsible for providing housing and social welfare benefits for asylum-seekers, have unitedly pushed for more restrictive legislation through the second federal legislative chamber, the Bundesrat. There was initially great variation among the *Länder* in the treatment of asylum-seekers. The southern *Länder* of Bavaria and Baden-Württemberg, conservative but also vulnerable to south–north migrations, spearheaded measures of deterrence, such as herding asylum-seekers in camps, providing in-kind benefits only, imposing work bans, and being quicker to deport rejected asylum applicants. The northern *Länder* of Lower Saxony and North Rhine–Westphalia and the city-states of Bremen and Hamburg, liberal but also more insulated, initially shied away from such negative measures. But the ensuing intra-German north–south pull of asylum-seekers forced the gentler north into a 'deterrence competition' (Münch 1992: 140) that eventually flattened such differences.

Tellingly, a Social Democratic (SPD) *Land* chief, Oskar Lafontaine of the Saarland, stung by a local episode of fierce popular opposition to Romanian refugees, was one of the first major politicians to question openly the constitutional right of asylum.[23] But his quick silencing by the national party leadership indicates that this second round of the German asylum debate, which focused on Article 16 of the Basic Law, was made of a different cloth. In this second round of conflict, the ideological left-vs.-right axis, as defined above all by different stances to the national past, was dominant: the 'left' arguing that the humanitarian obligations stemming from the Nazi past made Article 16 sacrosanct; the 'right' arguing that no such obligations existed, and that in the interest of political stability Article 16 had to be abolished.

Before the debate about Article 16 started in earnest, the first round of asylum conflict was about neutralizing the constitutional asylum right through fast-track legal procedures and measures of social deterrence.[24] This led to a curious disjuncture between a uniquely liberal asylum law and a harsh deterrence regime that a 1983 UN High

Commission for Refugees (UNHCR) report also found 'unique in Europe' (Wolken 1988: 60). Such deterrence must be seen in the context of Germany's zero-immigration policy after the oil crisis. After the halt on immigration of new guestworkers in 1973 (the *Anwerbestop*), asylum was the only legal avenue available for new entries. Immediately after the *Anwerbestop*, the number of asylum applications began to multiply.[25] The lifting of the general work ban in 1975 (issued to ease the financial burdens of municipalities and states) and the distribution since early 1974 of asylum applicants over the *Länder*, which made the industrial centres of the Ruhr and the Rhine–Main accessible for the new migrants, amounted to additional invitations to pursue the asylum strategy of immigration. When the number of new asylum-seekers grew to over 100,000 in 1980, more than half of them were Turks—the biggest group of guestworkers in Germany. This led to obvious inconsistencies: new Turks arriving on the asylum ticket were granted automatic work permits, while Turks arriving under the family reunification ticket had to wait four years before they were allowed to work (*Der Spiegel* 1980). There is ample evidence that the notion of 'bogus asylum-seekers' (*Scheinasylanten*), which was the focus of the first society-wide debate over asylum in 1980, was not the invention of vitriolic right-wingers. In the early 1980s Turkish newspapers reprinted the German government form required to claim asylum, and a market developed in South Asia (especially Pakistan) for 'package tours' that included one-way air fare and legal instruction on how to apply for asylum upon arrival (see Teitelbaum 1984: 79).

Between 1978 and 1991 no less than eight federal laws were passed to shorten the legal procedures and curtail the social incentives of asylum-seeking. Streamlining the legal process amounted to squaring a circle defined by the demanding legal requirements of constitutional law. Once the possibility of administrative appeal to the Federal Refugee Office was abolished, the administrative courts were flooded with asylum cases, creating a backlog that further lengthened the procedures and attracted new claimants in a vicious circle. In the first half of the 1980s, 80 per cent of all cases before the Federal Administrative Court were asylum cases, because most asylum-seekers (helped by a rather shady branch of the legal profession)[26] showed no hesitation in exhausting the full repertory of legal protection (*Der Spiegel* 1986). The introduction of a fast-track procedure for 'obviously unfounded' asylum claims in the Asylum Procedures Law of 1982, which limited but did not abolish administrative court review, amounted to 'a first significant tightening of the applicants' recognition practice' (Münch, 1992: 98). But further demands, raised by Bavaria, Baden-Württemberg, and the Christian Democrat (CDU) opposition, for single (instead of three) judges to decide asylum claims, enlarged competences for the Foreigner Offices, and a drastic shortening of judicial appeal procedures did not ensue.

The arsenal of legal fast-tracking and social deterrence was exhausted[27] when, from the late 1980s on, the number of new asylum applicants began to rise dramatically—103,076 in 1988, 121,318 in 1989, 193,063 in 1990, 256,112 in 1991, reaching the exorbitant level of 438,191 in 1992 (German Interior Ministry 1993: 106–7). By then, the Federal Republic was receiving 60 to 70 per cent of all refugees in western Europe, and in 1992 a staggering 80 per cent. This is when Article 16 itself came under attack. One of the last liberal lines of defence was a paradoxical one: rigorous deportations.[28] Germany was indeed a deportation laggard. Only 1–2 per cent of denied asylum applicants were eventually deported. But this is no accident, because state violence against foreigners had sad precedents in Germany—deportation is 'continuation of Nazi politics with other means', said a *gypsy* asylum activist (*Der Spiegel* 1992c).[29] Conservative asylum critics took a different line: the problem was not a deficit of deportations; the problem was automatic territorial access. The problem was Article 16, which amounted to a self-imposed abandonment of state sovereignty. It is no small irony that the threat of Chancellor Kohl, issued at the height of the German asylum crisis in November 1992, to seal the porous borders by emergency decree would eventually push the Social Democrats towards accepting a change to the Basic Law—'sovereign', Carl Schmitt (1934: 11) said famously, 'is who decides about the emergency'.

Helmut Quaritsch (1985: 21) had an early foreboding that the 'loss of sovereignty' (*Verlust der politischen Handlungsfähigkeit*) entailed by Article 16 might leave the state vulnerable to severe 'domestic unrest'. In fact, the unprecedented increase of asylum claims in the late 1980s and early 1990s triggered the most serious domestic crisis the Federal Republic has ever gone through. The situation was aggravated by the fact that, parallel to the new asylum-seekers (who were now predominantly from the civil war zones of post-communist south-eastern Europe), ethnic Germans from the Soviet Union, Poland, and Romania arrived in large numbers—close to a million between 1988 and 1990 (German Interior Ministry 1993: 123). In addition, the breakdown of East Germany entailed a third migration, with a peak of 340,000 in 1990. Taken together, the Federal Republic had to absorb 3 million new migrants between 1989 and 1992, almost twice as many as the American immigrant nation took in during the 1920s—no small thing for a country that defines itself as 'not an immigration country'. The parallel inflow of ethnic Germans (who were granted automatic citizenship according to Article 116 of the Basic Law) and asylum-seekers created particularly insidious distinctions. 'The coming home of Germans . . . has priority over the reception of aliens', wrote an influential conservative columnist (Fromme 1988). Because they competed for the same resources, welcoming ethnic Germans implied 'restricting the right of asylum'. In turn, Social Democrats and Greens favoured the dropping of Article 116, that anachronistic relic of *völkisch* nationhood, and the introduction of American-style immigration quotas, in which the ethnic Germans would be just another immigrant group.

While the politicians and intellectual élites became locked in a polarized and inconclusive debate about who should take priority, society felt the full impact of the unprecedented migrations. In a country with a housing shortage of 3 million units, there was simply no room to accommodate the new arrivals. Ramshackle container units were erected on the outskirts of almost every town or city, and mayors confiscated everything from gymnasiums, town halls, club halls, and vacant state-owned housing, even windowless air-raid shelters, to fulfil their quota obligations. From one point on, the SPD-governed city-state of Bremen simply refused to accept any more asylum applications by Poles and Romanians (whose recognition rate was zero). But the most fateful aggravation of societal stress was implied in a harmless-looking clause of the reunification treaty of October 1991, which allotted 20 per cent of new asylum-seekers to the new eastern *Länder*. This was in the spirit of burden-sharing, but culpably oblivious of a depressed society that had just escaped from two subsequent dictatorships and did not know how to deal with brown skin. Hoyerswerda and Rostock-Lichtenhagen, where the local population cheered the violent attacks of skinheads and neo-Nazis on asylum camps, were the beginning of the worst wave of xenophobic violence that Germany had seen since the end of the Third Reich, leaving more than forty people dead. The spectre of Weimar, the first German democracy destroyed by extremist violence, loomed above the reunified country (*Der Spiegel* 1992*a*). But the violent excesses of fringe groups, which were condemned by most, diverted attention from the real societal stress caused by uncontrolled migration. A 1992 survey showed that three-quarters of Germans were then demanding drastic action to contain the asylum flow, including the long-maligned change of the Basic Law (*Der Spiegel* 1992*b*).

Whose state is it? This key stake of asylum policy was never far from the surface during the German asylum crisis. The defenders of Article 16 saw the state in the first place obliged to human rights principles, and only secondarily to the people who constituted it. A leader of the Social Democrats refused to become 'the instrument . . . of popular sentiment (*gesundes Volksempfinden*)', warning that 'domestic considerations must not influence asylum policy'.[30] This delicate bracketing of democracy in favour of human rights is combined with the view that there is an inherent link between asylum and immigration.[31] Fusing both motives, Pro Asyl, an asylum rights organization, declared that the alternative was to 'wall ourselves in' or to 'share our wealth' (quoted in Bade 1994: 139). This conveys a resigned-cum-moralist attitude towards asylum-based immigration as in principle uncontrollable and retributive of global injustice. A Green asylum advocate flatly stated that 'the issue is not if we *want* immigration but how we *manage* it', adding that 'the population of this country will have to get used to the fact of permanent immigration'.[32] By contrast, conservative critics of Article 16, not without complacency, saw themselves as acting on popular mandate: 'my responsibility as a politician is to optimize the conditions for the people who live here. It is not my duty to treat all problems in the world equally.'[33] Conservative critics of asylum upheld the division of the world into sovereign states, each accountable to its own citizens first: 'Every state . . . has to serve its own citizens first, and only secondarily the rest of the world . . . Germany cannot become everyone's country (*Jedermannsland*).'[34]

Even though it was bullied by the street and by diabolic conservative campaigning, the SPD's final about-face in favour of constitutional change could draw upon one unambiguous demand of the day: European harmonization of asylum policy.[35] Since the European Union was obviously unwilling to go the German way,[36] Germany had to follow Europe. The initial stance of the SPD to 'adjust' Article 16 only *after* Europe had agreed upon 'humane' asylum standards was essentially hollow. Germany's neighbours profited from the status quo and showed no sign of accommodating German demands for substantive burden-sharing and stronger forms of co-ordination, not to mention that 'humane' standards would never see the light of day.[37] Constrained by its national constitution, Germany could only conditionally participate in the Dublin and Schengen treaties, which stipulate that one Union state was to process an asylum case on behalf of all others. Article 16 of the German Basic Law prohibited this procedure, commanding instead that asylum-seekers rejected in France or Britain would get a second chance in Germany. One of the reasons for the little enthusiasm among other member states for a harmonized asylum policy was that they could 'dump' their rejected applicants on Germany, while Germany was constitutionally prohibited from responding in kind. Germany was indeed, in the words of Interior Minister Wolfgang Schäuble, the 'reserve asylum country of Europe'. The point of the Interior Minister's ingenious European solution to the German asylum crisis was to turn the situation about: 'if we change our constitution, we would profit from the fact that we are surrounded by neighbours who can protect asylum-seekers from persecution . . . Then *we*, and not the others, would profit from our geographical location. Then our European neighbours, and not only we, would quickly want to find a joint solution' (Schäuble 1992).

The so-called 'asylum compromise' between government and opposition (excluding the Greens), which provided the required two-thirds parliamentary majority for a change of the Basic Law, avoided hard-line demands for a complete dropping of Article 16. But the insertion of proviso clauses now enabled the state to do what it could not do before: to reject apparently fraudulent would-be asylum-seekers at the borders (see Renner 1993). The amended Article 16 restricts access to territory and to the constitutional asylum process through two interrelated clauses: first, asylum-seekers arriving through 'safe third states' (which include Poland and the Czech Republic) are definitionally excluded from the asylum process and are denied entry or subjected to immediate deportation; secondly, asylum-seekers from 'safe countries of origin' are considered not politically persecuted and face a fast-track recognition procedure that generally ends in a rejection of their claims as 'obviously unfounded'. The cordon is finally sealed through the statutory 'airport regulation', which subjects asylum-seekers arriving by plane from safe countries of origin or without valid passports to a speeded-up recognition procedure in extraterritorial airport space, *before* they have legally entered the Federal Republic. In essence, only asylum-seekers arriving by plane or ship with valid papers and without debilitating third-country stops from countries of certified persecution are still entitled to claim the constitutional right of asylum. As a critic put it sarcastically, 'the right of asylum still exists—but not the refugees entitled to it' (Prantl 1994: 96).

What the same critic denounced as the 'most momentous political failure in the history of the Federal Republic' (p. 100) helped solve Germany's biggest political crisis after the Second World War. Refugees continue to arrive, but in numbers considered commensurate with the country's capabilities—around 125,000 in 1994 and 1995, which is 70 per cent less than in 1992. More importantly perhaps, the recognition quote has gone up to 25 per cent, indicating a return to more efficient and 'just' screening (see *Die Zeit* 1995). Related or not, right-wing violence against foreigners has passed its peak.[38] This is not to deny that the German recovery of border control has created new follow-up problems. First, the creation of buffer zones and the 'farming out' of refugee acceptance is now being copied by Germany's eastern neighbours, and the resulting chain deportations could entail the undermining of non-refoulement obligations. Secondly, curtailing legal entry has created the new problem of illegal immigration, which—given Germany's open land borders—may be inherently difficult to contain. Thirdly, more rigidly practised deportations have become continued bones of contention, gripping the country's moral conscience.[39] And fourthly, the Federal Constitutional Court has repeatedly stayed generic deportation orders, insisting on the constitutional principle of 'single-case examination' (*Einzelfallprüfung*).[40] Despite these reservations, few would doubt in retrospect that Germany, more drastically perhaps because initially more handicapped than other states, has only done what all Western states have done when confronted with mass asylum-seeking—forcefully reassert its sovereignty.

## UNBENDING SOVEREIGNTY: THE BRITISH CASE

There was no need for Britain to reassert sovereignty in asylum policy because it never showed the slightest inclination to give it up in the first place. Accordingly, the trajectory of British asylum policy shows no dramatic twists and turns, no epic battle between the double foundational principles of liberal nation-states, human rights and sovereignty. Britain is usually referred to as a (however dubious) model of successful immigration control, Europe's exceptional 'would-be zero immigration country' (Layton-Henry 1994). And in its firm resistance to a Europe without internal border controls, the country that was once the champion of subjecting princely powers to the control of Parliament is now the ardent defender of absolutism's most enduring fruit: state sovereignty.

The British case differs from the US and German cases in three basic respects: first, the lack of a written constitution and of domestically incorporated human rights conventions, which could provide a domestic foothold for the rights and interests of immigrants and asylum-seekers; secondly, a structural, not just rhetorical, conflation of immigration control and asylum policy; and, thirdly, the existence of a third category of migrant that, while sharing some elements of both, is neither immigrant nor asylum-seeker: British nationals without the right to settle in Britain.

It is paradoxical that the country that invented the idea and phrase of a 'bill of rights' doesn't actually have one. Britain is the only country in western Europe which has neither a written constitution nor international treaty rights incorporated in municipal law. As a result, there are no legally enforceable protections for the individual to be held against the state. Sovereignty is invested in Parliament, which has unlimited powers to make or unmake rights and to determine the law of the land. The principle of judicial review, well established in the United States and Germany, is relatively undeveloped in Britain. Bereft of a higher level of constitutional law, courts have no position from which to judge ordinary statute law, and thus to intervene in public policy. All courts can do is rectify procedural wrongs. For defenders of traditional 'British liberties' this is all right: a cumulative and concretist common law, they say, is better suited to protect individual liberties than abstract listings of rights, and wouldn't a bill of rights approach to law-making transfer powers from Parliament to unelected judges and thus be anti-democratic to the core?[41]

Only, the notion of well-protected British liberties is not free of complacency (Feldman 1993: 63). Britain is now known as one of Europe's most notorious human rights offenders. The European Court of Human Rights has decided thirty-seven cases against the United Kingdom, which gives it one of the worst records among all thirty-five signatories to the European Convention on Human Rights.[42] A good number of them have been immigration cases, touching upon key aspects of British immigration law. In 1972 the European Commission castigated the 1968 Commonwealth Immigration Act as 'racially discriminatory' (see Goodwin-Gill 1978, ch. 10). This Act had invented the principle (but not the word) of 'patrial'—the race-loaded core principle of British immigration law—to exclude former colonial subjects from access to Britain. In 1985 the European Court in Strasbourg found the family unification provisions of British immigration law 'sexually discriminatory', because they allowed settled husbands without citizenship to bring in their foreign wives, while not granting the parallel right to settled wives. The 1992 European Court of Justice decision in *Surinder Singh* put its finger on the so-called 'primary purpose' rule, which outlaws marriages of convenience and puts extraordinary high burdens of proof on the immigrant spouses-to-be. According to EC law, the Court argued, a British national has the unconditional right to bring in his foreign wife—which is more than British immigration law allows. Not only substantial, but also procedural, key aspects of British immigration law have been found wanting in Strasbourg: lack of enforceable rights and of effective appeal remedies, inadequate safeguards against deportations, and an over-dependence on executive discretion (Storey 1994: 112–13).

The human rights regime versus nation-state dualism, drawn by some human rights internationalists, is not all that inaccurate in the case of Britain. This is because the immigrant and asylum-seeker's best friend—the courts—which played so prominent a role in German and US immigration and asylum battles, have been largely absent from the British scene, at least domestically.[43] On the contrary, as the doyen of British immigration law, Ian Macdonald, put it sombrely, courts have helped 'tighten immigration control and extend the power of the state almost to the point of arbitrariness' (1983: 3). In reality, the sovereignty of Parliament is the sovereignty of the executive, with the Home Office the uncontested authority in immigration and asylum policy. On the opposite side, there is only Amnesty International, a handful of voluntary organizations, and a motley crowd of immigration lawyers attacking a government policy that falls short of 'international standards' (e.g. Amnesty International 1991). Not to much avail, because these standards *per se* have no teeth. EU standards are an exception, because they take precedence over national law and are legally enforceable. But the British government found a way to deal with them also: when faced with the 1985 European Court verdict regarding 'sexually discriminatory' marriage rules, it simply made it equally difficult for men to bring in their foreign wives—thus establishing an 'equality of misery' (Joint Council for the Welfare of Immigrants 1985). As Ian Macdonald (1987: 56) summarized the grim reality of British immigration law in which state interests rigorously cancel out individual interests, 'I know of no other body of law, especially one affecting human rights and civil liberties as immigration law does, where the interests of those affected by it have been so unrelentingly ignored and left out of account by the legislators and rule makers.'

Next to the lack of a domestic constitution protective of human rights, British asylum policy has been conditioned by its structural conflation with immigration control. Until the Asylum and Immigration Appeals Act of 1993, there were no separate asylum rules; asylum was processed according to the Immigration Act of 1971 and the non-statutory Immigration Rules (see Macdonald 1983, ch. 10). This meant that the shortcomings of immigration law and practice were *ipso facto* shortcomings of asylum determination: the lack of an in-country appeal procedure for would-be entrants rejected at the border, which entailed the generic possibility of refoulement (see Goodwin-Gill 1978: 119); and the wide discretion of the immigration officer, which enshrined the dominance of the executive over the judiciary in immigration and asylum policy alike. About the immigration officers a law lord had this to say: 'They cannot be expected to know or apply the [European] Convention [on Human Rights]. They must go simply by the Immigration Rules laid down by the Secretary of State and not by the Convention' (quoted in Storey 1994: 123). In a 1985 decision, the Law Lords (Britain's highest court) reaffirmed that refugee determination was an administrative, not a judiciary prerogative. Since Parliament had decided that *all* questions of entry and stay (including asylum) should be determined by an immigration officer and the Secretary of State, respectively, the courts had absolutely no say in the determination of refugee status: 'There was no basis on which any jurisdiction in the High Court could be found to determine the question whether a person was a refugee or should be granted asylum.'[44]

Inevitably, asylum policy became inflicted with the racially loaded control mentality of British immigration law and practice. Despite its official usage, 'immigration' is a misnomer in the British context. There never was any officially promoted, regular immigration to Britain. When larger numbers of New Commonwealth citizens arrived on British shores after the Second World War, they did so as British nationals with automatic right of entry and settlement. The logic of British immigration law is to adjust the anomalous (because privileged) status of Commonwealth citizens to the normal status of aliens, who are subject to strict entry and settlement conditions. This was achieved with the Immigration Act of 1971, which divides the world into two categories of people: 'patrials' with the 'right of abode' in Britain, and 'non-patrials' with no such right, their entry to Britain being contingent on an immigration officer's 'leave to enter' allowance. Unfortunately, the logic of 'patriality' is not to divide between British and non-British nationals, which would be uncontroversial, but to draw an insidious distinction between two groups of British nationals: those with 'substantial connections' with the United Kingdom and those without.[45] This was essentially a racial distinction, because its precise wording granted the right of abode to the descendants of (white) old Commonwealth settlers, while withholding it from the (coloured) new Commonwealth citizens.

The patriality clause is the revenge of empire, planting the virus of racial distinction deep into the heart of British immigration law. This law is geared towards keeping the non-patrials (read: blacks) out. As Ian Macdonald (1983: 12) put it, 'the main purpose of the law is to stop and if possible reverse coloured immigration to the UK'. When the arrival of Tamils in 1985 signalled Britain's entry into the age of mass asylum-seeking, the colour-couched control mentality of immigration law and policy instantly took hold of the new asylum field.[46] Home Secretary Douglas Hurd (1989) would even apply the government's old immigration policy logo to its new asylum policy: 'firm but fair'. In fact, the cleavages and discursive metaphors of immigration policy became exactly mirrored in asylum policy: asylum advocates calling 'racist' the government's assumption that most refugees were 'economic migrants', and the government defending its get-tough approach towards asylum-seekers as in the interest of 'good race relations'.

The institution of asylum establishes a link between an individual and a state that had not in any kind been linked before: it is a triumph of abstract moral over concrete communitarian obligations. Britain's hesitation to engage in such abstract linkage partially stems from its enduring trouble with fulfilling even its communitarian obligations stemming from the devolution of empire.[47] When it rammed through the 1968 Commonwealth Immigration Act to bar from Britain Asian British passport-holders facing mass expulsion in East Africa, the Labour government came close to violating one of the fundamental principles of international law: the obligation of states to accept their own nationals.[48] The 1981 British Nationality Act, which instituted a 'British citizenship' proper, put to an end the peculiar disjunction of immigration and nationality law. But the sense of 'special obligations' towards the remnants of empire did not go away, hovering in a strange middle position between asylum-granting and regular immigration. In fact, just when mass asylum-seeking became a pressing reality in the late 1980s, Britain faced the agonizing 'last chapter' (Douglas Hurd) of its empire: the release of Hong Kong, one of the last colonies of the Crown. After a heated debate over potential 'large-scale immigration' (Norman Tebbit), Britain's refusal of entry rights to all but a few hand-picked Hong Kong British nationals continued its defensive line established in 1968, and reaffirmed the stern imperative for élites not to tinker with the 'zero-immigration' maxim. Taking a hard line towards its own nationals, how could Britain display any generosity towards asylum-seekers?

Moving from the context to the content of British asylum policy, one is struck by its inclination to make maximal noise over minimal numbers. From 1980 to 1988 Britain received less than 38,000 asylum applications, the annual numbers rarely exceeding the 5,000 mark (Amnesty International 1991: 4). This makes Britain the country with the lowest per capita intake of refugees in Europe. The low numbers are partially the result of a tight and instantly imposed visa regime that perfectly complements Britain's geographical insulation. Low numbers have allowed Britain to reject relatively few asylum applicants: still in 1989, 30 per cent were granted refugee status, 60 per cent were granted 'exceptional leave to remain' (*de facto* refugee status), and only 10 per cent were rejected. But in a strange counterpoint to a mild recognition practice behind the scene, the front-stage was occupied by a few highly publicized deportation cases, some of which entailed proved violations of Britain's non-refoulement obligation. They may have been few, but they pointed at the crux of British asylum policy: the lack of effective in-country appeal procedures, and the quasi-absolute power of the executive in asylum determination.

Tamils have played a sad major part in such deportation cases. As an asylum advocate put it, the Tamils 'were ... typical of the very people that immigration law had been keeping out for decades. They were black, they were young men, they were from the Indian subcontinent.'[49] There was an instant reflex to brand the Tamils, who began arriving in larger numbers in 1985, as 'economic migrants' or 'bogus' refugees. Not without reason, because they came from the region where the 'pressure to immigrate' was highest and that was accordingly targeted by the government for a clamp-down on family-based immigration: the Indian subcontinent (see CRE 1985: 157). Getting tough on Tamils was indeed demanded by the need for consistency with tight immigration controls: 'queue-jumping' was no abstraction where the Home Office had imposed huge administrative delays upon family reunification from Bangladesh or India.[50] A hastily imposed visa requirement for Sri Lankans, the first ever for a Commonwealth country, was the initial measure for realigning asylum admissions with immigration control; precedent-setting deportations were the second.

The two major deportation cases involving Tamils were of radically opposite nature, and they epitomize the whole ambiguity of the asylum phenomenon—not only in Britain. The first case actually involved a Sinhalese communist supporting the Tamil cause, Viraj Mendis, who was forcibly returned to Sri Lanka in 1990 after having spent two years in church asylum. This most politicized deportation case of all is a classic case of 'bootstrapping' (Teitelbaum 1984: 80 ff.), the *ex post facto* creation of an asylum cause. Essentially an ex-student who had overstayed for eleven years, Mendis had applied for asylum in order to avoid a deportation order. A failed 'bogus' marriage with a British citizen on his record, Mendis's political engagement intensified just when his resident status in Britain became endangered. Not even the UNHCR supported his case. As a political commentator wrote sarcastically, 'he had failed his exams, his marriage to an Englishwoman was a sham, and most of all he had developed political views for the sake of convenience. All in all, you mused, he would make an ideal Tory MP' (Rawnsley 1989). Far from that, Mendis became a *cause célèbre* for Britain's race relations left, which supported him in a two-year-long, country-wide campaign that included 'guards' protecting his church shelter, weekly demonstrations and signature drives, and a Labour-initiated committee of inquiry at the Commons. But for the Home Office the shy yet determined Sinhalese represented that typical exemplar of 'law-dodger masquerading as genuine refugee' (*The Sunday Times* 1989), and it went after him with a vehemence that bordered on vengefulness. In Mendis, the government vindicated the central motive of its asylum policy: no mercy for 'bogus refugees'. After thirteen years on British soil (almost three times longer than normally required for being granted a 'vested right of residence'), Mendis was surprised one morning by a police squad which showed no scruples about demolishing church doors, and he was thrown onto the next plane to Colombo. What most liberal states would not have done for humanitarian reasons, the British showed no hesitation in doing.

The second Tamil deportation case is diametrically opposed, because it involved the refoulement of genuine refugees. In February 1988 the Home Office expelled five Tamil asylum-seekers who had arrived without entry clearance on various dates in 1987. The lack of proper visas excluded them from using the in-country appeals system—appeal they could, but only from back home! Their only remedy: a toothless judicial review could assess the procedural correctness, but not the substantial merits of the case. On these limited grounds, the Law Lords eventually upheld the Home Office's deportation order. Generically denounced by a Tory MP as 'liars, cheats, and queue-jumpers', three of the five deported Tamils had to endure torture and severe maltreatment by Sinhalese police and soldiers (*Guardian* 1989a). An immigration appeals adjudicator decided in their out-of-country appeal that all five were entitled to political asylum, ordering the Home Office to bring them back to Britain 'with the minimum delay' (*Guardian* 1989c). For Amnesty International, this was the first conclusive evidence that Britain was breaching the UN Convention, pointing out the 'pressing need' for statutory appeal rights *within* Britain (*Guardian* 1989b).[51]

Anticipating a European Court condemnation of Britain's dismal appeals practice, the 1993 Asylum and Immigration Appeals Act finally granted an in-country right of appeal for all asylum-seekers.[52] But this one liberalizing measure was more than offset by two restrictive features of the new Act: the removal of the right to appeal for refused short-term visitors and students, and the introduction of a fast-track procedure for 'manifestly unfounded' asylum claims (see Randall 1994; Stevens 1993). Giving a right to asylum-seekers while taking an established right away from another group subject to immigration controls epitomizes Britain's structural conflation of asylum and immigration policy. While the bill's (rather rocky) career had started in 1991 as an exclusive 'asylum bill', its final incarnation in 1993 was largely criticized as an 'anti-black family' measure that further curtailed the family reunion rights of Britain's settled immigrants (*Independent* 1993a). The Asylum Act's core provisions—fingerprinting of applicants, stiffer sanctions against carriers, and fast-tracking of 'manifestly unfounded' applications (which include applications by people arriving from a 'safe third country' and applications based on forged or destroyed documents)—are identical with the emergent EU asylum policy, and attuned to obliterate a future European adjustment of Britain's national policy. In fact, Britain, while jealously protecting its sovereignty on immigration from encroachment by the European Commission, has been an enthusiastic leader of the intergovernmental Trevi Group of EU immigration ministers, who in some secrecy have put the new British-cum-European asylum policy together. If Fortress Europe is being built on the foundation of its lowest common denominator, it is Fortress Britain opened out.

The Asylum Act's fast processing of 'manifestly unfounded' asylum claims has led to an unprecedented decline in Britain's refugee recognition rate. The rate of refused asylum applications leaped from 16 per cent in 1993 to 75 per cent in 1994, most of the refused facing involuntary repatriation (*Guardian* 1994*b*).[53] Those not deported immediately are increasingly put up in prison-like detention centres. Arbitrary detention of asylum-seekers has been standard practice since the first arrival of Tamils a decade earlier. But after the new Asylum Act, detentions acquired a new quality, the number of detainees doubling from 300 in 1993 to over 600 in 1994. In Campsfield House, Britain's newest and largest 'immigration detention centre' near Oxford, detained asylum-seekers felt 'treated like prisoners', initiating a wave of hunger strikes and riots that seized other detention centres as well.[54] While defended as in the interest of 'good race relations' (Home Secretary Kenneth Baker), the Asylum and Immigration Act's impact on black family life was no less negative. On Christmas Eve 1993 immigration officers detained a whole plane-load of Jamaican visitors; they had come to see their relatives, but eventually saw iron bars at Campsfield House, before being summarily returned to Kingston. This was possible because appeal rights for refused visitors no longer existed. What shocked the British public and caused a diplomatic row with Jamaica was stoically defended by a Tory MP: 'The Government has every right to send back anybody it wants' (*Guardian* 1993*b*). Such has been the British approach to immigration and asylum policy alike.

CONCLUSION

State sovereignty, the 'assertion of final authority within a given territory' (Krasner 1988: 86), has never been absolute. Contemporary diagnoses of sovereignty in decline, particularly those in the globalization mould, operate with simplified assumptions of what states could once do. Internally, the sovereignty of liberal states has always been limited by the rule of law, divided powers, federalism, or the autonomous functioning of societal subsystems, such as the capitalist economy.[55] Externally, sovereignty is more firmly established as the basic principle of international relations: here states are by definition sovereign, even if 'juridical' is not always matched by 'empirical' sovereignty (see Jackson and Rosberg 1982). But externally also, sovereignty is not absolute: while punctuated by wars, the post-Westphalian 'society of states' (Bull 1977) has mostly been an orderly one, respecting international treaty obligations and international law. States always had to cope with manifold interferences in internal affairs, from the religious toleration mandated by the Peace of Westphalia to the national minority protections of the Wilsonian order after the First World War. It is therefore correct to conclude, with Stephen Krasner (1993: 236), that 'the positive content of sovereignty, the areas over which the state can legitimately command, has always been contested'. . . . Sovereignty . . . has never been fixed or absolute.

The one novelty of the post-Second World War era—the rise of universal human rights claims and claimants that challenge traditional state sovereignty—has to be seen in this relativizing light. The lesson of Nazism has been to make individuals, and not just states, recognized subjects of international law (see Henkin 1990, ch. 1). This has put new limitations on state sovereignty, which no longer originate exclusively from the interdependence of states but also originate from the protection of human rights.[56] With regard to international migration, states are no longer free to determine at will the entry and residence of aliens: treaties and international law restrict the freedom of states to control immigration.[57] But the state system is still not built on the principle of justice. As Hedley Bull (1977: 146) put it, 'carried to its logical extreme, the doctrine of human rights and duties under international law is subversive of the whole principle that mankind should be organized as a society of sovereign states'. This is recognized in the fact that the one recent intrusion into state sovereignty—the right of asylum—has been made the sovereign right of states, not of individuals. Since the principle of human rights does not provide an organizational alternative, the sovereign state is still, if only by default, 'the only universally recognized way of organizing political life in the contemporary international system' (Krasner 1988: 90). Accordingly, the international law of human rights is 'soft law', granted by states in moments of ceremonial 'hypocrisy', and never really meant to be practised (Martin 1989). Still, hypocrisy can be put to use: 'The existence of the soft norm has increased the political costs of action contrary to the norm' (ibid. 555). This has provided a moral lever for non-governmental human rights organizations, now sometimes referred to as the international community, to exert pressure on states that fall short of these norms.

But if they didn't speak to the converted, all such moral appeals would come to nothing. Human rights internationalists (both political and academic) have drawn a flawed picture of an external human rights regime controlling egoistical nation-states, like a police helicopter circling above a group of delinquents. Gil Loescher (1989: 8), for instance, sees refugee policy determined by 'the conflict between international humanitarian norms and the sometimes narrow self-interest calculations of sovereign nation states'. While there may be truth in this scenario with regard to refugee resettlement, it does not apply to asylum policy. As I have tried to demonstrate, conflicts over asylum policy are in the first place domestic conflicts over competing principles of liberal nation-states: to be the state of their people while complying with their constitutional mandate to respect human rights. The first nation-state, after all, came into its own with a 'Declaration of the Rights of Man'. Such universalism is on the retreat today, but if it could not be invoked no state would take in a single refugee. Not external, but internal, constraints have prevented liberal states from shielding themselves completely from global refugee movements.

In the United States, the main inroad has been a constitution that makes no clear distinction between citizens and aliens. The trajectory of asylum policy has been largely a liberalizing one, moving from (morally indefensible) foreign policy tutelage to the source country universalism practised, since the civil rights reforms of the 1960s, in legal immigration. The blurring of the citizen–alien distinction, driven by the civil rights impulse and expressed in a communitarian immigration law, has left America bereft of a legitimate concept of national community, which explains some of its current agonies over 'uncontrolled' mass migration (see Brielow 1995).

In Germany also, the main constraint on state sovereignty has been home-made. In retrospect, it is astonishing how long Germany's unique constitutional right of asylum survived. For almost twenty years it had condemned the state to inactivity, making Germany the Western world's major asylum country. But then, sovereignty was an awkward concept in a country where Carl Schmitt's Führerstaat had been in place for a while. The sacrosanct Article 16 of the Basic Law, self-imposed atonement for the Nazi crimes against humanity, had to be neutralized by a unique deterrence regime, leading to the grotesque dissonance that the country with the world's most liberal asylum law was also the one with the most illiberal asylum practice. But after the 1993 change of the Basic Law, German exceptionalism in asylum policy (as in almost any other respect) is no more.

Britain showed how far a state with weak domestic human rights constraints can go in shielding itself from unwanted migrations. It is the one case that approximates the picture of a domestic state confronted with international human rights norms. Alas, it is also the case that demonstrates the impotence of such external norms, if not backed by a domestic bill of rights and independent courts. In a way, Britain has the most democratic immigration and asylum policies of all, forged by anxious élites that are well aware of the unfavourable mood of the majority population. Characteristically, European Court rules are viewed as 'undemocratic' restrictions on the institution where British sovereignty resides: Parliament. Only, unchecked parliamentary power becomes a vice if the boundary between citizens and non-citizens is at stake, because the 'ins' can dispose of the 'outs' at will. Britain shows that the risk in a world of international migrations is not too little but too much democracy.

Despite such domestic variations of asylum policy trajectories, there is convergence on the erection of doubly restrictive asylum regimes: restriction as deterrence, which minimizes the social incentives to come at all; and restriction as exclusion, which prevents the obstinately mobile from entering the territory (see Lambert 1995). The German experience has shown that even extreme deterrence may be insufficient to keep away today's huddled masses. Instead, exclusion is key. Exclusion, through visa requirements, 'safe country' rules, carrier liability, or high-seas interceptions, has one advantage for receiving states: it effectively neutralizes both international and domestic legal obligations, without openly violating them. Liberal states have learned from two decades of mass asylum-seeking that once an asylum-seeker is 'in', it is most difficult to get her 'out' again. Sadly, exclusion works indiscriminately against genuine refugees and economic migrants. Exclusive asylum regimes thus incorporated a migrant definition that may adequately reflect a situation where no clear line can be drawn between economic and political motives, voluntary and involuntary migrations. Slashing the refugees' former 'position of privilege' (Martin 1988a: 9) is the price that Western states have been willing to pay for dealing effectively with mass asylum-seeking.

Recent macro-analyses of international migrations have drawn effusive scenarios of a world beyond nation-states, in which universal personhood triumphs over parochial allegiances and identities. Such scenarios are not only wrong; they are dangerous because they elevate into a virtue the vice of statelessness, about which there should be no illusion after a 'century of refugees' (see Arendt 1951). This remains a world of bounded nation-states, in which the morally arbitrary fact of being born into a particular state decides about the life chances of most. My discussion of asylum policies in three Western states affirms Rogers Brubaker's (1994: 230) observation that the 'prosperous and peaceful states of the world remain powerfully exclusionary'. There is little reason to celebrate this fact, except for the lucky few living in the protected zones. Today's prosperous, perhaps post-national states have run out of overarching ideas to justify their exclusiveness; they perpetuate sheer facticity. The ideas, most notably of a world of universal justice, are with the human rights internationalists. States without ideas, ideas without organizational viability—this may be the saddest story of all.

## NOTES

This is a slightly reworked version of an article that first appeared in *Comparative Political Studies* (June 1997). It is reprinted here with the kind permission of Sage Publications.

1. 'Declining efficacy of immigration control' is the hypothesis of Cornelius *et al.* (1994). See also Hollifield (1992).
2. The linkage between the 'failure of state control' on migration and the rise of an international human rights regime is most explicitly made by Jacobson (1995: 2), who argues boldly that 'the basis of state legitimacy [in North America and Western Europe] is shifting from principles of sovereignty and national self-determination to international human rights'. Soysal (1994, ch. 8) is a bit more cautious, claiming that the 'global system' is structured by the 'institutional duality' of national sovereignty and universal human rights. But the root image is the same: an international human rights regime confronting nation-states from the outside. In the following, I call this position 'human rights internationalism'.
3. Miller and Castles (1993: 168) estimate that refugees and asylum-seekers constitute about one-quarter of recent international migration.
4. This is in line with Brubaker's rebuke of the 'declining capacity' hypothesis underlying Cornelius *et al.*'s (1994) volume: 'we see an increasing capacity and an increasing will to control unwanted flows—especially to deter unwanted asylum claimants' (Brubaker 1994: 229). A similar case for 'increasing capacity' is made by Freeman (1994).
5. A UN source estimated that over 80 per cent of the 700,000 asylum-seekers in western Europe in 1992 were *not* genuine refugees (*Independent* 1993*b*).
6. I owe this formulation to Thomas Faist.
7. The 1986 Immigration Act finally allowed the Haitians to convert to immigrant status.

8. Martin (1983: 171) speaks of 'procedural exuberance of the lower courts'.
9. Motomura (1990: 610) argues that courts have tended to avoid the plenary power doctrine 'through subconstitutional decisions that rely on phantom constitutional norms much more favorable to aliens'. The Supreme Court's cautious line in *Jean*, so Motomura, made it 'a potential landmark decision that never was' (p. 548).
10. This was the line taken by the liberal Ninth Circuit Court, responsible for the majority of asylum cases in the American South-west. Other courts did not follow. See Porter (1992: 251–2).
11. See the symposium in *Cornell International Law Journal*, 26 (1993), 495–818.
12. Still in 1989, 94 per cent of the 95,505 refugees approved for admission came from Communist countries (*New York Times* 1990*a*).
13. Since 1980 the government had denied 97 per cent of applications for political asylum by El Salvadoreans and 99 per cent of those by Guatemalans, while approving 76 per cent of Soviet and 64 per cent of Chinese applications.
14. So wrote the *New York Times* (1993*b*).
15. Quote by Muzaffar Chishti, boss of the pro-immigrant International Ladies' Garment Worker Union *(New York Times* 1993*c*).
16. Further legislation to summarily exclude asylum-seekers arriving in the US without documents and introduce a narrow time-limit for asylum requests by those already on US territory is currently pending in Congress (*Migration News* 1995).
17. The Federal Constitutional Court decided in Oct. 1975: 'The constitutional right of asylum . . . guarantees to a person seeking refuge from persecution . . . not to be rejected at the border of the state obliged to grant asylum . . .'. This court rule became incorporated in Paragraph 9 of the Asylum Procedures Law, which states that rejection at the border may occur only if the asylum-seeker enjoys alternative protection from persecution. See Pfaff (1992: 131).
18. So Burkhard Hirsch of the Liberal Democratic Party (FDP), one of the main protagonists in the German asylum debate (quoted in Wolken 1988: 105).
19. Heinrich Lummer of the CDU, quoted in *Der Spiegel*, no. 12 (1986), 68 and 66 respectively.
20. The municipal incorporation of international law has even the character of a constitutional principle. Article 25 of the Basic Law asserts: 'The general rules of international law (*Völkerrecht*) are part of municipal law (*Bundesrecht*). They are prior to the laws and create immediate rights and duties for the inhabitants of the Federal Republic.'
21. The first seven articles of the Basic Law uphold *Jedermann Grundrechte*. Article 1 asserts that 'the dignity of man is inviolable. To respect and protect it is the duty of all state authority.' There is, however, a tension in the Basic Law between universal human rights and *Deutschenrechte*, rights reserved for Germans. Article 8 of the Basic Law suddenly asserts: 'All Germans have the right [of free assembly].'

22. Article 2(1) of the Aliens Law of 1965 states: 'A residence permit may be issued if the presence of the foreigner does not impair the interests of the Federal Republic of Germany' (quoted in Hailbronner 1984: 749).

23. In July 1990 Lebach, a town of 22,000, was 'over-rolled' by the sudden arrival of 1,400 gypsy refugees from Romania. Local outrage included the mayor barricading town hall and public swimming-pool, and business people closing their shops; a protest march to the refugee camp was narrowly averted. In response, the Minister President conceded: 'The law of asylum must be made acceptable to the population' (*Der Spiegel* 1990).

24. Limiting territorial access through visa requirements, though practised since the mid-1970s, proved ineffective because of (West) Germany's open land borders.

25. Between 1973 and 1974 the number of new asylum claims jumped from 5,595 to 9,424 (Quaritsch 1985: 41). In addition, the post-oil crisis asylum-seekers came no longer from eastern Europe but from Third World countries. The proportion of non-European asylum-seekers increased from 7 per cent in 1968 to 75 per cent in 1977 (Münch 1992: 63). It should be mentioned that Germany also, not surprisingly perhaps for the front-line state in the Cold War confrontation, had double standards in accepting refugees: from 1966 to 1989 east European refugees were generally not deported. Only, it never aroused much public attention, not to mention criticism.

26. Such lawyers often co-operated with *Schlepper* (refugee-smuggling) organizations; they have no resemblance to the high-minded public interest lawyers in the United States, who are largely unknown in Germany (see *Der Spiegel*, no. 40 (1986), 84–96).

27. Compiling the elements of the restrictive asylum policy in place by 1987, *Der Spiegel* (3 Aug. 1987: 24–5) spoke of a 'catalogue of horror': visa obligations for most non-EU-countries; no recognition of so-called 'post-flight asylum reasons' (which had allowed what Teitelbaum (1984) called 'bootstrapping', the *ex post facto* creation of asylum causes), immediate departure in case of 'obviously unfounded' asylum claims; deportation also into countries of civil war (a specialitiy of Bavaria); forced encampment during the whole asylum procedures; a five-year work ban; and restrictive courts that did not automatically recognize asylum claims despite proved torture.

28. Commenting on the failure of seven asylum reforms since 1978 to stop the new movement of asylum-seekers, Burkhard Hirsch (FDP) said: 'In the end nothing is achieved if after a final legal decision no consequent deportation follows' (*Der Spiegel*, no. 45 (1990), 44).

29. The asylum recognition rate for Roma gypsies one of the biggest migrant groups in the early 1990s, was 0 per cent.

30. The Minister President of Lower Saxony, Gerhard Schröder (SPD), in *Der Spiegel*, no. 11 (1992), 59.

31. Jürgen Habermas (1992) speaks of a '*Junktim* [linkage] between the questions of political asylum and immigration'.

32. Lower Saxony's Minister for Refugee Affairs, Jürgen Trittin (Greens), in *Der Spiegel*, no. 37 (1992), 27, 28–9.

33. The Interior Minister of Bavaria, Edmund Stoiber (CSU), in *Der Spiegel*, no. 45 (1990), 52.
34. Alfred Dregger (CDU) in the parliamentary debate over the change of Article 16, *Das Parlament*, 11 June 1993.
35. Discussions of Germany's 'Euro-solution' to its asylum crisis are Kanstroom (1993*b*) and Neuman (1993).
36. The German government has repeatedly tried to make its asylum law international standard practice. At a Geneva UN Conference in 1977, only one state voted unconditionally for the (West) German proposal to adopt its subjective right of asylum: the Vatican (Quaritsch 1985: 18–19).
37. For instance, in 1991 the German campaign failed to delegate national competences for a unified asylum law and procedure to the European Commission.
38. Violent crimes motivated by xenophobia declined to 1,233 in the first eleven months of 1994, from 2,232 cases in 1993 and 2,630 in 1992 (figures provided by the Federal Office for the Protection of the Constitution, quoted in *International Herald Tribune*, 6 Apr. 1995, 6).
39. A recent example is the heavily publicized deportation of seven Sudanese asylum-seekers, which was loudly protested by the opposition parties. In the end, credible sources (from the Sudanese opposition) established that the asylum claims have indeed been fraudulent, and the Greens dropped their request for a parliamentary hearing (*Frankfurter Allgemeine Zeitung* 1995).
40. However, in its landmark decision of May 1996, the Court found the asylum compromise constitutional.
41. Along such lines has been the conservative response to a major European Court of Human Rights indictment of 'sexually discriminatory' British immigration rules. See *The Times* (1985*b*).
42. Accordingly, there is now a strong groundswell for a written constitution and bill of rights, including, most recently, *The Economist* (1995). See also Lester (1994).
43. A more positive interpretation of the role of British courts in the control of government is Sterett (1994). A general assessment of the pivotal role of courts in constitutional human rights politics is Shapiro and Stone (1994).
44. *Regina* v. *Secretary of State for the Home Department, Ex parte Bugdaycay* (see *The Times* 1985*c*).
45. 'Substantial connection' is the term used in the 1968 New Commonwealth Immigration Act; 'patriality' was first used in the 1971 Act. It connotes birth or naturalization in the United Kingdom, or the existence of a parent or grandparent born in the United Kingdom. For a precise definition of patriality, see Macdonald (1983: 43).
46. A *Times* editorial (1985*a*) warns of the 'possibility that the disturbances in Sri Lanka [are] being used as a pretext for evasion of the strictness with which our immigration controls are habitually enforced, a strictness that is one of the props of good race relations within Britain'.
47. Outlining the government's 'firm but fair' asylum policy, Douglas Hurd (1989) points out that most of the new asylum-seekers were from Asian

and African countries, 'some with few historical links with Britain'. This is an astonishing remark, because the institution of asylum is in principle independent of such 'historical links'. But it indicates the specifically British approximation of asylum and post-empire obligations.

48. Britain's face-saving concession was a voucher scheme that allowed a limited number of Asian British nationals to come to Britain every year. Britain never said not to accept the British Asians, but insisted that the inflow at any given time had to be commensurate with its absorption capacity (Goodwin-Gill 1978, ch. 6).

49. Interview with Ann Owers (formerly Joint Council for the Welfare of Immigrants), 18 July 1995, London.

50. As *The Economist* (1985) put it, the Home Office 'cannot afford to treat the Tamils better than those to whom it is already denying established rights'.

51. The list of deportation blunders could be easily prolonged, affecting each newly arriving refugee group. A High Court review found that twenty-three Turkish Kurds were 'unlawfully' deported in mid-1989, three of whom were later detained and tortured (Amnesty International 1991: 25–8). One of the most spectacular cases involved a Zaïrean asylum-seeker in 1991, who was deported despite a contrary court order (and has since disappeared). This made the responsible Home Secretary, Kenneth Baker, the first British minister in legal history to be found guilty of contempt of court. This Law Lords decision was in itself a landmark rule, because it subjects the absolute power of the executive to judicial control (*Guardian* 1993a).

52. Irony of ironies, the European Court of Human Rights eventually failed to accord with the five Tamils' charge that their denial of an in-country appeal possibility was in breach of the European Convention on Human Rights (see *Guardian* 1991).

53. The increase of the refusal rate has been at the cost of 'exceptional leave to remain' admissions, which have been down from 77 per cent in the first half of 1993 to 21 per cent in the first quarter of 1994 (National Council 1995: 28).

54. See the *Guardian* (1994a) documentation of life in Campsfield House, called a 'first-class facility' by the Home Office.

55. Carl Schmitt's (1934: 26) famous definition of sovereignty as 'highest, extralegal, non-derived power', while couched in the Boudinian continental European tradition, may apply to the totalitarian Führerstaat, but certainly not to the constitutional legal state.

56. As Plender (1988) outlines, the catalyst of this development is the changing views of the state's international obligation to admit its own nationals to its territory: the traditional view held that this obligation is the consequence of other states' rights to expel aliens; the more recent, 'radical' view sees it as the corollary of citizens' right to enter the territory of their own state (see also Macdonald 1983: 247).

57. The most notable sources of restricted state discretion over entry and exit are the principles of non-refoulement and non-discrimination (for the latter, see Goodwin-Gill 1978, ch. 5).

# REFERENCES

Abrams, Elliott (1983), 'Diluting Compassion', *New York Times*, 5 Aug., I. 23.
Aleinikoff, Alexander (1994), 'Safe Haven: Pragmatics and Prospects', *Virginia Journal of International Law*, 35/13: 71–9.
Amnesty International (1991), 'United Kingdom: Deficient Policy and Practice for the Protection of Asylum Seekers', London, mimeo.
Anker, Deborah, and Carolyn Patty Blum (1989), 'New Trends in Asylum Jurisprudence: The Aftermath of the US Supreme Court Decision in *INS* v. *Cardoza-Fonseca*', *International Journal of Refugee Law*, 1/1: 67–82.
Arendt, Hannah (1951), *The Origins of Totalitarianism* (New York: Harcourt).
Bade, Klaus J. (ed.) (1992), *Ausländer, Aussiedler, Asyl in der Bundesrepublik Deutschland*, 2nd edn. (Hanover: Niedersächsische Landeszentrale für politische Bildung).
—— (1994), *Ausländer, Aussiedler, Asyl* (Munich: Beck).
BRC (British Refugee Council) (1992), 'UK Asylum Statistics 1982–1992', London, mimeo.
Brielow, Peter (1995), *Alien Nation* (New York: Random House).
Brubaker, Rogers (1994), 'Are Immigration Control Efforts really Failing?', in Cornelius *et al.* (1994).
Bull, Hedley (1977), *The Anarchical Society* (London: Macmillan).
Cohn-Bendit, Daniel, and Thomas Schmid (1993), *Heimat Babylon* (Hamburg: Hoffmann & Campe).
Cornelius, Wayne, P. L. Martin, J. F. Hollifield (eds.) (1994), *Controlling Immigration* (Stanford: Stanford University Press).
CRE (Commission for Racial Equality) (1985), *Immigration Control Procedures: Report of a Formal Investigation* (London: CRE).
*Der Spiegel* (1980), 'Da sammelt sich ein ungeheurer Sprengstoff', no. 23: 17–18.
—— (1986), 'Asyl—"Bis an die Grenze des Zulässigen"', no. 31: 23–32.
—— (1990), 'Asylrecht: "Oskar quält sich"', no. 32: 32.
—— (1992*a*), 'Anklang an Weimar', no. 41: 18–29.
—— (1992*b*), no. 46: 34.
—— (1992*c*), 'Wer will Menschen das antun?', no. 46: 54.
*Die Zeit* (1992), 'Einmal Deutschland und zurück', 22 Sept., 17.
Dinh, Viet D. (1994), 'Law and Asylum', in Nicolaus Mills (ed.), *Arguing Immigration* (New York: Touchstone).
*Economist, The* (1985), 'Back-Door and Front-Door', 1 June.
—— (1994), 'Cubans First', 10 Sept., 56.
—— (1995), 'Why Britain Needs a Bill of Rights', 21 Oct., 44–6.
Feldman, David F. (1993), *Civil Liberties and Human Rights in England and Wales* (Oxford: Clarendon Press).

*Frankfurter Allgemeine Zeitung* (1992), 'Die Koalition spricht von drohendem Staatsnotstand', 2 Nov., 1.

—— (1995), 'Grüne verzichten auf aktuelle Stunde über Sudaner', 21 Sept., 1.

Freeman, Gary (1992), 'Migration Policy and Politics in the Receiving States', *International Migration Review*, 26/4: 1144–67.

—— (1994), 'Can Liberal States Control Unwanted Migration?', *Annals of the American Academy of Political and Social Science*, 534 (July), 17–30.

Fromme, Friedrich Karl (1988), 'Aussiedler und Asylbewerber', *Frankfurter Allgemeine Zeitung*, 26 Oct., 1.

Fuentes, José (1983), 'Immigration: Is U.S. Policy on Cubans Just?', *New York Times*, 2 Oct. XI. 30.

German Interior Ministry (1993), *Geschichte, Organisation, Aufgaben* (Bonn: Osang).

Goldstein, Judith, and Robert Keohane (eds.) (1993), *Ideas and Foreign Policy* (Ithaca, NY: Cornell University Press).

Goodwin-Gill, Guy (1978), *International Law and the Movement of Persons between States* (Oxford: Clarendon Press).

—— (1983), *The Refugee in International Law* (Oxford: Clarendon Press).

*Guardian* (1989a), 'Expelled Tamils Beaten in Sri Lanka', 7 May.

—— (1989b), 'Hurd "Deported Tamils Illegally"', 17 Aug.

—— (1989c), 'Deported Tamils Return to Britain', 5 Oct.

—— (1991), 'Expulsion of Tamils was Lawful', 6 Nov.

—— (1993a), 'Baker in Contempt of Court', 28 July, 1.

—— (1993b), 'Expulsion Row Grows', 27 Dec., 1.

—— (1994a), 'Welcome to Britain', 8 June.

—— (1994b), 'Britain "Barring more Refugees"', 1 Dec.

Habermas, Jürgen (1992), 'Die Zweite Lebenslüge der Bundesrepublik', *Die Zeit*, no. 51, 18 Dec.: 19.

—— (1994), 'Human Rights and Popular Sovereignty', *Ratio Juris*, 7/1: 1–13.

Hailbronner, Kay (1984), *Ausländerrecht. Ein Handbuch* (Heidelberg: C. F. Müller).

—— (1988), 'Nonrefoulement and "Humanitarian" Refugees', in Martin (1988b).

—— (1992), 'Der Ausländer in der deutschen Sozialordnung', *Vierteljahres- schrift für Sozialrecht*, 2: 77–98.

Helton, Arthur C. (1991), 'The Mandate of U.S. Courts to Protect Aliens and Refugees under International Human Rights Law, *Yale Law Journal*, 100: 2335–46.

Henkin, L. (1987), 'The Constitution and United States Sovereignty', *Harvard Law Review*, 100: 853–96.

—— (1990), *The Age of Rights* (New York: Columbia University Press).

Hollifield, James (1992), *Immigrants, Markets, and States* (Cambridge, Mass.: Harvard University Press).

Hurd, Douglas (1989), 'Firm but Fair Control on Asylum Builds Harmony in our Cities', *Independent*, 26 July: 18.

*Independent* (1993*a*), 'Asylum Bill Condemned as "Racist" Legislation', 12 Jan.

—— (1993*b*), 'Europe Shuts out Political Refugees', 4 June.

Jackson, Robert H., and Carl G. Rosberg (1982), 'Why Africa's Weak States Persist', *World Politics*, no. 1: 1–24.

Jacobson, David (1995), *Rights across Borders* (Baltimore: Johns Hopkins University Press).

Joint Council for the Welfare of Immigrants (1985), *Annual Report 1984–1985* (London: JCWI).

Kanstroom, Daniel (1993*a*), 'Wer sind wir wieder? Laws of Asylum, Immigration, and Citizenship in the Struggle for the Soul of the New Germany', *Yale Journal of International Law*, 18/1: 155–210.

—— (1993*b*), 'The Shining City and the Fortress: Reflections on the "Euro-Solution" to the German Immigration Dilemma', *Boston College International and Comparative Law Review*, 16/2: 201–43.

Keely, Charles B., and Sharon Stanton Russell (1994), 'Responses of Industrial Countries to Asylum-Seekers', *Journal of International Affairs*, 47/2: 399–417.

Kerridge, Roger (1983), 'Incorporation of the European Convention on Human Rights into United Kingdom Domestic Law', in M. P. Furmston *et al.*, *The Effect on English Domestic Law of Membership of the European Communities and of Ratification of the European Convention on Human Rights* (The Hague: Nijhoff).

Krasner, Stephen (1988), 'Sovereignty: An Institutional Perspective', *Comparative Political Studies*, 21/1: 66–94.

—— (1993), 'Westphalia and All That', in Goldstein and Keohane (1993).

Lambert, Helene (1995), *Seeking Asylum* (Dordrecht: Martinus Nijhoff).

Layton-Henry, Zig (1994), 'Britain: The Would-Be Zero-Immigration Country', in Cornelius *et al.* (1994).

Lester, Anthony (1994), 'European Human Rights and the British Constitution', in Jeffrey Jowell and Dawn Oliver (eds.), *The Changing Constitution*, 3rd edn. (Oxford: Clarendon Press).

Loescher, Gil (1989), 'Introduction', in Gil Loescher and Laila Monahan (eds.), *Refugees and International Relations* (Oxford: Oxford University Press).

—— and John A. Scanlan (1986), *Calculated Kindness: Refugees and America's Half-Open Door, 1945 to the Present* (New York: Free Press).

Macdonald, Ian A. (1983), *Immigration Law and Practice in the United Kingdom* (London: Butterworth).

Macdonald, Ian A. (1987), 'The Growth and Development of Modern Immigration Law', *Immigration and National Law and Practice* (Oct.), 54–9.

Martin, David (1983), 'Due Process and the Treatment of Aliens', *University of Pittsburgh Law Review*, 44; 165–235.

—— (1988*a*), 'The New Asylum Seekers', in Martin (1988*b*).

Martin, David (ed.) (1988*b*), *The New Asylum Seekers: Refugee Law in the 1980s* (Dordrecht: Martinus Nijhoff).

—— (1989), 'Effects of International Law on Migration Policy and Practice: The Uses of Hypocrisy', *International Migration Review*, 33/3: 547–78.

Marx, Reinhard (1992), 'The Criteria for Determining Refugee Status in the Federal Republic of Germany', *International Journal of Refugee Law*, 4/2: 151–70.

Meissner, Doris (1988), 'Reflections on the Refugee Act of 1980', in Martin (1988*b*).

*Migration News* (1995), 'New Asylum Rules', 2/8 (Aug.)

Miller, Mark, and Stephen Castles (1993), *The Age of Migration* (London: Macmillan).

Motomura, Hiroshi (1990), 'Immigration Law after a Century of Plenary Power', *Yale Law Journal*, 100/3: 545–613.

—— (1993), 'Haitian Asylum Seekers: Interdiction and Immigrants' Rights', *Cornell International Law Journal*, 26: 695–717.

Münch, Ursula (1992), *Asylpolitik in der Bundesrepublik Deutschland* (Opladen: Leske & Budrich).

Munir, Edward (1993), 'One Step Forward and Two Steps Back', *New Law Journal*, 6 Aug., 1149–50.

National Council for Civil Liberties (1995), 'The Last Resort: Violations of the Human Rights of Migrants, Refugees, and Asylum Seekers', London, mimeo.

Neuman, Gerald L. (1990), 'Immigration and Judicial Review in the Federal Republic in Germany', *New York University Journal of International Law*, 23: 35–85.

—— (1993), 'Buffer Zones against Refugees: Dublin, Schengen, and the German Asylum Amendment', *Virginia Journal of International Law*, 33: 503–26.

*New York Times* (1984), '1980 Cuban Refugees Gain on Citizenship Claim', 21 October, 1, p. 23.

—— (1985), 'Aid to Aliens Said to Spur Illegal Immigration', 23 Dec., 1.

—— (1990*a*), 'Study Asks New Safeguards for Refugees Asking Asylum', 16 Mar.

—— (1990*b*), 'U.S. to Make it Easier to Gain Asylum', 1 July.

—— (1990*c*), 'U.S. Adopts New Policy for Hearings on Political Asylum for Some Aliens', 20 Dec., B18.

—— (1992), 'System for Political Asylum is Improving, Report Finds', 14 Dec.

—— (1993*a*), 'Clinton Says U.S. will Continue Ban on Haitian Exodus', 15 Jan., 1.

—— (1993*b*), 'After Bombing, New Scrutiny for Holes in Immigration Net', 12 Mar., 1.

—— (1993*c*), 'Pleas for Asylum Inundate System for Immigration', 25 Apr.

—— (1993*d*), 'Fixing Immigration', 8 June, B2.

—— (1993*e*), 'High Court Backs Policy of Halting Haitian Refugees', 21 June, 1.

—— (1994*a*), 'Clinton Grants Haitian Exiles Hearings at Sea', 7 May, 1.

—— (1994*b*), 'U.S. Moves to Halt Abuses in Political Asylum Program', 3 Dec.

Pfaff, Victor (1992), 'Flucht und Einwanderung', *Kritische Justiz*, 25: 129–46.

Plender, Richard (1988), *International Migration Law*, rev. 2nd edn. (Dordrecht: Martinus Nijhoff).

Porter, Gregory (1992), 'Persecution Based on Political Opinion: Interpretation of the Refugee Act of 1980', *Cornell International Law Journal*, 25: 231–76.

Potelicki, Victoria (1981), 'US Asylum Procedures: Current Status and Proposals for Reform', *Cornell International Law Journal*, 14: 405–28.

Prantl, Heribert (1994), *Deutschland—leicht entflammbar* (Munich: Hanser).

Quaritsch, Helmut (1985), *Recht auf Asyl* (Berlin: Duncker & Humblot).

Randall, Chris (1994), 'An Asylum Policy for the UK', in Spencer (1994).

Rawnsley, Andrew (1989), 'Brando Hurd has them Raving in the Gallery', *Guardian*, 19 Jan.

Renner, Günter (1993), 'Asyl- und Ausländerrechtsreform 1993', *Zeitschrift für Ausländerrecht und -politik*, 3: 118–27.

Rottmann, Frank (1984), 'Das Asylrecht des Art. 16 GG als liberal-rechtsstaatliches Abwehrrecht', *Der Staat*, 3: 337–68.

Schäuble, Wolfgang (1992), 'Aylsrecht im europäischen Vergleich', in Bade (1992).

Schmitt, Carl (1934), *Politische Theologie: Vier Kapitel zur Lehre von der Souveränität*, 2nd edn. (Berlin: Duncker & Humblot).

Schuck, Peter (1984), 'The Transformation of Immigration Law', *Columbia Law Review*, 84/1: 1–90.

—— (1991), 'The Emerging Political Consensus on Immigration Law', *Georgetown Immigration Law Journal*, 5/1: 1–33.

Shapiro, Martin, and Alec Stone (1994), 'The New Constitutional Politics of Europe', *Comparative Political Studies*, 26/4: 397–420.

Sikkink, Kathryn (1993), 'The Power of Principled Ideas: Human Rights Policies in the US and Western Europe', in Goldstein and Keohane (1993).

Soysal, Yasemin (1994), *Limits to Citizenship* (Chicago: University of Chicago Press).

Spencer, Sarah (ed.) (1994), *Strangers and Citizens* (London: Rivers Oram Press).

Sterett, Susan (1994), 'Judicial Review in Britain', *Comparative Political Studies*, 26/4: 421–42.

Stevens, Dallal (1993), 'Re-Introduction of the UK Asylum Bill', *International Journal of Refugee Law*, 5/1: 91–100.

Storey, Hugo (1994), 'International Law and Human Rights Obligations', in Spencer (1994).

*Sunday Times, The* (1989), 'Britain Leads in Politics of Closed Door', 22 Jan., B3.

Teitelbaum, Michael S. (1980), 'Right versus Right: Immigration and Refugee Policy in the United States', *Foreign Affairs*, 59/1: 21–59.

—— (1984), 'Political Asylum in Theory and Practice', *Public Interest*, no. 76: 74–86.

*Times, The* (1985*a*), 'Tamil Fears', 29 May.

—— (1985*b*), 'Strasbourg Law', 1 June.

—— (1985*c*), 'Refugee Status Questions are for Administrators not Judiciary', 12 Nov.

Walzer, Michael (1983), *Spheres of Justice* (New York: Basic Books).

Wolken, Simone (1988), *Das Grundrecht auf Asyl als Gegenstand der Innen- und Rechtspolitik in der Bundesrepublik Deutschland* (Frankfurt: Peter Lang).

Zolberg, Aristide, A. Suhrke, and S. Aguayo (1989), *Escape from Violence: Conflict and the Refugee Crisis in the Developing World* (New York: Oxford University Press).

# 5

# European Union Migration Regimes, Established and Emergent

## REY KOSLOWSKI

In September 1992 British Foreign Secretary Douglas Hurd said that he and his fellow European Union foreign ministers deemed that migration, 'among all the other problems we face—is the most crucial'. Like nineteenth-century America, 'Europe is a magnet for people seeking greater opportunities, from the east and south . . . We have already seen, most obviously in Germany but also elsewhere in the Community, the tensions and antipathies which can result from the inflow.' But unlike nineteenth-century America, 'ours is not an empty continent' (quoted in Savill 1992: 10). The mere fact that foreign ministers, rather than labour ministers, were discussing migration demonstrated that migration in Europe had moved from the 'low politics' of international economic relations to the 'high politics' of international security.[1]

Not only is migration increasingly viewed as an issue of national security, policy-makers from EU member states have argued that challenges posed by migration should be best dealt with by European co-operation rather than by unilateral action. Wolfgang Schäuble, the Parliamentary Chairman the German Christian Democratic Union and Helmut Kohl's heir apparent, argued that no state could single-handedly protect its citizens from the new threats of mass migration, terrorism, ecological destruction, organized crime, and political religious fundamentalism. 'Therefore we cannot, and must not, be satisfied with the present degree of [European] integration. We must deepen integration, for we will solve neither today's nor tomorrow's problems with a Europe organized as a loose association based on inter-governmental, ad hoc agreements' (quoted in Binyon 1995).

Have such calls for action been met by European co-operation on migration? How effective has this co-operation been? Have EU member states been willing to transfer authority over migration policy-making to European institutions, thereby 'deepening' European integration in the process? If so, what does the phenomenon of migration and co-operative efforts to deal with it mean for the concept of state sovereignty?

In this chapter, I answer these questions by approaching the topic of migration in Europe from the perspective of international relations theory and examining the development of international regimes governing member state policy-making on migration within and to the European Union. Paraphrasing Stephen Krasner's definition,[2] EU migration regimes are implicit or explicit principles, rules, norms, and decision-making procedures around which European actors' expectations converge in the issue area of migration. A regime governing intra-EU migration was first articulated in the Treaty of Rome, reaffirmed in the Single European Act, and formally codified in the European Citizenship provisions of the Treaty on European Union signed at Maastricht. In contrast to the robust intra-EU migration regime, a regime governing migration into the European Union from non-member states is only beginning to emerge with the 1990 signing of the Dublin Convention on jurisdiction for asylum applications and the Schengen Convention on border controls as well as with the ongoing negotiations under Title VI of the Maastricht Treaty dedicated to Co-operation in Justice and Home Affairs.

EU governance of migration within the Union is closely linked to co-operation on migration to the European Union. Achieving a single European market comprising an 'area without internal frontiers in which the free movement of goods, persons, services and capital is ensured' has pressured member states to develop common policies on visas, border controls, asylum application, and illegal migration. Member state co-operation on intra-EU labour migration may have led to co-operation on dealing with migration to the European Union, but member states have diametrically opposed goals in the different issue areas. The objective of the intra-EU migration regime has been free movement across borders; member state co-operation on migration from without has focused on restriction. Given this focus on restricting migration, it appears that EU member states have been willing to give up their sovereignty with respect to the movement of their own nationals within the Union, but have been reluctant to do so for the migration of non-EU member state nationals to the Union. Still, the issue of sovereignty with respect to European co-operation on migration is much more complicated.

My argument proceeds in three steps. First, I review the place of European integration and migration regimes within international relations theory, demonstrating the theoretical significance of both by explaining the double challenge that European integration and international migration present to state sovereignty. Secondly, I describe the establishment of the intra-EU migration regime, noting the underlying neo-functionalist dynamic that drove it, evaluate the effectiveness of the regime and explain how it represents a transfer of member state sovereignty. Thirdly, I sketch out the emerging regime governing migration to the European Union, explain how it is best understood as the outcome of multilateral bargaining that was informed by the internal security ideology of transnational professional police networks, and evaluate the regime's effectiveness as well as its implications for sovereignty.

## EU MIGRATION REGIMES IN THEORETICAL PERSPECTIVE

European unification, or the lack thereof, has been a theme around which central debates over the nature of international politics have been organized from at least the time of Abbé Saint-Pierre and Rousseau (see Rousseau 1760). Traditional realist international relations theory was in large measure conceptualized in negative terms using the ideals of European unification, and later world government, as foils. A basic postulate of realist theory is that in the absence of European unity a balance of power among European states would prevail (Rousseau 1760/1991: 62–3). Subsequently, neo-realist scholars argued that international politics is conducted by sovereign states who, in an anarchical realm devoid of world government, pursue their self-interest of achieving relative gains in the balance of power among states. Neo-realists often begin with the premiss that European unification is next to impossible (see Waltz 1959: 183–4), depict EU member states as 'self-regarding units' of the international system whose close economic co-operation is a function of bipolarity (see Waltz 1979: 91, 70–1), and argue that this co-operation is destined to collapse with the end of the Cold War (see Mearsheimer 1990).

The founding of the European Community challenged the working assumptions of realist theory and inspired scholars to develop new approaches to understanding international politics which came to be known as integration theory, the most prominent being neo-functionalism. Neo-functionalist theory closely followed the strategic move of Jean

Monnet, who gave up on the dream of a European federation and prag-
matically shifted towards the economic integration of national industries
under supranational authorities. Neo-functionalists believed that integration of one sector of the economy would 'spill over' to other sectors
and this process of economic integration would eventually lead to the
political integration of European states into some sort of federation.[3]

While it has become clear that European integration has not followed the neo-functionalist trajectory, neither has integration 'rolled
back' (see Hoffman 1966) to the status quo ante of the classical system
of states that existed in Europe before the world wars. The European
Union can most usefully be viewed as an alternative to the states system that Hedley Bull termed 'the new medievalism'. This new medievalism is 'a system of overlapping authority and multiple loyalty' (Bull
1977: 254) in which states no longer are the primary locus of authority over territories and populations but rather share the loyalty of
individuals with subnational, regional, and global polities. From this
perspective, the European Union is not viewed simply in teleological
terms as a stage in the evolution towards a larger territorial state,
whether unitary or federal in organization. Rather it is seen as a new
form of political organization that is itself a point of reference for theory. The analytical objective then is not so much a matter of explaining the integration process and answering the question whether or not
some sort of United States of Europe will emerge—it may never happen. What is more useful is trying to understand the European Union
for what it is now rather than for what it might become. Hence, it is
useful to identify state practices that are indicative of political transformation, and it is in this regard that migration and EU member states'
responses to it become particularly significant.

European integration and international migration pose a double
challenge to state sovereignty. Jean Bodin initially conceived of sovereignty as the power to make law.[4] Following Bodin, realist international
relations theorists conceptualized world politics in terms of states that
have supreme 'law-making and law-enforcing authority' (Morgenthau
1973: 314) in a given territory. That is, realists assume states have both
juridical and empirically effective sovereignty. European integration
challenges the concept of state sovereignty in both senses when the
European Commission represents member states in trade policy negotiations with other sovereign states, when the European Union's Council
of Ministers issues single market directives based on qualified majority voting, and when the European Court of Justice issues rulings that
have direct effect and take supremacy over conflicting national laws.

From a realist perspective, sovereignty with respect to international migration means: that states control their borders and can decide whether or not to permit entry and exit; that even after admitting migrants the state can reverse its decision through expulsion, should it be deemed in the national interest; and that states choose which migrants will or will not receive nationality (see Hendrickson 1992). As Saskia Sassen's and Christian Joppke's contributions to this volume recount (Chapters 2, 4), the phenomenon of increasing 'unwanted' migration and the dissociation of civil, social, and even political rights of citizenship from the status of having the nationality of a state have challenged the traditional realist assumptions of state sovereignty over migration. Elsewhere, I have addressed the issue of citizenship and sovereignty in Europe (see Koslowski 1994*a*, 1995); here I will primarily focus on the dimension of sovereignty as control over migration within the context of European integration and co-operation.

The realist assertion that states are ultimately sovereign and have the capability to control their borders, while true, is not all that enlightening. States obviously have the *capabilities* to control their borders for unwanted migration (as the Soviet Union and east European states once so effectively demonstrated), the question is, 'Do they in practice?' One cannot impute practice from capabilities.

In response to the realist position, James Hollifield has argued that advanced industrial democracies, such as Germany, France, and the United States, have been reluctant to exercise state sovereignty and take extensive measures to halt migration or begin expulsions due to espousal of liberal economic ideologies and adherence to their own principles of human rights as well as international human rights treaties to which they are a party (see Hollifield 1992*a*). Taking a sceptical stance on this position, Gary Freeman (1994) argues that state capabilities of liberal democracies may in fact vary with respect to the various types of migration and vary from state to state, and there is evidence that during the early 1990s state capabilities in some liberal democratic states may be growing. Joppke (Chapter 4 in this volume) argues that, at least in the area of asylum policy, state capability in the United States, Germany, and Great Britain to control migration is not diminishing and the constraints of international human rights regimes on state sovereignty are overestimated.

The issue of migration and state sovereignty needs to be approached not only on a case-by-case basis of individual states but also within the context of the international system (beyond just human rights regimes) and for European states within the context of European integration.

From the outset, sovereignty denoted not only the state's supreme law-making and law-enforcing authority in a given territory, but also that such authority was recognized by the other states of the international system as expressed in the legal doctrine of sovereign equality. 'Sovereignty is not a concept that is sensibly applied to a single state or to numerous states in isolation from one another. It is inherently a relational concept' (Caporaso 1993: 78). Sovereignty is a social construct of states interacting in a system, and at the heart of this social construct is the seeming contradiction of bounded supreme authority (Kratochwil 1995: 23–5).

The common understanding of sovereignty as state autonomy to behave as it will is not just conceptually but empirically inaccurate. As Abram and Antonia Handler Chayes argue,

The largest and most powerful states can sometimes get their way through sheer exertion of will, but even they cannot achieve their principal purposes —security, economic well-being, and a decent level of amenity for their citizens—without the help and cooperation of many other participants in the system . . . for all but a few self-isolated nations, sovereignty no longer consists in the freedom of states to act independently, in their perceived self interest, but in membership in reasonably good standing in the regimes that make up the substance of international life. To be a player, the state must submit to the pressures that international regulations impose. Its behaviour in any single episode is likely to affect future relationships not only within the particular regime involved but in many others as well, and perhaps its position within the international system as a whole. (Chayes 1995: 27)

As the Chayes point out, in practice, most states comply with most international treaties, most of the time. Moreover, treaty compliance is largely not a function of supranational legal enforcement mechanisms, military or economic sanctions, but more often than not the state's desire to remain a member of the international system in good standing. Hence, when it comes to migration, sovereignty has two dimensions: expressions of sovereignty through independent actions such as increasing border checks, tightening asylum laws, deportations, etc.; as well as sovereignty *vis-à-vis* other states in co-operative efforts in issue areas, of which migration is only one.

Being a member of the international system in good standing with respect to migration is not exceptionally difficult because international co-operation on migration has been limited. As opposed to trade, arms control, and even the environment, there is little in the way of international migration regimes on the global level. Although there is an international refugee regime, an international labour migration regime has yet to develop. The international refugee regime is based on the norms of the 1951 Geneva Convention (see UNHCR 1993, Annex II.2: 163) and institutionalized in the office of the United Nations High Commissioner for Refugees. International co-operation has focused on: managing refugee flows to minimize conflicts between states; supporting countries of first asylum with the means to accommodate large refugee flows; facilitating resettlement of refugees from countries of first asylum to other states; assistance in voluntary repatriation to home countries once threats to personal security subside; and preventative action with respect to human rights abuses (see Loescher 1993). This co-operation has not significantly impinged on state sovereignty (except in the case of Third World states whose empirical sovereignty is already questionable at best; see Jackson 1990) because, contrary to common understandings, the international refugee regime only provides a modest framework for facilitating state management of refugees issues— it is not primarily concerned with the rights of refugees themselves. Moreover, since the end of the Cold War the refugee regime has been weakened by the unwillingness of the advanced industrial democracies to continue accepting the increasing numbers of refugees or to provide sufficient contributions for the support of refugees in countries of first asylum (see UNHCR 1993: 31–5; Loescher 1994).

In contrast to the global context, a regional labour migration regime is in place in the European Union, and it has important implications for state sovereignty. Over the decades EU member states have adopted an extensive set of principles, rules, norms, and decision-making procedures dedicated to providing labour mobility. Hollifield argues that the 'European Community functions as a weak international regime for migration at the regional level' (1992*b*: 587). This is possible because the European Union is an example of a type of international political economy Hollifield calls 'regional interdependence', which differs from international anarchy, embedded liberalism, and hegemonic stability 'in two important respects: the social purpose of the regime, in terms of norms and principles, is more fully institutionalized, and the legitimacy of the regime rests on institutions, ideas, and popular consent'. Unlike the relations among states in general, 'sovereignty with respect to the populations of member states has been ceded to the Community' (Hollifield 1992*b*: 580), given that most citizens of EU member states have freedom of movement among member states and rights to employment in fellow member states.

Hollifield's characterization of the European Community as a weak regime can be better elaborated if one differentiates between migration of EU member state nationals within the European Union and migration of non-EU member state nationals to the European Union. Governed by the principle of free movement and rules of non-discrimination, co-operation among member states regarding internal migration of workers from fellow EU member states was fairly well established by the beginning of the 1970s. Co-operation among member states regarding migration to the European Union is more recent and has been more *ad hoc* in nature. Following the definition stated at the outset, a regime governing migration to the European Union is developing because informal norms have facilitated member state co-operation, even if it is outside the EC Treaty framework and even if it is in advance of the formal ratification of multilateral agreements. This regime is still relatively incomplete and its influence on state behaviour is not necessarily immediate and direct.[5]

From the neo-realist perspective, the development of international migration regimes is not expected to happen at all. Neo-realists contend that international regimes reflect power relationships and are marginal in their consequences for state behaviour because states will not abide by rules aimed at fostering co-operation when state sovereignty and national interests are at stake (see Grieco 1988). For EU member states to transfer sovereignty with respect to populations of member states to a supranational body or 'pool' sovereignty in intergovernmental institutions (see Keohane and Hoffman 1991: 8–9) defies realist logic. Co-operation in response to east–west migrations made possible by the end of the Cold War is especially surprising when, according to the neo-realist vision, the end of bipolarity was to eliminate the external pressure for European co-operation. In this way, the establishment of an intra-EU migration regime and the emergence of co-operation on migration to the European Union not only demonstrates the significance of migration in international politics, it also demonstrates the persistence of European integration and its expansion.

## INTRA-EU MIGRATION

### The Intra-EU Migration Regime

The regime regulating the migration of workers within the European Union is based on the Treaty of Rome, a series of Council directives and regulations, and the securing of the right to free movement by the European Court of Justice (ECJ or 'the Court') (see Plender 1988). In conjunction with the principle of free movement of goods, capital, and services, the Treaty of Rome enunciates the freedom of movement of economic agents. That is, freedom of movement within the Community was not conferred to individuals given their status as citizens of member states, but rather as 'workers', whether through self-employment (Arts. 52–8) or as employees (Arts. 48–51), or as the providers or recipients of services (Art. 59). The principle of free movement of workers was realized in EC regulations that are generally applicable, are binding in their entirety, and take direct effect (Böhning 1972: 11–19). A 1961 regulation enabled workers from one EC member state to take a position in another member state if a suitable worker from that state could not be found within three weeks;[6] a 1964 regulation removed the need to search for local workers and augmented rights of family reunification;[7] and a 1968 regulation stipulated that workers from another member state had 'the right to take up available employment in the territory of another Member state with the same priority as a national of that State'.[8]

By referring to the free movement of 'persons' the 1986 Single European Act (SEA) acknowledged the degree to which the scope of the free movement principle had expanded—being applied to workers' families, for instance. In support of the principle of free movement, the ECJ rigorously applied prohibitions against discrimination based on nationality (see Johnson and O'Keefe 1994). Finally, European Citizenship formalized the *de facto* extension of the free movement principle from workers to all nationals of EU member states by detaching permission to reside in a fellow member state from employment (*Treaty on European Union* 1992, Part 2, Acts. 8–8e: 15–16).

The prospect of a frontierless internal labour market also gave impetus to harmonization of member state social policies. The Social Charter and Action Programme of 1989 essentially laid out a broad set of principles for member state policies on workplace regulations, worker benefits, unemployment insurance, etc., as well as specific measures necessary to realize social policy harmonization. Although the Maastricht Treaty includes an agreement expanding the scope of EU competence in social policy harmonization, the United Kingdom managed to negotiate an exemption from the agreement on the Social Charter. By drawing attention to the differing social costs per worker paid by employers in the various member states, intra-EU labour migration is encouraging member state action which may add further pressure for social policy harmonization.

For example, recent protests in Berlin by German construction workers have moved the Kohl government to put forward a law that would require foreign workers to receive the minimum wage paid to Germans as well as receive similar vacation time (see *Migrant News* 1995). While there are approximately 140,000 unemployed German construction workers, foreign workers from fellow EU member states constitute approximately 100,000 out of the 1.5 million German construction workforce. Given that German wages plus social costs makes German labour the most expensive of EU member states, unemployed German construction workers feel that they have been passed over by German employers who have hired construction workers from EU member states with lower wages and social costs, such as Portugal and the United Kingdom. The Kohl government argues that some firms, particularly British, provide documentation to unemployed workers enabling them to claim self-employed status and therefore offer their services throughout the European Union even while they received unemployment compensation. Should the law go into effect, German firms or foreign workers will most likely appeal to the ECJ for a ruling on the new law, thereby pitting the principle of non-discrimination against the lack of social policy harmonization. If the principle of non-discrimination is upheld, it will either pressure unions in member states with high social costs to accept more competitive wages and benefits or spur their governments to negotiate further social policy harmonization with low social cost member states.

Freedom of movement for EU nationals raises the issue of freedom of movement for third-country nationals already legally resident in the European Union.[9] To begin with, many third-country nationals enjoy a degree a free movement by virtue of being a member of an EU national's family. A national of one EU member state living in another can bring his or her spouse, dependent children, parents, and grandparents regardless of nationality.[10] With the relaxation of internal border controls, it would be, practically speaking, rather difficult to enforce controls on the movement of third-country nationals while allowing EU nationals to travel unimpeded. Third-country nationals for the most part remain in the EU state in which they possess work and resident permits and, even with the relaxation of internal border controls, it is questionable to what degree unemployed legal resident aliens who are entitled to social support would cross into another EU member state to work illegally.

The question then arises as to whether or not third-country nationals with work permits in one member state should be permitted to work in another. The Commission has proposed that member states should 'accord priority to third-country nationals permanently and legally resident in another Member State, when job vacancies cannot be filled by EC nationals' (see Commission of the European Communities 1994: 34). Although the Council has not acted on this proposal, expansion of mobility rights for third-country nationals has come through the Court's enforcement of the rule of non-discrimination. In the *Vander Elst* v. *International Migration Office* case, the ECJ ruled that a small Belgian demolition firm with a contract for work in France was wrongfully fined by French authorities for not having work permits for its Moroccan employees.[11] In this case, the rule of non-discrimination in applying the right of establishment became a vehicle for expanding mobility rights of third-county migrant workers.

Inasmuch as the SEA refers to an 'area without internal frontiers' the norms of the intra-EU migration regime include the right to cross borders unimpeded. Since border control is more central to state sovereignty than work and residence rights, member states were reluctant to approach the elimination of border controls within the framework of Community law. Hence, the elimination of border controls became the subject of multilateral negotiations by justice and interior ministers within the intergovernmental frameworks of European Political Co-operation, the Trevi group created in 1975 by the European Council and, after 1986, an *ad hoc* group of ministers responsible for immigration within the Trevi framework (see den Boer and Walker 1993: 6). The group of ministers examined questions of migration that would arise with the reduction of border controls within the European Union. They addressed visa policy co-ordination, asylum application abuse, and the development of an external common frontier to complement the relaxation of internal border controls. Although the group of ministers laboured on an external borders convention, conflict between Spain and the United Kingdom over Gibraltar side-tracked any agreement.

As the prospects for EC-wide co-operation on the elimination of border controls appeared rather dim, a subset of member states (Belgium, France, Germany, the Netherlands, and Luxembourg) signed a border control agreement in the Luxembourg town of Schengen in 1985. In the Schengen Agreement and the subsequent 1990 Convention, signatory states agreed to allow people to travel unimpeded by border controls among signatory states provided that they did not stay over three months, at which time national immigration policies would take effect.

Italy joined in 1990; Spain and Portugal joined in 1991; while Greece gained observer status; Austria joined in April 1995. Membership was initially limited to EU member states, but given the reluctance of Denmark, Sweden, and Finland to join Schengen if it meant abolishing free movement within the 40-year-old Nordic Passport Union, member states have agreed to permit Norway and Iceland to join even if they are not EU members (see Tucker 1995: 3).

As the Schengen Agreement went into effect on 26 March 1995 internal border controls were relaxed. On 1 July 1995 the signatory states were to stop passport checks at the borders between them while increasing controls at the external border bounding the signatory states as a group. Although France had been the first member state to ratify the Schengen Agreement and called for its extension to all fifteen EU member states, the French government stepped up border checks in the wake of a bombing of the Paris Metro and took advantage of a treaty derogation that permits border checks for another six-month period beginning 1 July 1995. Subsequently, French President Jacques Chirac said that France would probably request to have border checks maintained after 1 January 1996. Officials from fellow Schengen member states expressed their understanding of the French government's position, yet concerns arose that France may be using the situation to implement parts of the convention selectively (see *Migration News Sheet* 1995*a*: 2–3). In light of the French security concerns which have held up full implementation of the agreement, in October 1995 the Schengen group announced that it accepted a proposal to develop binational and multinational mobile patrol units that would conduct internal checks (*Migration News Sheet* 1995*b*: 1).

In sum, member state co-operation on intra-EU migration was often driven by spill-over from one area of functional co-operation to another. Realizing the goal of the free movement of workers in practice entailed member state co-operation on free movement of spouses and dependants. As the criteria for subjects of the principle of free movement expanded, liberal interpretation of these criteria in the adjudication of discrimination cases prompted expansion of the free movement principle to EU nationals in general. Free movement for EU nationals in turn creates pressures for social policy harmonization and the free movement within the European Union of migrant workers from non-EU member states. Once member states agreed on the objective of realizing the free movement of persons within the Community and defined free movement in terms of a frontierless area, it also prompted

TABLE 5.1. *Resident aliens in the European Union from EU member states* (000)

| Member state | 1987 | 1988 | 1989 | 1990 | 1991 | 1992 |
|---|---|---|---|---|---|---|
| Belgium | 495 | 474 | 446 | 497 | 551.5 | 554.6 |
| Denmark | 21 | 21 | 22 | 19 | 27.6 | 28.4 |
| Germany | 1,437 | 1,325 | 1,375 | 1,417 | 1,439.1 | 1,487.0 |
| Greece | 12 | 14 | 11 | 14 | 54.1 | 61.5 |
| Spain | 55 | 59 | 57 | 60 | 272.9 | 158.3 |
| France | 1,386 | 1,397 | 1,360 | 1,347 | 1,311.7 | 1,311.8 |
| Ireland | 60 | 65 | 62 | 61 | 68.5 | 73.3 |
| Italy | | | | | 149.4 | 111.2 |
| Luxembourg | 88 | 88 | 91 | 98 | 102.7 | 114.6 |
| Netherlands | 168 | 174 | 182 | 175 | 168.4 | 176.1 |
| Portugal | 10 | 12 | 11 | 13 | 28.7 | 30.0 |
| UK | 812 | 764 | 803 | 732 | 781.0 | 770.5 |
| Total EU 12 | 4,544 | 4,393 | 4,420 | 4,433 | 4,955.6 | 4,877.3 |

*Sources*: For 1987–90: Eurostat (1993*a*), selection 2.2.1.5. Statistics for Italy not reported. For 1991: Eurostat (1993*b*). For 1992: Eurostat (1994).

co-operation on external border controls. In this way, member state co-operation in labour policy has been linked to co-operation in the very different realms of foreign policy on refugees and policing.

## Rates of Intra-EU Migration and State Compliance

It was widely expected that relaxation of barriers to labour migration within the European Union would lead to increased migration, especially with the accession of less-developed member states such as Spain, Portugal, and Greece. Contrary to the expectations of the Commission (see Commission of the European Communities 1985), the SEA did not greatly increase intra-EU migration (see Table 5.1).[12] The removal of barriers to labour mobility did not increase the migration of industrial workers within the European Union in large measure due to the substitution of intra-EU capital mobility (see Molle and Mourik 1988; Straubhaar 1988; Werner 1993). It remains to be seen, however, if migration increases within other segments of the EU population as more barriers to movement drop. By separating the right to residence from employment, European Citizenship expands the potential pool of intra-EU migrants beyond that of traditional labour flows. By stipulating mutual recognition of professional credentials, the 1988 General Systems Directive (see Orzack 1991) not only enables professionals to work anywhere in the European Union, it frees students from career limitations imposed by academic degrees from other countries, and allows professionals nearing retirement to purchase homes abroad yet still practise part-time. Also, the 'Europeanization' of member state businesses facilitated by the SEA has led to a restructuring of firms and redeployment of personnel that fosters migration of highly skilled corporate employees (see Salt 1992). At this point, however, the overall effect of changes in rules governing intra-EU migration on migration rates has been marginal (see Hovy and Zlotnik 1994).

Changing rates of intra-EU migration should not be equated with the strength or weakness of the intra-EU migration regime because migration rates are not really indicative of state compliance with the regime. The objective of the regime is the elimination of barriers to free movement and the elimination of member state discrimination against EU nationals, not increased intra-EU migration itself. At issue is not the behaviour of individuals but rather the behaviour of states. Indeed, migration rates often go up in anticipation of impending restrictions in host countries. Guarantees of free movement reduce the rush to migrate before gates close as well as encourage return migration to the home country because migrants can rest assured that they may move again if they need to.

The strength of the intra-EU migration regime could be better assessed by examining member state discrimination against resident aliens from fellow EU member states. The fact that migrant workers from fellow EU member states keep their jobs despite persistent record-setting unemployment rates is testament to the strength of the intra-EU migration regime. Nevertheless, actions directed explicitly at foreign workers from EU member states, such as the proposed German law on minimum wages, do occur. Member states continue to violate the norms of the regime given the significant number of cases brought before the ECJ between 1989 and 1994 in which member states were found to have violated the rule of non-discrimination (see Johnson and O'Keefe 1994: 1327–9). Such member state actions, however, spur resolution of conflicting policies either through new rounds of harmonization or through adjudication by the Court. Not only has adjudication provided a means of gaining member state compliance, the Court has consistently reaffirmed the principle of free movement and rules of non-discrimination (ibid.). Given that EC law has direct effect, the prospect of Court action generally inhibits states from taking actions that are flagrant violations of the regime. Cases generally involve conflicting understandings of what actions constitute violations of regime norms and in this way their adjudication clarifies the rules of the intra-EU migration regime and makes it more effective in the long run.

Given that a frontierless area for free movement of persons was the objective stated in the SEA, the existence of border controls experienced by EU nationals is another good measure of regime compliance on the part of member states. On this front, the EU is far from achieving the SEA's stated goal given that internal border checks were relaxed over two years later than initially projected and then only among the Schengen countries. Still, an independent non-governmental organization assessment one month after the lifting of border controls among Schengen states on 25 March 1995 was rather positive. In advance of the implementation of the Schengen Agreement, the NGO, Euro Citizen Action Service, organized a hotline for EU nationals who wished to report the continuation of border checks or increased random internal checks. The ECAS survey indicated few abuses and, contrary to the expectations of the ECAS, border controls were not replaced by similarly systematic random internal checks directed particularly towards foreign-looking people (*Agence Europe* 1995*a*). The reluctance of states outside the Schengen Agreement, particularly the United Kingdom, to take measures necessary for eliminating internal frontiers (e.g. issuance of personal identification cards) and the reimposition of checks by France, however, raises doubts about the future effectiveness of the intra-EU migration regime with respect to border controls.

## Sovereignty

In general, member states have ceded sovereignty with respect to the migration of EU nationals within the Union. Sovereignty over the migration of permanent resident third-country nationals is eroding as well. However, important caveats are in order. Nationals from one member state may have the right to live and work in another, but they do not gain all the rights of nationals of their new state of residence. European citizenship extends the right to vote in local and European parliamentary elections to resident aliens from fellow EU member states, but member states have not similarly extended the right to vote in national elections and have evoked the principle of national sovereignty in doing so (see Koslowski 1994*b*).

Strictly speaking, it can be argued that the delayed and incomplete removal of border checks indicates a lack of free movement and a retention of sovereignty by member states (see Anderson *et al.* 1994). However, defining free movement in terms of an absence of border checks and defining sovereignty in terms of border control is misleading. For example, automobiles are stopped at the California–Arizona border and checked for contraband fruit and vegetables and the Pennsylvania State Police routinely stops automobiles crossing from New Jersey that are suspected of bringing in cheap New Jersey booze (Pennsylvania maintains a state monopoly on the sale of wine and liquor). Yet these border checks do not mean that free movement has not been realized within the United States, nor that California and Pennsylvania have retained their 'sovereignty'. A passport check at an internal EU border may slow crossing by a properly documented, law-abiding EU national, but it does not necessarily stop that person from moving to another member state because he or she has a legal right to do so.

With the Schengen group's acceptance of multinational mobile patrols to conduct internal checks, the nature of unimpeded movement among signatory states has also been significantly redefined. While this can be viewed as another *de facto* set-back in the realization of an 'area without internal frontiers', widespread institutionalization of multinational police units represents further functional integration via intersectoral spill-over that has important implications for the sovereignty of Schengen states. For example, one could easily imagine a situation in which a Spanish police officer confronting an armed suspect in France has authority to use deadly force against a French citizen. On the one hand, one could argue that such internal checks are practically equivalent to border checks and that member states have in fact retained sovereignty with respect to internal borders. On the other hand, extending jurisdiction and policing powers to other states could easily be viewed as an even greater abdication of sovereignty than removing border checks.

## MIGRATION TO THE EUROPEAN UNION

Until the 1970s net migration flowed out of western Europe (see Widgren 1990). Unlike classical immigration states such as the United States, Canada, and Australia, most EU member states do not have a tradition of immigration of permanent residents who then become citizens. Rather migratory flows to the EU have primarily been composed of guestworkers, their families, individuals from former colonies, co-ethnics with citizenship rights (e.g. ethnic Germans from Poland and the former Soviet Union), and asylum-seekers. Temporary labour migration and migration from former colonies predominated in the 1960s and early 1970s, family reunification in the later 1970s and early 1980s, and refugee flows came to the fore during the late 1980s and early 1990s, when increasing migration of co-ethnics and political refugees primarily from eastern Europe drove up the total number of resident aliens in the EU from non-EU member states (see Table 5.2).

Individual member states attempted to restrict entry of non-EU nationals by tightening visa policies and reducing support to asylum-seekers. Although such unilateral actions may have decreased the number of asylum-seekers, they diverted the flows to other countries and asylum-seekers turned away from one country simply reapplied in the next (see Funk 1995; Santel 1995). As unilateral measures proliferated, the extent of the marginal reduction in refugees experienced by one member state increasingly depended on other member states not enacting even more restrictivist policies.

## *Member State Co-Operation on Migration to the European Union*

In response to increasing numbers of refugees, and given the concern on the part of foreign policy-makers that the collapse of communism would unleash mass east–west migration, EU member states began to co-operate. The Schengen Convention harmonizes asylum application procedures and mandates that asylum-seekers may only apply in one country. It also calls for a common visa policy, harmonization of policies to deter illegal migration, and an automated information system so as to co-ordinate actions regarding individuals who have been denied entry. The 1990 Dublin Convention provided rules for determining which member state had jurisdiction in asylum applications governed by the principle that the state of entry would be responsible for any given application. If that state rejected the application, the asylum-seeker could not then apply in other member states. The objective was to eliminate abuse of member state asylum application processes through multiple application (asylum shopping). The Dublin Convention still has not been ratified by all member states.[13] In addition to the principle that the state of entry should process asylum applications, the Edinburgh Council of 1992 introduced the norm that asylum-seekers

TABLE 5.2. *Migration to the EU* (000)

| | 1988 | 1989 | 1990 | 1991 | 1992 | 1993 |
|---|---|---|---|---|---|---|
| Total net migration[a] | +622.5 | +1,017.4 | +1,076.1 | +1,054.4 | +1,344.5 | +1,037.6 |
| Non-EU resident aliens[b] | 7,911.3 | 8,487.2 | 9,542.9 | 10,438.9 | 12,098.3 | 12,251.2 |

[a] Total net migration is the total of net migration of the 15 EU member states. 'Net migration is the difference between the total population on January 1 and December 31 of the same year, minus the differences between births and deaths and including corrections (due to population censuses, register counts etc. which cannot be classified as births deaths or migrations)' (Eurostat 1995, table A-1, p. 4). Figures for EU 15, including Sweden, Austria, and Finland.

[b] Source for stock statistics on resident aliens in the EU from non-EU member states: Eurostat (1995, table A-5.1, p. 12). Figures for EU 15, including Sweden, Austria, and Finland. Stock statistics do not directly demonstrate migration flows but rather present yearly snapshots of the numbers of non-EU nationals resident in the EU on 1 Jan. of each year. Stocks may decrease due to the death or naturalization of non-EU nationals and increase due to births in countries in which the children of resident aliens do not gain citizenship.

should 'be encouraged to stay in the nearest safe area to their homes' (Presidency, European Council 1992: 44). Given that newly democratic east central European countries bordering member states were deemed to be 'safe countries', the criteria became a basis for rejecting asylum claims of those who crossed the EU frontier from these states (see e.g. Neuman 1993).

Title VI of the Maastricht Treaty formalized the process of inter-governmental co-operation among the member states on migration. Co-operation in the fields of Justice and Home Affairs formed one of three 'pillars' of the European Union along with the original European Community and Common Foreign and Security Policy. The pillar structure effectively kept most policies regarding migration to the European Union outside the Community legal order. Title VI does not promulgate specific rules to govern migration poicy but designates matters for common interest, including asylum policy, rules governing the crossing of external borders, and policies regarding third-country nationals (Art. K.1); stipulates compliance with the European Convention for the Protection of Human Rights (Art. K.2) and sets up a co-ordinating committee of senior officials (Art. K.4). A common visa policy was inserted in the EC Treaty itself (Art. 100c).

For the most part, member states have not utilized the new framework to go beyond previous intergovernmental co-operation until quite recently. The Justice and Home Affairs Council agreed to its first legally binding joint position at its November 1995 meeting when it stipulated a common definition of refugee. Based on the definition of the 1951 Geneva Convention as someone with a well-founded fear of being persecuted for reasons of race, religion, nationality, membership in a particular social group, or political opinion, the new common definition effectively excludes those who flee civil wars, generalized armed conflict, and persecution by 'non-state agents', such as armed militias and insurgent groups. Currently, Germany, France, Italy, and Sweden are the only member states that do not define those persecuted by non-state agents as refugees. The UNHCR criticized the common position as contrary to the spirit of the 1951 Convention and as a step backwards that could imperil refugee protection throughout the world (see *ANP English News Bulletin* 1995; *European Insight* 1995).

To understand why the regime governing migration to the European Union became increasingly restrictive, it is important to point out that member states avoided transferring authority in this area to the supra-national institutions of Commission and Court, and worked instead through the intergovernmental institutions of European Political Co-operation and the Council of Ministers[14] as well as through extra-Community multilateral forums such as Schengen. In the late 1980s and early 1990s liberal economic precepts held by centre-right governments in Germany and Great Britain as well as the free market-(re)orientated Socialist government of France called for realization of the SEA's provisions for a frontierless labour market. At the same time the lack of government response to growing public perceptions of migration as a threat played into the electoral designs of right-wing movements that challenged those governments. Given the collective action problems involved in unilateral restriction of entry and asylum application, co-operation became imperative. However, the lowest common denominator of agreement was co-operation on policing and assignment of asylum application responsibility, rather than on the more comprehensive co-operation advocated by the Commission in the areas of trade policy, foreign policy, and development co-operation aimed at the root causes of migration such as human rights abuses and civil war (particularly in the former Yugoslavia), economic disparities, population growth, and environmental degradation (see Commission of the European Communities 1994: 13–19).

Also, member state co-operation developed within the context of a growing web of multilateral forums and an explosion of international conferences and meetings on migration in the European region during the late 1980s and early 1990s.[15] In addition to the EU and Schengen frameworks, member states participated in meetings organized by the UNHCR, International Organization for Migration, Council of Europe, Organization for Economic Co-operation and Development (OECD), International Labour Office, the Intergovernmental Consultations on Asylum, Refugee, and Migration Policies in Europe, North America, and Australia (often referred to as the 'informal consultations'), the Berlin Process, and the Organization for Security and Co-operation in Europe. During the first half of 1993 there were approximately 80–90 such meetings, twice the number taking place two years before (see Council of Europe 1993). As use of the Schengen forum demonstrates, with a multitude of forums, multilateral co-operation can take the line of least resistance, adopting the lowest common denominator of agreement, and then become the basis for subsequent negotiations involving more participants and greater scope in issues. However, the basic norm of the regime is usually set in the initial agreement to which subsequent member states accede.

The characteristics of EU migration regimes can be further understood by considering the work of individuals and NGOs that have reached across state borders in common cause regarding a particular issue area. Such transnational efforts to gather information and publicize particular problems help place issues on the agenda of foreign ministries (see Risse-Kappen 1995). Moreover, provision of technical analysis and expert opinion by 'epistemic communities' informs the terms of debate in multilateral negotiations. 'An epistemic community is a network of professionals with recognized expertise and competence in a particular domain and an authoritative claim to policy-relevant knowledge within that domain or issue area' (P. Haas 1992: 3). The development of the regime governing migration to the EU was influenced by the agenda-setting of duelling epistemic communities—academic experts and NGOs committed to protecting human rights vs. transnational networks of police dedicated to using migration control to fight crime.

The many meetings and conferences on European migration brought officials from the European Union and other international organizations together with academics and NGO representatives who presented demographic analyses and predictions as well as offered policy analysis and prescriptions.[16] Moreover, NGOs have an important role in standard-setting, promoting ratification (see Niessen 1994), and, as will be discussed below, monitoring state compliance. The epistemic community committed to protecting human rights became particularly influential in the formation of policy proposals by the Council of Europe, European Parliament, and the Commission.

In contrast, transnational networks of police professionals that developed through contacts made under the auspices of Interpol and Trevi were critical to setting the agendas for member state co-operation by linking the problems of international crime and illegal immigration. As Monica den Boer and Neil Walker put it, 'The consistent association of the different themes in the language and practice of politicians and professionals has created a mutually reinforcive "internal security ideology"' (den Boer and Walker 1993: 9). This internal security ideology came to inform the development of the intergovernmental institutions which dealt with migration, most noteworthy being the third pillar of the Maastricht Treaty, which lumps immigration and asylum policy together with drug addiction and international fraud. In member state negotiations within the third-pillar framework, migration is addressed not in terms of human rights but in terms of internal security; resolutions focus on the instrument of policing rather than foreign policy and

TABLE 5.3. *Number of asylum-seekers in each EU member state*

| Member state | 1989 | 1990 | 1991 | 1992 | 1993 | 1994 |
|---|---|---|---|---|---|---|
| Belgium | 8,188 | 12,945 | 15,444 | 17,675 | 26,717 | 14,340 |
| Denmark | 4,588 | 5,292 | 4,609 | 13,884 | 14,347 | 6,651 |
| Germany | 121,318 | 193,063 | 256,112 | 438,191 | 322,599 | 127,210 |
| Greece | 4,033 | 10,569 | 5,944 | 3,822 | 862 | |
| Spain | 4,077 | 8,647 | 8,138 | 11,712 | 12,645 | 10,230 |
| France | 61,422 | 54,813 | 47,380 | 28,872 | 27,564 | 26,044 |
| Ireland | 36 | 62 | 31 | | 91 | 355 |
| Italy | 2,240 | 3,570 | 24,490 | 2,589 | 1,323 | 1,834 |
| Luxembourg | 87 | 114 | 238 | 120 | 225 | |
| Netherlands | 13,898 | 21,208 | 21,615 | 20,346 | 35,399 | 52,576 |
| Austria | 21,822 | 22,789 | 27,306 | 16,238 | 4,744 | 5,082 |
| Portugal | 116 | 61 | 233 | 655 | 2,090 | 614 |
| Finland | 179 | 2,743 | 2,137 | 3,634 | 2,023 | 849 |
| Sweden | 30,335 | 29,420 | 27,351 | 84,018 | 37,581 | 18,640 |
| UK | 16,775 | 38,200 | 73,400 | 32,300 | 28,500 | 41,000 |
| Total EU 15 | 289,114 | 403,496 | 514,428 | 674,056 | 516,710 | 305,425 |

*Source*: Eurostat (1996, no. 1, table 1, pp. 2–3).

trade and development (see Funk 1995). In this sense, the tug of war pitting the Commission and Parliament against the Council for authority over EU migration policy is also a contest in the battle of ideas.

### Regime Effectiveness: Migration Rates and Member State Policy Changes

Since the objective of the emerging regime governing migration to the European Union is not free movement but rather reducing illegal migration and eliminating asylum abuses, co-operation should reduce migration flows. Illegal migration is difficult to measure, but figures for asylum-seekers in the European Union since the signing of the Schengen and Dublin Conventions are very enlightening. Although the number of asylum-seekers continued to increase during the first two years after the agreements were signed, they dropped in the third, as member states, most notably Germany, put stricter asylum policies into place (see Table 5.3). Still, absolute decreases in migration flows cannot be the sole criteria for regime effectiveness because, without whatever co-operation that did exist, migration rates could have been even higher, especially since the primary objective of co-operation was to eliminate abuses of asylum application procedures, rather than arbitrarily limit the number of political refugees accepted in the European Union.

Germany accounts for close to, if not more than, half of the European Union's asylum-seekers in any given year and changes in the overall EU number reflect German trends. The recent drop in the number of asylum-seekers in Germany can be attributed to the introduction of a new asylum law that went into effect on 1 July 1993, which stipulated that asylum-seekers entering Germany from countries that offer asylum should make their application there and that those coming from countries considered 'safe' would have to provide evidence of selective individual persecution.

Strictly speaking, Germany's action was unilateral in nature.[17] However, it is better understood in the context of the changing European norms enunciated in the Dublin Convention and the Edinburgh Summit Declaration. The emerging EU migration regime was useful to the CDU–CSU–FDP governing coalition in justifying a restrictivist policy that required constitutional amendment. As Chancellor Helmut Kohl put it, 'The new regulation of the right to asylum of 1 July was an important precondition for the fact that Germany can fully participate in a common European asylum policy' (International Intelligence Report 1994, quoted in Ucarer 1997). Moreover, given that Schengen rules generally give responsibility for asylum-seekers without visas to states of first entry (even if illegally), it put additional pressure on member states with external borders to maintain strict border controls and adopt restrictive asylum policies lest they bear a disproportionate burden of asylum-seekers (see Neuman 1993: 508). Hence, Germany's accession to the Dublin and Schengen Conventions provided international legitimization as well as a practical incentive for domestic political action.

Generally speaking, even though not all EU member states have signed the Schengen Convention nor ratified the Dublin Convention, these agreements have had an indirect effect on migration rates via changes in the asylum policies of individual member states. Given that efforts to enact restrictivist migration policies are hampered more by domestic economic interests and human rights concerns, changes in international norms within an international migration regime may be useful in changing domestic policies. In this case, multilateral cooperation can be viewed as part of a 'two-level game' (see Putnam 1988) in which states justify the curtailment of certain rights and increased state interference in the domestic economy in terms of prevailing international norms and adherence to multilateral commitments, much in the way leaders in developing states who wish to effectuate painful economic reforms find it politically useful to blame the International Monetary Fund for their actions.

## *Sovereignty*

While member states have transferred sovereignty with respect to the migration of EU nationals within the Union, they have resisted a similar transfer of sovereignty over migration of non-EU nationals into the Union. Generally speaking, member state sovereignty has for the most part been retained with respect to external border control, illegal migration, and asylum policy because some member states have either not become parties to certain agreements (e.g. Schengen) or when member states did negotiate and sign agreements in these areas, they did so primarily in multilateral state-to-state forums or in intergovernmental institutions of the European Union. Co-operation agreements in these areas remained outside the Community legal order and the jurisdiction of the ECJ.

Again, a few caveats are in order. First, co-operation in Justice and Home Affairs (the third pillar of the Maastricht Treaty) is separated from the community framework. However, the Commission is associated with the work in this area (Art. K.4) and shares a right of initiative with the member states (Art. K.3). In addition, the Council may apply Article 100c of the EC Treaty to actions in the area of migration (Art. K.9), in effect 'communitarizing' parts of the third pillar. There were early indications from the Reflection Group preparing for the 1996 Intergovernmental Conference that a majority of member states favour a communitarization of parts of the third pillar (see *Agence Europe* 1995*b*). British protest over the European Union's ban on beef suspected of infection with 'mad cow disease' stalled IGC negotiations on co-operation in Justice and Home Affairs, and British resistance will most likely block wholesale communitarization of the third pillar. A compromise that is applicable to all member states put forward by France and Germany that some member states go ahead with integration in some areas of Justice and Home Affairs while allowing some member states, such as the United Kingdom, to opt out, is more likely (Gaunt 1996). Hence, the institutional and legal framework set up by Title VI is actually a mixture of simple intergovernmental co-operation and integration within the Community, and that mixture could well become less intergovernmental in the near future. There-fore, member state sovereignty is somewhat more compromised than in other multilateral forums dealing with migration, and it may soon become even further compromised.

Secondly, to determine the location of sovereignty by drawing a sharp line between the community legal order and international treaties result-ing from multilateral or intergovernmental negotiations is somewhat problematic. Theoretically speaking, one can say that member states retain their sovereignty when signing multilateral or intergovernmental agreements because there is no legal enforcement mechanism similar to the ECJ and these agreements are not binding because they can ultimately be broken by states. As pointed out above, however, this traditional definition of sovereignty as complete state autonomy to act as it will does not even really hold for international relations in gen-eral outside the European Community context. Member states may retain sovereignty by negotiating intergovernmental agreements on migration instead of utilizing the Community legislative process to do so. How-ever, this does not necessarily mean that member states will comply any less with the agreements made. The retained sovereignty may be much more symbolic than substantive.

Finally, one must be careful not to confuse restrictivist common policies with retention of sovereignty. When individual states step up border checks and deport visa overstayers and rejected asylum-seekers they demonstrate state sovereignty through its exercise. However, when a group of states harmonize their migration policies or integrate their migration policy-making institutions, they cede sovereignty regardless of whether the objective of that co-operation or integration is to restrict immigration or encourage it. Co-operation is co-operation; integration is integration. A restrictivist common policy might enable a partici-pating state to assert its sovereignty in the particular area in question, as the Dublin Convention facilitated the change in Germany's asylum law. The co-operation required to enact that common policy, however, itself constrains the range of state actions and can require states to do what they would not otherwise do had the co-operation agreement not been in place. Hence, states may actually sacrifice sovereignty in one dimension in order to exercise it in another.

A hypothetical example may help to clarify this point. If almost all EU member states agreed that the goal of co-operation should be a common policy that opened their common external border and encouraged migration to the European Union and one member state refused to co-operate and stepped up border controls, it would be clear that that state was demonstrating its territorial sovereignty through its exercise as well as retaining its sovereignty *vis-à-vis* the other members of the European Union. But if almost all states agreed to the goal of a restrictivist common policy and one state refused to co-operate and it eliminated border checks at its portion of the common external border, that state may be abdicating territorial sovereignty with respect to migration but it would also be retaining its sovereignty *vis-à-vis* the other EU member states. Although this hypothetical example may seem farfetched because few, if any, individual EU member states have recently encouraged immigration, one could easily see how a very restrictivist common policy on migration would infringe on an individual member state sovereignty in the area of nationality and citizenship.

With the institution of European citizenship, the nationality laws of one EU member state effectively become the boundaries of residence and employment rights of all member states. For example, free movement in the European Union is effectively extended to ethnic Germans from Poland, Romania, Russia, and Khazakhstan because the expanded understanding of German citizenship as delineated in Article 116(1) of the German Basic Law[18] is in effect for community purposes (Plender 1988: 198). A Pole of German ancestry who speaks fluent English, but little German, can claim German nationality, retain his or her Polish nationality, and, as an EU citizen, have the right to reside and work in the United Kingdom. Similarly, having an Irish grandparent entitles one to Irish nationality and therefore EU citizenship. Spain has dual nationality agreements with most Latin American states; nationals from these states do not need visas to enter Spain and they have been able to gain access to the EU labour market via special accelerated naturalization provisions in Spain.[19] Nationals of Portuguese-speaking countries and individuals of Portuguese descent can be exempted from Portugal's residency requirements for naturalization, and those who do not have the requisite ancestry have been able to accelerate naturalization by virtue of purchasing property.[20]

If internal free movement was paired with a highly restrictivist common policy on asylum and external border control which effectively cut potential migrants' existing points of entry to the European Union, potential migrants would have greater incentives to gain access via acquiring a member state nationality. Much as differing asylum policies of individual member states prompted 'asylum shopping', differing nationality laws could prompt 'citizenship shopping', among member states. A restrictivist response of EU member states to harmonize their nationality laws would put pressure on states with relatively open access for particular categories of third-country nationals to change their nationality laws. Fellow EU member states have already put pressure on Portugal to curtail easy naturalization of foreigners who purchase property (O'Nes 1990: 109), and Spain has been under pressure to stop preferential treatment of Latin Americans since the immigration of members of Colombian drug cartels (Starchild 1993: 19). Inasmuch as sovereignty means that a state can make anyone it chooses a citizen, such harmonization represents a loss of sovereignty *vis-à-vis* other member states.

## CONCLUSION

The member states of the European Union have taken international co-operation on migration further than any other states in the world. Member state co-operation on migration not only exceeds that of international co-operation on a global level, it also goes beyond that of other regional organizations of comparable advanced industrialized states. For example, the North American Free Trade Agreement does not directly impinge on member state actions that regulate migration aside from co-operation on the mobility of managerial staff associated with foreign direct investment. In contrast to the Treaty of Rome, NAFTA does not affirm the principle of free movement of workers.[21] When Canada and the United States engaged in negotiations on an agreement that would enable one state to return asylum-seekers who entered via the other they consciously looked to the Dublin Convention as a model (see Neuman 1993: 504).

Unlike international co-operation on migration among other states, EU member state relations are conditioned by a multitude of principles, norms, rules, and decision-making procedures that have become institutionalized in the course of over four decades of practice. In William Wallace's memorable words, the European Union 'is less than a federation, more than a regime' (see Wallace 1983). Likewise, EU regulation of migration can be characterized as not quite that of a federation but also more than that of an international regime. Member state sovereignty with respect to migration within and to the European Union is just as ambiguous: the Union is not quite sovereign over intra-EU migration but more so than the member states; member states are for the most part sovereign over migration from outside the Union, but not as sovereign as non-EU member states owing, in large part, to the constraints of EU membership and the demands of continuing integration in general.

Advocates of European integration generally view increasing co-operation among member states in a positive light. But the consequences of greater co-operation may run counter to other simultaneously held values. Human rights advocates point out that greater co-operation among EU member states may ultimately result in human rights violations if co-operation means increasingly restrictive policies that bar entry of legitimate asylum-seekers, and racist overtones if enforcement is directed at migrants from non-European countries and governed by ascriptive physical characteristics (see Percival 1994; Joly 1992: 107–16). Moreover, given that member state co-operation on migration to the European Union has for the most part remained outside the Community framework, the secrecy and lack of parliamentary oversight that such co-operation entails increases the democratic deficit (see Curtin and Meijers 1995), especially with respect to the rights of the migrants themselves (see Geddes 1995). Hence, from a perspective focusing on human rights and democratic legitimacy, increasing European integration may, in this case, be anathema to the values espoused by member states, individually as liberal democracies under the legal obligations of the European Convention for the Protection of Human Rights (to which all member states are signatories) and collectively as a Union whose criteria for membership includes democratic practice. In short, with the integration of democratic polities, the compromise of sovereignty in co-operative efforts can well mean the compromise of popular sovereignty, regardless of the overall objectives, be they liberal or not in nature.

While increasing co-operation has come at the expense of restrictive policies and decreasing transparency and democratic accountability, the European Parliament and Commission are viewing the IGC revisitation of the Maastricht Treaty with the hope that increasing harmonization of member state migration policies can be achieved without these undesired side-effects. If migration and asylum policy is indeed brought under community competence and into the community legal order, it would be a major step in the development of a regime governing migration to the European Union. While the convergence of member state positions may not be any greater than is currently the case in the various multilateral forums, the increased transparency of legislative processes within the Community framework would work against epistemic communities imbued with the internal security ideology and in favour of epistemic communities focused on developing comprehensive immigration policies dealing with the root causes of migration while carefully protecting human rights. At the same time, bringing immigration and asylum policy under the jurisdiction of the Court would introduce a powerful means of enforcing agreements made, clarifying the rules of the regime, and expanding integration into related areas.

## NOTES

Many thanks to Thomas Heller, Christian Joppke, and an anonymous reviewer for their helpful comments on previous drafts. I also greatly appreciate the financial support for the process of revision provided by the Center for German and European Studies at Georgetown University.

1. On 'high' and 'low' politics, see Aron (1966) and Mark Miller's discussion of Aron's position on migration in Miller (1992: 300–1).
2. 'Regimes can be defined as sets of implicit or explicit principles, norms, rules and decision-making procedures around which actors' expectations converge in a given area of international relations. Principles are beliefs of fact, causation and rectitude. Norms are standards of behaviour defined in terms of rights and obligations. Rules are specific prescriptions or proscriptions for action. Decision-making procedures are prevailing practices for making and implementing collective choice' (Krasner 1983: 2).
3. On the concept of 'spill-over', see E. Haas (1958: 283–317); Nye (1971: 200). On the implicit federal goal of neo-functionalism, see Groom (1978).
4. The sovereign 'cannot in any way be subject to the commands of another, for it is he who makes law for the subject, abrogates laws already made and amends obsolete law' (Bodin 1576/1967: 28).
5. For analytical purposes it is useful to differentiate between migration within the European Union of member state nationals and migration to the European Union of non-EU nationals and attribute different patterns of regime formation to each. This division, however, is problematic because there are many grey areas in between—such as the intra-EU migration of permanent resident aliens from non-EU countries and co-operation on border controls which simultaneously deals with both borders between EU member states and their common external border.
6. Regulation no. 15/61 of the Council of 16 Aug. 1961, cited in Böhning (1972: 11).
7. Regulation no. 38/64 of the Council of 15 Mar. 1964 on the freedom of movement for workers within the Community (*OJ* 1964).

8. Regulation no. 1612/68 of the Council of 15 Oct. 1968 on freedom of movement for workers within the Community *(OJ* 1968).

9. For an overview, see Hailbronner (1994).

10. See Art. 10 of Regulation no. 1612/68 of the Council of 15 Oct. 1968 on freedom of movement for workers within the Community *(OJ* 1968).

11. According to the Court ruling, 'Articles 59 and 60 of the EEC Treaty must be interpreted as precluding a Member State from requiring undertakings which are established in another Member State and enter the first Member State in order to provide services, and which lawfully and habitually employ nationals of non-member countries, to obtain work permits for those working from a national immigration authority and to pay the attendant costs, with the imposition of an administrative fine as the penalty for infringement' (see *Reports of the European Court of Justice*, Case 43/93).

12. Measuring migration using the stock statistics in Table 5.1 must be approached with a degree of caution. They present yearly snapshots of the numbers of EU nationals in each member state. Stocks may change due to deaths of resident alien EU nationals and births in countries in which the children of resident alien EU nationals do not gain citizenship. Also, gathering accurate statistics on recent trends in intra-EU migration becomes difficult because the work and resident permits which previously provided data are often no longer required by host countries. Free movement also permits short-term stays and frontier work in which migrants do not officially register a change in residence.

13. As of the end of Nov. 1995 the Netherlands, Ireland, Austria, Finland, and Sweden had not yet ratified the Convention.

14. For a perspective that stresses member state use of intergovernmental institutions, see Moravcsik (1991).

15. For an overview, see Ucarer (1997).

16. For example, the Mar. 1991 OECD International Conference on Migration, the Nov. 1991 conference, 'The New Europe and International Migration', organized by the Giovanni Angelli Foundation and the Center for Migration Studies, or the Nov. 1993 conference on 'The Use of International Conventions to Protect the Rights of Migrants and Ethnic Minorities', organized by the Churches' Commission for Migrants in Europe, and International Movement against all forms of Discrimination and Racism, under the auspices of Mrs Catherine Lalumière, Secretary-General of the Council of Europe, with the support of the Commission of the European Communities.

17. For a good account of unilateral, bilateral, and multilateral actions regarding asylum policy, see Ucarer (1997).

18. 'Unless otherwise provided by law, a German within the meaning of this Basic Law is a person who possesses German citizenship or who has been admitted to the territory of the German Reich within the frontiers of 31 December 1937 as a refugee or expellee of German stock (*Volkszugehörigkeit*) or as the spouse or descendant of such person.' See the Basic Law printed in Hucko (1987: 255).

19. Nationals of certain Spanish-speaking Latin American states have only a one- or two-year residence requirement for naturalization instead of the usual ten (see Council of Europe 1995: 126).
20. The residency requirement of nationals of Portuguese-speaking states is six instead of ten years; however 'individuals who . . . are reputed to be of Portuguese descent or are members of Portuguese communities abroad, and foreigners who have carried out important work for the Portuguese State or who will be requested to do so in the future' may be dispensed from fulfilling residency and language requirements or demonstrating a 'genuine link to the community' (see Council of Europe 1995: 107). On accelerating naturalization through property purchases, see O'Nes (1990: 107–10).
21. When the Mexican government suggested labour migration be included in negotiations, the United States quickly rejected the idea, knowing full well that any inclusion of labour migration into the Agreement would make ratification impossible (see Weintraub 1992: 507).

# REFERENCES

*Agence Europe* (1995a), 'ECAS Reports Globally Positive Results on Schengen', 29 Apr.

—— (1995b), 'IGC Reflection Group: Majority in Favor of a Clause on Non-Discrimination', 27 Sept.

Anderson, Malcolm, Monica den Boer, and Gary Miller (1994), 'European Citizenship and Cooperation in Justice and Home Affairs', in Andrew Duff, John Prinder, and Roy Price (eds.), *Maastricht and Beyond* (London: Routledge).

*ANP English News Bulletin* (Stichting Algemeen Nederlands Persbureau) (1995), 'Some in EU Share Criticism of its Refugee Policy', 27 Nov.

Aron, Raymond (1966), *Peace and War* (Garden City, NY: Doubleday).

Binyon, Michael (1995), 'Kohl "Heir" Backs EU Army', *The Times*, 2 Nov.

Bodin, Jean (1576/1967), *Six Books of the Commonwealth*, trans. Jean Tooley (Oxford: Oxford University Press).

Böhning, Wolf R. (1972), *The Migration of Workers in the United Kingdom and the European Community* (London: Oxford University Press).

Bull, Hedley (1977), *The Anarchical Society* (New York: Columbia University Press).

Caporaso, James A. (1993), 'International Relations Theory and Multilateralism: The Search for Foundations', in John Gerard Ruggie (ed.), *Multilateralism Matters* (New York: Columbia University Press).

Chayes, Abram, and Antonia Handler (1995), *The New Sovereignty: Compliance with International Regulatory Agreements* (Cambridge, Mass.: Harvard University Press).

Commission of the European Communities (1985), 'A People's Europe: Reports from the *ad hoc* Committee', *Bulletin of the European Communities*, suppl. 7/85.

—— (1994), *Communication from the Commission to the Council and the European Parliament on Immigration and Asylum Policies*, Com (94) 23 final, Brussels, 23 Feb.

Council of Europe (1993), *Existing Fora for Inter-Governmental Co-Operation on Asylum, Refugee and Migration Problems in the European Region, Strasbourg*, 15 Oct. CDMG (93) 20 rev.

—— (1995), *European Bulletin on Nationality*, DIR/JUR (95)1, Strasbourg, 1 Jan.

Curtin, Deirdre, and Herman Meijers (1995), 'The Principle of Open Government in Schengen and the European Union: Democratic Retrogression?', *Common Market Law Review*, 32: 391–442.

den Boer, Monica, and Neil Walker (1993), 'European Policing after 1992', *Journal of Common Market Studies*, 31/1 (Mar.), 6.

*European Insight* (European Information Service) (1995), 'EU Makes Protection of Refugees Less Secure', 1 Dec.

Eurostat (1993*a*), Eurostat CD-ROM database.

—— (1993*b*), *Rapid Reports*, Population and Social Conditions, no. 6 (Luxembourg: Office for Official Publications of the European Communities).

—— (1994), *Demographic Statistics 1994* (Luxembourg: Office for Official Publications of the European Communities).

—— (1995), *Migration Statistics 1995*, Population and Social Conditions (Luxembourg: Office for Official Publications of the European Communities).

—— (1996), 'Asylum-Seekers in Europe 1985–1995', *Statistics in Focus*, Population and Social Conditions, no. 1 (Luxembourg: Office for Official Publications of the European Communities).

Freeman, Gary P. (1994), 'Can Liberal States Control Unwanted Migration?', in Mark J. Miller (ed.), *Annals of the American Academy of Political and Social Science*, 534 (May), Special Issue: *Strategies for Immigration Control*, 17–30.

Funk, Albrecht (1995), 'Immigration Policy of the EU: Common Challenges, Common Responses, Common Policies', paper presented at the Fourth Biennial International Conference of the European Community Studies Association, Charleston, SC, 11–14 May.

Gaunt, Jeremy (1996), 'Flexible Europe is Problem for EU Negotiators', *Reuters European Community Report*, 31 May.

Geddes, Andrew (1995), 'Immigrant and Ethnic Minorities and the EU's "Democratic Deficit"', *Journal of Common Market Studies*, 33/2 (June), 197–212.

Grieco, Joseph M. (1988), 'Anarchy and the Limits of Cooperation: A Realist Critique of the Newest Liberal Institutionalism', *International Organization*, 42 (Aug.), 485–507.

Groom, A. J. R. (1978), 'Neofunctionalism: A Case of Mistaken Identity', *Political Science*, 30/1 (July), 15–28.

Haas, Ernst (1958), *Uniting of Europe: Political, Economic, and Social Forces 1950–1957* (London: Stevens & Sons).

Haas, Peter M. (1992), 'Epistemic Communities and International Policy Coordination', introd. to *International Organization*, 46/1 (Winter), Special Issue: *Knowledge, Power and International Policy Coordination*, 1–36.

Hailbronner, Kay (1994), 'Visa Regulations and Third Country National in EC Law', *Common Market Law Review*, 31: 969–95.

Hendrickson, David C. (1992), 'Migration in Law and Ethics: A Realist Perspective', in Brian Barry and Robert E. Goodin, *Free Movement in the Transnational Immigration of People and of Money* (University Park: Pennsylvania State University Press).

Hoffman, Stanley (1966), 'Obstinate or Obsolete? The Fate of the Nation-State and the Case of Western Europe', *Daedalus*, 95: 862–915.

Hollifield, James F. (1992a), *Immigrants, Markets, and States* (Cambridge, Mass.: Harvard University Press).

—— (1992b), 'Migration and International Relations: Cooperation and Control in the European Community', *International Migration Review*, 26/2 (Summer), 568–95.

Hovy, Bela, and Hania Zlotnik (1994), 'Europe without Internal Frontiers and International Migration', *Population Bulletin of the United Nations*, no. 36: 19–42.

Hucko, Elmar M. (1987), *The Democratic Tradition: Four German Constitutions* (New York: Berg).

*International Intelligence Report* (1994), 'Kohl Views 1993 Achievements, 1994 Tasks', 3 Jan.

Jackson, Robert H. (1990), *Quasi-States: Sovereignty, International Relations and the Third World* (Cambridge: Cambridge University Press).

Johnson, Esther, and David O'Keefe (1994), 'From Discrimination to Obstacles to Free Movement: Recent Developments concerning the Free Movement of Workers 1989–1994', *Common Market Law Review*, 31: 1313–46.

Joly, Daniele (1992), *Refugees: Asylum in Europe?* (Boulder, Colo.: Westview Press).

Keohane, Robert O., and Stanley Hoffman (1991), 'Institutional Change in Europe in the 1980s', in R. O. Keohane and S. Hoffmann (eds.), *The New European Community: Decisionmaking and Institutional Change* (Boulder, Colo.: Westview Press).

Koslowski, Rey (1994a), 'International Migration, European Political Institutions and International Relations Theory', Ph.D. diss., University of Pennsylvania.

—— (1994b), 'Intra-EU Migration, Citizenship and Political Union', *Journal of Common Market Studies*, 32/3 (Sept.), 378, 387–9.

Koslowski, Rey (1995), 'Dual Nationality in Germany, Changing European Norms and International Relations', paper prepared for the Fourth Biennial International Conference of the European Community Studies Association, Charleston, SC, 11–14 May.

Krasner, Stephen D. (1983), 'Structural Causes and Regime Consequences: Regimes as Intervening Variables', in S. D. Krasner (ed.), *International Regimes* (Ithaca, NY: Cornell University Press).

Kratochwil, Friedrich (1995), 'Sovereignty as *dominium*: Is there a Right of Humanitarian Intervention?', in Gene M. Lyons and Michael Mastanduno, *Beyond Westphalia: State Sovereignty and International Intervention* (Baltimore: Johns Hopkins University Press).

Loescher, Gil (1993), *Beyond Charity: International Cooperation and the Global Refugee Crisis* (Oxford: Oxford University Press).

—— (1994), 'The International Refugee Regime: Stretched to the Limit?', *Journal of International Affairs*, 47/2: 351–77.

Mearsheimer, John J. (1990), 'Back to the Future: Instability in Europe after the Cold War', *International Security*, 15 (Summer), 5–56.

*Migrant News* (1995), 'Germany: Asylum, Illegals, and Ethnics', 2/9 (Sept.).

*Migration News Sheet* (1995*a*), 'Paris still Mistrusts the External Border Checks Made by its Partner', no. 51/95–10 (Oct.), 2–3.

—— (1995*b*), 'More Mobile Police Checks', no. 152/95–11 (Nov.), 1.

Miller, Mark J. (1992), 'Evolution of Policy Models for Regulating International Labour Migration', in Mary M. Kritz, Lin Lean Lim, and Hania Zlotnik, *International Migration Systems: A Global Approach* (Oxford: Clarendon Press).

Molle, W., and A. W. van Mourik (1988), 'International Movements of Labour under Conditions of Economic Integration: The Case of Western Europe', *Journal of Common Market Studies*, 26/3: 317–42.

Moravcsik, Andrew (1991), 'Negotiating the Single European Act: National Interests and Conventional Statecraft in the European Community', *International Organization*, 45/1: 651–88.

Morgenthau, Hans (1973), *Politics among Nations*, 5th edn. (New York: Knopf).

Neuman, Gerald L. (1993), 'Buffer Zones against Refugees: Dublin, Schengen, and the German Asylum Amendment', *Virginia Journal of International Law*, 33/3 (Spring), 503–26.

Niessen, Jan (1994), 'The Role of Non-Governmental Organizations in Standard Setting and Promoting Rectification', in Julie Cator and J. Niessen (eds.), *The Use of International Conventions to Protect the Rights of Migrants and Ethnic Minorities* (Strasbourg: Churches Commission for Migrants in Europe).

Nye, Joseph S., Jr. (1971), 'Comparing Common Markets: A Revised Neofunctional Model', in Leon N. Lindberg and Stuart A. Scheingold (eds.), *Regional Integration: Theory and Research* (Cambridge, Mass.: Harvard University Press).

*OJ (Official Journal of the European Communities)* (1964), no. 965/64.
—— (1968), no. L257/2.

O'Nes, D. (1990), *The Guide to Legally Obtaining a Foreign Passport* (New York: Shapolsky Publishers).

Orzack, Louis (1991), 'The General Systems Directive and the Liberal Professions', in Leon Hurwitz and Christian Lequesne (eds.), *The State of the European Community: Policies, Institutions, and Debates in the Transition Years* (Boulder, Colo.: Lynne Rienner Publishers).

Percival, Debra (1994), 'Europe—Human Rights: Amnesty Attacks EU Asylum Seeker Laws', *Inter Press Service*, 22 June, *Nexis* release.

Plender, Richard (1988), *International Migration Law* (Dordrecht: Martinus Nijhoff).

Presidency, European Council (1992), Conclusions of the Presidency, European Council in Edinburgh, 11–12 Dec.

Putnam, Robert D. (1988), 'Diplomacy and Domestic Politics: The Logic of Two Level Games', *International Organization*, 42 (Summer), 427–61.

Risse-Kappen, Thomas (ed.) (1995), *Bringing Transnational Relations back In: Non-State Actors, Domestic Structures and International Institutions* (Cambridge: Cambridge University Press).

Rousseau, Jean-Jacques (1760/1991), 'Abstract and Judgement of Saint-Pierre's Project for Perpetual Peace', in Stanley Hoffmann and David P. Fidler, *Rousseau on International Relations* (Oxford: Clarendon Press).

Salt, John (1992), 'Migration Processes among the Highly Skilled in Europe', *International Migration Review*, 26/2: 484–505.

Santel, Bernard (1995), 'Loss of Control: The Build-Up of a European Migration and Asylum Regime', in Robert Miles and Dietrich Thränhardt (eds.), *Migration and European Integration* (London: Pinter Press).

Savill, Anika (1992), 'Hurd Urges EC to Focus on Migration', *Independent*, 16 Sept., 10.

Starchild, Adam (1993), *Second Passports and Dual Nationality* (Baltimore: Agora).

Straubhaar, Thomas (1988), 'International Labour Migration within a Common Market: Some Aspects of EC Experience', *Journal of Common Market Studies*, 27: 45–62.

*Treaty on European Union* (1992) (Luxembourg: Office for the Official Publications of the European Communities).

Tucker, Emma (1995), 'Schengen Pact Open to Non-EU Members', *The Financial Times*, 25 Oct., 3.

Ucarer, Emek M. (1997), 'Europe's Search for Policy: Asylum Policy Harmonization and European Integration', in E. M. Ucarer and Donal J. Puchala (eds.), *Immigration in Western Societies: Problems and Policies* (London: Pinter Press).

UNHCR (United Nations High Commission for Refugees) (1993), *The State of the World's Refugees* (New York: Penguin).

Wallace, William (1983), 'Less than a Federation, More than a Regime: The Community as a Political System', in H. Wallace, W. Wallace, and C. Webb (eds.), *Policy-Making in the European Community* (New York: John Wiley).

Waltz, Kenneth (1959), *Man, the State and War* (New York: Columbia University Press).

—— (1979), *Theory of International Politics* (New York: Random House).

Weintraub, Sidney (1992), 'North American Free Trade and the European Situation Compared', *International Migration Review*, 26/2 (Summer), 507.

Werner, Heinz (1993), 'Migration Movements in the Perspective of the European Single Market', in Organization for Economic Co-operation and Development, *The Changing Course of International Migration* (Paris: OECD).

Widgren, Jonas (1990), 'International Migration and Regional Stability', *International Affairs*, 66/4 (Oct.), 749–66.

# PART II

# The Challenge to Citizenship

# PART II

## The Obligations of Citizenship

# 6

# The Re-Evaluation of American Citizenship

## PETER H. SCHUCK

Citizenship is very much on America's collective mind. Congress is busily redefining it. Intellectuals are writing books about it. Citizens are debating whether it has lost its meaning. Aliens are lining up to apply for it in unprecedented numbers. What, one may ask, is going on here?

Citizenship talk proceeds through several different tropes. Sometimes we advance it as a powerful aspirational ideal. In this normative usage, it serves as a proxy or place-holder for our deepest commitments to a common life. Citizens, in this view, mutually pledge their trust and concern for each other and their full participation in shared civic and civil cultures. Sometimes—perhaps even at the *same* time—we also deploy citizenship as a positive concept. In this positive usage, it describes a legal–political status that some individuals enjoy, some can only aspire to, and still others have little hope of ever attaining. Here, citizenship defines a relationship between individuals and the polity in which citizens owe allegiance to their polity—they must not betray it and may have to serve it—while the polity owes its citizens the fullest measure of protection that its law affords, including (except for minors and some convicted felons) the right to vote.

These two uses of citizenship—the normative and the positive—are linked rhetorically, and perhaps even psychologically. Like the serpents on a caduceus, they are tightly intertwined. We often use the ideal of citizenship as a standard against which to evaluate the actual conduct of others, hurling the ideal as an accusation, bitterly condemning what we do not like about contemporary life and ascribing it to the defects of our fellow citizens. Whether the offence is the despoilment of public spaces in our cities, the failure to vote in our elections, the violence in our schools and neighbourhoods, or the erosion of our families, we indict not only the individual perpetrators but the polity that, by debasing citizenship, has fostered or at least countenanced these wrongs. At times —and today seems such a time—our despair may be so great that we wonder whether we remain one people dedicated to common purposes. The most disillusioned of us may conclude that citizenship should be a privilege that requires us to be better in order to claim it, a prize that can be earned only through greater rectitude.

It is precisely at these censorious moments, however, that citizenship's positive meaning can check the harsh, exclusionary impulses that its normative meaning reflexively arouses in us. When we are tempted to say (or feel) that our fellow citizens should 'shape up or ship out', or should 'love our country or leave it', we may recall that our law does not view citizenship as a reward for civic virtue. The target of criticism may respond with what he imagines is a rhetorical trump: 'It's a free country'. But far from silencing the critic, this reply simply invites a rebuttal in which he invokes his underlying conception of freedom—and of citizenship. So the conversation goes.

In the United States today, this conversation is particularly heated. Not since the McCarthy era in the early 1950s, when many Americans aggressively questioned the loyalty of their fellow citizens, relatively few immigrants were admitted, and relatively few of those sought to become citizens, has citizenship talk been so energetic and morally charged. In Congress, at the bar of public opinion, and even in the courts, citizenship in both its normative and positive dimensions is being closely re-examined. Indeed, Congress adopted welfare reform and immigration control laws in 1996 that were intended, among other goals, to increase sharply the value of American citizenship while reducing the value of permanent legal resident status. As of June 1997, moreover, some members of Congress were calling for legislation that would restrict the availability of naturalized citizenship, birthright (*jus soli*) citizenship, and plural citizenship.

In this chapter, I explore the reasons why Americans are arguing more passionately about citizenship today, and why some of the rules that have long structured this status are under vigorous assault. I shall argue that the intensity of this debate reflects the tensions that arise within and among three analytically distinct relational domains, each of which is characterized by a distinctive problematic, a wrenching conflict between competing and deeply held values.

The first domain is international law and politics. Here the nation defines the scope of its sovereignty by classifying all individuals as either insiders or outsiders. By insiders, I mean those whom the polity brings into its constitutional community by granting them legal rights against it. The American constitutional community includes citizens, legal resident aliens, and in some cases illegal aliens. Outsiders are everybody else in the world. The United States defines its sovereignty in this international domain largely, but not exclusively, in terms of its power over territory; its constitutional community embraces virtually all individuals within its national borders and territories, as well as some who are outside them but to whom the United States has acknowledged some special political and legal relationship. The distinctive problematic in this domain is a tension between the values of national sovereignty and autonomy and the reality that many outsiders possess the power to transform themselves into insiders without the nation's consent and beyond its effective control.

The second domain is national politics. Here, public law classifies the body of insiders into different categories, defining what the polity owes to each of them and what they in turn owe to the polity. Its distinctive problematic is a tension between the values of equal treatment and communal self-definition, and the reality of limited resources. This tension is particularly delicate because it encourages the marginalization not only of outsiders but of some insiders as well. The meaning of citizenship in the national political domain is highly controversial in the United States today because it is intimately connected to bitterly divisive questions about the welfare state—its essential legitimacy, its moral character, its purposes, its programmatic scope, and its availability to citizens and to various categories of aliens.

The third domain is federalism—the structural division of the American polity into multiple, overlapping sovereignties. (As I note below, I mean to include in 'sovereignties' both public and private governance regimes to which individuals may be subjected.) Each individual possesses a civic status in the national polity and in a state polity. She may also live in a private enclave in which her status is regulated, often extensively, by contract. Different rights and duties attach to these diverse statuses. Federalism's distinctive problematic is a tension between the values of equality and uniformity, which the nation can promote through its power to unify the same policy throughout its territory, and the value of diversity among, and responsiveness to, the policies advanced by different states and contractual regimes. In this domain, as in that of national politics, Americans are bitterly debating the meaning of citizenship in the most divisive of contexts: a fundamental reconsideration of the welfare state. In August 1996 the United States adopted a welfare reform law—forged through a remarkable bipartisan consensus—that constitutes perhaps the most far-reaching change in American social policy since the foundations of its welfare state were established during the New Deal. I discuss these reforms in a later section on citizenship in the federal system.

The chapter is divided into three parts, corresponding to these three domains of citizenship. In each, I discuss how changing conditions, ideas, and values have provoked a re-evaluation of American citizenship by deepening its characteristic tensions. Before concluding the chapter, I offer some brief and tentative observations on the notion, which has recently come into academic vogue, of what is commonly called 'post-national citizenship'.


## CITIZENSHIP IN THE INTERNATIONAL DOMAIN

In dividing up the world's population into insiders and outsiders, the United States is remarkably inclusive, at least relative to other polities. This inclusiveness takes a number of different forms. First, the United States has adopted a very liberal legal immigration policy, admitting approximately 800,000 aliens each year (the precise number fluctuates considerably) for permanent residence. (The number of legal immigrants actually admitted was 915,000 in 1996, 720,000 in 1995, 804,000 in 1994, and 904,000 in 1993.) This annual influx probably exceeds the legal admissions totals of the rest of the world combined. Moreover, the United States has increased its legal admissions during the 1990s, a period during which other countries have been restricting it. When Congress overhauled US immigration laws in 1996, it resisted intense political pressures to reduce the number of legal admissions. Hence the post-1990 growth in the legal immigration system remains in place. Secondly, the United States in the late 1980s and early 1990s extended legal permanent resident status to nearly 2.7 million illegal aliens through a massive amnesty, a programme to legalize their dependants, and more conventional immigration remedies. Thirdly, a combination of expansive *jus sanguinis* and *jus soli* rules extends citizenship very broadly— to essentially all individuals who are born on US soil, regardless of their parents' legal status, all children born abroad to two American parents, and many children born abroad to one American parent. Fourthly, US naturalization requirements are relatively easy—indeed, some say, too easy—to satisfy. From 1990 to 1995 the United States naturalized between 240,000 and 446,000 aliens a year; approximately 1.3 million naturalization petitions were filed in 1996, the largest in history. Propelled by welfare law changes that restrict many benefits to citizens, further increases in petitions—up to an estimated 1.8 million in 1997—are expected. (The Immigration and Naturalization Service (INS) rejected 200,000 petitions in 1996; 965,000 petitions were pending in March 1997.) Fifthly, dual (and even triple) citizenship is increasingly common, and the State Department no longer opposes it in principle.

Finally, more than 1 million aliens enter the United States illegally each year; some 250,000 to 300,000 of these remain in illegal status more or less permanently, producing an illegal population now estimated at over 5 million. Simply by virtue of their presence in the United States, they can claim extensive procedural rights, and in some cases substantive entitlements as well, under the Constitution, statutes, and administrative rules, although the 1996 amendments to the immigration statute severely limited some of these rights, especially for those who entered the United States illegally. Even excludable aliens stopped at the border, who possess only the most elementary constitutional rights (e.g. access to the courts; freedom from physical abuse), can claim many statutory rights under US law.

In the international arena, the principal force reshaping Americans' conceptions of citizenship is the growing anxiety aroused by their perception that their national sovereignty is under serious challenge. Three recent developments are particularly salient: the globalization of the US economy; the increase in immigration, particularly illegal immigration; and a more general diminution of American autonomy in the world.

## Globalization

The integration of the world economy—its 'globalization', in the already hackneyed phrase—has proceeded at an ever-quickening pace. This integration, moreover, is comprehensive, encompassing all factors of production, distribution, and communication including goods, services, capital, technology, intellectual property rules, and (most pertinent for present purposes) labour. The US economy, while primarily focused on its enormous domestic market,[1] has in recent years become a nimble exporter and importer of capital and, to a lesser extent, of jobs. A number of factors strongly suggest that this trend will continue. Powerful economic and political interests are driving it, while enfeebled labour unions lack the bargaining-power to arrest, much less reverse, it. American producers, no longer able to count on policies protecting them from foreign competition, are rationalizing their operations by sending low-skill jobs abroad while importing high-skill technicians, managers, and professionals where needed.

Nowhere is the force of this globalization dynamic more apparent than in the formation of regional free trade blocs and their gradual extension—through the inclusion of new members, merger with other such blocs, and coverage of additional goods and services. This dynamic first occurred in Europe with the progressive expansion of the Treaty of Rome leading to the European Union and its absorption of much of the former European Free Trade Area and its addition of other new members and trade sectors. For the United States, of course, the crucial development has been the creation of the North American Free Trade Agreement (NAFTA), which is likely to be enlarged eventually to include Chile and perhaps other hemispheric nations, as well as being extended to include other areas of economic activity. Long before NAFTA, of course, the United States and Mexican governments had concluded a number of formal and informal arrangements involving economic activities in the border areas and the control of migration to the United States from South and Central America. NAFTA has altered and extended these arrangements, with consequences that will not be well understood for years to come.

For present purposes, the important point is that these developments signal a growing recognition by the US government that America's fate is increasingly linked to that of her neighbours, her other trading partners, and the rest of the world. These linked fates are not merely economic but are also demographic, social, and political. The United States is increasingly vulnerable to the immense migratory pressures being generated by conditions beyond both her borders and her control. These 'push' factors are magnified and reinforced by powerful, indeed tidal, 'pull' factors: a vast and burgeoning American economy that often prefers foreign workers to domestic ones, a dynamic American culture that promises immigrants great personal freedom and mobility, and grooved pathways of kinship-based chain migration that constantly creates and replenishes immigrant and ethnic communities in the United States.

## *Migration*

Since 1965 immigration to the United States has been transformed in virtually every vital aspect.[2] The legal immigration streams have swelled both in absolute terms and as a percentage of the overall population. Even more important than the size of these streams, the 'look and feel' of American society has changed dramatically with the changing mix of the newcomers' national origins, races, and languages. All of this has occurred in a relatively short period of time, generating cultural, economic, and social anxieties among many Americans.

But it is *illegal* migration that is primarily driving the political dimension of this debate. The volume of illegal migration has grown fairly steadily during the last three decades except for the period immediately following the enactment of the employer sanctions provisions of the Immigration Reform and Control Act of 1986, when the number declined. This decline, however, proved to be brief; by 1990 the number had already returned approximately to its pre-1986 level; the permanent illegal population now exceeds 5 million. Even the extraordinary growth in the resources devoted to border control during the last five years, especially when compared to the retrenchment in other federal programmes, shows no clear sign of stemming this influx (as opposed to rechannelling it). The continuing ineffectiveness of border control is a source of enormous frustration to Americans and their politicians, especially in the relatively small number of communities with high concentrations of illegals. At the same time, Americans have become both more dependent on illegal workers and more aware of this dependence, which for many employers, consumers, and communities can approach an addiction. This can produce hypocrisy of comical dimensions. California Governor Pete Wilson, for example, sought to build a political movement by denouncing illegal aliens, only to be caught employing them in his household and then failing to pay their social security benefits!

Because many Americans feel beleaguered and victimized by illegal immigration, it is profoundly affecting their political identity. These feelings are intensifying as the large cohort of former illegal aliens who received amnesty in the late 1980s begin to become US citizens in large numbers, many impelled by a desire to assure their access to welfare state benefits. Moreover, the families of these amnestied illegals are now exerting strong pressures on the *legal* immigration system, competing with the more compelling claims of legal immigrants' relatives who wish to join their families in the United States. Congress is also considering whether to eliminate automatic birthright (*jus soli*) citizenship for the US-born children of illegal alien parents. None of these proposals, however, is likely to be enacted. In 1997 Congress may take up the question of whether the naturalization law should be changed in light of concerns that many immigrants are naturalizing fraudulently, for the wrong motives, or too easily.

As the number of illegal aliens grows, their position in the American polity becomes increasingly anomalous. Americans admire the tenacity, hard work, and resourcefulness of illegal aliens (at least the majority who do not commit crimes in the United States) but at the same time deeply resent their furtive success in penetrating US territory, working in US jobs, earning (and exporting) dollars, and securing legal status—even the ultimate prize, citizenship—for themselves and their families. As the voting for California's Proposition 187 demonstrated, many legal resident aliens and recently naturalized citizens are also strongly opposed to illegal migration (Schuck 1995). The fact that the United States has long countenanced illegal migrants, derived tax revenues and other economic benefits from them, and built important sectors of her economy around their continued flow arouses cognitive dissonance, but it does not really alter the resentment. Although the number of illegals residing in the United States now is probably higher than the number whose plight prompted the 1986 legalization, Congress will certainly not propose a new amnesty in the foreseeable future. Americans believe that illegal aliens impose large costs on American society, but even if they did not believe this they would still demand the interdiction and expulsion of illegals. After all, illegals are like trespassers; they have no right to enter or remain. Control of illegal migration, then, is not merely a pragmatic policy goal; it assumes the character of a legal duty and a moral crusade, as evidenced by the far-reaching immigration control legislation enacted in 1996. Americans' conceptions of citizenship reflect these imperatives.

### Diminished Autonomy

The massive breaching of American borders by illegal aliens is most vivid evidence of her vulnerability; 'invasion' and 'flood' are the metaphors that are conventionally used to describe the influx. Americans, however, are experiencing a more general sense of unease that their national destiny is moving beyond their control. This anxiety springs from many sources. I have already mentioned growing US reliance on the global economy; American prosperity now depends almost as much on public and private decisions in Tokyo, Bonn, and Hong Kong as it does on those in Washington or Wall Street. But the loss of control is not confined to the economic realm. The protracted trauma of the Vietnam War convinced many Americans that the United States can no longer work its will in the world militarily. The geopolitical fragmentation with the end of the Cold War has left the United States as the sole remaining superpower, yet the American Goliath is now at the mercy of myriad ethnic rivalries and subnational conflicts that defy international intervention and order. Even threats to public health, traditionally the province of national governments, increasingly cross national borders, as the recent examples of AIDS, dengue fever, tuberculosis, and other communicable diseases suggest. Public concern with international terrorism, galvanized by several notorious bombing incidents, adds to Americans' anxieties about this loss of control.

The world has always been a dangerous place. Most Americans probably believe that it is more dangerous today than ever before, although precisely the opposite is true—at least for them but also for many others. They evidently feel growing insecurity about their jobs, marriages, safety, and personal future. People in such a state of uncertainty naturally search for safe havens from these storms. Their citizenship serves as a dependable anchorage; it gives them a secure mooring in an increasingly intrusive, turbulent, uncontrollable 'worldwind'. A valuable legal status, it can never be taken away. It defines who is a member of the extended political family, which, like its natural counterpart, offers some consolation in a harsh world. We imagine that we can count on the company of citizens to join us in a search for the common good. Our concern for our fellow citizens is usually greater than that for the rest of humankind. They share our lifeboat and are in it for the long haul.

Citizenship thus imparts to the polity a special shape and expectancy —in the United States, a common claim to enjoy the 'American way of life'. The more perplexing and menacing we find the world and the more buffeting its gales of change, the more tenaciously we cling to our citizenship's value and insist on maintaining it.[3] David Jacobson, drawing on the conceptions of Mircea Eliade and Benedict Anderson, suggests that this tenacity is driven by an even more profound disorientation—a crisis of what he calls the desacralization of territory.

'The nation', he writes, 'is the primordial center, the ultimate point of reference, for its members. . . . In being boundary oriented, the (nation)-state depends on those boundaries being effectively maintained. The entry of undocumented or illegal immigrants, or the settlement of guest workers, is not simply a violation of the law of the recipient country. It is a violation of sacred space and of a primordial category' (Jacobson 1996: 131).

## CITIZENSHIP IN THE DOMESTIC DOMAIN

If citizenship provides succour to Americans in their confrontation with the outside world, it also promises them political and social standing and national identity in the domestic one. Here, citizenship crowns a hierarchy of statuses, with each one bearing a distinctive set of legal rights and obligations.[4] David Martin has suggested that this domain may be represented metaphorically by concentric circles; a community of citizens at the central core is surrounded by a series of more peripheral status categories with ever more attenuated ties to the polity, weaker claims on it, and more limited rights against it (Martin 1983). Citizenship's normative meaning can be inferred from (among other things) the magnitude and nature of the gap between citizens and those in the outer circles with respect to their rights and duties.

American citizenship, as Alexander Bickel (1975: 54) famously observed, 'is at best a simple idea for a simple government'. By this, he meant that the ratification of the Fourteenth Amendment to the Constitution made membership in the American polity widely and easily available, that the legal rights and duties associated with citizenship have long ceased to be an important or divisive public issue, and that this consensus has been both firm and highly desirable. In an article published in 1989, I found merit in Bickel's point and suggested that it was probably even truer then than it had been in 1973 when he asserted it.[5]

Today, however, Bickel's (and my) confident assurances seem embarrassingly premature. In a radically altered political environment, the question of citizenship is now both salient and divisive. To understand the larger significance of what has transpired, it is necessary to describe the basic structure of US citizenship law, and the differences between the rights and duties of citizens and those of legal permanent residents (LPRs). I shall then discuss the re-evaluation of citizenship that is now occurring in the United States in the shadow of more funda-mental debates—notably, debates concerning the role of immigration in America's future and the legitimacy and shape of the welfare state.

### The Structure of US Citizenship Law

US citizenship can be acquired in three ways. The most common way—citizenship by birth in the United States—reflects the Anglo-American tradition of *jus soli* (although the United Kingdom no longer strongly adheres to it, while France does; Weil 1995), and it is pro-tected by the Fourteenth Amendment's Citizenship Clause.[6] Judicial interpretation of the Citizenship Clause has long been understood as extending this status to the native-born children of aliens who are in the country, even if illegally or on a temporary visa. This interpreta-tion has never been seriously questioned in the courts, although it has recently come under scrutiny, and some criticism, from some politi-cians, commentators, and scholars (Schuck and Smith 1985).[7]

A second route to citizenship is through naturalization. In 1994 more than 407,000 individuals naturalized; this represented a 30 per cent increase over the 1993 figure. The total for 1995 reached 446,000, approximately the record level set in 1944 during the Second World War. To naturalize, an LPR must have resided in the United States with that status for five years, be of good moral character, demonstrate an ability to speak, read, and write English; and demonstrate a basic knowledge of US government and history. More than 85 per cent of all naturalizations take place under these general provisions, although some people are permitted to use less restrictive procedures. Spouses of American citizens can naturalize after only three years; children who immigrate with their parents can be naturalized more or less automat-ically (simply by obtaining a certificate) when their parents naturalize; and adopted children of US citizens can also naturalize in that fash-ion. Certain aliens who served with the American military during past wars may naturalize easily. Some individual or group naturalizations are effectuated directly by statute. It is significant that a large number of citizenship-eligible aliens choose not to naturalize.[8]

The third route to citizenship is through descent from one or more American parents. The principle of *jus sanguinis* is codified in the statute. For example, a child born outside the United States of two citi-zen parents is a citizen if one of the parents resided in the United States prior to the child's birth. If one of the parents is an alien but the citizen parent was physically present in the United States or an outlying possession for a period or periods totalling five years, two of which were after the age of 14, the child is a citizen. Over time, Congress has liberalized these eligibility requirements.

Plural citizenships are quite common in the United States due to the combination of the American *jus soli* rule with the various *jus sanguinis* rules of other countries. Thus aliens who naturalize in the United States must renounce their prior allegiance. This renunciation may or may not effectively terminate that foreign citizenship under that state's law, but US naturalization law—unlike Germany's—does not require that the renunciation actually have that legal effect. In this sense, and also by permitting US citizens to naturalize elsewhere, the US government tolerates and protects plural citizenships.[9] Since most of the countries of origin from which the largest cohorts of immigrants to the United States come—Mexico, the Philippines, the Dominican Republic, Canada, and India—recognize children born to their nationals abroad as citizens, plural citizenship among Americans is rapidly increasing (Spiro 1997; Schuck 1998).

US citizenship, once acquired, is virtually impossible to lose without the citizen's express consent. Supreme Court decisions since the 1960s have severely restricted the government's power to denationalize a citizen for reasons of disloyalty, divided allegiance, or otherwise. Today, the government cannot prevail against a birthright or *jus sanguinis* citizen unless it can prove that the citizen specifically intended to renounce his or her citizenship. This standard is difficult to satisfy— as it should be. Relatively few denationalization proceedings are brought and the number of successful ones is probably declining. Denaturalization proceedings against citizens who procured citizenship by misrepresenting their back-grounds or through other illegality are largely directed against Nazi and Soviet persecutors, and under a 1988 decision of the Supreme Court (*Kungys* v. *United States*), the standards that the government must satisfy to prevail are quite demanding.

### Advantages of Citizenship Status

Until the statutory changes adopted by Congress in 1996, the differences between the legal rights enjoyed by citizens and those enjoyed by LPRs were more political than legal or economic, and those differences had narrowed considerably over time. In the same 1989 article referred to earlier, I argued that the narrowing of these differences constituted a 'devaluation' of citizenship, one that raised important questions about the evolving political identity of the United States. Today, partly in response to widespread dissatisfaction with this devaluation, a *re-evaluation* of citizenship is in progress, one in which the differentiation of the rights of citizens and LPRs is a central theme.

The power of Congress to treat citizens and LPRs differently is subject to certain constitutional constraints. First, US courts have established that the constitutionality of government-imposed discriminations between citizens and aliens turns in part on whether the discrimination being challenged is imposed by the federal government or by a state. In several Supreme Court decisions during the 1970s, the Court held that Congress could exclude resident aliens from public benefits under Medicare (and presumably under other federal programmes as well), but that the states could not do so without the federal government's blessing. Since then, the constitutional rationale for decisions restricting the states' power to discriminate may have changed. The Court originally seemed to view state law discriminations on the basis of alienage as a 'suspect classification' like race, which under the Equal Protection Clause would impose a very heavy, probably impossible, burden on the state to demonstrate that its interest in discriminating against aliens was 'compelling' and narrowly tailored to achieve its purpose. In subsequent cases, however, the Court rested its decisions on a different constitutional theory based on the Supremacy Clause, not the Equal Protection Clause. This latter theory, known as 'federal pre-emption', is discussed below and in the next section, 'Citizenship in the Federal System', as are the recent developments in federalism reflected in the 1996 welfare reform law.

Despite these constitutional constraints on discrimination against aliens, some noteworthy differences in legal right were established long before the 1996 changes which significantly increased those differences were enacted. Three are political in nature: the right to vote, the right to serve on federal and many state juries, and the right to run for certain high elective offices and to be appointed to some high (and not-so-high) appointive ones. Each of these restrictions seems to be premised on one or more of the following assumptions: that aliens' political socialization is too fragmentary and embryonic to be trusted in matters of public choice; that confining political participation of this kind to citizens carries an important symbolic message about the value and significance of full membership; and that exclusion of aliens from such participation encourages them to naturalize as soon as possible.

Although aliens enjoyed the franchise in many American states during the nineteenth century, only US citizens may exercise it today—a rule that applies in virtually all other countries as well, at least in national elections. A number of local communities have allowed aliens (some even include illegals) to vote in some or all of their local elections, and proposals to extend the franchise to aliens have been advanced in several large cities, including Washington and Los Angeles. In addition, some academic commentators support such a change, drawing on the historical precedent for alien voting and on liberal, republican, and natural rights theories (Rosberg 1977: 1092; Raskin 1993: 1391; Neuman 1992: 259, 291–335).

Most individual LPRs (as distinct from immigrants' rights advocates) probably do not view their inability to vote as a major disadvantage, although they may well resent the second-class status that this disability implies. (US citizens, it should be noted, usually decline to vote; only 49 per cent of those eligible to vote in the 1996 presidential election and 38 per cent of the eligibles in the 1994 congressional elections cast their ballots—a higher rate than in recent off-year elections.) Their collective political identities have focused far more on ethnicity than on alienage *per se*; most empowerment campaigns have been mounted by ethnic organizations and promote naturalization, not legal changes to allow aliens to vote. (Indeed, Congress in 1996 made it a federal crime for aliens to vote in federal elections, and made voting in violation of any federal, state, or local law and ground for removal.) But now that Congress is changing the law to disadvantage legal aliens as a class, the political salience of alienage *per se* and hence the value that aliens place on the vote are likely to increase in the future.

Citizenship requirements for jury service are less of an issue in the United States. In the framing of the Bill of Rights, which protected the right to trial by jury in both criminal and civil cases, the jury service was seen as an important political, as well as legal, institution protecting the people from the oppression of governmental and private élites. Prior to the notorious O. J. Simpson trial, Americans esteemed the institution. Although most serve on it conscientiously, many also view it as less a privilege than a burden. Unlike the right to vote, the notion of extending jury service to aliens has not surfaced in the recent public debate about improving the jury system.

Aliens' ineligibility for federal employment, which is similar to the practice in virtually all nations,[10] is likely to be of greater concern to many of them than their inability to serve on juries. Few if any LPRs are likely to seek high elective or appointive offices during the period prior to naturalization. Many LPRs, however, might want to pursue employment in the federal, state, and local civil service systems. In two Supreme Court decisions in the mid-1970s, the Court applied the constitutional principles relating to discrimination against aliens in the civil service setting. It held that the Constitution permitted Congress and the President to limit federal civil service jobs to citizens (which has been done since the 1880s) but that the states could not impose citizenship requirements for their own civil service systems. The Court emphasized the exclusive federal interest in regulating immigration, a principle that is discussed more fully below. It recognized, however, the state's power to exclude LPRs from particular job categories that represented the state's 'political function', such as schoolteachers and police officers. This distinction has proved exceedingly difficult to apply but continues to enjoy the Court's support.

Two other disadvantages to LPRs are worth mentioning. First, LPRs have a lesser right to sponsor their family members for immigration. As noted earlier, 'immediate relatives' of citizens receive a preferred immigration status without regard to numerical quotas, and citizens' siblings and adult children have a preferred status under the numerical quota system. In contrast, the spouses and unmarried children of resident aliens qualify for only a numerically limited preference, and their siblings receive no preference at all.

Many policy-makers, including the US Commission on Immigration Reform, are concerned about the potential chain migration effects triggered by the large overhang of imminent naturalizations by many of the almost 2.7 million illegal aliens who were legalized under the 1986 amnesty programme, are now LPRs, and will soon be citizens, enabling their immediate family members—and in turn *their* family members—to immigrate legally to the United States in large numbers. Congress, under considerable political pressure to reduce legal immigration, could decide to limit LPRs' family immigration rights further, or even to limit the family immigration rights of *US citizens* who achieved that status only by virtue of the amnesty programme enacted in 1986. Such a policy, which has not yet been adopted, would raise novel and important constitutional questions concerning whether Congress possesses the authority to discriminate against US citizens based on their prior immigration status.

In addition to different sponsorship rights, citizens and LPRs differ with respect to their right to remain in the United States. LPRs are subject to deportation (after the 1996 immigration control legislation, the term is 'removal'); citizens (whether by birth, naturalization, or statute) are not. Deportation of a long-term resident can wreak enormous deprivation upon aliens and their families and friends. Although the Supreme Court has repeatedly held that removal is not punishment and therefore does not implicate the Due Process and other constitutional guarantees that surround the imposition of criminal sanctions, the fact is that as Justice Douglas once put it, removal 'may deprive a man and his family of all that makes life worthwhile'.[11]

Still, it is important to place this risk in realistic context. The actual risk of removal for non-criminal LPRs has been vanishingly small.[12] Even after the 1996 immigration control legislation, formal removal of legal aliens, especially non-criminal LPRs, remains a costly process for the INS to effectuate. Beyond the applicable statutes and regulations, which confer extensive procedural safeguards on removable LPRs, the courts require the agency to observe high standards of procedural fairness in adjudicating whether LPRs may remain in the United States. Severe administrative failures further limit the INS's ability to implement even the relatively few formal removal orders and the far more numerous informal departure agreements that it does manage to obtain. Except at the border, where the INS can often effectuate the 'voluntary departure' of aliens, the agency has been notoriously ineffective in actually removing aliens who want to remain—even including the 'aggravated felons' against whom Congress has provided special summary enforcement and removal powers (Williams and Schuck). As a legal and practical matter, then, a long-term, non-criminal LPR's chances of remaining in the United States if he wishes has been almost as great as that of a citizen. The 1996 law, which is designed to facilitate the removal of aliens who are inadmissible, commit crimes in the United States, lack credible asylum claims, or are otherwise out of status, is unlikely to alter this risk significantly.

Today the most controversial issue concerning the rights of LPRs concerns their access to public benefits to which citizens are entitled. Prior to the 1996 welfare reforms, LPRs and some other aliens who were present in the United States legally and who would probably gain LPR status in the future but did not yet enjoy it (e.g. family members of amnestied aliens, refugees and asylum-seekers, parolees, and Cuban–Haitian entrants) were eligible for many cash assistance, medical care, food, education, housing, and other social programmes, albeit subject to some restrictions.[13] (In addition, LPRs were often eligible for benefit programmes under *state* law such as low tuition in state university systems.) The 1996 welfare reforms significantly limit LPRs' eligibility for all or virtually all federal cash assistance programmes.[14]

These legal differences between the social programme benefits that are available to citizens and to LPRs have no parallel in the welfare states of the European Union. In the United States, however, these differences are somewhat palliated by several facts. Some states and cities (New York is a notable example) have been lax and even obstructionist in their enforcement of these limitations. Many LPRs and illegal aliens have managed to circumvent them through fraudulent applications. Most importantly, the vast majority of LPRs can easily remove the limitations in five years (three if they have a citizen spouse) by naturalizing. Much of the remarkable surge in naturalization petitions since the 1994 election apparently reflects precisely this kind of calculation on the part of LPRs, who anticipated the kinds of restriction on their entitlements that Congress adopted in 1996.

## The Re-Evaluation of Citizenship

In recent years, public discourse about citizenship has returned to first principles: its nature, sources, and significance. So fundamental are these principles that the new discourse amounts to a re-evaluation of American citizenship in both its normative and its positive dimensions. This re-evaluation has been prompted by deep concerns about the unity and coherence of the civic culture in the United States, concerns that flow from five developments on the post-1965 era. They are the accumulation of multicultural pressures; the loss of a unifying ideology; technological change; the expansion and consolidation of the welfare state; and the devaluation of citizenship.

### Multicultural Pressures

With the enactment of the 1965 law, the composition of the immigration stream to the United States changed radically. Of the ten top source countries, only the Philippines and India were sending immigrants who speak English well. Bilingual education thus became a major curricular issue in public education, and teaching in dozens of languages became necessary in many urban school systems. With the growing politicization of ethnicity and widespread attacks on the traditional assimilative ideal, anxieties about linguistic and cultural

fragmentation increased. These anxieties have led to public referendums establishing English as the official language in California and
other states and proposals to restrict the rights of aliens. As genuine
racial integration proved elusive, the civil rights movement took a
turn towards separatism. Blacks, already severely disadvantaged, were
increasingly obliged to cede political and economic influence to more
recently arrived Hispanic and Asian voters. Many of the newer groups
qualified for affirmative action programmes, which exacerbated tensions among the groups and which also magnified fears that immigration and affirmative action were fragmenting American society. Certain
economic sectors came to depend almost entirely upon immigrant
workers, legal and illegal. Relatively parochial immigrant enclaves
grew larger. These multicultural pressures caused many Americans to
feel more and more like strangers in their own country.

### Loss of Unifying Ideology

The end of the Cold War deprived the United States of an ideology,
anti-communism, that had served for many decades as a unifying,
coherent force in American political culture and as an obsessive preoccupation and goal in US foreign policy. No alternative ideology has
yet emerged to replace it. Only constitutionalism, our civic religion,
seems potentially capable of performing this function of binding together
a nation of diverse peoples.

### Technological Change

Rapid changes in transportation and communication technologies have
transformed a world of sovereign nations into a global web of multinational enterprises and interdependent societies. Migration has become inexpensive. Immigrants no longer need to make an irrevocable
commitment to their new society; they can more easily retain emotional and other ties to their countries and cultures of origin. On the
other hand, there is growing evidence that television helps to assimilate second-generation immigrant youths into an underclass culture
rather than into the mainstream American culture.

### Welfare State Expansion

In the United States, the welfare state—especially the creation of entitlements to income support, food stamps, medical care, and subsidized

housing—grew enormously during a remarkably brief period of time, at least when compared to the more gradual, long-term evolution of European social support systems.[15] With this growth, the behaviour, values, and economic progress of immigrants became matters of great fiscal significance and public policy concern. Some observers noted that in contrast to the historical pattern, immigration no longer ebbed and flowed with the business cycle—presumably because of the growth of the social safety-net. Immigration increasingly pitted citizens and aliens against one another as they competed for scarce public resources. The perennial debate over how the polity should conceive of community, affinity, and mutual obligation took on a new significance as the stakes in the outcome grew larger. Demands that Americans' obsession with legal rights be balanced by an equal concern for their social responsibilities and civic behaviours were increasingly heard in the land. Among academics, Lawrence Mead (1986) and Mary Ann Glendon (1991) were two of the most outspoken advocates for this position.

In August 1996 this long-simmering debate culminated in the enactment of a radical restructuring of the Aid to Families with Dependent Children (AFDC) programme (known and often stigmatized in the United States as 'welfare') and some other federally funded cash and social services programmes. In the next section, I analyse in some detail the implications of this change for US citizenship in a federal system.

## Devaluation of Citizenship

The egalitarian thrust of the welfare state, its nourishing of entitlement as an ideal, and the repeal of the military draft led to a progressive erosion of citizenship as a distinctive status bearing special privileges and demanding special commitments and obligations. The rights of LPRs converged with those of citizens until there was little to separate them but the franchise, the greater immigration sponsorship privileges that citizens enjoy, and eligibility for the federal civil service. Americans began to feel that US citizenship had lost much of its value, that it should somehow count for more (Schuck 1989: 1). These developments, which have parallels in other countries (Canada, House of Commons), have prompted calls for a revitalization of citizenship. One type of proposal, which led to the enactment in 1993 of the National Community Service Corps, looks to the creation of a spirit among young people of public service to their nation. Another type of proposal, a centrepiece of the welfare reform legislation enacted in 1988 and in

1996, seeks to combat the entitlement mentality by insisting that those able-bodied applicants for cash assistance perform some kind of socially useful work as a condition of receiving it. A third approach, exemplified by the 1996 restrictions in immigrants' rights to public benefits, is largely motivated by the desire to save scarce public resources and to favour citizens in the allocation of those resources. Its incidental effect, however, will be to increase the value of citizenship by widening the gap between the rights of citizens and aliens, thereby creating stronger incentives for the latter to naturalize. Whether this incentive is the kind of motivation for naturalization that proponents of a more robust citizenship have in mind is a question that is seldom asked.

Two other types of reform are aimed directly at citizenship itself. An incremental change, one to which the current INS Commissioner is firmly committed and to which there is no discernible opposition, seeks to enhance the attractiveness of the naturalization process, thereby encouraging more LPRs to acquire citizenship. This effort, however, has been caught up in a Congressional review of fraud in and partisan manipulation of the naturalization process before the 1996 elections, a review that may prompt changes in the naturalization law.

A more radical proposal, not at all inconsistent with encouraging naturalizations, takes a very different approach: it would deny citizenship to some who would otherwise obtain it. This approach would alter the traditional understanding of the *jus soli* rule, embodied in the Citizenship Clause of the Fourteenth Amendment, under which one automatically becomes a citizen merely by being born in the United States, even if the child's parents are in the country illegally or only as temporary residents. Such proposals, which have also been advanced in Canada (Canada, House of Commons: 17) take the form of legislation that would eliminate this form of automatic birthright citizenship either by constitutional amendment or by statute. Advocates of such a change emphasize the importance of mutual consent—the polity's as well as the alien's—in legitimizing American citizenship. They also point to the irrationality of permitting a Mexican woman with no claims on the United States to be able to confer American citizenship on her new child simply by crossing the border and giving birth, perhaps at public expense, in an American hospital. Defenders of birthright citizenship stress the importance of avoiding the creation and perpetuation of an underclass of long-term residents who do not qualify as citizens, a situation that applies to many guestworkers and their descendants stranded in countries that reject the *jus soli* principle.

For this reason, Congress is unlikely to eliminate birthright citizenship *per se*, although, as noted earlier, political support for this idea has grown recently. Many other nations already apply a birthright citizenship rule. Some others, notably Germany, have been moving towards (although remaining well short of) the American position. Nevertheless, some modification of the traditional birthright citizenship rule might attract wider support in the United States. For example, the law might deny automatic citizenship for those who are born in the United States in illegal status but still enable those native-born illegals who continue to reside here more or less permanently to naturalize at some point. Alternatively, it might reduce somewhat the perverse incentive effects of the current birthright citizenship rule by denying to the illegal parents any immigration benefits derived through their birth-right citizen child.

## CITIZENSHIP IN THE FEDERAL SYSTEM

Among the most striking features of contemporary geopolitics is the fragmentation of national political authority, and its devolution—through the collapse of centralized regimes, civil wars, negotiated agreements, and other decentralizing processes—to smaller, subnational, often ethnically defined groups. This devolution, of course, is still very much in flux; it has not yet reached an equilibrium. Indeed, as the economic, military, and political disadvantages of radical decentralization become more manifest, some recentralization is bound to occur. Nevertheless, the rapidity and militancy with which devolution has proceeded are remarkable. This has been most famously true in the former Soviet Union, which fissioned in the aftermath of the Cold War. But even before the dissolution of the Soviet Empire, the weaker states of Africa and Asia had been disintegrating into chaos. Devolution is also occurring, albeit more slowly and less dramatically, in stronger nation-states like Italy, Belgium, and Mexico, and even in paradigmatically strong ones like the United Kingdom and France. It is even occurring in nation-states like Canada with highly decentralized federal systems already in place.

The United States falls into this last category. Devolution to the states is perhaps the most prominent area of policy innovation pursued by the Republican congressional majority since the 1994 elections. The programmes that comprise the modern welfare state are being reassessed and in some cases fundamentally reshaped to give the states control of central aspects of the policy process: policy design, financing, eligibility, administration, evaluation, and enforcement. The recasting of the AFDC programme is the most dramatic example of a fundamental curtailment of federal power and augmentation of the states' authority. Although the Medicaid, food stamp, and supplemental security income (SSI) programmes have not yet been as thoroughly overhauled as AFDC, the precise division of authority between the federal and state governments remains the subject of bitter struggle and intense negotiations. Devolution of social support programmes, along with deregulation and privatization initiatives in a number of other policy areas, constitutes a substantial repudiation of the New Deal and Great Society, and it is one in which a substantial number of Democratic Party office-holders have joined. The spasmodic but unmistakable nationalizing trajectory of American political development has not merely been interrupted; it has been reversed.

These changes are no mere ephemera. They do not simply mark a discontinuity in the ongoing evolution of the American polity, a temporary aberration after which the ascendancy of national power at the expense of the states will continue. The changes instead reflect deep and abiding forces in US society[16]—and, on the evidence elsewhere, perhaps in the world. They are likely to be long-lived, if not permanent, for the structures supporting national power will be almost impossible to restore once they are dismantled. This task of restoration would require the convergence of three unlikely conditions: a convulsive national crisis equivalent to the Great Depression that spawned the national regime; a growth in public confidence in the efficacy of centralized power and of national governmental solutions; and a surrender by the states of their hard-won powers.

In emphasizing the changing conceptions and roles of national and state citizenship, one must also take note of another institutional development—the private residential enclave—that is becoming an increasingly significant locus of civic membership and governance in the United States.[17] Whether these enclaves take the form of urban apartment condominiums, suburban home-owners' associations, or other co-operative community arrangements, they are territorial organizations that create new kinds of governance regimes that exercise far-reaching powers over millions of Americans. That such enclaves are more creatures of private law than public law, that the relationships of people and activities within them are structured more by contracts than by political constitutions, does not alter the fact that they regulate important aspects of their members' lives in ways that closely resemble the powers of government. This is another domain in which devolution of authority—here, from the states, which ordinarily regulate property rights and community development, to private organizations— is proceeding.

These reconfigurations of governance and authority relationships amount to a reconstruction of American citizenship. By redefining the relationships between the citizen and the nation, the citizen and the states, and the citizen and his or her community, this devolution is fundamentally transforming the rights and duties of membership in the various layers of American polities. In doing so, it is also transform-ing the meanings that attach to those memberships and those polities.

An important, if relatively unremarked, aspect of this devolution-driven redefinition of citizenship is its possible effect on the status of aliens. The role of the states in defining the rights of aliens in the United States has a somewhat complex history. Until 1875, when the first federal statute restricting immigration was enacted, the states exercised broad authority over aliens' entry and legal rights. Although a Supreme Court decision in 1849 (the *Passenger* cases) had indicated that the states could not regulate immigration *per se*, they still pos-sessed a residual constitutional responsibility for protecting the health, safety, and morals of those within its jurisdiction, including aliens. As a number of scholars have shown, the states often exercised this re-sponsibility during this period in ways that had the effect of limiting immigration, especially by aliens who were poor, ill, or were other-wise considered undesirable (e.g. Neuman 1993: 1833; Skerry 1995: 71). Even after the federal government entered and occupied the field of general immigration control and the Supreme Court invalidated some state laws regulating aliens, the states continued to enforce local laws that limited aliens' rights with respect to employment, property owners-hip, use of public resources, eligibility for public benefits, and other matters. With some exceptions, these statutes were generally upheld by the courts until the 1970s, when the Supreme Court began to apply strict scrutiny to such statutes, except for those that limited aliens' rights to certain public jobs involving 'political functions'. The exclusive federal authority over immigration—its 'plenary power', in the words of a seminal Supreme Court decision on the subject—went so far as to invalidate state laws that tended to reinforce federal policies against illegal aliens by disadvantaging them. In perhaps no other area of legisla-tion has the federal government's primacy been more firmly established and the power of the states more clearly circumscribed.[18]

This 'plenary power doctrine' is a double-edged sword. It has received sustained criticism from legal scholars who find no textual warrant for it in the Constitution and who contend that the structural and policy justifications that have been used to support it, such as the need for a single voice in foreign affairs, are either weak or over-broad (Schuck 1984: 14–30; Legomsky 1984: 255; Spiro 1994). These scholars (and I count myself among them) believe that the federal government's power over aliens, while broad, cannot be complete but must instead be subject to some constitutional limitations. On the other hand, the courts have used the federal pre-emption logic of the plenary power doctrine to constrain the power of *states* to regulate and discriminate against aliens, a result that scholars generally applaud. This tension is deepened somewhat by the fact that the main alternative doctrinal route to constraining state law alienage discriminations—heightened scrutiny under the Equal Protection Clause—is itself problematic, although perhaps not insuperably so. The question, then, is how fair treatment of aliens can be assured in a federal system in which the national government possesses plenary, or at least primary, responsibility for regulating aliens, while the states, which sometimes have fiscal and political incentives to discriminate against them, possess some degree of policy autonomy.

Today, however, this old question has taken on new coloration. The United States has entered a period of extraordinary constitutional ferment in which the federal government's constitutional authority— even over subjects over which it has long played the exclusive or dominant policy-making role—is being increasingly called into question. The most dramatic example of this ferment occurred in the Supreme Court's *United States* v. *Lopez* decision, rendered in 1995. In *Lopez*, a sharply divided Court invalidated a federal statute that prohibited the possession of firearms near schools. It did so on the ground that the federal power to regulate under the Commerce Clause of the Constitution did not extend to such a local activity. Although the decision's scope and significance remain unclear, it cast doubt on almost sixty years of jurisprudence that construed the Commerce Clause to permit virtually any regulation that Congress wished to enact. *Lopez* has already provoked new challenges to long-established laws in policy areas involving highly localized impacts—for example, environmental regulation, drug enforcement, and abortion—that had previously been considered well within the ambit of federal power.

Federal regulation of immigration, of course, would survive a constitutional challenge under *Lopez*. As noted above, more than a century of Supreme Court decisions has emphasized the national sovereignty and foreign policy implications of immigration law, the exclusive federal prerogatives in this area, and the dangers of state encroachment. There is much to be said for the traditional approach on the merits, and it is difficult to imagine that this conservative Court, ironically radical as some of its conservatism is, would jettison it as a matter of constitutional law.

It is not the Constitution, however, that has been the main barrier to greater state responsibilities in the immigration field. In a series of decisions invalidating state laws on federal pre-emption grounds, the Court has clearly indicated that Congress remains free as a matter of *policy* to authorize, or perhaps even require, the states to act in this area. The real impediment to a larger state role is Congress, which has chosen essentially to occupy the fields of immigration policy through federal legislation. In recent years, Congress has recognized only a very limited role for the states in immigration policy—largely that of providers of federally mandated social services for refugees. The decision by a lower federal court invalidating most of California's Proposition 187 on pre-emption grounds is simply the most recent example of this confinement of state policy discretion where it seems to conflict with federal policy concerning even illegal aliens.[19]

This situation, however, could change. Nothing in the nature of immigration policy requires that it be an exclusively national-level responsibility. Although immigration control is a national function in all countries, subnational units in some federal systems—Canada and Germany, for example—do exercise important policy-making functions with respect to immigration. With devolution occurring in so many other areas of public policy traditionally controlled at the centre, can devolution of immigration regulation be impervious to the trend? And if the states were to assume a more significant, independent role in immigration policy, a role that Congress might encourage and that the courts might therefore sustain, how would this development alter the nature of citizenship in the American polities?

These questions are by no means academic. Some of the same economic, social, political, and ideological forces that are propelling devolution in other policy areas also affect the politics of immigration. Immigrants are not distributed randomly across the nation. Quite the contrary; immigration is a largely *regional* phenomenon, with the vast majority of immigrants tending to live in a handful of states and metropolitan areas. However great the economic and other benefits of immigration to the nation as a whole may be, its costs—especially those resulting from immigrants' use of schools, hospitals, prisons, and other public services—are highly concentrated in these few high-impact states and metropolitan areas, while the rest of the country need not incur immigration's costs in order to enjoy many of its benefits. The disproportionate stakes of immigrant-receiving areas prompted Proposition 187 in California and similar anti-illegal immigration proposals in some other states. For the high-impact states, immigration is as salient as any policy area with which they deal.

That these state-level impacts also have enormous *political* significance is obvious when one considers (as politicians surely do) that the seven states with the largest immigrant populations account for two-thirds of the electoral votes needed to win the presidency (Skerry 1995: 84). This fact places immigration reform high on the *national* political agenda—and it is from the national level, principally the Congress, that devolution of power over immigration policy must ultimately issue.

Signs of movement in this direction appear in the 1995 federal law limiting unfunded national mandates on states and localities, and in the 1996 welfare reform legislation discussed earlier. One of the practices prompting the unfunded mandates law was the federal government's recent policy of admitting a growing number of refugees while at the same time reducing its funding for resettlement support, forcing states, localities, and non-governmental organizations to pick up the increasing deficit (ibid. 78–9). The unfunded mandate law will presumably limit, if not eliminate, this practice. The 1996 welfare reform law restricts federal policy initiative even further, transmuting AFDC into block grants and leaving the states largely free to determine how to distribute those funds among US citizens while barring the states from spending them on some (but not all) broad alien categories. State laws that impose restrictions on state-financed programmes that track the new federal restrictions will almost certainly survive constitutional challenge in the courts.

In a recent article, Professor Peter Spiro develops a more sweeping rationale for the devolution of immigration policy to the states (1994: 121). He argues that the interests in national uniformity and control over foreign relations, which constitute the traditional justifications for federal pre-emption in immigration policy, are no longer decisive in 'a post-national world order'. In that order, according to Spiro, states are the major fiscal and political stakeholders in immigration policy. They also play larger, more independent roles in their dealings with foreign nations. He attributes the more robust state role in foreign relations to the globalization of information, communications, and travel, and to the economic and cultural ties that states have increasingly forged with foreign governments and communities. 'This international engagement on the states' part', Spiro writes, 'has inevitably undermined the [traditional pre-emption] doctrine's more fundamental underpinning, viz., that other countries will not distinguish the states and their actions from the nation's' (p. 162).

Spiro's argument is less important for his prescriptions, which I find quite problematic, than for his empirical claim that the federal government's monopoly of authority and influence in foreign relations and immigration is steadily (and, in his view, irrevocably) eroding, as the states (and private non-governmental organizations) operate more independently of Washington.[20] Assuming that he is correct about this, however, it does not follow that Congress would devolve immigration policy to the states—even if it continues its efforts to devolve power in a broad range of other policy domains. Congress may instead conclude that immigration is simply *different*, perhaps because it believes, contrary to Spiro, that immigration's foreign policy implications and the need to speak with one voice are considerations of overriding importance.

Alternatively, Congress might adopt a middle path. It might decide that, *as a matter of national policy*, it is prepared to tolerate greater diversity among, and discrimination by, states in their treatment of aliens. By adopting an affirmative national policy that allows states to discriminate against aliens in certain areas such as welfare benefits or student loans, Congress could continue to uphold the principle of federal pre-emption while encouraging policy diversity among the states. Such a national policy might well pass constitutional muster as an exercise of Congress's plenary federal power, and discriminatory state laws that would otherwise raise serious constitutional questions might also be upheld by the courts because it would be consistent with, and in furtherance of, this plenary federal power. *Graham* v. *Richardson* and other court precedents that invalidated state law discriminations might be distinguished on the ground that those discriminations were not authorized by this kind of clearly expressed congressional policy.

In the welfare reform legislation enacted in August 1996, Congress took precisely this middle path on the question of aliens' eligibility for welfare and other public benefit programmes. The structure of the legislation is very complex; it creates a new legal category ('qualified aliens'), differentiates among particular programmes, governmental levels, and alien categories, carves out many exceptions, contains 'grandfather' clauses, and provides special transitional rules. Consequently, its specific meanings will remain uncertain for years to come. For purposes of this discussion, however, what is of greatest interest is that Congress has sought to 'revalue' US citizenship by adopting a firm new national policy favouring discrimination against LPRs (not just illegal aliens) in the distribution of public benefits and by conscripting the states into the implementation of that new policy.

In the 1996 law, Congress defined four different modalities along the spectrum running from policy prescription to complete policy deference. Interestingly, these modalities do not simply track the distinction between federal and state programmes (although that distinction is obviously at work in the level of prescription), and Congress is somewhat prescriptive even where it is deferential. In the first modality, Congress is dealing with federal benefits (which it defines broadly) and is highly prescriptive, precluding any contrary state policies. Its general rule bars from all federal benefits all aliens other than LPRs, refugees and asylum-seekers, and a few other categories; it then bars all *current* LPRs and other aliens with legal status (except for three favoured groups[21]) from the fully federal SSI and food stamp programmes;[22] and it bars *new* LPRs and other legal aliens (other than those three groups) during their first five years in the United States from all federal means-tested programmes such as AFDC but with a large number of exceptions including emergency Medicaid, disaster relief, child nutrition, some training and education, etc.

In its second modality, Congress is more deferential to the states' policies towards aliens—even relating to some federal programmes. It *allows* (but does not require) states to bar aliens from three federal programmes (block grant for temporary assistance for needy families, social services block grant, and non-emergency Medicaid), but *requires* the states to provide these benefits—which in the case of Medicaid benefits are very costly—to the three favoured alien groups.

In its third modality, Congress adopts a prescriptive mode regarding most *state and local* benefit programmes. Here it *prohibits* states from allowing any aliens other than LPRs, temporary visitors, and some other categories to receive state and local public benefits (except for certain emergency programmes), although it *allows* states to make *illegal* aliens eligible for those state and local benefit programmes (but only if they do so by new, specific legislation). Oddly, this empowers states to place illegal aliens in a better position than certain categories of legal aliens to whom, under the new law, the state may not provide state and local benefits. A fourth modality—deference to state programmes—*allows* states to bar legal aliens (other than the three favoured groups) from state programmes altogether.

This crazy-quilt pattern is not aberrational; it is emblematic of the complexity of US politics, federal structure, and public administration. From the perspective of the polity's valuation of citizenship, however, two aspects of the new law's treatment of aliens are particularly striking. First, the federal government has now made a clear, comprehensive choice (albeit confusing in its details) in favour of a national policy to discriminate against aliens in its own public benefit programmes, and to either require or permit the states to do so in theirs. This policy fundamentally reverses the recent law in this area. With a few exceptions such as the wholly federal programme at issue in *Mathews* v. *Diaz*, the federal government had long since abandoned the practice of discriminating against aliens and, because Supreme Court decisions held the states to the same rules as a matter of constitutional law, the states could not discriminate either. New York City, Florida, and other plaintiffs have challenged these new discriminations on equal protection grounds; in July 1997, a federal district court in New York upheld the statute as being rationally related to the federal government's interests in controlling programme costs, encouraging aliens to naturalize and to be self-sufficient, and removing an incentive for immigration.[23]

The second noteworthy feature of this new federal mandate to discriminate is that it is part of a statute that, like many other laws enacted by the Republican-controlled Congress, vastly enlarges the states' discretion over most other aspects of welfare policy. This means that the new policy on alien benefits is unusual not only substantively (it requires discrimination that in other contexts would be unconstitutional) but also structurally (it presumes, contrary to the now-dominant thinking about federalism, that Washington knows best and should enforce its 'one-size-fits-all' policy preferences on the states).

Outside the area of public benefits for aliens, however, more deference to the states will be the rule. In the future, the rights and obligations of individuals—US citizens and aliens alike—will depend more on state law and less on federal law than at any time since the New Deal. This world will be even more unfamiliar to the extent that Congress devolves immigration policy to the states, but it will be novel in any event. In such a world, *state* citizenship could become more salient than in the past, and the constitutional limits on states' power to discriminate—constraints derived from state constitutions as well as from the US Constitution—will become more significant. State citizenship is a status that has received little scholarly attention of late; it ceased to have much practical significance once states barred aliens from voting in their elections, American Indians received US citizenship, and the Supreme Court interpreted the Constitution's Privileges and Immunities Clause to limit the states' power to discriminate against citizens of other states.

Should Congress expressly permit the states to favour their own state citizens over aliens in areas other than those public benefits covered by the 1996 welfare reform law, however, this might change. The plenary power doctrine might then preclude aliens from challenging Congress's decision to do so under the US Constitution; in that event, aliens' only recourse might be to challenge the state law discrimination under the applicable state constitution. State constitutions typically contain equal protection clauses, and those clauses proscribe many kinds of discrimination—in some cases more completely than the federal Constitution does. But the extent to which they would limit *alienage* discrimination is uncertain. It will be particularly uncertain where the constitutional issues arise in a novel devolution context in which states exercise new powers and operate outside the shadow cast by traditional federal pre-emption principles—or indeed in perfect harmony with federal policies limiting aliens' entitlements.

If devolution thus transforms the structure of American federalism, the nature of citizenship in the American polities must also be transformed. The legal, political, and social relationships between an individual alien and the larger juridical communities that affect her relative status and well-being—the national government, state governments, local self-governing enclaves—will in effect be redefined.

Like so much else in this new devolutionary regime, it is difficult to predict how aliens will fare under it. Some aliens will be better off than they are now, while others will be worse off. Some states and local communities already embrace legal aliens at least as warmly as the federal government does. In such states, this favourable reception is driven by enduring forces and will probably continue even after the 1996 changes in the welfare and immigration laws. These communities regard the newcomers as valuable economic and cultural assets. Community leaders recognize that the immigrants and their families and friends may soon become voters and citizens; the community may also wish to mollify the immigrants' many co-ethnics who are already such.

The state governments in Texas and New Jersey, for example, seem to view legal immigrants as beneficial to their states (McCartney and Blumenthal 1995; Espenshade 1997); even Pete Wilson, the California governor who promoted Proposition 187, has defended the welfare benefit rights of legal aliens, extending their entitlements under federally funded programmes as long as possible. Politicians in New York (both state and city) and Massachusetts have welcomed even *illegal* aliens (see e.g. Schmitt 1996).[24]

Many other states and communities, however, may view at least certain types of immigrant as unwanted invaders, as fiscal and political burdens that the state can hope, through discriminatory policies, to shift to other states. The possibility of this dynamic—of a so-called 'race to the bottom' in which states seek to discourage some categories of immigration by adopting more discriminatory policies than its sister states—is a powerful argument in favour of pre-empting state immigration policies in a federal system or at least for imposing limits on permissible state discriminations.[25] It is a possibility, moreover, which the 1996 welfare reform magnifies. The experience of other federal nations in dealing with this risk of immigration policy fragmentation should be of special interest to the United States in this devolutionary era.

## A BRIEF NOTE ON 'POST-NATIONAL CITIZENSHIP'

In recent years a number of scholars have pointed to a new development in thinking about citizenship—what Yasemin Soysal and others have called the idea of 'post-national citizenship'. Its 'main thrust', according to Soysal, 'is that individual rights, historically defined on the basis of nationality, are increasingly codified into a different scheme that emphasizes universal personhood' (Soysal 1994: 136).[26] In this conception, transnational diasporic communities of individuals bearing multiple, collective identities make (and, it is hoped, enforce) claims against states. In contrast to a traditional 'national' model of citizenship, individuals—simply by virtue of their personhood—can legitimately assert these claims on the basis of their universal human rights (as defined by evolving principles of international law) whether or not they are citizens, or even residents, of those states.

In somewhat similar terms, David Jacobson notes the emergence of 'a deterritorialized identity' that is transforming the nature of, and relationships among, the community, polity, and state, and he cites some judicial decisions that seem to be propelling this transformation. A new dispensation, Jacobson believes, is ineluctable: 'The multiplicity of ethnic groups and the absence of contiguity of such groups make any notion of territorially based self-determination patently impossible. However, in so far as such groups can make claims on states on the basis of international human rights law and, hence, become recognized actors in the international arena, territoriality becomes less critical to self-determination.' He quickly adds that this bright promise of post-national citizenship is being realized only in western Europe and North America, acknowledging that eastern Europe is experiencing the very opposite: 'the territorialization of communal identity' (Jacobson 1996: 126–7).

These visions of post-national citizenship are undeniably attractive. A just state will respect and vindicate minority groups' claims to cultural diversity and autonomy. Detaching the legitimacy of these claims from their conventional territorial mooring in 'normal politics'[27] and traditional citizenship law, as post-national citizenship seeks to do, may sometimes promote their recognition, as Soysal's own work on the progress of Muslim communities in western Europe demonstrates (see Soysal 1996). Moreover, some court decisions do seem to point in this direction, requiring polities to extend some procedural and even substantive rights to strangers who come within their jurisdiction and claim judicial protection.[28]

Those decisions, however, remain exceptional and some have been overturned by recent legislation in the United States. But a more important set of questions about the character and implications of post-national citizenship are raised by recent events elsewhere in the world. Bosnia (and Somalia, Rwanda, Burundi, Cambodia, and all too many other areas of conflict) should remind us that the ostensible goals of post-national citizenship—human rights, cultural autonomy, and full participation in a rich civil society—are tragically elusive, and that its achievements are exquisitely fragile.

The problem is not merely that the parochial partisans of exclusion and discrimination will oppose post-national citizenship at every turn and often succeed in establishing illiberal policies in traditional nation-states. The more fundamental problem is that the possibility of an instantiated ideal of post-national citizenship ultimately depends on its ability to transcend, or at least enlarge, the domains of normal politics and law. After all, if those domains would accept the post-national agenda, there would be no need to advocate it as an alternative to traditional national citizenship and hence no problem. Such a transcendence of normal politics, however, would leave post-national human rights naked and vulnerable with no firm political and institutional ground-ing. Without such a grounding, national courts enforcing international law principles are unlikely to provide durable, reliable protection (see Schuck 1993: 1763).[29] The often feckless international human rights tribunals are even less plausible guarantors of those principles.

Soysal and Jacobson might acknowledge this point yet respond that some protection for post-national citizenship, however episodic, is bet-ter than none. But this response does little to shore up post-national citizenship, for its grounding only in adjudication would risk more than an incomplete fulfilment. The problem is not simply that courts are institutionally ill-equipped to defend their rulings in the political arena, or even (as Mr Dooley famously put it) that the Supreme Court fol-lows the election returns (Dunne 1901: 26). The greater risk is that the normative foundation of a post-national citizenship may be so thin and shallow that it can easily be swept away by the tides of tribalism or nationalism. As formulated by Soysal in her work on civil society, post-national citizenship (unless it includes rights already established under national laws) possesses only a limited institutional status, largely confined to some courts. (If it were more fully institutionalized than this, the new ideal would be superfluous.) Beyond this, Soysal argues, post-national citizenship is built on a 'discourse of rights', one that explicitly renounces the Habermasian effort to fuse reason and will in pursuit of a non-coercive consensus. Instead, this discourse chooses 'to focus on agendas of contestation and provide space for strategic action, rather than consensus building' (see Soysal 1996).[30]

I am not at all certain what this means, but it strikes me as omin-ous. I worry when normative commitments on which the lives and welfare of vulnerable minorities depend is premissed on something as insubstantial, transitory, and manipulable as a 'discourse', even (or per-haps especially) a discourse of rights. Discourses of rights are double-edged swords, and my metaphor is grimly apt. The slain in the former Yugoslavia call out an unmistakable warning from their mass graves. Their murderers, after all, were—are—participants in a discourse of rights. They too are transnational communities which plausibly invoke universal human rights to legitimize their claims to group autonomy, cultural integrity, and political self-determination. They too believe that these rights are threatened by other communities, even as those other communities, with tragic irony, claim similar rights and perceive similar threats. In this furious competition for communal power, the dis-course of rights—universal in form but fatally tribalistic in practice—

has legitimized genocidal holocausts. This discourse has been far more destructive of human life, property, and values than all of the well-known limitations of normal politics in democratic polities.

In reasonably democratic states—and post-national citizenship is only possible and meaningful in such states—even an imperfect constitution recognizing minority rights, and even a majoritarian politics in which groups must compete for acceptance of their communal aspirations, are likely to be surer guarantees of liberal human rights than a discursive ideal. This is especially true to the extent that the post-national, trans-national ideal is institutionally grounded only in politically isolated courts and lends itself (by reason of its substantive indeterminacy) to repressive applications. A discourse whose success necessitates overleaping the messy exigencies of normal politics where expansive conceptions of human rights must contend for legal recognition seems destined to be either irrelevant or anti-democratic.

There is a valuable role that the notion of post-national citizenship can and should fulfil. It should serve as a compelling vision of tolerance, diversity, and integration that people of good will can aspire to, that normal politics in democratic states can sometimes realize, and against which their failures can be fairly judged and condemned. This is the role that it has begun to play in the United States. To claim more for it—to promote it as an alternative to, or a cure for, the weaknesses of democratic politics—would ultimately discredit the humane agenda that its proponents advocate. If it can succeed in mobilizing normal politics to win that recognition in positive law, however, it will be truly transformative even as it thereby ceases, in an important sense, to be 'post-national'.

## CONCLUSION

Citizenship is a status whose meaning in any particular society depends entirely on the political commitments and understandings to which its members subscribe. In the United States, many of these commitments and understandings have always been tenuous, contestable, and contested; some still are.[31] Of no political arrangement is this more true than the American welfare state. It was first established only sixty years ago and it only reached its current form in the 1970s and 1980s, with the rapid expansion of the food stamp, Medicaid, and social security programmes (Schuck 1997). In this mature form,[32] then, the welfare state is less than three decades old. During most of that period, moreover, its legitimacy has been under constant attack by much of the political and intellectual establishment; the present political struggle will determine precisely how firm its hold on the public's allegiance actually is.[33]

This feverish debate over the welfare state, which has continued and in some ways deepened since its inception in the New Deal era, has inevitably shaped Americans' conceptions of the meaning and incidents of citizenship. In this sense, the American debate might be seen as yet another example of what has tendentiously been called 'American exceptionalism'—the notion that, for a variety of complex historical reasons, some of the patterns that have shaped the character of European democracies do not apply, or apply quite differently, to the United States. In this case, however, I believe that such a perception would be mistaken. More likely, the American debate prefigures a re-evaluation of citizenship in Europe.

Such a re-evaluation appears to be inescapable in light of a number of extremely important developments: the enlarged scope and ambition of the European Union, the migration and asylum pressures unleashed by the fall of the Iron Curtain, the recognition among many European leaders that recent budget deficits are both unsustainable and inconsistent with further monetary (not to speak of political) integration, and the sclerotic performance in recent years of the high-cost European economies in the intensely competitive global markets. Although this debate will surely resemble the American one in some respects, it will be distinctively European in many others. As the social, economic, and political conditions of Europe and the United States increasingly converge, we shall have unprecedented opportunities to learn from one another—from our triumphs as well as our mistakes.

## NOTES

1. The globalization phenomenon, while important, is easily exaggerated. According to a very recent study, US-based firms' share of world output outside the United States actually declined from 3 per cent to 2 per cent between 1977 and 1993, even as the domestic US economy expanded (Lipsey *et al.* 1996).
2. For a discussion of these developments, see Schuck (1996*a*).
3. Some commentators maintain that the justifications for citizenship lie primarily in the international law realm; this status, they believe, has—or ought to have—little significance inside a nation's borders. See e.g. Legomsky (1994: 279, 300).
4. For each status, these rights are more expansive and valuable than the rights of those who occupy the status beneath it. The obligations attaching

to these statuses, however, are not calibrated or distributed in quite the same way as the rights. The obligations owed by citizens are not necessarily greater than those owed by lesser statuses; in some respects—e.g. the resident alien's paperwork obligations to the INS—citizens' duties may actually be *less* onerous.

5. Much depends, of course, on what one means by membership and how full it must be in order to satisfy Bickel's terms. Women, for example, were citizens but lacked the franchise, at least in federal elections, until the ratification of the Nineteenth Amendment in 1920. Young adults only obtained it in 1971 with the adoption of the Twenty-Sixth Amendment. A full, robust citizenship, moreover, demands more than the right to vote. See Shklar (1991); Smith (1997).

6. Customary exceptions to the *jus soli* rule exist; they include, for example, children born on foreign-flag vessels and children of diplomatic personnel.

7. Legislation to eliminate birthright citizenship in these circumstances was considered (but not adopted) in 1996 and the 1996 Republican Party platform called for a constitutional amendment for this purpose. I have opposed such measures under current conditions (Schuck 1995–6; Schuck and Smith 1996).

8. An INS study of the cohort of aliens who immigrated to the United States in 1977 found that 54 per cent still had not naturalized by the end of 1995, eighteen years later, when they had already been eligible for well over a decade. Moreover, most aliens who do naturalize do not apply until well after they become eligible; their median period of US residency is now nine years. There are, however, important regional and country variations in speed of naturalization.

9. See generally Neuman (1994: 237); Schuck (1994: 321, 326).

10. Canada's citizenship preference was upheld against a constitutional challenge (*Lavoie* v. *The Queen*, 1995).

11. *Harisiades* v. *Shaughnessy*, (1952) 342 U.S. 580.

12. In 1995 only 45,000 aliens were formally deported or removed 'under docket control' and virtually all of these were illegal entrants, out-of-status non-immigrants, violators of narcotics laws, or convicted criminals. The proportion of aliens removed who were charged with crimes or narcotics activity was 70 per cent. A far larger number (1.3 million) were expelled without formal proceedings, but almost all of these fell into the same four categories. (US Department of Justice 1995.) Moreover, relatively few of those who were deported or expelled had been in the United States for a long period of time. (US Department of Justice 1993: 156.)

13. First, so-called 'deeming' provisions apply to many federal and state benefit programmes. Even an alien with a visa to enter as an LPR can be excluded if he is 'likely at any time to become a public charge' (i.e. receive means-tested public assistance), and an LPR or other alien already in the United States can be removed if he has become a public charge within five years after entry, unless he can show that his poverty was caused by conditions that arose after entry. Very few removals have been enforced under this provision. Entering aliens (except for refugees) must show that they will have a steady source of support through employment, family resources, or other-

wise. If they cannot do so, a portion of the income of their US resident sponsors (in the case of family-based immigrants) is deemed to be available to the alien for a number of years after arrival, which will ordinarily render him ineligible for public benefits. An alien who receives welfare would also encounter difficulty in sponsoring other family members as immigrants.

The 1996 welfare reform law extends the reach and enforceability of these deeming provisions, making fewer LPRs eligible for benefits even if they can survive the other new, more categorical restrictions on eligibility for new immigrants and for those already admitted but not yet naturalized as citizens.

14. LPRs do enjoy the benefits of a special programme, adopted as part of the compromise that led to the 1986 employer sanctions provisions, which bars job discrimination against aliens who are legally authorized to work. The 1996 amendments make proof of discrimination more difficult by requiring the alien to show the employer's discriminatory intent.

15. Indeed, this growth continued (except in the case of Aid to Families with Dependent Children) during the Reagan and Bush years (Schuck 1997: 575).

16. For a discussion of these social forces, see Schuck (1996*b*).

17. For leading, and contrasting, discussions of this development, see McKenzie (1994); Ellickson (1982: 1519); Ford (1994: 1841).

18. If anything, the courts, led by the Supreme Court, have reaffirmed this primacy in the last decade. For a review of some of the recent cases, see Legomsky (1995: 925).

    For an argument favouring a broader state role in immigration policy, see Spiro (1994). This article is discussed below.

19. *League of United Latin American Citizens* v. *Wilson* (1995) WL 699583 (C.D. Cal., 20 Nov. 1995). The 1996 federal statute requiring the states to discriminate against illegal aliens in certain programmes will surely affect this decision.

20. This development is not confined to the United States but is occurring in other developed nations as well.

21. The favoured groups are: refugees and asylum-seekers in their first five years in the United States, veterans and soldiers, and those who have worked in the United States for ten years and stayed off public assistance during that time.

22. As part of the budget compromise negotiated by President Clinton and Congress in July 1997, some of the SSI benefits were restored to legal immigrants who were receiving benefits on or before 22 August 1996.

23. *Abreu.* v. *Callaghan*, 1997 U.S. Dist. Lexis 10676.

24. Some of these same states (as well as others) have sued the federal government to recover billions of dollars that states have expended to educate, incarcerate, and hospitalize illegal aliens. All such suits have been dismissed and appeals are pending.

25. A similar analysis has been applied, *mutatis mutandis*, to many other areas of public policy in the United States. See e.g. Romano (1993); Esty (1996); *Yale Law and Policy Review*, Symposium Issue on Federalism (1996).

26. Soysal notes that the idea of post-national citizenship has developed since the Second World War and especially during the last two decades.

27. I borrow this phrase and its connotation from Ackerman (1983).
28. I developed this theme almost fifteen years ago in an article that called attention to these judicial stirrings (Schuck 1984). Jacobson (1996, ch. 5) discusses some of them. In hindsight, I believe that my conclusion that a 'transformation' was occurring may have been somewhat premature, although important changes in judicial doctrine and attitude clearly did occur during the 1980s.
29. The swift overruling and narrowing of most of the 'post-national' US court decisions on behalf of long-detained criminal aliens that Jacobson cites confirms this point (Schuck 1993: 98–100). And while *Plyler* v. *Doe*, probably the most important 'post-national' decision cited by him, remains intact, both its narrow majority and its reasoning leave it vulnerable to being either reversed or distinguished away, perhaps in the pending litigation challenging the constitutionality of Proposition 187. See Schuck (1995).
30. Although Soysal does not expressly refer here to the idea of post-national citizenship developed in her other work, she is clearly invoking it, as when she concludes: 'This shift in focus from national collectivity to particularistic identities . . . points to the emergence of a new basis for participation and the proliferation of forms of mobilization at various levels of polity, which are not imperatively defined by national parameters and delimited by national borders' (1996: 16).
31. For a magisterial account of these contests, see Smith (1997).
32. Even in this mature form, most European (and American) analysts consider it a limited, laggard example of the species.
33. The most recent evidence hearing on this question is the decision to create a large new federal programme to provide health care coverage to children who are uninsured (Clymer).

# REFERENCES

Ackerman, Bruce A. (1983), 'The Storrs Lectures: Discovering the Constitution', *Yale Law Journal*, 93/6: 1013–72.

Bickel, Alexander M. (1975), *The Morality of Consent* (New Haven: Yale University Press).

Canada, House of Commons (1994), 'Canadian Citizenship: A Sense of Belonging', Report of the Standing Committee on Citizenship and Immigration.

Clymer, Adam (1997) 'White House and the G.O.P. Announce Deal to Balance Budget and Trim Taxes' *New York Times*, 29 July, A1.

Dunne, Finley Peter (1901), *Mr Dooley's Opinions* (New York: R. H. Russell).

Ellickson, Robert C. (1982), 'Cities and Homeowners' Associations', *University of Pennsylvania Law Review*, 130: 1519–80.

Espenshade, Thomas J. (ed.) (1997), *Keys to Successful Immigration: Implications of the New Jersey Experience* (Washington: Urban Institute Press).

Esty, Daniel (1995), 'Revitalizing Environmental Federalism', *Michigan Law Review*, 95: 570–653.

Ford, Richard T. (1994), 'The Boundaries of Race: Political Geography in Legal Analysis', *Harvard Law Review*, 107: 1841–1921.

Glendon, Mary Ann (1991), *Rights Talk: The Impoverishment of Political Discourse* (New York: Free Press).

Jacobson, David (1996), *Rights across Borders: Immigration and the Decline of Citizenship* (Baltimore: Johns Hopkins University Press).

Legomsky, Stephen H. (1984), 'Immigration Law and the Principle of Plenary Congressional Power', *Supreme Court Review*, 1984: 255–307.

—— (1994), 'Why Citizenship?', *Virginia Journal of International Law*, 35: 279–300.

—— (1995), 'Ten More Years of Plenary Power: Immigration, Congress, and the Courts', *Hastings Constitutional Law Quarterly*, 22: 925–37.

Lipsey, Robert, Magnus Blomstrom, and Eric Ramstetter (1996), *Internationalized Production in World Output*, NBER Working Paper no. 5385 (Cambridge, Mass.: National Bureau of Economic Research).

McCartney, Scott, and Karen Blumenthal (1995), 'Texas Strives to Avoid California's Mistakes, and it is Prospering', *Wall Street Journal*, 13 Sept., A1.

McKenzie, Evan (1994), *Privatopia: Homeowner Associations and the Rise of Residential Private Government* (New Haven: Yale University Press).

Martin, David A. (1983), 'Due Process and Membership in the National Community: Political Asylum and Beyond', *University of Pittsburgh Law Review*, 44: 165–235.

Mead, Lawrence M. (1986), *Beyond Entitlement: The Social Obligations of Citizenship* (New York: Free Press).

Neuman, Gerald L. (1992), 'We are the People: Alien Suffrage in German and American Perspective', *Michigan Journal of International Law*, 13: 259–335.

—— (1993), 'The Lost Century of American Immigration Law 1776–1875', *Columbia Law Review*, 93: 1833–1901.

—— (1994), 'Justifying U.S. Naturalization Policies', *Virginia Journal of International Law*, 35: 237–78.

Raskin, Jamin (1993), 'Legal Aliens, Local Citizens: The Historical, Constitutional and Theoretical Meanings of Alien Suffrage', *University of Pennsylvania Law Review*, 141: 1391–1470.

Romano, Roberta (1993), *The Genius of American Corporate Law* (Washington: REI Press).

Rosberg, Gerald (1977), 'Aliens and Equal Protection: Why not the Right to Vote?', *Michigan Law Review*, 75: 1092–1136.

Schmitt, Eric (1996), 'Giuliani Criticizes G.O.P. and Dole on Immigration', *New York Times*, 7 June, B3, col. 5.

Schuck, Peter H. (1984), 'The Transformation of Immigration Law', *Columbia Law Review*, 84: 1–90.

—— (1989), 'Membership in the Liberal Polity: The Devaluation of American Citizenship', *Georgetown Immigration Law Journal*, 3: 1–18.

—— (1993), 'Public Law Litigation and Social Reform', *Yale Law Journal*, 102: 1763–86.

—— (1994), 'Whose Membership is it Anyway? Comments on Gerald Neuman', *Virginia Journal of International Law*, 35: 321–31.

—— (1995), 'The Message of 187', *The American Prospect* (Spring), 85–92.

—— (1995–6), 'Testimony before House Judiciary Subcommittees on Immigration and Claims and on the Constitution', US Congress, 13 Dec. 1995 and suppl. letter 14 Feb. 1996.

—— (1996*a*), 'Alien Rumination', *Yale Law Journal*, 105: 1963–2012.

—— (1996*b*), 'Introduction: Reflections on the Federalism Debate', *Yale Law and Policy Review*, 14: 1–22.

—— (1997), 'Against (and for) Madison: An Essay in Praise of Factions', *Yale Law and Policy Review*, 15: 553–97.

—— (1998), 'Dual Citizenship in an Era of Migration', in Schuck, *Citizens, Strangers, and In-Betweens: Essays on Immigration and Citizenship* (Boulder, Colo: Westview Press).

—— and Rogers M. Smith (1985), *Citizenship without Consent: Illegal Aliens in the American Polity* (New Haven: Yale University Press).

—— —— (1996), Letter to the Editor, *New York Times*, 11 Aug., A14.

Shklar, Judith N. (1991), *American Citizenship: The Quest for Inclusion* (Cambridge, Mass.: Harvard University Press).

Skerry, Peter (1995), 'Many Borders to Cross: Is Immigration the Exclusive Responsibility of the Federal Government', *Publius*, 25: 71–85.

Smith, Rogers M. (1997), *Civic Ideals: Conflicting Visions of Citizenship in U.S. Public Law* (New Haven: Yale University Press).

Soysal, Yasemin (1994), *Limits of Citizenship: Migrants and Postnational Membership in Europe* (Chicago: University of Chicago Press).

—— (1996), *Changing Parameters of Citizenship and Claims-Making: Organized Islam in European Public Spheres*, Working Paper no. EUF 1996/4 (Florence: European University Institute).

Spiro, Peter J. (1994), 'The States and Immigration in an Era of Demi-Sovereignties', *Virginia Journal of International Law*, 35: 121–78.

—— (1997), 'Dual Nationality and the Meaning of Citizenship', *Emory Law Journal* 46.

US Department of Justice (1993), Immigration and Naturalization Service, *Statistical Yearbook for 1993* (Washington: US Department of Justice).

—— (1995), Immigration and Naturalization Service, *Statistical Yearbook for 1995* (Washington: US Department of Justice).

Weil, Patrick (1995), *La France et ses étrangers* (Paris: Calmann-Lévy).

Williams, John and Schuck, Peter H. (forthcoming), 'Deporting Criminal Aliens: The Pitfalls and Opportunities of Federalism', *Harvard Journal of Law & Public Policy*, 21.

*Yale Law and Policy Review* (1996).

# 7

# Reconfiguring Citizenship in Western Europe

MIRIAM FELDBLUM

In contemporary Europe, citizenship policies and practices have undergone dramatic changes.[1] Europe has witnessed a proliferation of citizenship and nationality reforms. Numerous west European states, including Great Britain, Belgium, the Netherlands, Spain, Switzerland, Germany, and France, have revised or attempted to revise their citizenship, naturalization, or nationality provisions and criteria.[2] Some state revisions have appeared restrictive, including tightening nationality acquisition and redefining citizenship categories; others have been expansive, including facilitating the naturalization process, enabling dual nationality, and enlarging the eligibility criteria for citizenship. In the past decades European polities have extended many rights previously associated with formal state citizenship, such as rights to access the social service system and the market-place, and rights to residency. New policies to incorporate immigrants have included variations of multicultural policies and legislation extending the right to vote, at least on the local levels, to non-citizens.

At the same time, the continuing process of European integration and the provisions of the 1992 Maastricht Treaty have produced new categories of European citizenship and its associated rights for the nationals of EU member states. With all these changes, conflict over the practice and understandings of national membership has intensified. Beyond disputes over formal policies, various debates continue to arise over the meaning of national identity and community, the integration of immigrants—who may or may not be foreigners—and minority groups, and the definition of the nation. At various times in recent history, west European states have proposed, and often passed, policies to restrict the access and incorporation of foreigners.[3] In the broader conflicts over immigration and immigrants, the defence of national and restrictive models of membership are often contrasted with calls for immigrant rights and other forms of membership.

The character, consequence, and direction of these citizenship changes are greatly contested.[4] Some studies advance the view that recent developments indicate that traditional understandings and operation of citizenship have become displaced, as different kinds of 'post-national' trends in citizenship and society increase.[5] Others, to the contrary, focus on how current trends demonstrate the adaptability of existing citizenship schema and the persistence of 'national models' of state citizenship.[6] Finally, others still point out that what is significant today are patterns of convergence across west European polities.[7]

This chapter seeks to address two questions about the changes in citizenship in Europe: Do trends in domestic and international policy-making, public discourse, and political practices signal important transformations in citizenship development in western Europe? And, to what extent has a convergence emerged across these European countries? I argue here that national citizenship is being reconfigured in two distinct directions. The first is in the direction of what has been called 'post-national' membership (Soysal 1994). By 'post-national', I mean to refer to developments that move beyond the formal state, or where the state is no longer the sole site for citizenship. However, transformations in citizenship are not simply moving from old national forms of membership to new, emergent post-national forms of membership. Instead of a dichotomy between the existing national citizenship and post-national citizenship, there is another set of citizenship outcomes in the direction of what I call 'neo-national' membership.[8] By 'neo-national', I mean to refer to developments whose effects are to reconfigure cultural, national, and transnational boundaries to ensure closure.

In this chapter, I argue that the two developments—post-national and neo-national membership—constitute limited or glancing kinds of convergence among European states. On the one hand, across western Europe, seemingly convergent or common outcomes in nationality reforms, incorporation policies, and European citizenship are apparent. But, the substance of these developments reveal very different angles and directions. One of the ways to understand such convergence is to identify the dominant strategies which have contributed to its emergence. In the contemporary developments a wide array of actors ranging from subnational, national, transnational, to international levels have pursued actions and ways of ordering and organizing membership. I call these actions and ways 'citizenship strategies'.[9] The actors include national governments, political parties, immigrant associations, transnational movements, and EU institutions. Actor-centred strategies imply a narrow sense of agency, choice, and power relations: Whose strategies? To what end or for what purpose?[10] Taken together, however, dominant sets of strategies are neither confined nor reducible to individual political actors or deliberative actions (Crow 1989). For the purposes of this analysis, I am interested in identifying the changing strategies that are evident in policies, public discourse, collective action, and other political and institutional outcomes.

## CITIZENSHIP DEVELOPMENT: POST-NATIONAL AND NEO-NATIONAL TRENDS

Traditional citizenship has meant full membership in a polity. In the modern world, the polity has been understood to be a nation-state; that is, citizenship is integrally linked to a territorial state and to the people (or nation) belonging to that state. In other words, citizenship has been regulated by states to specify a single and singular membership. Membership has been institutionalized by rights, benefits, and obligations which distinguish members from non-members. It has been identified by substantive understandings of membership and community, and located in an authoritative nation-state. How different is this initial capsulation of state citizenship from current developments? Well, there is no doubt that citizenship matters have become more complex. A brief review of citizenship regulations, institutionalization, ideologies, and locus can underscore the changes.

Citizenship regulations cover the formal state membership policies, which set the legal procedures and parameters of state membership. In an administrative, legal sense these rules tell us who is a citizen and who is not. Variation in these rules among the European states have certainly existed, and continue to persist. Despite variations, European states generally have relied on the presumption that the regulation of modern citizenship has meant the regulation of a single citizenship, and the coincidence of bounded citizenries with territorial nation-states. The institutionalization of citizenship is another central dimension in state citizenship. This is defined in terms of incorporation, rights, benefits, and obligations. Such elements enforced the consequentialness of membership status. It delineated distinctions between nationals and non-nationals. It also underscored distinctions between effective, full citizens and those without full membership citizenship. T. H. Marshall defined modern citizenship as a status denoting full membership in a community to which are attached rights and duties. He outlined three elements of citizenship development: civil, political, and social rights (Marshall 1953: 74–90). Like citizenship regulations, citizenship insti-tutionalization has evolved historically and varied cross-nationally.[11] Despite the dissimilarities, institutionalization in modern Europe was mainly about incorporation of bounded citizenries into national citizen-ship, which took place within the national parameters of a territorial nation or single state.[12] It featured national referents, including the single state, shared nationhood, and bounded rights. Developments often were seen as driven by national agents, including political élites and economic groups.

The ideology of a national citizenship is another dimension of state citizenship. These ideologies have presumed that membership is situ-ated in the nation-state and that citizenries are defined by these national boundaries and identities. While noting the analytical difficulty of defin-ing homogeneous and specifically distinctive national sentiments, Max Weber emphasized that 'one can only do so by referring to a tendency toward an autonomous state' and that 'sentiments of solidarity, very het-erogenous in both their nature and origin, are comprised within national sentiments' (1946: 179). Finally, the authority over citizenship and the capacity to regulate it has been traditionally located in a sovereign, auto-nomous nation-state. In all the dimensions of citizenship outlined above, the role of the state has been integral. The nation-state set the bound-aries for citizenship, ensured the bounded citizenry, organized mem-bership incorporation, and perpetuated the distinctions between nationals and non-nationals. The historical basis for this 'model' or characteriza-tion of citizenship has been in fact the west European experience.

Yet, the recent developments to which I referred speak of very dif-ferent citizenship matters. What led from the coincidence of citizenship and the nation-state to contemporary trends? Yasemin Soysal (1994) has offered a broad analysis of the array of domestic and international factors which have generated new developments. These include the changing nature of membership in the modern world, increased flows of labour migration to Europe in the post-war period; European changes in the matter of national sovereignty and identity, particularly within the European Union; the increase in international organizations and international regulations, including the dissemination of an international discourse of human rights. David Held has argued that in the European Community 'any conception of sovereignty which assumes that it is an indivisible, illimitable, exclusive, and perpetual form of public power

—embodied within an individual state—is defunct' (1996: 412). He too points to the rise of international law that has arisen to constrain national governments. For example, the European Convention on Human Rights created human rights legislation that, in principle, was transferable across national borders without restriction, was not subject to large variations of national legislation, and was guaranteed by supranational institutions limiting the sovereignty of the state. A recent article on the European Court of Human Rights remarked on the ire provoked when the court ruled against British legislation (*New York Times* 1996). International conventions, agreements, and directives expanded the rights of foreigners even if they did not eliminate discrimination against non-nationals or foreign residents. While the European Convention on Human Rights extended protection to non-nationals, it was still premised on the distinction between national and non-national.[13] Such factors have mediated the previous power of traditionally national determinants, such as state institutional arrangements, political and cultural tradition, domestic social structure, historical context, geography, or colonialist legacies.[14]

Likewise, the emergence of regional and other new social movements in the 1960s and 1970s helped to introduce new conflicts, agents, and referents in citizenship. The formation and experiences of immigrant or minority communities introduced changes in ethnic and multicultural politics. The extension of universal suffrage to women, and the extension of social rights within the citizenry may be considered simply as extensions of existing citizenship institutionalization. However, the issues of women's rights, minority recognition, and identity that arose in the new contexts have also been considered incapable of being handled by the existing institutions. Social movements in west European polities as elsewhere sharply critiqued the limited universalism of liberal or republicanist democratic citizenship. They have critiqued the capacity of state citizenship to deal with pluralist politics (cf. Mouffe 1992; Castles 1994: 4, 7). Feminists continue to argue that women have not experienced the full membership, equality, and standing of citizenship (Young 1990; Yuval-Davis 1991). Taken as a whole, the new social movements have striven to redefine the import of national parameters and institute new referents of transnational, local, and international membership. Regardless of outcomes, they also introduced new agents, including women, foreigners, racial or ethnic minorities, and transnational movements and organizations.

Yasemin Soysal's institutionalist analysis of membership and immigrant incorporation in Europe identifies a general, pervasive transformation of the European state institutional framework. Soysal contends that contemporary citizenship developments are indicators of an emergent 'post-national membership'. Indeed, numerous changes in citizenship do reconfigure national citizenship in post-national directions. The emergence of these trends are evident in a variety of state policies, international discourse, public definitions, and collective action. They move membership beyond the parameters of a particularistic, territorial, or nationally bound citizenry. Frequently, the conflicts associated with such developments have international or transnational origins. They are often defined as struggles over identity, where the authority status of the nation-state is either contested or deemed less relevant than other criteria. Sources of the logic driving these changes have been both domestic and international. A closer examination of recent developments can provide a better understanding of emergent post-national trends.

One of the more salient developments has been the proliferation of citizenship reforms. Some have been highly politicized while others have been less so. Revising citizenship laws is not novel. What has been striking about the current spate of reforms is the new kinds of convergence visible among the European states, including a loosening of citizenship regulations. Numerous west European states have passed various kinds of expansionist reforms of their naturalization, citizenship, dual nationality, and voting rights policies. Belgium and the Netherlands, for example, revised their laws in 1985, supplementing their traditional descent or lineage-based criteria for membership with qualified territorial rights to citizenship. They facilitated naturalization and dual nationality, and extended local suffrage to long-term foreign residents. In 1991 Belgium granted the automatic acquisition of citizenship to children born in Belgium of foreign parents. Germany facilitated access to German citizenship in 1991 and 1993, and other states have enacted similar revisions (Çinar 1994). The expansionist nationality reforms point in the direction of post-national membership in several ways. Reforms facilitating access to citizenship can modify the ties between national identity and formal citizenship. Facilitating the acquisition of citizenship also enables in practice the increasing incidence of multiple memberships. The reforms arose in the aftermath of post-war labour migration to western Europe. They acknowledged, albeit reluctantly and only recently in certain cases, the permanent immigrant settlement in these polities. It is important to note that characterizing these reforms as expansionist or leading to post-national outcomes does not delimit the varied politics driving these reforms.

Consider more closely the phenomenon of dual nationality. Multiple nationality has traditionally been discouraged and banned by states.[15] Nevertheless, the incidence of dual nationality in western Europe has continued to rise, and is now estimated in the millions. Gender equity reforms, and transnational migration and immigrants who retain the nationality of their countries of origin, account for part of the growing numbers. Several west European states in the past decade or so have changed their national laws to permit dual nationality. In fact, according to Dilek Çinar, 'the availability of dual nationality has now become a matter of course in Western Europe', with some exceptions (1994: 62). In 1992 it was estimated that 18–19 million legal foreign residents were living in western Europe, up from 5 million in 1950. Thus, the incidence of dual nationality will increase (Fassman and Münz 1994: 5). Even those states long opposed to dual nationality have softened their opposition. With close to 2 million Turks in Germany, Germany and Turkey have engaged in inter-state discussions about dual nationality. This phenomenon is not specific to western Europe alone. For example, debates have arisen in Mexico over enabling dual nationality for Mexican nationals in the United States. Likewise, both Turks in Berlin and Mexican immigrants in California have engaged in their own campaigns for the right to dual nationality, and, at the same time, for the right to vote in their countries of origin, and still again, for the extension of voting rights in their place of residence, regardless of their nationality. The emergent fluidity of memberships— local, national, and transnational—has meant that citizenries are less defined by one state border or identity.

Dual nationality breaks with the logic and practice of national state citizenship. For different reasons, the European Parliament called for EU member states to permit dual nationality, and the Swedish and French governments struggled to rescind the 1963 Strasbourg Convention —a treaty to discourage dual nationality—in the Council of Europe. Unlike the Swedish, the French efforts were driven by government officials and French emigrant groups who bemoaned the inequities of the legitimate dual national status of a Franco-non-European, such as Franco-Algerians, and the problematic dual national status of a Franco-European, such as a Franco-German, whom they considered 'culturally closer'. On the other hand, Portugal in 1981 loosened restrictions on dual nationality for its numerous emigrant groups abroad, who did not want to forfeit Portuguese nationality. In a very different context, Germany allows ethnic Germans (*Aussiedler*) who acquire Germany nationality to retain their previous citizenship. Regardless of the intentions of policy-makers, therefore, the proliferation and legitimization of dual and multiple nationality transforms the function of citizenship.

Beyond nationality revisions, the practice of extending rights and benefits to non-citizens—in other words, citizenship rights without citizenship—has signalled important changes in the institutionalization of citizenship. In western Europe, long-term foreign residents have the economic, legal, and social rights of citizens, including rights to welfare, rights to social services, unemployment benefits, and medical insurance. Nor are such access and rights limited to long-term foreign residents. While asylum-seekers, short-term foreign residents, and those without legal papers have certainly had a more precarious status, they too have been granted more rights. This has meant in part that state citizenship has become less determinative; it matters less. Tomas Hammar and other scholars have called the new rights for long-term foreign residents 'denizen' rights (Hammar 1990; Layton-Henry 1990). Other interpretations have classified contemporary policies granting 'denizen'-style rights as extensions of national citizenship. For example, suffrage has been a right traditionally associated with formal legal citizenship, and conflict over suffrage was a key feature in national citizenship development. Rainer Bauböck (1992) has called the extension of voting rights to foreigners an extension of citizenship. But, I would argue, the effect of these policies do not really extend citizenship to foreigners along the logic of national citizenship. The extension of local suffrage to non-nationals translates into more fluid national boundaries, but does not transform the status of foreigners into a status analogous to that of previously disfranchised classes within these polities. Overlapping citizenship rights can extend from subnational to transnational levels, and cut across several categories of citizens and foreigners. For example, EU citizenship covers nationals of those member states. At the same time, several European states had already extended local suffrage rights to their long-term foreign legal residents. Further, select dimensions of EU citizenship, such as the right to appeal to the European Union Ombudsman, can actually extend to all legal residents within the Union, not only EU nationals.

For Soysal, the enactment of legislation granting rights or facilitating incorporation on criteria other than formal citizenship status is an important indicator of an emergent post-national model of membership. She cites that one of the emergent bases for extending rights rests on the notion of 'personhood', the foreigner is considered a person, a human even if not a national. Soysal links the extension of rights for non-nationals to the concurrent rise of human rights discourse and policies in international and transnational regimes and to transformations in state sovereignty (1994: 140–3). The principle of personhood is a post-national norm, in so far as it is not based on institutionalized national status nor generated by the state; however, the policies and discourse about human rights need not originate outside the state.[16] In European states, as in the United States, national courts have played important roles in striking down government actions to restrict rights and benefits as violating human rights of these people, regardless of their citizenship status.[17] In the case of the passage of the 1993 French reforms on immigration and citizenship, the French Constitutional Council ruled that some aspects of the government's legislation violated the rights of foreigners as individuals. As a lead article in *Le Monde* (1993) stated, 'foreigners are not French but they are people'. At the same time, international organizations as well have called for the protection of the human rights of foreigner populations.

The decoupling of membership ideologies from formal state citizenship has been another indicator of a reconfiguration of citizenship. As immigration and citizenship became politicized topics, immigrant activists and others have attempted to redefine the national identity. They talk about transnational loyalties or multiple memberships, rather than a singular citizenship. In fact, numerous immigrant associations have pursued explicit and self-conscious kinds of post-national strategy, such as calling for new citizenship, voting rights for foreigners, and the dissociation of citizenship and nationality. The impetus to dissociate citizenship from nationality has long been advocated by immigrant activists who claim the right to engage in 'citizenship' activities in the locality where they live while retaining their nationality. Interestingly, one can consider that such logic was appropriated by the European Intergovernmental Conference of 1992 in its formulation of an EU citizenship. In other ways, the questions of membership and identity raised in the contemporary wave of citizenship politics recall those raised by feminist and other social movements. They are not subsumed easily under traditional conceptions of citizenship rights and obligations.[18]

Finally, EU citizenship is certainly not delimited to the nation-state. Part of the drive underlying the new EU citizenship has been that the European Union is giving its member nationals the new status to generate loyalty and identity to itself, to the European Union. From this perspective, EU citizenship can be considered not simply as complementing national membership, but as displacing national citizenship. Some scholars argue that to speak of a European identity challenges 'nationalist conceptions of political citizenship' (Turner 1994: 157; Habermas 1994: 20–35). Examining the emergence of different social and political rights in the European Community, Elizabeth Meehan has argued that once we separate citizenship from nationality, 'the European Community can be thought of as, and already is, a polity in which more than one set of standards can be invoked—a kind of three dimensional framework for the exercise of the rights, loyalties, and duties of citizenship' (1993*a*: 173).[19] As a whole, European integration process continues to shift decision-making upward. At present, many rules regarding labour flow, population movements, social policies, and rights are being defined at level of EU institutions, including the Commission, Council, and Court.

Post-national developments are not simply extensions of national development of citizenship. They break with its logic by moving citizenship beyond or outside of the parameters of a territorial nation-state. They underscore how citizenries are no longer bounded as they once were. However, even as post-national reconfigurations of membership and trends have been the product of both international and domestic processes, other reconfigurations and trends have also arisen. From a post-national perspective, nationalist and exclusionary dimensions of citizenship development are backlash phenomena. They are often considered reflective of old, persistent national membership models. They are reactionary trends and not new in a significant way.[20] But, are the constrictive trends in citizenship development an indicator only of resistance by the old order? Post-national arguments can appear to imply an irreversibility to the diminishment of national membership. They can underestimate a reconfiguration of national membership that resembles national citizenship. Institutionalist arguments also relegate specific political responses as secondary to the institutional outcomes. Yet, the political processes of membership, immigration, and citizenship policies have generated new political conflicts and debates, with institutional implications. The intensity and kind of political responses in the new European citizenship politics has varied considerably, even when outcomes have appeared convergent, such as with nationality reforms. Indeed, the contrasting types and intensities of political response appear to be an important site to examine in order to understand fully the new citizenship politics and its ramifications.

The emergence of what I call 'neo-national' membership can be discerned in current citizenship developments, and, in particular, in the political processes of the new citizenship politics. The term 'neo-national' is used to distinguish these trends from the existing national order of citizenship and from traditional nationalist trends. Neo-national membership is a reconfiguration of cultural, national, even supranational boundaries to ensure new closures. Like post-national developments, neo-national trends also break with the logic of extension within a bounded citizenry; they too involve boundary settings within or beyond the national territorial state. In other words, if one defines traditional state citizenship as delimited by the formal state, neo-national membership may encompass a larger transnational space outside the state or a smaller cultural space within the state. Neo-national reconfigurations of membership are often assemblages of nationalist sources and state citizenship traditions. Yet, they demonstrate the malleability of such sources and citizenship (see e.g. Whitney 1996; Crossette 1996). As with post-national outcomes, this set of developments has been shaped by cross-cutting transnational factors as well as specific domestic processes. And it too can be examined in each of the central dimensions of citizenship.

Alongside the slew of expansionist nationality reforms have come several important constrictive revisions of membership. In France in 1993, for example, a ten-year national debate on citizenship culminated in a restrictive reform of the Nationality Code. The 1993 revision tightened France's traditional territorial criteria for citizenship. It required that second-generation immigrants—those born and raised in France of foreign parents born elsewhere—file formal requests to become French—to integrate into French national community. The reform also restricted the applicability of other territorial criteria, which had facilitated attribution of citizenship to its post-colonial populations. In Britain, the Nationality Act of 1981 formalized a series of efforts to redefine British nationality in a newly and narrowly national and culturalist bounded citizenship (Cesarani 1996). In the United States, the national Republican Party has recently called for the repudiation of the scope of the (post-Civil War) fourteenth Amendment so as to deny birthright citizenship to children born in the United States of foreign parents who are not either legal or long-term foreign residents. Constrictive reforms point in the direction of neo-national membership in several ways. The reforms reinvigorate a bounded citizenry by breaking with the historical national order, such as breaking with long-standing precedent, revising historical criteria, or creating new boundaries. Of course, the rhetoric of the reforms may stress that they are the culmination of historical loyalty. As a practical effect, the reforms are often exclusionary and not expansive reconfigurations of citizenship. They may buttress the new cultural and racial nationalisms.

Recent efforts to restrict and rescind the institutionalization of citizenship rights without citizenship can be considered a response to ongoing post-national trends. These efforts cut across the different levels of overlapping memberships, to include the undocumented or 'illegal' immigrants, marginalized asylum-seekers, 'denizens' or longer-term foreign residents, as well as others with ties to the old national membership order. For example, there have been crack-downs against illegal immigration in numerous European countries, as well as specific efforts aimed at asylum-seekers. Britain's Immigration and Asylum Bill in autumn 1995 called for restricted access to services for certain groups of asylum-seekers. The rightist Germany party the Christian Social Union (CSU) called for payment cuts to refugees and asylum-seekers.[21] Thus, even when citizenship as a status has appeared to matter less, new patterns of exclusion have arisen. They are constituted by boundaries that are both within and without the nation-state (see e.g. Blitz 1995; Eager 1995; *Financial Times* 1996; Ying 1996). In this respect, neo-national membership is not solely domestic. Like post-national membership, it has domestic consequences, but also transnational implications.

Efforts to define national membership in exclusive, cultural nationalist terms have been visible across western Europe. The efforts are often spearheaded by far-right groups in Europe. The sharp rise of far-right nationalist, anti-immigrant parties in many west European states has been dramatic. But, the generation and promotion of culturalist rhetoric and restrictive access spans the political spectrum. Its logic is not defined solely by the nation-state. For example, the rightist rhetoric about citizenship in the French debates drew variously on human rights discourse and the right to difference, and a culturalist Europe. Likewise, left and centrist proponents of citizenship reform drew from reconstructed national traditions of citizenship and transnational references. These efforts have been characterized as the 'new nationalist republicanism' (cf. Feldblum 1993; Lorcerie 1994; Favell 1997). The integrationist strategies of immigrant associations in France also coincided with the logic of the new citizenship reforms. The president of France Plus, a politically active immigrant group, approved of the stress on national integration of immigrants and the definition of national identity advanced by a national Commission on Nationality: the Commission upholds 'the republican model, the values of the Revolution . . .

they propose to reinvigorate the Francophone space' (interview in *Libération*, 1 January 1988). While francophone space implies the extension of French membership, the actual reform of 1993 entailed an exclusion of the traditional francophone citizens. The reform sharply curtailed the privileged lien—in terms of 'double *jus soli*' of former colonial populations.[22]

The conflation of citizenship and immigration issues, and in particular of immigrant, national membership and identity issues, has been another dimension of neo-national developments. There are now 10–13 million Muslims living in western Europe, a significant portion of whom are nationals of European countries; the largest populations are 5 million in France, of whom at least 2 million are French nationals or dual nationals, 1 million in Britain, of whom most are nationals, and 2 million in Germany, of whom almost none are nationals. During highly visible affairs—including the Rushdie affair in Britain and the Islamic scarves affair in France—the issue became in part the suspected transnational memberships of the resident Muslim population. The links between citizenship and immigrants have become both more salient and obscured in Europe and elsewhere, because certain immigrants—whether illegal, legal, or citizens—are considered foreign and 'illegitimate', be it their origin or religion that is rendered suspect.

Indicators of an emergent neo-national membership are visible across western Europe in the efforts to tighten and restrict access into the countries—what has been called by some the phenomenon of a Fortress Europe. Interestingly, part of that rhetoric derives its logic from transnational trends often associated with post-national outcomes. Arguments for Fortress Europe have included reference to Europe's right to be different, that is its cultural and historical rights. In other words, the promotion of a culturalist Europe has drawn upon an international discourse of rights and identity. Other arguments are based on the new political economy of the post-war order so that European states are said to be responding in necessary ways to the pressures generated by the internationalization of markets and the globalization of labour. National closures are now built on similar foundations. For example, efforts to create a Fortress America have translated into actual construction of concrete walls and wire; they are also built on 'English only' legislation that seeks to uphold America's 'rights' to difference and identity.

Thus, boundary-setting and closure have taken place at various levels: access for immigrants within the polity, national citizenship, and international borders. There is, in fact, a dynamic between the increasing membership fluidity and new closures. For example, the language of European integration speaks of 'l'espace homogène'; the phrase could be translated as a 'border-free territory', but it also contains the meaning of a space without foreign elements. While Germany and other states have facilitated access to citizenship, they have dramatically closed off physical access to themselves. Germany in 1993 dramatically restricted its refugee policy, and accelerated deportations. In fact, the deportation of asylum-seekers and undocumented immigrants generally has increased in European countries. In France, governmental efforts to deport hundreds of African immigrants in the summer of 1996 became a national crisis when 300 immigrants sought refuge in a Parisian church, with some undertaking hunger-strikes. The legal status of many African immigrants had become complicated following the restrictive immigration and citizenship revisions of 1993. By late August government officials had retreated somewhat from their hard-line position by declaring that about a third of the targeted immigrants would be allowed to remain in France. They argued both the European implications if their efforts failed and the fact that the Council of State—the institution that in the past defended the 'human rights' of immigrants—upheld their right to expel the immigrants. The crisis over the African immigrants clearly highlighted the exclusion of immigrants from ex-colonial territories from French membership. Besides humanitarian concerns, protestors decried the constriction of French 'national' boundaries; as one Mali immigrant argued, 'we're here to stay . . . for us, we're not immigrants. We are in our native land' (cited in Rosenblum 1996; see also Reuters 1996*a*,*b*).

The locus of authority in neo-national membership, unlike traditional citizenship, is not limited to the nation-state. Earlier, EU citizenship provided an instance of post-national membership. Yet, an alternative interpretation is also possible. European citizenship has been based on a strong presumption of national citizenship, and is most frequently understood as complementing the national memberships of its member states. In fact, for the coming revision of the Maastricht Treaty, all member states as well as the European Parliament and other European entities proposed explicit clarifications to that effect, that EU citizenship supplements without replacing national citizenship. At times, to speak of a European citizenship or identity has been to construct western Europe as a historical-organic collection of nation-states necessarily banded together to protect their cultural particularities (cf.

Martiniello 1994; Ferry 1992). Even those efforts formulated for the 'promotion of European citizenship' can be redefined to promote cultural particularities. For example, the project of 'Europe in Fifteen Towers', sponsored by the European Pegasus Foundation, revolves around schools in the fifteen member states adopting local monuments and then creating collages of the monument pictures. The press release for the project asked, 'But the European citizens, will they feel more European?' The solution, according to this project, was selected monuments, many religious and patriotic in nature, to discern the constituent components of the 'European' culture and identity (Summit 1996). Thus, EU citizenship and European identity can be understood as a reformulation of nationalist ideas. Notwithstanding the strong opposition of many nationalist parties in Europe to the European Union, the integration process can be see as redrawing the lines around a culturalist and physical Europe so to ensure the exclusion of non-European foreigners, an exclusion that actually can no longer be effectively or easily accomplished at the level of the nation-state.

Neo-national trends are more than replays or extensions of national and nationalist developments. They can break with the logic of the historical development of national citizenship. Their referents and parameters extend beyond the state. They underscore innovative conflations of identity, citizenship, and immigration issues.[23] To summarize the arguments thus far, I have identified two distinctive trends in citizenship development. The first being the reconfiguration of national state citizenship in terms of post-national membership, and the second the redefinition of national membership in terms of neo-national membership. Are post-national and neo-national memberships competing, contradictory developments? The answer is not straightforward.

From the different types of evidence given here, there are at least three ways in which the two sets of developments can be seen to be causally linked. First, in some respects, the developments are like two sides of a coin, shaped by the same phenomena. Thus, the rise of transnational forces, new social movements, and changing demographic, political, and economic factors have produced post-national phenomena as well as neo-national pressures. Secondly, several recent developments in the direction of neo-national membership have constituted a response to emergent post-national reconfigurations of membership. Finally, at times, both sets of developments appear as components of what Yasemin Soysal has called the 'dialectic of the post-war global system', which refers to the 'institutionalized duality between the two normative principles of the global system: national sovereignty and universal human rights' (1996: 24).

## CONVERGENT OUTCOMES, DIVERGENT STRATEGIES

Why focus on citizenship strategies? There are several reasons for this. First, strategies highlight the interactions of political actors, institutions, and ideologies. In other words, they bring the political process of citizenship developments back into focus. A focus on strategies, therefore, illuminates one of the factors contributing to changing citizenship in Europe. I argue that identifying and understanding the divergent strategies sharply qualifies the current convergence. I do not contend that divergent citizenship strategies constitute the sole explanation for new citizenship developments. As noted earlier, an array of factors, including broad structural and institutional changes, have shaped the new developments. Finally, citizenship strategies underscore the actions pursued by a variety of actors on the tiered and cross-cutting levels of contemporary citizenship, including national, subnational, transnational, and specifically European levels. In the following cases, I aim to identify the dominant sets of citizenship strategies. Clearly, neither domestic nor European citizenship politics have featured monolithic strategies, but I am interested here in those strategies or ways of pursuing membership issues and priorities that helped define the outcomes. In the following pages, I examine the dominant citizenship strategies in three instances of apparent convergence: nationality reform and incorporation policy, using the 1993 French and German cases, and the establishment and ongoing revision of EU citizenship.

Consider more closely the nationality reforms enacted by Germany and France, each of which modified the traditional order. In Germany, citizenship traditionally has been based on lineage criteria or the rules of *jus sanguinis*, whereby one is automatically attributed German citizenship if one's parents or ancestry are German; if not, then a procedure of naturalization must be undertaken. Thus, 'ethnic Germans' from Russia and other parts of eastern Europe are granted citizenship automatically upon entry into Germany. At the same time, second- and third-generation immigrants of Turkish origin born in Germany have neither been attributed citizenship at birth nor automatically been given it at any point later on. Under the citizenship law, they must undergo a naturalization process and renunciation of their previous citizenship to obtain German citizenship. In France, the Nationality Code contained a mixture of territorial and lineage criteria, whereby second-generation immigrants—those born in France of foreigners born elsewhere—acquired French citizenship semi-automatically at their majority; and third-generation immigrants—those born in France of foreigners born themselves on French territory—were attributed French citizenship at birth.

Recent reforms indicate that whereas Germans now discuss moving towards a combination of descent and territorial criteria and lessening the ethno-cultural presumptions of citizenship, the French have moved towards a tighter combination of territory and descent and increased the culturalist connotations of citizenship. As the Germans seek a type of 'French solution' to citizenship processes, the French seek greater political and cultural closure.[24] The direction of the French and German reforms not only contradicts rhetoric about their respective 'national models', it also points to a convergence of sorts in citizenship policy. Yet, the strategies driving the two reforms are at odds with each other.

For the past several years the German government has continued to institutionalize a liberalization of naturalization procedures and conditions for both long-term foreign residents and foreigners born and raised in Germany. A 1991 Act Amending the Aliens Law gave these groups a claim to naturalization. In July 1993 new revisions, which were in many ways a reiteration of the earlier liberalization, gave both groups an 'absolute entitlement to naturalization', in other words, a right to citizenship (Federal Ministry of the Interior 1993: 38).[25] The most recent German naturalization revisions came amidst several events that accentuated the absence of citizenship access for Turkish foreigners and long-settled immigrants: the continuing attacks against foreigners in Germany, the large influx of ethnic Germans who are granted German citizenship automatically, the unification of East and West Germany, and the government's passage of a severely restrictive asylum reform. Facilitating naturalization was considered partly compensation to immigrant workers and the families long settled in Germany, in particular those originating from Turkey, who had been targets of fire-bombing. Opening the door to German citizenship was also compensation for political support for harsh closures at the border. Chancellor Kohl in June 1993 asserted that German citizenship law, whose foundations date back to 1913 and are based solely on lineage criteria, needed radical overhauling, and underscored the case of second-generation youth.[26]

While the Kohl government held back from introducing a legislative proposal at that point, other parties, including the major opposition, the Social Democratic Party (SPD), and the centrist party, the Free Democratic Party (FDP), floated citizenship reforms. Since that time, citizenship reform has become an increasingly salient topic in German national politics, with the German far-right parties and movements generating a rhetoric of German identity and anti-immigrant sentiments. At stake in the policy debates since 1993 have been the institution of qualified territorial criteria for citizenship for foreigners born in Germany, and the acceptance of dual nationality; also debated has been the extension of local suffrage and other civic rights to all long-term foreign residents (and not only EU nationals).[27] Turkish immigrant associations have called for easier access to Germany citizenship, but their other priorities are the extension of local suffrage and the availability of dual nationality. In June 1996 Germany's Commission for Foreigners predicted that legislation to enable dual nationality for second-generation immigrants would pass the Bundestag because a majority of parliamentary members support such a reform.

German strategies and debate have been situated in the context of dispersed memberships within and beyond Germany. By 'dispersed memberships', I mean to refer to different levels of formal and informal membership, including intranational membership, as in East or West German or ethnic German; national membership, as in German national or foreign national; and transnational membership, as in European national, or ethnic or religious identifications. The reasons for these varied dispersed memberships and their particular salience in Germany are several. First, German reunification and the influx of ethnic Germans generated cultural dissonance within the imagery of German citizenship. It also created pragmatic dissonance. For example, ethnic Germans are permitted to retain their nationality of origin. Secondly, the changing German immigration and citizenship policies have been formulated with reference to the European Union. For example, the 1993 revision of the asylum law in Germany was partly propelled by the restrictive Dublin Accord on asylum as well as by restrictive crack-downs on asylum-seekers instituted by other west European countries. In addition, given that second-generation immigrant youth in some other European countries accede to citizenship more easily, German laws have transnational implications. Germany itself has also been divided about EU citizenship. A *Europinion* survey (EC 1996*a*) issued by the European Commission showed that while 65 per cent of West Germans view themselves as both German and European, less than 50 per cent of East Germans do so. Thirdly, Germany has embarked on a series of bilateral negotiations with Turkey on issues such as dual citizenship. Likewise, immigrant activists in Germany stress transnational integration, such as dual nationality and voting in Germany and Turkey, rather than singular citizenship.

In certain ways, therefore, the dominant effect of recent citizenship strategies in Germany has been an evasion of the parameters of national-cultural membership. Strategies of singular cultural citizenship have not been the predominant focus. Indeed, it is arguable that the increasing political support for dual nationality by some is a form of resistance or preventative measure against a more substantive reconfiguration of German citizenship. Since 1989, in particular, the dominant German strategies in citizenship politics have become increasingly dispersed. It is important to note that the array of actors contributing to the general emergence of dispersed citizenship strategies in Germany have been driven by variegated, and often competing, concerns and interests. To differing degrees, the German government, federal and state officials, political parties, far-right, domestic, and transnational immigrant movements, and European-level groups have all contributed to the shape of German citizenship strategies.

At the same time in 1993 a newly elected French government passed a restrictive revision of the French nationality code.[28] Since the early 1980s there has been a series of intensifying electoral and policy debates over the criteria and meaning of citizenship. Far-right leaders and immigrant activists, conservatives, and socialists all have debated the relationship between immigrants (in particular those of North African Muslim origin) and French citizenship. Over the past years the leading parties in France have supported a new commitment to integrationist voluntarism in citizenship. The 1993 French reform reflected the changed political commitments to citizenship. It modified the mode of nationality acquisition to require that second-generation immigrants—those born and raised in France of foreign parents born elsewhere—file formal requests to become French.[29] That is, the state now demands a voluntaristic step by these youth. More controversial were the parts of the new law which restricted access by ex-colonial populations. The law rescinded a 1974 reform that extended the territorial criteria for citizenship access to the children born in France of parents born in former French colonies before their independence. The 1993 reform also restricted the provisions as they concerned Algeria, which until its independence was considered a French department, not simply a colony. For Algeria, the government established new conditions of prolonged legal residence in France for parents in order for 'double *jus soli*'—third-generation attribution—to apply to their children born in France (*Official Journal of the European Community*, 31 Dec. 1993; Bernard 1994).

In contrast to Germany, French strategies were situated within a context of a culturally singular integrated membership within France. While the actual nationality reform only took place in 1993, French citizenship strategies were already shaped by the debates, conflicts, and policy efforts of the previous decade. For example, the 1987 Nationality Commission, established to review the proposed nationality code revisions of 1986, held publicly televised hearings. And it ultimately issued a report that combined a defence of national identity, an insistence on a national integration of immigrants (the 'French' model), the valorization of a voluntarist citizenship, and a reaffirmation of statist perspectives.

A dispersal of public memberships, as in public multicultural membership, was explicitly rejected in the French conflicts. While the debates featured acknowledgement of European integration, any sort of European identity was defined in supplemental terms. From this perspective, a series of tiered memberships was visible in France: private identity, public French citizenship, and supplemental European membership. Though immigrant associations in France have also pushed for the extension of local suffrage to foreigners and the decoupling of nationality and active citizenship or civic engagement, some of the most visible immigrant groups during the citizenship reform conflicts promoted cultural and national integration. Thus, the Commission's report was hailed by the left and right, including immigrant associations, who applauded the integrationist appeal of the Commission. The Commission's recommendations did not differ much from the rightist 1986 proposals, and in fact laid the groundwork for the 1993 reform. Overall, culturalist and centred interpretations of membership were the dominant French strategies.

The emergence of German and French multicultural policies can provide another example of the different dominant strategies. Multicultural incorporation policies are another indicator of the changing institutionalization of membership. They may suggest that identity and incorporation are no longer situated at the level of the nation-state or within a bounded citizenry. But, multiculturalism itself is ambiguous. For example, in describing multiculturalism in Australia, Stephen Castles has written, 'multiculturalism maintains that it is no longer necessary to be culturally assimilated to be an Australian citizen' (1994: 7). Nevertheless, from an Australian perspective, and more generally from the perspective of traditional state citizenship, access to formal citizenship is the first step of multicultural citizenship. Indeed, in Australia and Canada, multicultural policies are closely linked to formal citizenship acquisition campaigns (e.g. the Year of Citizenship in Australia).

In Germany, on the other hand, many multicultural policies are tied to foreign nationality groups, residence, or activity, and not to a rhetoric of nationality acquisition or national integration. Multicultural policies in Germany are not aligned with efforts of 'national community'. Consider a multicultural billboard put up by the mayor of Solingen after the fire-bombing of a Turkish family's house, in which five women and children were killed, some of whom were second-generation immigrants in Germany. The board read, 'Your Christ [is a] Jew; your auto, Japanese; your pizza, Italian; your democracy, Greek; your coffee, Brazilian; your vacation, Turkish; your numbers, Arabic; your letters, Latin . . . and only your neighbour is a foreigner?' On the one hand, the multiculturalism underlying this public campaign fragments and externalizes immigrant identity. It depoliticizes their membership. On the other hand, the campaign assumes fragmentedness and foreignness of cultures. In effect, it bypasses the nation-state membership to configure a new model of post-national incorporation.

The domestic processes in Germany constructing citizenship politics provide further insight into the determinants of post-national transformations of citizenship. Post-national citizenship outcomes in Germany have been shaped, at least in part, by the interaction of historical rules, institutional practices, and political strategies. Germany's traditional understandings of membership presumed a strategy of maintaining a closed national community based on ethnicity, which is not easily open to reconfiguration. On the other hand, Germany's existing corporatist state structure has provided foreigner groups such as the Turkish population with collective recognition and social and economic incorporation into the existing order. Given their status and relation to the state, immigrant groups in Germany have pursued incorporation strategies that use their transnational linkages and resources, rather than those which aimed as primarily integrationist into some type of national community —neither an open nor a profitable alternative.[30]

In contrast, the changing politics of French formal citizenship were very favourable to cultural nationalist arguments. 'Republican nationalism' was seen as at once a political tool and a legitimate analytical model in France. The French statist institutionalization of citizenship diminished the opportunities for the recognition of immigrant populations as collectivities. It encouraged the bifurcation of a political individualism in the national community and private identities. Thus, multiculturalism in France has been closely tied to the promotion of 'national integration' of immigrants; multicultural public citizenship is explicitly rejected. Whereas in Australia the content of national citizenship expands, in France the identity and transnational referents are redefined either to coincide with French cultural parameters or to be relegated external to citizenship. French state multicultural policies have supported items such as 'ethnic festivals' and at the same time insist on the public predominance of a individualist, distinctively French model of citizenship. In contrast to an incorporation that bypasses the nation state, multiculturalism in France has the effect of reifying a supposed national model of state citizenship. Immigrant strategies reflect this configuration of constraints and opportunities. For groups like France Plus, a Franco-Maghrebi electoralist association, the strategies are primarily integrationist and complement dominant rhetoric, even as their frames of reference include more transnational human rights or immigrant rights emphases.

Taken together, the nationality reforms and multicultural policies in Germany and France demonstrate the importance of identifying the divergent strategies in the current convergence of European citizenship policies. Dissimilar, even competing, strategies are also visible in another dimension of apparent convergence in western Europe: the creation and continuing push for European citizenship. While talk of a European citizenship or European identity can be traced throughout much of the period of European integration, efforts to propose a formal category accelerated in the 1990s (Meehan 1993*b*; Ugur 1995; Martiniello 1994; Triandafyllidou 1995). The Maastricht Treaty established the status of European citizenship. Every citizen of an EU state was now also a citizen of the Union. For EU member state citizens, that meant that the scope of citizenship has expanded, and in some ways converged as well. EU citizenship entailed the new extension of local and European voting rights to all foreign residents who are citizens of other member states; and the right to stand as a candidate in those elections. Other rights gathered or created under EU citizenship include rights to free movement and residence, rights to consular protection by EU member states, and the right to appeal to a European Ombudsman about 'maladministration in the activities of Community institutions'.

The extension of these rights to third-country nationals in the European Union was not addressed by the new citizenship category. Since its inception, some politicians and commentators have called for the extension of EU citizenship to these foreign residents. The article on the European Ombudsman in the Maastricht Treaty (Arts. 8d and 138E) does extend the citizenship; complaints to the European Ombudsman may be made by 'any person, regardless of whatever nationality, who resides in a member state' (European Ombudsman 1995, part 1, sect. I.3). However, the entire article was orientated towards widening rights of EU nationals, rather than extending EU citizenship to non-EU nationals. The extension of EU citizenship in such directions has not appeared to be a popular cause (Martiniello 1994: 31–2; Triandafyllidou 1995; Ugur 1995: 988). For some commentators, EU citizenship accentuated the inconsistencies among and within states with regard to its foreign resident populations.[31]

Thus, the category of European citizenship for EU nationals acquired more substantive content, and gave citizenship rights for these populations some transnational consistency. But, the existence and potential of citizenship rights tied to the European Union also acquired more resistance and ambiguities. Certainly, complete opposition to any sort of European citizenship can be found across the European states for disparate sets of reasons and in particular as voiced by some far-right and nationalist groups.[32] Yet, the support for EU citizenship also brings into focus the operation of divergent sets of citizenship strategies in the seemingly convergent outcome of a supranational membership. As one of the topics under discussion in the 1996–7 Intergovernmental Conference (IGC) on the European Union Treaties—on the revision of the Maastricht Treaty—EU citizenship has attracted much explicit attention. As evidenced in documents produced in preparation for the IGC, varied strategies are pursued by subnational groups, parties, and movements, national governments, transnational movements, and organizations, as well as specific EU institutions and groups.

The calls to enlarge and strengthen European citizenship have gained particular visibility. Proposals to establish a generalized citizenship have been increasingly advanced by a diverse set of transnational and EU-level groups (Wiener, forthcoming). Some of the proposals include calls to incorporate non-EU nationals in EU citizenship and to disperse European citizenship through a series of practices and rights. For example, the Socialist Group of the European Parliament sponsored a petition by Socialist youths, entitled, '*A letter from Brussels: 217 European Young people ask for European Citizenship "for all"* ' (Socialist Group

1996). The letter called for the extension of European citizenship to be 'granted to non-EU citizens who live in the Union the right to work under the same conditions as EU citizens' (Socialist Group, 1996: 3). The Permanent Forum of the Civilian Society, which is an organization representing seventy non-governmental 'progressive democratic' organizations issued '*A Warning to Governments*'. In the document, the Civil Society called for 'a guarantee of civil rights for all (men, women, nationals, immigrants), and any other person who is legally resident in any of the member states ... which will mean real status at the European level for Non-Governmental Organizations, and a recognition at the European level of the right of association' (Civil Society 1996). The European Parliament has been another source of strategies to expand and disperse citizenship rights. In 1995 a reflection group set up by the European Council called for the expansion of EU citizenship to spell out the 'fundamental rights' covering citizens and third-country nationals in the European Union. A minority among the group 'proposed that the citizens of third countries established in the Union be given a special status with certain rights (right of free movement and right of residence)' (European Parliament 1995, sect. 38).

A majority of the states in the European Union also appear to support a strengthened EU citizenship, but mainly for member state nationals (Shaw 1997: 9–10). In a document issued by the European Commission which summarized member state position papers on EU citizenship, most member states called for the incorporation of new rights, including a 'charter of European citizenship' (European Commission 1996). Germany has endorsed a stronger and 'better-defined' statement on fundamental rights and civil liberties (German Government 1996). Italy has proposed the incorporation of civil and political rights (Italian Government 1995, 1996; also Greek Government 1996). The Belgian government would include adhesion to the European Convention of Human Rights and to a Social Charter under EU citizenship (Belgian Government 1995). All the Benelux countries called for the revision to include clauses supporting the principle of language equality and cultural diversity (Benelux Government 1996). The French government, while much more opaque on the issue of EU citizenship, declared it wanted 'to better guarantee citizenship rights' (French Government 1996). The 'Presidency Conclusions' (Italy) presented at the Florence European Council in June 1996 called for the next presidency to prepare a draft revision of the treaties that would include 'strengthening European citizenship, without replacing national citizenship and while respecting the national identity and traditions of the member states' European Council (1996: 6).

Britain has continued to offer the starkest dissenting voice. A British White Paper on the subject, certainly in accordance with Britain's long-standing opposition to supranational trends, states that the British government 'does not consider . . . that the European Union is the right context for the protection of fundamental human rights . . . or prohibiting discrimination . . . the Government is concerned that the creation of rights would eventually lead to pressure for reciprocal duties . . . [such duties] have not been developed . . . and they should not be . . . The European Union . . . is not a state, and should take care not to develop ideas which feed people's fears that it has a vocation to do so' (1996, sects. 55, 56, 58). Advocates for European citizenship have tried to counter such critiques. Jacques Delors, former President of the European Commission, has argued that 'criticism of the idea of a European citizenship is unjustified. I have always felt that nations will survive; they are a natural reference point and will remain so . . . But European citizenship will emerge through a process and will be subordinated to national citizenship. It will represent common territory in the form of social and citizenship rights and a feeling of belonging to a wider community without tearing down national feelings of affinity' (Delors 1995).

Most of the proposals for expanding and strengthening EU citizenship rely on dispersed strategies or centred and tiered strategies. Not surprisingly, among those who support European citizenship, transnational actors and organizations have pursued more dispersed strategies, by which I mean the generalization of citizenship practices among different membership spheres. In current proposals, some suggested practices include more associational rights on the European level, and increased anti-discrimination rights. In contrast, member states have pursued more tiered-style strategies, by which I mean the extension of citizenship rights (except for fundamental rights) based upon a centred (and central) state citizenship. The strategies trace the expansion of EU citizenship through several tiers of membership, from local, regional, national to transnational and European. Thus local citizenship is linked to European citizenship, and European citizenship is usually premissed on national citizenship. From this perspective, the distinctions between dispersed and tiered strategies in the European context roughly invoke the distinctions sketched out earlier between the dispersed and tiered citizenship strategies in Germany and France. At the same time, it is worth while to note the trend towards 'dispersing' citizenship for EU nationals through a variety of practices. Already the Maastricht Treaty has envisioned dispersed practices of voting for EU member state nationals in local, national, and European elections. Majority acceptance for tiered and dispersed citizenship as they pertain to EU nationals is visible in EU member states. *Eurobarometer* surveys of European and national identity show that in most member states (twelve of the fifteen), the majority are willing to see themselves as identified with the national identity, and then with the European identity; the exceptions were Britain, Finland, and Sweden, as well as eastern Germany. In only six member states—Luxembourg, Germany, Belgium, France, Italy, and Spain —are more than a fifth of the population willing to identify themselves first with the European identity and then with the specific national identity. According to another *Europinion* poll, 77 per cent of the respondents thought that strengthening EU citizenship with a 'European Charter of the Rights and Duties of the Citizen' was a 'good thing'. Furthermore, a majority supported the extension of local and European election suffrage to other EU nationals (*Europinion*, no. 6, October 1996, sect. 6).

That dispersed citizenship strategies have been confined to intra-EU nationals has had institutional and political implications. Mehmet Ugur contends that different strategies become available when issues become more 'transparent' and 'divisible', and public pressure or assertiveness increases (1995: 970–1). According to Ugur, the decoupling of the issue of EU citizenship and rights for European nationals from the issue of non-EU nationals has enabled the continued push for EU citizenship (pp. 992–4). At the same time, the continued rise of anti-immigrant parties and movements and the linkage of the so-called illegal migration problem with all aspects of immigration in the domestic politics of the member states have disabled the pursuit of dispersed or tiered strategies with regard to non-EU nationals. Ugur notes that extension of rights to third-country nationals have been considered by the European Commission and other bodies. But, the predominant policy trend has been marked by harsh immigration and asylum measures and the 'exclusion' of third-country nationals. Member states have pursued centred and statist strategies to co-ordinate the international closures to non-EU nationals. Such strategies shaped the Dublin Accord, the Schengen Accord, and its modifications, as well as the continuing negotiations of the Working Group on Immigration (Convey and Kupiszewski 1995: 940–3; Ugur 1995). There are indications of 'an emergent European identity defined against non-EU nationals . . . EU nationals not only are less inclined to see the rights of third country immigrants being tackled at the European Union level, they also tend to be in favor of restricting those rights or leaving them as they are' (Ugur 1995: 978). Taken together, tiered and dispersed strategies for European citizenship expansion (for EU nationals) have been buttressed by centred or statist and persistently nationalized citizenship strategies for the constriction of immigrant access.

These divergent strategies intersect in interesting ways with the current debate between 'intergovermentalists' and 'multi-level governance' or 'new polity' analysts about the nature of governance in the European Union.[33] Intergovernmentalists have stressed national state co-ordination of European policy, and the domestic constraints and preferences that shape policy. Multi-level governance analysts have stressed the emergence of subnational and supranational actors, and understand European policy formation as defined by conflicts involving 'contending coalitions of governments, supranational actors, and domestic interests' (Hooghe and Marks 1996: 36). At the same time, this terminology is also part of the political talk of Eurocrats and European politicians. The analytical and political dimensions of the debate easily blur. For example, in preparation for the 1996 IGC, the General Assembly of European Municipalities and Regions issued a declaration that calls the coming revision of the Maastricht Treaty 'a decisive state in the transformation of the current intergovernmental Europe in a Europe which is an autonomous political entity' (Council of European Municipalities and Regions 1996: 1). From the perspective of this debate, does European citizenship attest to convergent inter-state policy-making? Or, does European citizenship signal the emergence of a 'new polity', namely the European Union, which features multi-level governance?

For certain observers of the European Union, the different dimensions of European citizenship, including but not limited to the formal EU citizenship created by the Maastricht Treaty, do indeed affirm the emergence of multi-level governance and a 'new polity' in Europe. In their study of the European integration process, Hooghe and Marks speak of the 'birth of a new polity'. They emphasize that the democratic development of the European Union has been 'exclusively in one direction: towards the creation of a European citizenship and the upgrading of democratic channels at the supranational level' (1996: 21). The initial drive to create and implement EU citizenship and some of the recent efforts to expand it have been characterized as 'citizenship from above', and not a product of mobilization from below

(Martiniello 1994: 36; Bryant 1991). Nevertheless, it must be noted that the proliferation of transnational groups and movements pursuing dispersed and tiered citizenship strategies through EU citizenship has been striking, as evidenced through the current surge in proposals to revise European citizenship.

To qualify the question of multi-level governance in terms of the divergent strategies driving European citizenship presents a more complicated picture. While EU citizenship for nationals has displayed multi-level policy-making, the policy-making around EU citizenship for non-EU member nationals has been dominated by intergovernmentalist and state-centred policy-making (Ugur 1995). In fact, the development of EU citizenship is constituted by a similar dynamic evident in other citizenship changes. The post-national features of EU citizenship interplay with neo-national features. Dispersed citizenship, blurred boundaries, and increasingly irrelevant state citizenship are enabled by and enabling centred membership, closed borders, and increasingly relevant exclusionary policies. Overall, member states have pursued centred and statist, even if internationally co-ordinated, strategies in areas concerning citizenship regulations for non-EU nationals, asylum policy, border control, and entry and residence policies. Within the context of the 1996 IGC, some member states have explicitly proposed transferring authority over immigration and asylum issues upward, but other states, including France and Germany, have maintained support for more upward but inter-state co-ordination. It is important to note that centred strategies do not imply a continuation of old national strategies; and the pursuit of intergovernmentalist strategies does not mean the absence of multi-level governance. The targeted closures are as much about transnational boundaries as national boundaries, as evidenced by the Dublin and Schengen Accords. These closures call for an 'espace homogène', as Chancellor Kohl and President Chirac underscored in a joint declaration before the European Council (European Council 1995). Moreover, the state-centred and persistently nationalized strategies have been shaped by supranational processes and actors. And, certainly much of the autonomy (even if not sovereignty) over these issues have been shifted to European-level organizations.[34]

## CONCLUSION

The examination of the different citizenship developments brought out varied kinds of citizenship strategies, which were pursued by varied actors. The actors identified here include national governments, political parties, European Union institutions and associated organizations, immigrant associations, and an overlapping array of transnational movements and actors. The citizenship strategies can actually be categorized into two distinctive sets of dominant strategies. The first set is of dispersed strategies. The second set is of centred and tiered strategies. These strategies do not correspond to static, ideal citizenship models. Rather, they refer to dynamic political processes. While the two sets of strategies do not usually overlap, the combination of dispersed and tiered strategies visible for EU nationals demonstrates their flexibility. In the national cases of convergence—the convergence of French and German nationality policies and of their incorporation policies—identifying the different strategies illuminates the impact of the political processes of each of the polities. Divergent strategies explain the apparent convergence between states with historically different membership schema.[35] In the case of European citizenship, the divergent strategies driving the strengthening and expansion of EU citizenship help differentiate the dual-tracked and multi-levelled political processes of European citizenship and immigration policies. They also help explain how convergence around a supranational citizenship has continued.

These two sets of strategies—dispersed on the one hand and centred on the other—are integral factors shaping the emergence of post-national and neo-national membership trends sketched out earlier. As shown in the case-studies, dispersed citizenship strategies have contributed to the emergence of post-national membership, while centred strategies have contributed to the emergence of neo-national membership. However, generalizations about the actors pursuing these strategies are very difficult to make. Can one assume that national governments (because of the presumption of sovereign interests and preferences) always pursue centred and statist strategies? In the case of German nationality reform and incorporation, I sought to show how and why Germany pursued dispersed strategies. Historical, institutional, and structural factors in part determine the character of the dominant strategies. Can one assume that immigrant associations always pursue dispersed citizenship strategies? Overall, transnational immigrant groups and European-level organizations have been more likely to pursue dispersed strategies. But, in the case of French nationality reform and incorporation, I sought to show how some of the most visible immigrant strategies were, in effect, integrationist and centred strategies. Moreover, some transnational movements, such as European-level movements constituted by numerous far-right, nationalist groups, have been diametrically opposed to the incidence of post-national membership. In fact, their innovative use of transnational references and bases, even as they advocate nationalized, singular citizenships, demonstrates some of the novelty of neo-national trends.[36]

This analysis does not presume a direct linkage between intentionality underlying the pursuit of different strategies and post-national and neo-national membership outcomes. Returning to the example of the integrationist strategies of French immigrant activists, their strategies buttressed the national cultural, centred, and statist strategies that dominated the reform process. But, that does not mean that the intentions of these groups, or of others in the process, coincided with neo-national membership. The strategies pursued by EU member states and the actual direction of EU citizenship constitutes another example. On the one hand, the exact character and direction of EU citizenship—whether it is an indicator for post-national or neo-national membership—is currently being debated (contrast Martiniello 1994; Turner 1994; Habermas 1994; Bauböck 1994*a*; Soysal 1996; Shaw 1997; Weiner, forthcoming). On the other hand, most member states have pursued tiered and dispersed strategies to strengthen EU citizenship for EU nationals. These strategies arguably lay the groundwork for a more generalized post-national membership. A future dispersed citizenship extended through different membership levels and groups (denizens, nationals, etc.) has not been the intention of most member states; one could argue that such an outcome would be against many of the member states' interests and preferences at this stage in European integration.[37]

The continuing process of EU citizenship also provides further evidence of the causal relationship between the post-national and neo-national developments in Europe. The dualistic trends of post-national and neo-national membership have constituted new dynamics of a glancing convergence. Constrictive revisions of entry and membership rules, creation of transnational and international closures, obsessive preoccupation with national models, and increasing salience of anti-immigrant politics rebound off the growing incidence of dual nationality, increased citizenship rights for non-nationals, emergence of transnational norms, and the erosion of the 'imaginary walls' of the Western nation-states. The divergent sets of citizenship strategies underscore how old conceptual frameworks of citizenship and national identity can obscure the emergence of new dynamics. I have sought to show that, as the nature of citizenship has changed, an array of actors have pursued strategies shaped from multiple sources: the still-existing order of national citizenship as well as the emergent developments of post-national and neo-national membership. In turn, these strategies have contributed to the ongoing dualistic developments and the moments of convergence. Finally, as seen in the cases of nationality revisions, incorporation policies, and European citizenship, the interplay of these strategies continue to have domestic and transnational consequences.

## NOTES

1. This chapter addresses changes in citizenship and nationality policy. While the terms 'citizenship' and 'nationality' are technically and ideologically distinctive, they are often used interchangeably in popular discourse. Here, I distinguish the terms when appropriate, and otherwise use them interchangeably.
2. The scope of this chapter is limited to western Europe. The proliferation of citizenship reforms, however, is very visible among the new states in eastern Europe and the former Soviet Union. See the journal *Migration News* for monthly summaries of recent immigration and citizenship developments in Europe and elsewhere.
3. By 'foreigners', I refer to the broad range of immigrants, including labour migrants, family reunification entries, asylum-seekers and refugees, and undocumented migrants.
4. That the concept and practice of citizenship is in flux, and its character and direction contested, has been widely discussed. For recent works on the transformations of citizenship in the context of immigration, see Cesarani and Fulbrook (1996); Soysal (1994); Bauböck (1994*a,b*); Kymlicka (1995); Hammar (1990).
5. Several recent studies have discussed changes in citizenship in terms of 'post-national' or 'transnational' trends. For example, see Soysal (1994: 136–62); Bauböck (1994*a*: 210–12, 216–21); Hammar (1990); Ferry (1991); Habermas (1994). It also should be stated at the outset that there is disagreement about the terminology. There are several different definitions of 'post-national', 'transnational', and 'supranational'. For example, in contrast to the usage of the terms here, Rainer Bauböck reserves the term 'post-national' for those phenomena for which nation-state institutions are fully bypassed and irrelevant, and uses the term 'transnational' for those phenomena which extend beyond the nation-state and for which nation-state institutions are still presupposed (Bauböck 1994; personal communication). For other definitions of post-national phenomena, see Soysal (1994), Martiniello (1994), Ferry (1991, 1992).
6. There is an array of studies that situate changes in citizenship and immigration politics in terms of differentiated national models. See e.g. Brubaker (1992); Weil (1991); Hollifield (1992); Schnapper (1990); also see Schmitter Hiesler (1992).

7. Some studies have focused on convergent expansionist tendencies, while others have focused on the rise of new nationalisms and racial politics. See Freeman (1995) on the expansionist convergence of liberal democratic polities. The study of racial politics has become a growth industry. See e.g. Cohen (1994: 186–91); Santamaria (1989); Anthias and Yuval-Davis (1992); Wrench and Solomon (1993).

8. In other versions of this essay, I have used the term 'neo-nationalist' membership, rather than 'neo-national' membership. My reasons for changing the term were largely to avoid the confusion the original term provoked. For some readers, 'neo-nationalist' meant to refer exclusively to the extreme right and new nationalist movements of western Europe, which was not the intention here. For other readers, the lack of symmetry with 'post-national' meant that 'neo-nationalist' was an evaluative expression, and not a descriptive category, which, again, was not the intention here. Both post-national and neo-national membership are meant to be distinguished from traditional national membership in the course of the essay. My thanks to Christian Joppke for his suggestion of 'neo-national membership'.

9. The definition and usage of the term 'strategies' in this chapter are drawn from different sources, including from Swidler's term 'strategies of action', which she defines as 'persistent ways of ordering action through time' (1986: 273), and her understanding of strategies as 'larger ways of trying to organize a life . . . within which particular choices make sense, and for which particular, culturally shaped skills and habits . . . are useful' (p. 276). The term also recalls Mann's (1987) use of the term to delineate historical citizenship patterns. See n. 11.

10. For example, Riker (1986) has discussed the 'art of political manipulation' in terms of strategies; thus individuals can 'manipulate outcomes by manipulating the agenda' (p. 11).

11. The institutionalization of citizenship has been reconsidered since Marshall. For example, writing as a corrective to Marshall's configuration of citizenship development, Mann (1987) traced varied historical paths of citizenship practices as constitutive of different kinds of 'strategies'. Whereas Marshall identified change in the development of citizenship in terms of the consecutive enlargement of sets of rights (civil, political, social) and the extension of rights to different classes in the nation-state, Mann argued that such a pattern reflected only one kind of strategy. Mann, like Marshall, related the modern development of citizenship to national class conflict and efforts to institutionalize and control such conflict. But, Mann used the concept of citizenship strategies to differentiate ruling-class and regime action among the European states: he argued that five different types of citizenship strategy were actually visible in different countries and at different points in time: 'liberal, reformist, authoritarian monarchist, Fascist, and authoritarian socialist' (pp. 339–41). Turner (1990) identified state and collective patterns in the development of citizenship; he differentiated the institutionalization of citizenship from above and below, and analysed 'passive' and 'active' variations of membership rights and incorporation.

12. Marshall, Mann, and Turner represent, of course, only one dimension of literature on historical models and understandings of citizenship and

citizenship practices as well as on the changes in these models and practices. For a sampling of recent studies, see Soysal (1994), Bauböck (1994a), Brubaker (1989), Spinner (1994), Barbalet (1988); Habermas (1992).

13. I am grateful to Daniele Lochak for this point.

14. See Layton-Henry (1990) on the rights of foreign workers, and Yasemin Soysal (1994) on the influence of international trends on domestic policies.

15. For example, in 1963 ten European states signed the Strasbourg Convention on the 'reduction of cases of multiple nationality'. The aims of the Convention were to prevent the further incidence of dual nationality by enumerating the conditions leading to the forfeiture of nationality for a variety of cases. Its aims also were to deal with the already growing problem of male dual nationals and military service. Britain, one of the signatories of the Convention, signed only the section regarding military service. The other signatories were France, Germany, Austria, Denmark, Sweden, Norway, the Netherlands, Italy, and Luxembourg.

16. For a domestic policy process approach for examining the extension of citizenship rights to non-nationals, see Ch. 8 in this volume, by Guiraudon.

17. In the United States, for example, state and federal courts in California delayed implementation of Proposition 187, the public referendum designed to authorize harsher measures against undocumented immigrants, increase state powers, and rescind rights of undocumented immigrants to education and medical services. In other cases, US courts have ruled that government actions have violated the human rights and due process of migrants. See Weinstein (1996).

18. For a sampling of the discussions about modern changes in the understanding of citizenship and the growing importance of identity conflicts, see Hall and Held 1989; Yuval-Davis 1991.

19. Also see Meehan (1993b) for a fuller argument; Guild (1996) offers a detailed analysis of the distinguishing features of national and EU citizenship.

20. While Soysal considers that the 'explosion of nationalisms' and new 'appeals to nationhood' are part of the 'dialectic of the post-war global system', she identifies only one new mode of membership, namely post-national membership, which is the 'new mode of membership ... [that] transgresses the national order of things' (Soysal 1996: 25–6).

21. For recent and excellent compilations of press reviews of these new efforts and legislation, see *Migration News* (1995a,b; 1996a,b).

22. See below for a more detailed discussion of the 1993 reform.

23. Husbands (1994) argues that the contemporary debates over citizenship, including the nationalist rhetoric, is a function of displacement of new 'moral panics' about European resilience and national identity.

24. Based on the author's interviews in Germany (Mar. 1994).

25. The 1991 amended aliens law facilitated naturalization procedures and gave the groups a claim to naturalization (German Bundesminister das Innern 1991: 8). The July 1993 revisions (the Act to Amend the regulations Governing Legal Questions of Asylum Procedure, Work Permits and Aliens Law) further diminished the discretionary features of the naturalization process, and specified an absolute right to naturalization, as long as the applicants fulfilled the necessary conditions (pp. 37–9); On 23 Nov.

1995 Germany's Foreigners' Commissioner, Cornelia Schmalz-Jacobsen, released a report on the status of foreigners which reiterated that certain groups of foreigners had the right to German citizenship (*Migration News* 1996c). Nevertheless, the substantive advance of the 1993 revisions over the 1991 reform can be dependent on the particular *Länder* administration.

26. Kohl, in a speech to the Bundestag (16 June 1993), stated, 'we should change our citizenship laws so that the possibility of naturalization is more heavily used. I am thinking primarily of the young Turks who have been born here, who see Germany as their home, and would be prepared to perform the duties of a citizen in our democratic state.' While Kohl announced that his party, the CDU (Christian Democratic Union), would submit a legislative proposal to revise the 1913 citizenship law, no proposal was actually submitted to the Bundestag. On the other hand, in spring 1994 the major opposition party, the SPD, introduced a legislative proposal for discussion in the Bundestag, which introduced modified territorial criteria for citizenship. The SPD reform has the general support of the centrist FDP, and is opposed by the CDU and rightist party, the CSU.

27. On recent debates on citizenship reforms and dual nationality, see Rittstieg (1994); *Agence France Press* (1995); also Cowell (1995a,b).

28. Legislative proposals to reform the French nationality code have been electoral stakes in French national politics since 1986. But, citizenship issues were already salient in French politics after 1983.

29. Under the existing code of nationality, children born in France to foreigners acquire French citizenship quasi-automatically at the age of 18. Under the new law, youth between the ages of 16 and 22 would have to 'manifest their wish' for French citizenship.

30. An episode that highlighted such strategies was the recent local election in Berlin, where Turkish immigrants called for, at once, the right to dual nationality, local suffrage for all non-nationals in Berlin, and suffrage in Turkey for nationals living abroad, in Germany.

31. For an detailed analysis of the new EU category and its possible ramifications for third-country nationals, see Triandafyllidou (1995); also Guild (1996).

32. But note that numerous European far-right parties do not feature blanket opposition to European integration or unity; rather, there can be opposition to the specific characteristics of the European Union or the direction of the current integration process.

33. For an overview of the debate, see Hooghe and Marks (1996); Pierson (1996).

34. See Held (1996: 411) for a discussion of state autonomy as capacity and state sovereignty as authority.

35. In contrast, cultural political explanations that rely on mostly static citizenship models and historical membership idioms are often unable to explain reforms and politics that flout or manipulate historical traditions. See e.g. Brubaker (1992), and for a more extensive critical discussion of political–cultural approaches, see Feldblum (forthcoming, esp., ch. 5).

36. For example, commenting on the recent electoral success of his far-right 'Freedom Party' in the elections for the European Parliament in Austria,

the Austrian nationalist politician Jörg Haider focused on the possibility for a new pact among rightist politicians in the European Parliament to fight against the Maastricht Treaty and the European Union as the way in which European integration should progress (*Los Angeles Times* 1996; also see Frey 1996).

37. For recent discussions about the need to look beyond intergovernmentalist intentions to explain outcomes in European integration processes, see Hooghe and Marks (1996), Pierson (1996), and Schmitter (1996).

# REFERENCES

*Agence France Press* (1995), 'Euro-Foreigners have Right to Vote in Berlin Municipal Poll', 20 Oct.

Anthias, Floya, and Nira Yuval-Davis (1992), *The Racialized Boundaries: Race, Nation, Gender, Colour, and Class and the Anti-Racist Struggle* (London: Routledge).

Barbalet, J. M. (1988), *Citizenship Rights, Struggle and Class Inequality* (Minneapolis: University of Minnesota Press).

Bauböck, Rainer (1992), *Immigration and the Boundaries of Citizenship* (Coventry: Centre for Research in Ethnic Relations).

—— (1994*a*), *Transnational Citizenship: Membership and Rights in International Migration* (Aldershot: Edward Elgar).

—— (ed.) (1994*b*), *From Aliens to Citizens: Redefining the Status of Immigrants in Europe* (Aldershot: Avebury).

Belgian Government (1995), *Belgian Government Paper to the Parliament concerning the IGC 1996*, Oct. (Brussels: European Commission).

Benelux Governments (1996), *Mémorandum Bénélux en vue de la CIG*, 7 Mar. (Brussels: European Commission).

Bernard, Philippe (1994), 'Nationalité française, nouveau mode d'emploi', *Le Monde*, 1 Jan.

Blitz, James (1995), 'Asylum Benefit Laws will Starve People out of Britain', *Financial Times*, 19 Dec.

British Government (1996), 'White Paper. A Partnership of Nations: The British Approach to the European Union IGC 1996', 12 Mar.

Brubaker, W. Rogers (ed.) (1989), *Immigration and the Politics of Citizenship in Europe and North America* (Lanham, Md.: University of America Press).

—— (1992), *Citizenship and Nationhood in France and Germany* (Cambridge, Mass.: Harvard University Press).

Bryant, C. (1991), 'Europe and the European Community 1992', *Sociology* 25/2: 189–207.

Castles, Stephen (1994), 'Democracy and Multicultural Citizenship: Australian Debates and their Relevance for Western Europe', in Bauböck (1994*b*).

Cesarani, David (1996), 'The Changing Character of Citizenship and Nationality in Britain', in Cesarani and Fulbrook (eds.), *Citizenship, Nationality and Migration in Europe*.

—— and Mary Fulbrook (eds.) (1996), *Citizenship, Nationality, and Migration in Europe* (London: Routledge).

Çinar, Dilek (1994), 'From Aliens to Citizens: A Comparative Analysis of Rules of Transition', in Bauböck (1994*b*).

Civil Society (1996), *A Warning to Governments*, 21 June.

Cohen, Robin (1994), *Frontiers of Identity: The British and the Others* (Harlow: Longman).

Convey, Andrew, and Marek Kupiszewski (1995), 'Keeping up with Schengen: Migration and Policy in the European Union', *International Migration Review*, 29/4 (Winter), 939–63.

Council of European Municipalities and Regions (1996), XXth General Assembly, 'Thessaloniki Declaration: A Europe for its Citizens', Thessaloniki, 25 May (Internet site: http://www.europa.eu.int/en/agenda/igc-home/eu-doc/regions/ccreen.htm).

Cowell, Alan (1995*a*), 'Turks Seek Acceptance of Culture in Germany', *New York Times*, 14 Dec.

—— (1995*b*), 'For Turks, Life (or Death) in Germany still Offers no Respite', *New York Times*, 8 Dec.

Crossette, Barbara (1996), 'Citizenship is a Malleable Concept', *New York Times*, 11 Aug.

Crow, Graham (1989), 'The Use of the Concept of "Strategy" in Recent Sociological Literature', *Sociology*, 23/1 (Feb.), 1–24.

Delors, Jacques (1995), 'As Japan and America Explode, Europe will Endure,' *New Perspectives Quarterly*, 12/1 (Winter).

Eager, Charlotte (1995), 'Exiles' Dream of Freedom Turns to Dust', *Observer*, 17 Dec.

EC (European Commission) (1996*a*), 'Continuous Tracking Survey', *Europinion*, no. 8 (March), table 10.

—— (1996*b*), *La Citoyenneté de l'union—fiche thématique*.

European Council (1995), *Déclaration du chancelier Helmut Kohl et du Président Chirac, au président du Conseil européen*, 6 Dec. (Brussels: European Council).

European Council (1996), 'Florence European Council, 21 and 22 June 1996: Presidency Conclusions' (Internet site: http://europa.eu.int/en/record/florence/flore-en.htm).

European Ombudsman (1995), 'Report for Year 1995' (Internet site: http://europa.eu.int/europarl/mediateu/report95/rep95_1.htm).

European Parliament (1995), 'Reflection Group's Report', Brussels, 5/12 (Internet site: http://europa.eu.int/lu/en/agenda/igc-home/eu-doc/reflect/final.html).

Fassmann, Heinz, and Rainer Münz (eds.) (1994), 'Patterns and Trends of International Migration in Western Europe', in H. Fassmann and R. Münz (eds.), *European Migration in the Late Twentieth Century: Historical Patterns, Actual Trends and Social Implications* (Aldershot: Edward Elgar).

Favell, Adrian (1995), 'Citizenship and Immigration: Pathologies of a Progressive Idiom', paper prepared for presentation at the ECPR Workshop, Bordeaux, 27 Apr.–2 May.

—— (1997), *Philosophies of Integration: Immigration and the Idea of Citizenship in France and Britain* (New York: St Martin's Press).

Federal Ministry of the Interior (1993), *Survey of the Policy and Law concerning Foreigners in the Federal Republic of Germany* (Bonn: Federal Ministry of the Interior, July).

Feldblum, Miriam (1993), 'Paradoxes of Ethnic Politics: The Case of Franco-Maghrebis in France', *Ethnic and Racial Studies*, 16/1: 52–74.

—— (forthcoming), *Reconstructing Citizenship: The Politics of Citizenship Reform and Immigration in Contemporary France* (Albany, NY: SUNY Press).

Ferry, Jean-Marc (1991), 'Pertinence du postnational', *Esprit*, 176: 80–3.

—— (1992), 'Une "Philosophie" de la Communauté', in J.-M. Ferry and Paul Thibaud, *Discussion sur l'Europe* (Paris: Calmann-Lévy).

*Financial Times* (1996), 'Bonn Concern at Asylum Seekers', 11 Jan.

Freeman, Gary P. (1995), 'Modes of Immigration Politics in Liberal Democratic States', *International Migration Review*, 29/4 (Winter), 881–902.

French Government (1996), *Débat à l'Assemblée Nationale sur la CIG: Discours du Ministre Délégué aux affaires européennes, M. Michel Barnier* (13 Mar.), Paris.

Frey, Eric (1996), 'Austria: Right Wing Gains in European Poll', 14 Oct.

German Bundesminister das Innern (1991), *Das Neue Ausländerrecht der Bundesrepublik Deutschland*, V II 2–125 312/22 (Brussels: European Commission).

German Government (1996), *Statement by the German Government to the Ministerial Meeting of the Intergovernmental Conference*, 22 Apr.

Greek Government (1996), *For a Democratical European Union with Political and Social Content*, 22 Mar. (Brussels: European Commission).

Guild, Elspeth (1996), 'The Legal Framework of Citizenship of the European Union', in Cesarani and Fulbrook (eds.), *Citizenship, Nationality and Migration in Europe*.

Habermas, Jürgen (1992), 'Citizenship and National Identity: Some Reflections on the Future of Europe', *Praxis International*, 12/1: 1–19.

—— (1994), 'Citizenship and National Identity', in Bart van Steenbergen (ed.), *The Condition of Citizenship* (London: Sage).

Hall, Stuart, and David Held (1989), 'Citizens and Citizenship', in S. Hall and M. Jacques (eds.), *New Times* (London: Verso).

Hammar, Tomas (1990), *Democracy and the Nation-State: Aliens, Denizens and Citizens in a World of International Migration* (Aldershot: Avebury).

Held, David (1996), 'The Decline of the Nation-State', in Geoff Eley and Ronald Grigor Suny (eds.), *Becoming National: A Reader* (New York: Oxford University Press).

Hollifield, James (1992), *Immigrants, Markets, and States: The Political Economy of Postwar Europe* (Cambridge, Mass.: Harvard University Press).

Hooghe, Liesbet, and Gary Marks (1996), 'Birth of a Polity: The Struggle over European Integration', paper presented at the Tenth International Conference of Europeanists, Chicago, 14–16 Mar.

Husbands, Christopher (1994), 'Crises of National Identity as the "New Moral Panics": Political Agenda-Setting about Definitions of Nationhood', *New Community*, 20/2 (Jan.), 198–9.

Italian Government (1995), *Italian Government Statement of 23 May 1995 on the Intergovernmental Conference* (Brussels: European Commission).

—— (1996), *Position of the Italian Government Conference for the Revision of the Treaties*, 18 Mar. (Brussels: European Commission).

Kymlicka, Will (1995), *Multicultural Citizenship: A Liberal Theory of Minority Rights* (Oxford: Oxford University Press).

Layton-Henry, Zig (ed.) (1990), *The Political Rights of Migrant Workers in Western Europe* (London: Sage).

Lorcerie, Françoise (1994), 'Les Sciences sociales au service de l'identité nationale', in Denis-Constant Martin (ed.), *Cartes d'identité: Comment dit-on 'nous' en politique?* (Paris: Presses de la Fondation National des Sciences Politiques).

*Los Angeles Times* (1996), 'Far Right Wins High Marks in Austria Vote', 14 Oct.

Mann, Michael (1987), 'Ruling Class Strategies and Citizenship', *Sociology*, 21: 339–54.

Marshall, T. H. (1953), *Class, Citizenship, and Social Development* (Westport, Conn.: Greenwood Press).

Martiniello, Marco (1994), 'Citizenship of the European Union: A Critical View', in Bauböck (1994*b*).

Meehan, Elizabeth (1993*a*), 'Citizenship and the European Community', *Political Quarterly*, 64/2 (Apr.–June), 172–86.

—— (1993*b*), *Citizenship and the European Union* (London: Sage).

*Migration News* (1995*a*), 'British Immigration Reform', 'Italian Immigration Reform', 'Austria: Immigration and Elections', 2/11 (Nov.).

—— (1995*b*), 'British Immigration Plan', 'Italian Decree', 'Germany: Asylum', 'Swedish Guest Workers and Refugees', 'Immigration: Top Priority in France', 2/12 (Dec.).

—— (1996*a*), 'Reducing Immigration in Britain and Italy', 3/1 (Jan.).

—— (1996*b*), 'Britain: More Safe Countries', 'Spain's Grand Borgain', 'Italy Immigration Decree not Enough', 3/3 (Mar.).

—— (1996*c*), 'Germany Immigration Reforms Expected', 3/8, Aug.

*Le Monde* (1993), 'La Nouvelle Législation sur les étrangers comporte des "atteintes excessives" aux droits fondamentaux', 16/8: 1.

Mouffe, Charal (1992), 'Feminism, Citizenship and Radical Democratic Politics,' in Judith Butler and Joan W. Scott (eds.), *Feminists Theorize the Political* (New York: Routledge).

*New York Times* (1996), 'Rights Panel Stirs Anger in Britain', 5 June, A4.

Pierson, Paul (1996), 'The Path to European Integration: A Historical Institutionalist Analysis', *Comparative Political Studies*, 29/2 (Apr.), 121–63.

Reuters (1996*a*), 'Hunger Strike Divides French Ruling Coalition', 20 Aug.

—— (1996*b*), 'Juppe Rejects African Immigrants' Demands', 22 Aug.

Riker, William H. (1986), *The Art of Political Manipulation* (New Haven: Yale University Press).

Rittstieg, Helmut (1994), 'Dual Citizenship: Legal and Political Aspects in the German Context', in Bauböck (ed.), *From Aliens to Citizens*.

Rosenblum, Mort (1996), 'France Views African Immigrants', AP News Briefs, 16 Aug.

Santamaria, Ulysses (1989), 'Introduction: Racism in Europe', *New Political Science*, nos. 16–17 (Fall–Winter), 7.

Schmitter, Philippe (1996), 'Imagining the Future of the Euro-Polity with the Help of New Concepts', in Gary Marks, Fritz Scharpf, Philippe Schmitter, and Wolfgang Streek (eds.), *Governance in the Emerging Euro-Polity* (London: Sage).

Schmitter Heisler, Barbara (1992), 'The Future of Immigrant Incorporation: Which Models? Which Concepts?', *International Migration Review*, 26/2 (Summer), 623–45.

Schnapper, Dominique (1990), *La France de l'intégration, sociologie de la nation en 1990* (Paris: Gallimard).

Shaw, Jo (1997), *European Citizenship: The IGC and Beyond*, European Integration Online Papers, 1 (no. 003).

Socialist Group (1996), 'A Letter from Brussels: 217 European Young People Ask for European Citizenship "For All" (at the initiative of the Socialist Group at the European Parliament)', 14 May 1996.

Soysal, Yasemin Nuhoglu (1994), *Limits of Citizenship: Migrants and Post-national Membership in Europe* (Chicago: University of Chicago Press).

—— (1996), 'Changing Citizenship in Europe: Remarks on Postnational Membership and the National State', in Cesarani and Fulbrook (1996).

Spinner, Jeff (1994), *The Boundaries of Citizenship, Race, Ethnicity, and Nationality in the Liberal State* (Baltimore: Johns Hopkins University Press).

Summit (of Heads of State and Government in Florence) (1996), 'Europe in Fifteen Towers', Press Release, 21–2 June.

Swidler, Ann (1986), 'Culture in Action: Symbols and Strategies', *American Sociological Review*, 51 (Apr.), 273–86.

Triandafyllidou, Anna (1995), 'A Supra-National European Citizenship: Implications for Migration Policy', paper prepared for presentation at the ECPR Workshop, Bordeaux, 27 Apr.–2 May.

Turner, Bryan S. (1990), 'Outline of a Theory of Citizenship', *Sociology*, 24/2 (May), 189–217.

—— (1994), 'Postmodern Culture/Modern Citizens', in Bart van Steenbergen (ed.), *The Condition of Citizenship* (London: Sage).

Ugur, Mehmet (1995), 'Freedom of Movement vs. Exclusion: A Reinterpretation of the "Insider"–"Outsider" Divide in the European Union', *International Migration Review*, 29/4 (Winter), 946–99.

Weber, Max (1946), 'Structures of Power', in Gerth H. H. and C. Wright Mills, *From Max Weber: Essays in Sociology* (New York: Oxford University Press).

Weil, Patrick (1991), *La France et ses étrangers: L'aventure d'une politique de l'immigration 1938–1991* (Paris: Calmann-Lévy).

Weinstein, Harvey (1996), 'Rulings could Reopen Many Deportee Cases', *Los Angeles Times*, 10 Oct., 1.

Whitney, Craig (1996), 'Europeans Redefine what Makes a Citizen', *New York Times*, 1 Jan. 1996.

Wiener, Antje (forthcoming), *Building Institutions: The Developing Practice of European Citizenship* (Boulder, Colo.: Westview Press).

Wrench, John, and John Solomos (eds.) (1993), *Racism and Migration in Western Europe* (Oxford: Berg Publishers).

Ying Hui Tan (1996), 'Asylum Seekers can only Make One Claim', *Independent*, 24 Dec.

Young, Iris (1990), 'Polity and Group Difference: A Critique of the Ideal of Universal Citizenship', in Cass R. Sunstein (ed.), *Feminism and Political Theory* (Chicago: University of Chicago Press).

Yuval-Davis, Nira (1991), 'The Citizenship Debate: Women, the State and Ethnic Processes', *Feminist Review*, 39 (Aug.), 58–68.

# 8

# Citizenship Rights for Non-Citizens: France, Germany, and the Netherlands

VIRGINIE GUIRAUDON

During the last two centuries larger segments of the population in western Europe—in particular, the lower classes and women—have gained access to citizenship, i.e. a set of rights and obligations relating the state and the individual in a bounded political unit. Citizenship rights have also come to encompass a wider array of rights: socio-economic rights along with civil liberties and rights of political participation.[1] This development of citizenship coincided with the building of national communities. In T. H. Marshall's words, it found its origins in 'the first stirrings of a sense of community membership and common heritage' (1965: 93).[2] This marriage of *dēmos* and *ethnos* consecrated national citizenship, which linked the enjoyment of rights in a polity with belonging to the nation.

Yet, foreigners[3] residing in western Europe have come to enjoy many of the rights[4] of nationals (Brubaker 1989; Layton-Henry 1990) pushing further the 'frontiers of citizenship' (Vogel and Moran 1991). Now, 'there is a continuum of rights attached to membership of a state rather than a sharp distinction between citizen and non-citizen' (Layton-Henry 1990: 118). Tomas Hammar coined a word for this historical evolution and speaks of settled legal immigrants as 'denizens', waiting in the antechamber of full citizenship (Hammar 1990). The extension of civil, political, and social rights to foreigners took place in an order which reverses T. H. Marshall's: welfare benefits were secured early on while political rights remain contested (Soysal 1994; Bauböck 1995).

This phenomenon is a puzzling one given the adverse political context which foreigners have confronted. First, it seems counter-intuitive given the restrictionist goals of European governments regarding migration flows after the first oil crisis. Many of the changes described above made immigration a more attractive prospect for immigrants while it limited the ability of governments to lower their numbers (civil rights made it more arduous to expel foreigners; the right to lead a normal family life enabled migrants to bring their families). Secondly, since the 1970s a number of elements including economic and social restructuring have favoured a rise in xenophobia within public opinion and in media representations.

Thirdly, certain reforms (the advent of equal industrial rights and a freer access to the labour market) went against the logic of post-war labour migration as a mobile army of cheap labour since they narrowed the difference between native and foreign workers. This logic conceived of migrant workers as 'birds of passage' creating a dual labour market, acting as shock-absorbers in capitalist economies and preventing the inflation of wages (Piore 1979). The consolidation of their labour and industrial rights as well as of their residence status contributed to persuading the birds of passage to stay 'here for good' (Castles 1984). Why governments submitted to changes which led to a *rapprochement* between foreign and native labour is what we must understand.

Fourthly, the inclusion of foreigners in the welfare state after the long boom is also puzzling. During the first waves of labour migration, it was in the interest in the states to do so because migrant workers were mostly young, healthy men, who contributed more than they received from welfare services and who did not stay long enough to qualify for benefits based on seniority or length of residence. This ratio changed as family regrouping took place and welfare provisions extended to family dependants and the first waves of workers grew old. Yet, the move towards inclusiveness continued. The granting of welfare rights is also counter-intuitive because the principles of the welfare state require non-members to justify a departure from free market mechanisms through a community-based solidarity (Freeman 1986). Unlimited migration would undermine the high level of benefits in advanced industrialized countries; thus, the replacement of porous geographical borders by a guarded entry to the welfare state would seem logical.

Policy and socio-economic and political elements thus militated against the consolidation of citizenship rights for foreigners. Nevertheless, the advent of citizenship rights can be observed in a number of countries regardless of their policy on naturalization or integration.[5] How and why non-nationals acquired new rights and benefits and a more secure legal status since the 1970s is the main issue of this chapter. The chapter discusses the causal mechanisms which account for the degree of convergence in the area of foreigners' rights that can be observed in western Europe. It draws upon a comparative study of the evolution of the rights of foreigners in France, Germany, and the Netherlands since 1974. Among the three cases, the Netherlands is the country that has gone furthest in granting rights to foreigners, since they can vote at local elections and cultural rights are guaranteed under the country's minority policy. The question of remaining cross-national variance will thus be addressed. The first section is devoted to a discussion of existing explanations, both domestic and international,[6] that can be inferred from the scholarly literature on immigration and citizenship. The second section outlines an alternative explanatory framework which focuses on the impact of the scope and locus of political debate on policy outcomes.

## DOMESTIC EXPLANATIONS: A CRITIQUE

### The Role of Partisanship and Ideology

Casual observers may not find the question of foreigners' rights and benefits puzzling. They may consider that immigrant rights are predominantly an issue on the agenda of the post-materialists as incarnated by the new left. Or they may argue that more traditional parties or labour unions[7] of the left favour these rights because they want to appeal to constituencies protective of civil liberties or because they consider that equalizing the conditions of foreign and native workers is a means of reducing the competitive advantage of the former while invoking class solidarity.[8]

During numerous electoral campaigns the immigration issue has appeared as a means of distinction between the left and the right. For instance, this was the case in 1986 and 1993 in France, in 1983 in Germany, and in 1991 in the Netherlands, when right-wing parties accused left-wing governments of having been lax *vis-à-vis* immigration and too generous towards foreigners. This should not come as a surprise given the fact that issues such as economic policy and state ownership which used to structure political cleavages are not very different from one party to another. Moreover, in hard times, when parties no longer want to focus on social and economic problems for which they might be blamed, identity politics and 'moral panic' discourses resurface, placing ethnic minorities at the centre of debate (Husbands 1994).

Yet the evidence belies any systematic link between partisanship and the granting of rights to foreigners. Public divergence often masks an underlying policy consensus. Many pro-foreigner laws were passed under right-wing governments, and there was often policy continuity when there was a change of governmental colour. Most major laws adopted in the last two decades on this issue were voted by democratic parties or by mixed coalitions (in France in 1984, in the Netherlands in 1983 and 1985, in Germany in 1990 and 1993).[9] The same phenomenon can be observed in other European countries of immigration such as Sweden (Hammar 1985) and Britain (Messina 1989; Saggar 1992). This 'general agreement across the political spectrum on basic immigration policy' is a most striking instance of cross-national convergence, according to Yasemine Soysal (1994: 35). Gary Freeman argues that this convergence is set within the 'boundaries of legitimate discussion' in liberal democracies that preclude xenophobia (1995). Another way of construing this phenomenon is to consider that attempts at rolling back alien rights are constrained by domestic legal norms and judicial oversight, while the wishes of politicians who want to augment alien rights are sometimes nipped in the bud by the electoral calculus of politicians who believe it is easier to alter one's position on an issue than to shift public attitudes towards aliens. Parties of the right are more likely to feel the former constraint and parties of the left the latter as they affect their party platforms. In any case, this tacit consensus among parties leads at least to a reformulation of the question 'Under what circumstances would partisanship be an accurate predictor?'

One should also take into account proposals that do not reach a bill form. For instance, local voting rights for foreign residents was one of Mitterrand's 110 platform proposals in 1981. However, as a result of strong disagreement within the Socialist Party, a bill to that effect was not put before Parliament. In Germany, officials from the governing coalition such as the Christian Democratic Union (CDU)'s Barbara John at the Office for Foreigners in Berlin and the Free Democratic Party (FDP)'s Federal Commissioner for Foreigners' Affairs have been pushing for an improvement in the status of immigrants in the 1980s, yet they have been largely unsuccessful—prompting one of them, Lieselotte Funcke, to resign in protest in July 1991. There are numerous signs of internal party division which weaken the partisanship hypothesis.[10]

## The Role of Political Mobilization

Perhaps one should not discount what James Scott has called the 'weapons of the weak' (1985): unorganized action outside the boundaries of institutionalized politics and other forms of group mobilization. They constitute an important tool for lower-status groups who need to counteract the greater resources of the mighty. The mobilization hypothesis posits that policy-makers grant rights to foreigners because they fear the disruption of public order and the social tensions brought about by immigrant militancy.

Patrick Ireland's recent book on the form and impact of immigrant mobilization in France and Switzerland (1994) argues that immigrant militancy in the 1970s led to an institutional response which included the granting of more rights along with repressive measures: 'If host-society officials hoped to prevent a dangerous escalation of resentment and alienation, they had to respond to the immigrants' outrage' (p. 254). At first, reform drew from the existing repertoire of participatory channels: governments in both countries expanded trade union rights and the French made the welfare state more inclusive. Later, new avenues of integration emerged as part of the platform of opposition parties who had been alerted to the needs of immigrants through their protests.

It cannot be denied that migrants emerged as political actors and moved immigration-related issues up in the national agenda in the 1970s. The various conflicts in which immigrants took place in the 1970s such as the strikes at the Ford plant in Cologne or the Société Nationale de Construction de Logements pour les Travailleurs (Sonacotra) rent strikes in France drew attention to the conditions in which aliens lived. In this way, these happenings served as 'focus events' and their effect can be likened to the hijackings and occupations by young Moluccans in the mid-1970s in the Netherlands (Penninx *et al.* 1994). They were agenda-setting media-covered events, yet it is unclear what kind of policy response they induced.

The process of migrant political mobilization should have continued with the settling down of migrant populations. The fact that they were here with their families for a long time should have heightened their interest in local affairs (as opposed to homeland-orientated political activity). In fact, the situation in the 1980s and 1990s has been more complex. Among immigrants, political mobilization remains relatively low and is made difficult by the very heterogeneity of the character and demands of the foreign population and their dispersion. This is perhaps best exemplified by the German case, in which the largest immigrant population of Turkish nationality is still divided among ideological and ethnic lines. The structure of political opportunity in Germany makes it difficult for them to participate (naturalization remains limited and voting rights have not been granted). Moreover, the neo-corporatist character of the German political system does not favour the incorporation of new actors. Consequently, it keeps the Turkish community turned inwards rather than mobilizing for full incorporation into the German polity.

There are recent instances of increased political involvement in Europe, but they occurred *after* more rights of participation had been granted, for example after the freedom of association was extended in 1981 in France (Ireland 1996). A vicious circle seems in place which can be described using Albert Hirschman's terminology (1970): to be heard, one already needs to have a right to 'voice'. This is especially the case when the other option, 'exit', is no threat because it is exactly what the government wants you to do, i.e. repatriate.[11]

The French case also provides examples of failed mobilization. Although this was the one country in Europe which saw the emergence of a large social movement of second-generation immigrants in the early 1980s, their civil rights demands were not met. In brief, even if one could establish that there was pressure from below, this would not imply that it had a significant impact on policy change.[12] Furthermore, foreigners do not necessarily target a reform in status. The focus of associations, or of the most spectacular urban riots that captured national attention, were mostly local. They resulted in the guaranteeing of public funds for local projects rather than in national reforms in status (Body-Gendrot 1993).

The role of mobilization for the extension of rights to aliens should also be questioned given that major changes in this area took place without immigrant involvement or consultation of the minorities concerned. This was the case in the Netherlands. Jan Rath, writing on local voting rights reform in the Netherlands, underlined that it 'had not been the result of a struggle on the immigrants' part: although they welcomed the implementation of this political right, their support only manifested itself after the amendment to the Constitution had been voted' (1993: 340). Few aliens knew of the reform, and a wide-scale information campaign had to be launched to make them aware of this new political right.

Immigrant political action also risks creating a government back-lash rather than helping to push for liberal reforms. The Ford strike in Cologne in the 1970s confirmed German authorities in their belief that the recruitment of *Gastarbeiter* had to be halted (Herbert 1990). The same applies to the rent strikes in France and urban riots in the Netherlands (Wihtol de Wenden 1988; Penninx *et al*. 1994) in the same period. A political counter-offensive also followed the blossoming of anti-racist movements in France in the early 1980s. These groups advoc-ated 'le droit à la différence' (the right to be different). The extreme-right-wing party the National Front perverted their arguments and argued that foreigners were too different to be assimilated. Mobilization by the opposite camp greatly reduces the margin of manœuvre of govern-ments unwilling to alienate native xenophobic constituencies.

## The Role of Nation-Building Legacies

There is yet another way of approaching the issue of foreigners' rights and benefits. Governments do not operate from a *tabula rasa* per-spective and the shadow of the past looms large. The order in which rights were granted in each country, as well as the persistence of cross-national differences, reflected the countries' histories of nation-building and citizenship. Historical comparative studies such as Rogers Brubaker's (1992) have insisted on the importance of past citizenship traditions in understanding present debates on immigration.

It may be fruitful to compare the societal incorporation of foreign residents with that of other groups in the past for several reasons. First, studies such as Giovanna Zincone's study comparing the integration of the periphery, of women and of immigrants, into the polity (1992) and Jan Rath's work comparing the treatment of 'asocials' and of for-eigners (1991) shed a new light on the specificity of the foreign minor-ities question. The arguments used in the past to exclude women or the poor from full participation are now reiterated against the integration of foreigners. Secondly, critical junctures in nation-building have become part of the mythology of today's nation-states and thus still inform the terms of the debates about state membership.

Thirdly, beyond its discursive potential, the history of nation-building has left an institutional legacy, namely particular means of organizing state–society relations which make certain measures more or less com-patible with national tradition. They are generally embodied in the Constitution or in the legal tradition invoked by the courts. This may explain why some rights arose and took hold almost as 'natural' solutions in some nations long before other nations even considered them (such is the case for political rights). The foreigners' right to vote in local elections has been the object of political controversy in France, and the right to associate was only granted in 1981. In the Netherlands, all the aforementioned provisions have been passed with multipartisan support. One could argue that these variations stem from differences in nation-building and reflect past political struggles of the kind Lipset and Rokkan emphasized (1967), struggles which were not linked to immigration concerns at the time. In brief, if one takes into account the French distrust of intermediary bodies since 1789 and the long struggle between the Church and secular forces, one would understand the reluctance of the French in extending association rights and the vehemence of the numerous controversies over the wearing of *hijabs*.

In the Netherlands, it is interesting to note that the three historic pillars, or *verzuiling* (Catholic, Protestant, and liberal), which had ordered the political and social system faded during the post-war period with the decline of religious attendance and the rise of other issues. Nevertheless, it is this particular heritage which was used to set up policy towards minorities—a new migrant pillar with its own voting constituencies and demands, a new Muslim pillar with its own schools —and specific claims were built as other religions (older pillars) lost their significance. What this suggests is the endurance of old paradigms even in a changing context. In fact, faced with the new challenge of foreign minorities, European nations clung to old solutions and re-enacted past nation-building struggles.

The decoupling of nationality and citizenship thus may be easier in countries with a tradition of functional representation (the 'Dutch pillars' ideal type), whereas it may not where assimilationist policies have historically prevailed (the 'peasants into Frenchmen' ideal type). One caveat is that very different historical legacies sometimes yield similar results: both Germany and France refuse to grant local voting rights to foreigners. Thus countries classified as displaying 'civic nationalism' display the same reluctance to give non-nationals political rights as do countries where the legitimacy of the nation lies elsewhere (Germany).

To explore the national legacy hypothesis, one must rely on historical material and scholarly characterizations of the country cases to determine how they rank as far as the importance of Church–state conflict, corporatist tradition, and nation-building are concerned. There is the temptation to select a historical reference-point to fit the data and infuse too much determinism in the analysis. Germany offers another illustration of analytical bias. The portrayal of Germany as an organic nation, a community of destiny, unable to surmount its historical peculiarity (late unification, late democratization) and to include non-ethnic Germans may be partially true. Yet it fails to capture the evolution which took place within major German political parties in the 1980s paving the way for a more political conception of the nation (Murray 1994). Another analytical risk consists in taking official rhetoric at face value when political actors exploit history to frame an issue to their advantage. When French politicians invoke *laïcité* as the backbone of France's identity as a nation to prevent the institutionalization of Islam or condemn the veil, they conveniently forget that the separation of Church and state was never total: the state helps fund private religious schools and there are chaplaincies in public schools; and in the 1970s state authorities actually encouraged the creation of prayer-rooms in factories and helped pay for imams and Korans (Kepel 1987). Many contrasting interpretations of the lessons that historical events had for the treatment of foreigners today can be drawn.[13]

National legacy is perhaps only an intervening variable which weighs on the outcome in highly politicized situations by determining which issue will become more salient.


## INTERNATIONAL VARIABLES


While cross-national differences in the rights of foreigners remain, all nations have made advances in this policy area. This suggests that the evolution of the rights of foreigners is a transnational phenomenon and that it may have been driven by international forces. Especially in an institutionally 'thick' environment such as western Europe, it is plausible that international institutions and transnational actors were able to diffuse shared understandings about the treatment of foreigners so as to change and shape the views of domestic state and societal actors, as has been the case in other areas (Wapner 1995). In fact, this kind of argument has been presented by Yasemine Soysal (1994) to explain how citizenship rights were granted to non-citizens. Soysal states that the post-war elaboration of an international human rights discourse functions as a powerful norm-guiding behaviour at the domestic level. In her view, the basis and legitimacy of state membership has shifted from nationality to residence and personhood, and this new normative discourse has been diffused by transnational actors and international institutions. This would explain why a similar evolution towards a new 'post-national' model of citizenship can be observed across European countries:[14] 'The universalistic conceptions of individual rights and personhood become formally institutionalized norms through an array of collectivities . . . These collectivities, by advising national governments, enforcing legal categories, crafting models and standards, and producing reports and recommendations, promote and diffuse ideas and norms about universal human rights that in turn engender a commanding discourse of membership' (1994: 152).

Therefore, national actors, governments, and immigrant groups adopt the human rights rhetoric, although the causal mechanisms whereby one leads to another are unclear.[15] Soysal points to the creation of a number of international institutions, charters, and declarations providing nation-states with guide-lines for the treatment of non-citizen populations on their territory. This is a theoretically tempting argument that has also gained currency in international political economy studies. Scholars in this discipline argue that the post-war era has been characterized by a regime of embedded liberalism in which domestic liberal norms are institutionalized in the international system in such a way as to constrain the autonomy of states where they first emerge (Ruggie 1982; Hollifield 1992*b*).

Yet, as Soysal herself underlines, it is still up to nation-states to abide by international norms (1994: 143). Even when there is a shift in international discourse, national variations in its application abound and policy reversals or restrictions occur. As political scientists have regained interest in transnational ideas, they have also highlighted the ways in which domestic structures influence their infiltration so as to create significantly different outcomes (Hall 1989). Kathryn Sikkink's study on human rights policy in Europe and the United States has demonstrated that, in spite of a similar international normative commitment, the time at which this commitment led to domestic action and the nature of the policies generated were very different (Goldstein and Keohane 1993). International texts are applied by state administrations and courts, who do so according to their own national values and with national interest in mind (Noiriel 1991). The nation-state is designated as responsible for organizing state membership and implementing human rights principles. Sociologist Saskia Sassen, who has also argued for the importance of international legal instruments, nevertheless acknowledges that 'various components of the state have been key agents for the incorporation of human rights in domestic law' (1996: 60).[16]

Legal scholar Olivier Beaud reminds us, 'considering international law as a source of limitation of national sovereignty ignores the fact that it originates from the will of the states themselves and they carefully control its content' (1993).[17] This is indeed what can be deduced from the study of the many human rights conventions signed after the war.[18] Although signatories are meant to protect the fundamental freedoms of people within their jurisdiction regardless of nationality, there are *in the texts themselves* a number of limits to their universal application. Political rights are reserved for citizens (Art. 25 of the 1966 International Covenant on Civil and Political Rights; Art. 16 of the European Convention on the Protection of Human Rights and Fundamental Freedoms). National security and public order are deemed legitimate reasons to restrict liberties (a reason often invoked in cases involving foreigners). What is not included in international texts is equally telling: the prerogatives of a nation-state when it comes to refusing access, residence, or naturalization to its territory has not been put into question.[19] The International Convention on the Elimination of all Forms of Racial Discrimination (1966) also specifically mentions that discriminations on the basis of nationality do not apply (Art. 1.2).

The leitmotif in these texts is that the principle of national sovereignty of the contracting parties is not to be challenged. International law does put restrictions on states who want to prevent their nationals from *exiting*, but the state can decide who enters, who participates in the 'general will', who can become part of the nation; it can legitimately prefer 'its own' in legislation.[20] The same remark applies to conventions which focus on socio-economic rights in so far as the latter justify laws aiming at the protection of the national labour market.[21] It should also be underlined that the universal character of human rights is undermined in international conventions which restrict the enjoyment of rights to specific nationalities because they are based on the principle of reciprocity (such as the 1977 European Convention on the Legal Status of Migrant Workers) or only concern European Union member country citizens (European Social Charter, Treaty of Rome, Treaty on European Union).

International agreements do not all have a legal value. When they do, it sometimes takes decades before they are ratified and states may do so only partially and/or may fail to ratify controversial protocols. Individual petition is not always possible. Then domestic actors, judges, or lawyers who might use them need to be aware of the potential of international agreements. In other words, the influence of international norms can only be the result of a slow, diluted process. Studying a 'critical case', the European Commission and Court of Human Rights (ECHR), which was the first international jurisdiction of human rights protection in history, is a fruitful way of measuring the impact on the domestic legal statuses of non-nationals of international organizations which have a real monitoring and enforcement power.

The ECHR record in relation to about ten rulings on the civil rights of foreigners (*circa* 2.5 per cent of its decision between 1959 and 1990) shows that not only is there a limited legal basis on which to protect non-nationals but, even where the Convention provided such a basis, the European Court of Human Rights was reluctant to use its judicial capital in a politically explosive dossier. The judges did rule on certain very specific areas but not on the core of foreigners' rights. The Court has not ruled on discriminations on the basis of alienage. Article 14 of the ECHR, which bans discrimination of many grounds including race, colour, language, religion, and national origin, is sometimes invoked by litigating parties yet has so far been deemed irrelevant by the judges (Krüger and Strasser 1994). The Court has not pronounced itself on dispositions which specifically protect foreigners: against expulsion (Art. 1, Protocol 7)[22] and against collective expulsion (Art. 4, Protocol 4). The contribution of the Court has been in two areas. The first is the need to take into consideration the family ties of an alien mainly in deportation cases and in granting residence permits. It is based on Article 8, on family life, starting with a 21 June 1988 decision (*Berrehab* vs. *Netherlands*). The other significant jurisprudence is based on Article 3, on inhuman treatment, and provides guarantees against expulsion or extradition to countries that perpetrate such treatment. The timing of the ECHR decisions are significant since, at that point, many of the reforms extending rights to aliens had been enacted domestically, invalidating a causal argument about their impact on the policy of receiving countries.

What about the ways in which the ECHR has been 'institutionally co-opted' at the domestic level (Moravcsik 1994), i.e. instances when national courts refer to international human rights standards in their pronouncements? It took a long time for national high courts to start incorporating ECHR jurisprudence, at which point they had already developed their own jurisprudence on alien rights based on constitutional and general legal principles. France only ratified the European

Convention of Human Rights in 1974 and waited until 1981 to permit individual petition under Article 25. It was only in 1988 that the French Council of State recognized the applicability of the Convention in the Arrêt Nicolo. What can be inferred from this delayed effect of the Convention? First, it should be said that French judges were already defending the rights of foreigners on human rights grounds before 1988 and, in particular, their right to lead a normal family life, which the Council of State had declared to be a general legal principle as of 1978 (Wihtol de Wenden 1988).

In countries with strong judicial review and human rights protection, such as Germany, the effect of international human rights norms is practically invisible. Very few complaints have been filed with the European Commission of Human Rights.[23] Furthermore, the Federal Constitutional Court can only base its decisions on the Constitution and has held that a constitutional complaint cannot be based on an alleged violation of the European Convention. It only allows interpretation of the Convention in cases in which a court has violated a plaintiff's fundamental right to equality before the law under Article 3 of the Basic Law by *arbitrarily* misapplying or overlooking the Convention (Steinberger 1985). This reduces the impact of the ECHR domestically. As in the French case, the ECHR jurisprudence on the aliens' right to lead a normal family life post-dates German jurisprudence on the same issue. The latter is based on Article 6 of the 1949 Basic Law. As early as 1966 the Federal Constitutional Court stated that the family situation of an alien had to be considered in deportation cases and the Court reaffirmed this special constitutional protection of the family in landmark cases in 1973 and 1978 (Neuman 1990).

In the Netherlands until the 1980s courts did not deem the ECHR self-executing and preferred to apply a comparable provision of Dutch law and, in cases when they did apply the Convention, they did so in a very restrictive way. The attitude of the courts towards human rights treaties evolved in the early 1980s and the Supreme Court took a few landmark decisions invoking the ECHR. It is within this context that a 1986 ruling of the Supreme Court should be seen, which stated that the President of a District Court had been right to annul a deportation order based on the right to a normal family life. This ruling came after the Netherlands had been condemned in Strasbourg in a similar case mentioned above—*Berrehab* vs. *The Netherlands*. The activism of public interest law organizations such as the Working Group on Legal Aid to Immigrants has been instrumental in ensuring that foreigners benefited from the provisions of international law. They have done so by filing suits to create case-law and through parliamentary lobbying (Groenendijk 1980).

National implementation of human rights norms requires a combination of factors that are demanding enough to hinder further the effects of international norms in domestic contexts. One pre-condition seems to have been the presence of pre-existing national norms compatible with international ones. It is not fortuitous that the ECHR's main contribution has been made via the right to a normal family life since, in all the countries studied, this right was already included in constitutional texts and law and/or actively applied. Other factors include formal rules, the favourable attitude of national courts towards international law, and knowledgeable domestic lawyers willing to draw upon international law to multiply litigation and create case-law. Even when the Court did condemn a signatory state on a particular issue, only the condemned states reflected on the Court's decision and only in the narrow area on which the Court had ruled. In any case, there is no uniformity in the interpretation and incorporation of international norms which supports the idea of a top–down impact of human rights norms.

Even if one takes for granted that politics in west European states have been pervaded by a universalistic post-national discourse on rights, one must still determine empirically whether this rhetoric results in a praxis among policy-makers. Even in the case of immigrant groups, human rights are a tool in a larger repertoire, a mere rhetorical weapon in a struggle to defend their interests. Notwithstanding, one should not confuse the means with the reasons of a struggle.

A number of other possibilities must not be overlooked. First, national policy-makers speak in terms of transnational rights when they promote pro-foreigner laws, but this is not what motivates them. For example, when French authorities extended industrial rights for migrant workers after a series of strikes by immigrant workers made them fear further social unrest, they were not doing so to align France with International Labour Organization standards or to uphold a basic right. More generally, governments may be concerned with social peace rather than with human rights compliance. Secondly, national policy-makers do not consider all provisions for foreigners as rights *per se* but simply as benefits. Their decisions thus obey a different logic, based on economic calculations, interest group pressure, or a desire to diminish the attractiveness of immigration. For instance, this is the case for certain social services (services for asylum-seekers and non-contributive welfare programmes especially in the less 'decommodified' European welfare states) and for work authorizations. Thirdly, improvements in the status of foreigners sometimes occur because of national traditions embodied in law prior to the emergence of the post-war human rights discourse. This is the case of family reunification guarantees in Germany, which were secured because a right to family life is inscribed in the Basic Law of 1949. Its Article 6 reflects a concern for traditional family values as constitutive of the national character which antecedes the war.

For each measure extending a right to non-citizens, one needs to assess whether the debate was shaped by a universalistic discourse emphasizing the rights of individuals or if other considerations were present: national traditions of pluralism or tolerance; pragmatic rather than normative reasons. In legislative minutes, official reports, press coverage, and in interviews with civil servants and politicians in charge of alien issues, references to international human rights standards are actually very rare. The post-national discourse is not the only operative one at work. A nation-state-centred discourse is still a powerful contender. 'Neo-national' rhetoric has successfully infiltrated mainstream politics in a number of European countries. Miriam Feldblum (Chapter 7 in this volume) argues that a neo-national strategy focusing on the revalorization of national boundaries and identity coexists with a post-national strategy. In brief, it is the struggle between two contradictory discourses that is being waged in European countries over a range of issues including immigration. In order to see which one of these two has prevailed, one needs to scrutinize the policy process in each case of rights extension.

In the end, international pressure on governments and administrations is fairly constant. It remains to be established when it is more likely to affect policy outcomes. The impact of international-level variables should be strongest when domestic pressure is low and debate is contained within the gilded doors of official buildings. When this is not the case, the cost of alienating foreign partners or facing international disapproval may be lower than that of forsaking domestic allies or losing support at the polls from galvanized anti-immigrant voters. This makes international-level variables fairly unpredictive on their own.

## DOMESTIC AND INTERNATIONAL EXPLANATIONS: CONCLUSION

Since I would like to argue that the factors invoked in the literature should be understood as relevant in only certain parts of the political

process, modelling the institutional trajectories of reforms is very important. One can narrow the range of likely policy outcomes by pinning
down the political venues that a reform will go through. This implies
taking into account how their *modus operandi* biases the decisions they
make. Therefore, a bureaucrat in the Interior Ministry, one sitting in
an agency for integration policy, a politician running for re-election,
and an administrative judge need not think about foreigners' rights in
the same way and use the same criteria. All of them will have notions
of what it is appropriate to say and/or think; all of them will also have
their own perception of what the national interest is and their own
definition of the nation.[24] Yet, there is no obvious reason to think that
these conceptions should be the same. More importantly, each of the
different factors listed above (international norms, fear of mobilization
and unrest, nation-building legacies, and so forth) are not equally important in each institutional context. Judges may be aware of international
human rights standards when deliberating on a case, but they are not
concerned with social peace in the same way a government official is.
In sum, the 'why' of reform depends on the 'where' of reform.

## A NEW MODEL: CONTROLLING THE EXPANSION OF POLITICAL DEBATE ON FOREIGNERS' RIGHTS

More explanatory leverage could be gained by approaching the question of rights and benefits extension using a different framework, one
focusing on the policy process through which the status of foreigners
changed. Different types of provision followed distinctive political
trajectories: some were the object of intense political mobilization or
public debate, others were not; some aspects of the status of foreigners
were discussed only within the bureaucracy, while others depended ultimately on judicial pronouncements. The following section develops a
model which underlines that the success of reforms affecting the rights
of foreigners depends on the scope of political debate.

Whether measures affecting non-nationals are adopted within an
open or closed political arena matters because it changes the actors
and the processes involved. Eric Schattschneider has pointed out that
the scope of a debate is an important determinant of outcome: 'conflicts
are frequently won or lost by the success that the contestants have in
getting the audience involved in the fight or in excluding it, as the
case may be' (1960: 4). In his view, it is the weaker party in a closed

debate that seeks to expand the roster of participants to more sympathetic ones. Using a playground analogy, he states that 'it is not the bully, but the defenceless smaller boys who "tell the teacher" ' (p. 40). In the case of foreigners, however, given the lack of support they enjoy in the public at large, there is reason to believe that the teacher will not act as a neutral arbiter but will side with the bully.

## The Risks of Politicization: The Less Said the Better?

Gary Freeman has recently argued that, in order to understand immigration policy change, 'we need to investigate how public officials interact with organized groups between elections because immigration politics in liberal democracies is dominated by the organized public' (1995: 885). His reasons are twofold. First, he believes that immigration has concentrated benefits and diffuse costs and that those most likely to compete for jobs and housing with aliens are the least-advantaged part of the population. This implies, in his view, that the bearers of the costs are less likely to mobilize politically than the beneficiaries of immigration. Secondly, he states that public opinion has only incomplete information about immigration and also only has inadequate means to mandate policy choices even at election time, thereby giving state actors and politicians a free hand in dealing with immigrant-related issues (p. 885).

I agree with Gary Freeman's analysis that many decisions granting migrant rights depended upon a relative insulation of policy-makers from the public at large (e.g. in small policy circles and courts). Notwithstanding, there is room for disagreement when it comes to understanding why and how much the public can be kept in the dark. Gary Freeman's description fits well the first phase of foreign labour recruitment in Europe. As Tomas Hammar has commented, immigration policy was made in administrative contexts, without public participation and with little parliamentary supervision (1985: 277–87). However, in the 1980s and 1990s in Europe, there have been instances of politicization and electoral use of the immigration issue and extensive national debates on citizenship and the place of ethnic minorities in the national fabric.[25]

The central question then becomes: 'What happens when the issue spills over in a larger public arena than the client politics[26] one would expect from a policy yielding concentrated benefits and diffuse costs?' (see Wilson 1980 for typology).[27] One consequence is a change in the perception of these costs and benefits and the involvement of new groups who in turn change the balance of forces in the policy debate.[28] At first, migrants had been discussed by small numbers of participants in terms of numbers and economic input. Yet, starting in the late 1970s, previously uninterested constituencies became involved in the debate as the issue of alien rights was framed using well-known agenda-setting techniques. Politicians who wanted to exploit the issue electorally succeeded in 'making creative and credible linkages . . . to a broader political issue' (Baumgartner 1989: 215), and presented the problem as a social one rather than as a technical issue,[29] as had been the case until the 1970s (when the discussion centred around labour market statistics). Politicians who wish to expand debate participation are likely to adopt a highly emotional tone (Riker 1986) and, in the case of foreigners, politicians generalized about the future of national identity and culture so as to involve larger and larger constituencies in the debate (Cobb and Elder 1983).

Examples abound. When two girls who wore Islamic veils in a Creil high school in 1989 were expelled, the case was redefined as an issue about cultural rights, secularism, French national identity, and the future of the public school system; and it involved every national political group during two months of intensive media coverage. In the Netherlands, it was the crashing of a plane on an Amsterdam suburb which sparked an emotional and confused debate on illegal aliens (many were believed to be among the victims) and their status in Dutch society. A recurring motif of these debates is the link between immigration and crime, drugs, urban decay, unemployment . . . Thomas Faist (1994*a*) discussing the German case calls this turning migrant rights into a 'meta-issue' linked to a range of domestic problems.

Emphasizing the importance of rhetoric goes against the idea that the substantive implications of an issue will determine the scope of debate. It means that issues with symbolic value rather than material value take on importance. Frank Baumgartner insists that 'those issues that affect the most people, cost the more money, or would result in the most radical changes' are not necessarily those which will lead to intense political mobilization (1989: 213). It seems that, in fact, foreigners' access to social services has been less problematic than their right to participate politically, to naturalize, to cultivate their cultural identity. In brief, whereas Gary Freeman would argue that the beneficiaries of immigration outweigh in resources the cost-bearers, I would argue that there are non-cost-bearers who will oppose immigrant rights on symbolic grounds, which is one reason why an expanded scope of debate will not result in more rights for aliens.

Why should a move from a closed to an open debate be detrimental to measures aimed at improving the status of foreigners?[30] A number of interrelated elements make politicization or high issue salience risky for the extension of rights to foreigners. They can be grouped under the following categories: (1) the electoral calculus of politicians during 'hard times'; (2) negative media coverage; (3) the state of public opinion.

The conduit between politicians and the voting public is of course the media. Key players in the construction of an issue, the media have been described as biased and reductionist in their portrayal of foreigners in recent studies on press reporting in Europe (Bonnafous 1991; Faist 1994a; Van Dijk 1993). Recent research in this area has shown that opinion leaders who appear in the media and 'influentials' who read the press and diffuse the ideas therein significantly mould the general public's views on immigration and asylum issues (Weimann and Brosius 1994; Thränhardt 1994; Van Dijk 1993). The way these issues are covered, however, cannot help the foreigners' cause: stereotypical or violent images are often placed next to stories (veiled women, riots, fires, begging gypsies); emotive metaphors are used to describe the numbers of foreigners ('flows', 'tides', or 'hordes'); and the numbers themselves are easily manipulated (most typically asylum requests and criminal statistics)—to mention but a few of the characteristics of media coverage (Battegay and Boubeker 1993; *Médiascope*, 4 (1993); Ruhrmann and Kollmer 1987; Blanke 1993).

The combined effects of political and media representations of foreigners on public opinion completes the circle and reinforces the chances that restricting foreigners' rights will be electorally lucrative. The first reliable comparative data available on public opinion and foreigners was gathered by Eurobarometer in 1989. In that year 51 per cent of those polled believed that there were too many 'Others' in their country and 37 per cent thought that there were too many foreigners (Eurobarometer 1989). Since 1989 Eurobarometer has continued to monitor attitudes towards non-nationals in the European Union, and survey results demonstrate an increase in the number of negative attitudes towards foreigners. They reach a peak in 1993, particularly in countries with large numbers of immigrants such as those studied here.[31] This increase cannot readily be attributed to a significant worsening of socio-economic conditions. In fact, this increase corresponds to periods of intense political discussions and media coverage of foreigner-related issues after 1989 (over Muslim migrants in France, over asylum-seekers and the reform of Article 16 in Germany, and to a lesser extent in the Netherlands over illegals and the failures of minority policy). In other words, 'prejudice' grew 'as a response to perceived group threat' (Quillian 1995: 586) fuelled by political debate and heightened by biased coverage.

Another feature that characterizes an expanded scope of debate is the presence of marginal actors such as extreme-right parties who do not have channels of access to restricted policy venues. The balance of forces between different interest groups is different in a bureaucratic style of policy-making and in a society-wide policy debate. As Ellen Immergut has argued, 'depending upon the logic of the decision process, different political strategies are available to interest groups, and different groups are privileged by the political institutions in each country' (Immergut 1992: 66–7). Diffuse groups in society or actors on the margins (the extreme right, for instance) which may not benefit from secure institutional linkages with the state have a better chance in an open debate.[32]

Given the bias in press coverage and the xenophobic potential in public opinion, politicians who seek to seize power are confident that anti-immigrant rhetoric can be electorally lucrative, especially in times of socio-economic restructuring, when there is a need to assign blame. This is borne out by the fact that calls for *restrictions* or rights generally occur at the end of a government's term of office, i.e. close to major (parliamentary or presidential) elections,[33] whereas reforms that *extend* rights to foreigners are more likely to occur after a major election, when the time horizon of elected officials is not too limited. Just as governments are said to inflate the economy before elections and deflate it after elections in a phenomenon known as the 'political business cycle' (Nordhaus 1975), governments inflate anti-foreigner rhetoric before elections and then deflate the rhetoric and produce liberal reforms soon after they occur.

Here are a few instances of this 'election–migration policy cycle'. In Germany, the Social Democratic Party (SPD) had postponed immigrant reform just before the 1980 elections for fear of voter retaliation. In 1982–3 the CDU–CSU successfully raised the issue of foreigners during the the parliamentary campaign and undermined the SPD's political base as Helmut Kohl promised that restricting immigration and encouraging repatriation would be one of three main planks of his new policy (Meier-Braun 1987).[34] In fact 'after winning the elections, the government programme of the second Kohl government in spring 1983 mentioned *Ausländerpolitik* only scarcely . . . The issue had been successfully used, now it was dropped. The debate on "foreigners" died down' (Thränhardt 1994: 7–8).

In France, the same phenomenon took place. Reforms granting rights immediately followed a major election. When the left came to power in 1981, the government acted very quickly in enacting some important reforms that granted foreigners full rights of association in 1981 and unrestricted industrial rights (in 1982) and in publishing circulars that put a momentary stop on expulsions,[35] and organized the regularization of illegal aliens and elaborated a more flexible policy towards family reunification.[36] The head of staff of the 1981–2 State Secretariat for Immigrants, Patrick Weil, attributed the rapidity of these actions to the fact that 'the relevant decision-makers—cabinet members, ministerial staff members—have the feeling that the timing is propitious, immediately after a victory that has singularly weakened the Right, but that the "window of opportunity" can quickly close in a policy area where public opinion support is not insured' (1991: 142–3). They were correct in their assessment of the situation to the extent that, during the next major campaigns, the right-wing parties who sought to recapture a majority or the Elysée Palace took on the immigrant issue and proposed to restrict the conditions of entry and stay and of access to citizenship for foreigners (in 1986 and again in 1993).

There is a self-reinforcing negative dynamic between the press, public opinion, and the electioneering politician. On this account, elections are tricky, especially for pro-migrant groups and associations who want to speak out so that the issue of foreigners is not forgotten yet are afraid to see their ideas manipulated and perverted. Policy-makers are also aware of this problem. In the Netherlands, even when all major democratic parties had agreed to grant local voting rights to foreigners, they feared a backlash among native Dutch people: 'To avoid uselessly provoking public opinion, almost all the parties agreed to avoid a "hot" debate. Because of this moderating decision, divergences could only be expressed within Parliament' (Rath 1993: 144). Mishandling the media coverage of a reform project is a guarantee of failure. In France, a famous blunder was made when Claude Cheysson, the Foreign Relations Minister, told the press on 9 August 1981 that the foreigners' right to vote locally would be in effect for the 1983 municipal elections. There was a public outcry: the press covered it as its lead story for several weeks and the Ministry of Social Affairs was deluged with hostile 'citizens' letters', and a poll showed 58 per cent of the electorate were opposed to the measure.[37] The government was coerced into publicly denying that it had ever contemplated any such project.[38]

Therefore, alien rights are best discussed in restricted loci of debate. Scholars have stressed the importance of this locus of debate—what Frank Baumgartner and Bryan Jones call 'policy venues', i.e. 'institutional locations where authoritative decisions are made concerning a given issue' (1993: 32). They posit that strategically minded policymakers on the losing side of a debate will not just try to appeal to larger and larger groups, they will search for a more receptive institutional venue. A change of institution will not only mean a different audience but also different internal dynamics and rules and thus possibly different 'structurally-induced equilibria' (Shepsle 1986: 27–59). The main relevant 'policy venues' can be found in the executive realm (administration and government), and the judicial sphere (national and European courts, administrative and constitutional courts, as well as bodies with overseer powers such as the Council of State in France). Each sphere possesses its own rules of the game and its own priorities; therefore, passage from one sphere to another will redefine the stakes involved in the issue.

### Keeping the Debate behind Closed Doors: The Bureaucratic Sphere

Can we predict when there will be politicization of immigrant rights in a way that is more systematic than attributing it to the uneven rhetorical skills of political entrepreneurs? Institutional constraints play a role. Ellen Immergut (1992) has argued that the ability of the political executive to enact reform depends on the existence of 'veto points' in each political sphere. The latter include constitutional rules which determine which political arenas a reform has to go through.[39] There are several instances in which we should expect that measures regarding the rights of foreigners will not be confined to the executive realm.

### Rule-Induced Debate Expansion

Instances when an open debate is unavoidable due to institutional constraints should be distinguished from instances where political strategists have room for choice. If a government can extend a particular right for foreigners with a decree or a circular, it is plain sailing. However, if it requires legislative approval, the issue enters a new sphere which the government does not fully control (if its majority is not cohesive, if counter-mobilization makes the law a political liability forcing the withdrawal of the project). That sphere has the potential to be a 'veto point' à la Immergut.

Granting voting rights to foreigners entails constitutional revision and thus legislative passage by a large coalition. This means that public discussion on the issue is almost inevitable and bound to be long and divisive as all sorts of larger debates (e.g. on the definition of the nation) will resurface, thus hampering chances for reform. Welfare benefits do not obey the same rules. In their case, regulatory changes often suffice; or they can be provided by a bill that includes many social measures so as to divert attention from the benefits attributed to foreigners; and they need only be adopted by a simple majority. In a number of cases, legal texts are neutral as far as nationality is concerned and the issue is to render these written rights effective rather than to adopt new laws. These facts facilitate the adoption of social benefits and the extension of rights for which there already exists legislation. It should be noted that rules here vary across types of right rather than across countries.[40]

## Conflict-Based Debate Expansion

Although rules go a long way towards explaining why certain rights reforms are bound to spill over from the executive arena, they sometimes allow flexibility in the way policy change is enacted. In these cases, the expansion of debate is more likely to come from the existence of conflict among policy-makers since, 'where there is little or no conflict, policies tend overwhelmingly to be made by small groups of experts in specialized policy communities far from the view of the public' (Baumgartner 1989: 213). In the present context, this refers to the government agencies in charge of immigrants. It is in their interest to do their work stealthily, and it is significant that the main mode of change has been the enactment of unpublicized decrees and circulars. Stealth becomes arduous, however, when agencies have competing aims, for instance, between ministries in charge of social issues and ministries in charge of border controls. The rights to family reunification, freedom of movement, and access to the labour market are examples of provisions which agencies in charge of migration flow control consider as having direct impact on their efforts, thereby sparking intra-governmental feuds. Disagreements over priorities have also arisen between public health and finance ministries, and between economics and labour ministries.

Therefore, the character of the institutions responsible for migrant policy is important—whether they are centralized, parapublic, unitary, politically insulated, or under judicial scrutiny—and whether consultation with interest groups is institutionalized. This influences their outlook as well as the risk of intrabureaucratic conflict and spill-over. The Dutch case is illuminating as it constitutes the least likely case of debate expansion because of its unitary and co-ordinated character. The Co-ordination of Minorities Policy within the Ministry of the Interior is a means of containing and resolving possible divergence behind office doors. Moreover, the Dutch administration has managed to co-opt and institutionalize a number of actors who could oppose the official dogma: researchers whose projects are commissioned and funded by the government (Penninx *et al.* 1994) or ethnic élites who are nominated to special oversight or consultative boards. A few experts, who often alternate between government and academic positions in the Netherlands, were given a lot of leverage to elaborate an integration policy in the early 1980s. Their competence and knowledge were needed in what had been an neglected field of policy. Finally, there is also a surprising lack of interaction between incorporation policy and migration policy (that of the Ministry of Justice).

There is another reason beside the structure of policy-making that explains why Dutch political élites were able to restrain debate to a small 'policy community' or 'issue network' (Marsh and Rhodes 1992). The coalition character of governments minimizes open conflict and turnover of personnel. Furthermore, because no single camp can outvote another in a coalition system, political battles are waged over details. The consensus on equal treatment for foreigners in the Netherlands (one of the three objectives in the 1983 Minorities Report) and its parallel lack of politicization and intense media coverage make sense if one takes into account the enduring features of the Dutch political system. Arend Lijphart's famous study on consociational democracy included 'depoliticization' and 'secrecy' as two essential features of the politics of accommodation in the Netherlands (1975: 129–34). These features were still at play during the early 1980s, when minority policy was elaborated.

The Netherlands has both a unitary, co-ordinated policy-making structure and consensual élites. Are these elements absent in the other cases so as to explain why there was a politicization of alien issues? Turning first to Germany, it may be argued that Germany's political system resembles that of the Netherlands with respect to coalition governments and one should find similar methods of consensus-building behind the scenes. Experts on German politics stress that the absence of an hegemonic party, for instance, and the pivotal role of the FDP lead to delayed or incremental policy-making and that Germany is a *Verhandlungsdemokratie* in which policy is subject to complex negotiations among coalition partners (Schmidt 1992; Czada and Schmidt 1993; Katzenstein 1987). In contrast with what happened in the Netherlands, however, conflict between members of the governing coalition such as the FDP Commissioner for Foreigners' Affairs and the CDU Interior Minister on the foreigners' issue was open and public.[41]

This can be explained by the fact that, in Germany, there is no unitary structure or co-ordinating unit on immigrant policy within the state apparatus. Conflict arises between different levels of government as well as between agencies in charge of foreigners and federal ministries. The federal organizations who assist foreigners have traded off independence for influence. The only federal-level public office is the Federal Commissioner for Foreigners (physically situated within the Ministry of Labour and Social Affairs). Its task consists in issuing guide-lines; it has a very small staff and budget and it continually suffers from a lack of 'attention from the government' so that 'when similar agencies in other countries are considered, the Federal Commissioner has a much weaker position *vis-à-vis* both the state and migrant groups' (Soysal 1994: 78). There is no immigration nor immigrant policy as such in Germany and no federal agency to administer immigrant-related tasks.[42] The parapublic institutions[43] who do (Caritas, Diakonisches Werk, Arbeiterwohlfart) exert pressure for reform from outside the state apparatus using public channels. Therefore conflict over migrant issues cannot be voiced within the state structure.

Another factor that explains why debate on alien rights is not confined behind ministry doors is the multi-level character of the German polity. Alien law is federal in Germany and the *Länder* do not have much leeway in applying the Federal Act.[44] Yet, certain areas such as social policy, education, and culture fall within the prerogative of the *Länder*, so that states can regulate on the rights of aliens in these domains. The federal system multiplies the number of policy venues in which differing views can be heard, allowing for multiple points of entry to the debate (local, state, and Bundesrat).

If one compares France with the Netherlands, the difference lies not so much in the structure of policy-making as in the differences in the political system that make French political élites more competitive than Dutch ones. Conflict at government level may appear likely in France because of the organization of immigration policy. The management of the latter is scattered among a plethora of ministries and agencies, some with overlapping competence. The centralization of the bureaucracy, however, makes up for its lack of unity. Conflict between different agencies and ministries can often be resolved by co-ordinating units or by Cabinet arbitrage.[45] The main difference between France and the other cases lies in the political system. France is a majority democracy with a bipolar party system. Rather than encourage consensus, it exacerbates the contrast between the positions of the two main camps. Consequently, ideological differences over immigration are inflated.

In brief, the two dimensions of cross-national variation that affect the likelihood that debate on alien rights will spill over in the electoral sphere are the level of co-ordination of policy-making and the degree of competitiveness of the political élites. Within each nation, however, rights of certain types, such as social rights, are more easily obtained than others since the rules guiding reform are more compatible with stealth.

### 'Second Chances' for Reforms: Shifting to the Judicial Sphere

There is still a 'second chance' for changes in foreigners' rights outside the bureaucratic sphere. A constitutional court or a high administrative tribunal can be asked to pass judgment on its conformity to basic principles embodied in a higher law, and the reform outcome can be reversed. The record of higher courts in Europe shows that they guarantee civil liberties and non-discrimination, and in almost all cases this leads them to protect foreigners' rights. Since the late 1970s there are more legislative and regulatory texts for courts to give their opinion; there are also more opportunities for pro-immigrant actors to sue the administration. Therefore, a large body of jurisprudence has developed on alien rights that highlights the importance of courts as 'quasi-legislators' (Stone 1992) and as full-time actors in social reform (Horowitz 1977; Schuck 1993).[46] There is one important exception to equality of treatment between foreigners and nationals, namely voting rights, because constitutional texts generally make it clear that these are reserved for citizens.[47]

All immigration scholars agree that until the end of the 1970s the handling of immigration was characterized by 'infra-droit' (meaning 'sublaw'; see Lochak 1985) and the arbitrary power of the administration. Catherine Wihtol de Wenden, noting that apart from the 1972 law on racism and the 1975 law on the eligibility and voting rights of trade union delegates, no law on migration questions had been passed until 1980,[48] sums up the situation in 1970s France as follows:

Between 1945 and 1980 (the Bonnet bill on the entry and stay of foreigners was passed on 10 January 1980) a maze of decrees, circulars, departmental memos or even telexes regulated the foreigners' situation in a complex, dense and obscure way; they are generally not published and often change. *On navigue à vue*, often without respecting the rule of law, without judicial control and sometimes in an arbitrary fashion. Expulsions and refusal of entry without the control of a judge, excessive ID checks, delays in processing naturalization and asylum requests are vehemently denounced by associations defending the rights of immigrants. (Wihtol de Wenden 1993: 168)

The height of this type of policy-making can be traced back to 1977 and 1978, when thirty-seven decrees, circulars, and memos regarding foreigners were issued. They all contributed to making foreigners' situation more precarious. This was perhaps too much too fast, since it was also in 1978 that the judicial sphere entered the scene to remedy the arbitrariness of the administration. The Council of State annulled all or part of the measures that it considered most detrimental to human rights in four landmark decisions. By the 1990s alien-related cases made up about 15 per cent of the now more than 10,000 cases a year before the Council, which shows just how important litigation strategies had become for migrant rights groups,[49] and the Council's 'important jurisprudence on aliens, refugees, expulsions, extraditions, typically protective of human rights' was held to be one of its major jurisprudential developments (Costa 1993: 39). The Constitutional Council followed suit as legislative developments in the area of immigration after 1980 increased and were referred to the Council, striking down, for instance, eight of the dispositions of the 1993 so-called Pasqua laws on the entry and stay of foreigners.

Both high courts drew on the French Constitution and Bill of Rights to guarantee equality before the law for aliens and to reduce discrimination on the basis of alienage. The Council of State confirmed on 30 June 1989 that no benefit could be denied on the basis of nationality in an instance when the Paris Municipal Council had sought in 1986 to exclude aliens from a family policy non-contributive benefit.[50] The Constitutional Council then reaffirmed that exclusion of foreigners from welfare benefits is against 'the constitutional principles of equality' when, on 22 January 1990, they struck down a legislative measure that extended a benefit ('l'allocation adulte handicapé') to non-nationals but *only* to EU nationals.

The situation in Germany was very similar to that of France until the early 1970s. The 1965 Federal Aliens Act regulated the stay of foreigners only in broad terms and had no formulated legislative aim. It used deliberately vague expressions such as 'the interest of the Federal Republic of Germany' as reasons to cancel a residence permit. The Aliens Act was to be completed by executive decrees and circulars, yet no procedure was delineated by law for their enactment except when state approval was required (Dohse 1981). Some of these circulars were not made public and remained unknown to lawyers (Hailbronner 1989: 35). As Tugrul Ansay points out, 'consequently, it left foreign migrants at the bureaucratic mercy of those sitting in state ministries and preparing such specific circulars, or those in alien bureaus who were using their discretion on a case-by-case basis' (1992: 835).[51] This also resulted in great variations in practice within Germany (Franz 1975: 46).

At the same time as in France, in the mid- to late 1970s, decisions by the Federal Constitutional and Administrative Courts stated that under the rule of proportionality (Article 20.3 of the Basic Law), the interest of the state had to be balanced against the constitutional interests of the foreign worker (and thus, for instance, foreigners should no longer be deported for committing a small traffic offence).[52] Furthermore, courts affirmed that residence and permit renewal guarantees had to be granted to foreigners, who have a right to develop freely their personality as stated in Article 2 of the German Constitution and thus must be given the opportunity to plan their future (Schwerdtfeger 1980). In a landmark case in 1978, the Federal Constitutional Court stated that prior routine renewals of an alien worker's residence permit had created a constitutionally protected reliance interest in continued residence that could not be overridden by the official thesis that 'the FRG was not an immigration country'.

The Federal Constitutional Court also took into consideration the family situation of the alien, basing itself on Article 6 of the Basic Law, which provides for explicit protection of marriage and the family (paragraphs 1 and 2), which are defined as 'natural rights' as aforementioned.[53] Finally, the Federal Constitutional Court also came to issue rulings on discriminations on the grounds of alienage. The Court forbids 'arbitrary discrimination' on the basis of alienage, based on Article 2 of the Basic Law, which establishes equality before the law. The constitutional judges invalidated a federal statute that excluded aliens from the enjoyment of pension payments should they no longer reside in the Federal Republic. German constitutional law sets as a government goal a just social order known as the *Sozialstaat* principle, and the court underlined that it applied to all regardless of nationality.[54]

Evidence of arbitrariness could also be found in the Dutch case in the early 1970s. For instance, until the mid-1970s immigrant workers only received unemployment benefit for six months, and it was a customary administrative practice to take away their residence rights and expel them if they had not found a job after three or six months. Dutch workers are entitled to two and a half years of benefits but nowhere in unemployment legislation was it stated that legally employed foreigners were a special category (Groenendjk 1980: 170). Intense lobbying by legal groups in Parliament succeeded in overturning this practice without going through the courts. In other instances, however, they had to go through the courts, when, for instance, municipalities would distribute benefits *à la tête du client* rather than the full legal amount—300 or 400 guilders instead of 1,000, for instance.[55] The Judicial Division of the Council of State plays an important role in the judicialization of policy-making by, for instance, providing criteria and definitions for family reunification. The Supreme Court's rulings on asylum, conditions of detention, and deportation have emphasized the need to respect due process.

As governments were trying to restrict and control the entry and stay of foreigners, they set in motion a new political process. They sought to regulate immigration further and, by thus placing the issue higher on the political agenda (as a means of diffusing the economic crisis), they publicized it and allowed other actors to enter the debate. At the same time, because this new focus on migration led to more regulations (and, in the case of comprehensive policies, new legislation), albeit unwillingly they left a window open for the judicial sphere to intervene, define human rights standards, and circumscribe the limits of state power in its handling of foreigners' rights. Politicization and judicialization coincided, usually sparked by government initiatives to restrict flows.

In the United States, the rise of a new legal culture in the 1970s convinced the federal judiciary to curb the sweeping exclusionary powers that executive authorities had been able to exercise with respect to aliens (Schuck 1984). Although, in Europe, the role of the judiciary may not be generally believed to be as pervasive as in the United States, there is a remarkable convergence with the American experience (Hollifield 1992*a*: 186). My research shows that the role of judicial institutions has been more prevalent in the area of rights extension than one would anticipate in countries such as France, where it is considered a junior partner in the hierarchy of powers, a politically weak or dependent body. Judges became involved in decisions concerning the definition of who is an alien and who is entitled to membership in the polity.

It should be pointed out that the treatment of aliens was not the only area in which the role of judiciary institutions was felt more strongly. Administrative courts in particular made inroads against the discretionary power of public agencies in other policy areas. So this is part of a long-term movement which included the development of a new post-war jurisprudence, the evolution of the mentality of judges *vis-à-vis* the limits of state power, and the time that it took them to make a place for themselves in the balance of power. Therefore, the judicial sphere has become important as a venue of debate.

Courts are institutions with a relatively autonomous cognitive structure known as 'legal tradition', i.e. long-term repertoires of thought and behaviour. This implies that, although judges in pronouncing themselves on alien rights were very much aware of the 'judicial capital' they were spending and of their need not to tread on politicians' toes, their decisions exemplify that courts 'were less determined and more insulated both from concrete social interests and from political struggle taking place in other state institutions' (Stone 1992: 13). It is to be expected that the *modus operandi* of courts will be distinct from that of other venues of debates and shifting to the judicial sphere will redefine the stakes.

### Learning Strategies over Time: Recent Developments in Immigrant Policy

The process of rights extension is relevant to our understanding of learning processes in politics, and 'policy feedbacks' (Pierson 1993). My research covered the last twenty years. I was therefore able to investigate signs of political learning. When devising strategies for reform, political actors try to learn from past political mistakes. In other words, the outcome of a particular struggle for reform leads to a revising of the losers' means and channels of action. Political actors learn from previous policy changes what channels to avoid and they factor it in when launching new reforms.

Recent evidence shows the ways in which governments and activists have sought new institutional venues and/or found new linkages to the issue so as to tip the balance of forces in their favour.[56] For instance, national governments who want to restrict the rights of foreigners and have realized that national and international courts impede their actions explore new policy venues and have done so mainly by shifting the level of decision-making—*upwards* to intergovernmental international forums and *downwards* to local authorities—as well as *outwards* by delegating the implementation of policy to private actors.[57]

At the international level, this has led to the multiplication of co-operation groups on immigration, asylum, police, and border control which do not have to answer to a more representative body or international courts (such as the Shengen Agreement, and the European Union Justice and Home Affairs working groups). The lack of transparency of these negotiations also makes it difficult for national actors to oversee the process. Supranational bodies are thus used to circumvent national protection of rights. In order to eschew legal constraints, governments also rely on 'remote control' immigration policy or the creation of international zones in airports, where intervention by lawyers and human rights associations is almost impossible, and thus the civil rights guaranteed by domestic laws are less likely to be respected in this juridical 'no man's land'. Furthermore, governments have sought to curb the realm of judicial intervention either by diminishing the time allowed to examine cases or by narrowing the possibilities for appeal.

At the domestic level, it is significant that national governments have delegated substantial decision-making powers to local authorities such as mayors and the local police in the area of immigration policy in a way altogether detrimental to foreigners' rights.[58] National actors can use dencentralization to induce two main effects: (1) decentralization creates or facilitates intranational variations which are contrary to the universalism understood in the idea of equal rights, and (2) national actors can count on local elected officials who, because they are under financial stress and wish to attract attention to receive more funds or to gain votes, will take exceptionally harsh measures against immigrants.

Another phenomenon consists in the 'privatization' of policy implementation, whereby governments hand over the monitoring of alien status to 'non-state actors'. Examples include airline companies or ships, who will be fined should they transport aliens without proper documentation, or private companies who run detention centres for deportable aliens. Privatization does not always meet policy goals, as the case of sanctions on employers for hiring illegal aliens has shown in many countries. Yet, in the aforementioned instances, the state delegation of control has actually facilitated the efficiency of restrictive migration policy.

Political actors fighting on behalf of foreigners' rights have sought to counter these tactics, which seek to undermine the earlier consolidation of non-nationals' status. The role of courts in the protection of foreigners' rights has increased (as demonstrated by the number of cases opened) as proponents have become aware of the consistent record of this institutional recourse and of the dangers of politicization and the public opinion sphere. It is more common now to find domestic activists training in Brussels so as to unearth international legal means to win cases at home; and the legal departments of pro-migrant groups have greatly expanded to keep up with the increasing complexity of foreigners' law. Efforts by migrants and their supporters to set up transnational networks are also more numerous (Kastoryano 1994).

## CONCLUSION

My claim that containing debate behind closed doors (the doors of ministries or of courtrooms) is necessary for the success of a reform may be relevant in other policy areas. There has been a debate spurred by 'the return of the state' in political science, and 'state-centric' studies such as Hugh Heclo's (1974) work on social policy-making in Britain and Sweden stress and analyse 'autonomous state contributions to policy-making even within constitutional polities nominally directed by legislatures and political parties' (Skocpol 1985: 12). The main tenet of 'statists' is the insulation of policy-making from external actors in society. What this study suggests is that in some cases, policy change is indeed only possible if it is elaborated by officials without much publicity[59] or if actors such as courts who are also relatively insulated from electoral politics are called upon.

Some scholars have emphasized the ability of policy-makers to use a strategy of stealth in order to avoid blame as opposed to strategies of high policy visibility when they expect to get credit for certain developments (Arnold 1990; Weaver 1986; Pierson 1994). These strategies have been in evidence in the area of alien rights, and many incremental changes in regulations that furthered the legal security of aliens in this respect were often masked by tough campaign talk on public order issues. The executive's ability to prevent an open debate on alien rights, however, is not unconditional. As I have suggested above, it depends, in the case of foreigners' rights, first, on the type of rights at stake. Political rights, because they are clearly reserved for citizens in fundamental laws, and constitutional revision is required to open them to aliens, are less likely to avoid large-scale debates. Secondly, cross-national variations in the level of co-ordination of policy-making and in the modes of political élite co-operation account for varying degrees of politicization.

The positive correlation between aliens' access to citizenship rights and a lack of mobilization and politicization is counter-intuitive in certain ways. Historically, the incorporation of groups such as women and the lower classes into the polity in the nineteenth and twentieth centuries has been the result of mass mobilization, struggles, and societal debates. Perhaps because the question of the incorporation of aliens occurred after the expansion of state bureaucracies, the development of liberal democratic norms, and the coming of age of courts, other channels were open for reform. It may seem paradoxical that alien rights are hindered by a lack of political debate in part because of the state of public opinion since a further acceptance of aliens in the public a priori requires public discussion and debate. The past experience of Italians and Poles in France or the Irish in the United States suggests that it takes several generations for migrants to be fully accepted by society and not make for lucrative political controversy. Consequently, it is not so surprising that, in the short term, improving the status of post-war migrant groups in Europe was achieved away from the public eye.

# NOTES

I would like to thank Peter A. Hall, Paul Pierson, and Andy Moravcsik for their suggestions and comments on the draft version of this chapter. I am also very much indebted for their insightful comments to the participants of the 1995 joint sessions of the European Consortium for Political Research and the participants of the 1996 European University Institute workshop 'Immigration, Citizenship and Ethnic Conflict', as well as to Christian Joppke and an anonymous reviewer. I would like to thank the Social Science and Humanities Research Council of Canada, the Program for the Study of Modern France, and the Program for the Study of Germany and Europe at Harvard University for providing funding for research and writing.

1. There are as many meanings of the concept of modern citizenship as there are political theorists—or, at least, theories (liberal, communitarian, 'republican' . . .), ideologies, and countries. See Van Steenbergen (1994b) on 'four conceptions of citizenship'. Liberal conceptions generally see the citizen as a bearer of rights and stress the instrumentality of citizenship, in particular as a means of protection against the power of the state. Other schools of thought stress political participation and participation in the community as the key component of citizenship. For this project, I have chosen to draw from T. H. Marshall's understanding of citizenship rights (1965), which goes beyond that dichotomy since it comprises both civil rights and political participation; he includes social rights as well. In spite of the reservations that one may express concerning his famous 1949 lecture, his framework is useful in disaggregating the different aspects which tie the state and the individual, and it also helps understand citizenship as an ongoing historical process which can expand and contract (see also Bendix 1977; Turner 1986).

2. Or, as Jürgen Habermas once wrote, 'nationalism . . . founded a collective identity that played a *functional* role in the implementation of citizenship' (1994: 23).

3. I use the words 'foreigner' and 'non-national' interchangeably here to mean: anyone who does not have the nationality of the state in which s/he resides, anyone who is not a full-fledged citizen. These terms correspond to a legal category. This is not the case for the more sociological notion of 'migrant' or 'immigrant' and the terms do not cover the same population. This needs to be clarified since many migrants have been naturalized (in France and the Netherlands), and some of the ex-colonial migrants were already nationals. Moreover, some foreigners never 'immigrated'. I am referring to non-naturalized children or grandchildren of migrants such as young Turks in Germany who were born on European soil.

4. The word 'right' is often laden with normative assumptions; here it refers to legal provisions granting access to the welfare state, education, and the political realm and, in the case of certain civil rights, protecting individuals against the arbitrariness of the state by giving them access to the legal system. In the simplest of terms, it can be understood as what is not forbidden to non-nationals, what foreigners are included in.

5. In fact, when studying rights rather than immigrant policy as a whole, we can better assess the contradictions between the official policy discourse on integration and attempts at restricting rights that contribute to the successful incorporation of migrants.

6. The three countries studied here belong to the same international and European institutions and have signed the same international conventions. Therefore, they are exposed to the same international factors.

7. As Stephen Castles and Godula Kosack have pointed out, the unions face a dilemma: they oppose immigration at first for bringing wages down yet, once migrants have settled, it is imperative that unions organize them and defend their rights to avoid a split of the working class—although by then foreign workers will be distrustful (1985: 127–8).

8. This argument gains credibility if one considers that the segments of the population mostly likely to feel directly threatened by immigrants are also

less likely to put pressure on the leftist agenda because they are less likely to participate politically. It is often argued that the unemployed do not vote or participate in politics and nor do the poor (see e.g. Eichengreen and Hatton 1988).

9. In cases when the opposition does not vote the reform, it is interesting to see whether they vow to undo it should they come to power. The French Socialists, for instance, who criticized the 1993 laws on immigration, stated during the 1995 presidential campaign that they would not seek to change them.

10. Intra-party division is also the case when it comes to the recognition of religious and cultural rights for foreigners (see the veil issue in France or the question of Muslim primary schools in the Netherlands).

11. Therefore, it is in countries like Great Britain, where most immigrants vote, or in the Netherlands, where foreign residents can vote after five years, that ethnic élites have emerged and been able to achieve some bargaining leverage.

12. A recent study (McClain *et al.* 1993) showed how difficult it was for minorities to get their issues on the agenda and influence policy because of the structure of the political system, lack of group cohesion, or the original framing of the issue.

13. See Guiraudon (1994) on the present use of the French Revolution in political discourse.

14. This type of argument stems from the sociology of organization literature and elaborates on the concept of institutionalized norm. For sociologists like John Meyer, norms and rules are not structures of incentives and constraints which determine the calculus of actors but rather function as templates for behaviour as in the case of routines, standards of appropriateness, cultural symbols, and cognitive schema (Thomas *et al.* 1987). Organizational theorists contend that the latter enable actors to find solutions to their problems by providing clues to what constitutes a legitimate form of action (Powell 1990). In their view, strategies of action emerge from a process whereby shared models of appropriate action are constructed socially and diffused through the organizational environment (Spreng and Meyer 1993; Scott and Meyer 1994).

15. Much as with other works coming from Meyer and Boli's 'Stanford School' which are large-N studies and do not lend themselves to process-tracing, the approach in her book is mainly structural in the sense that it assumes the impact of norms on state behaviour with little agency on the part of the state incorporating or resisting those norms. Jeff Checkel, who also studies the impact of international norms on citizenship debates, points out that this type of research 'still suffers from a lack of attention to actual diffusion mechanisms and domestic political processes' (1995). A specification of the links between international and national developments is what is needed to asses the validity of Yasemine Soysal's argument.

16. The page number refers to that of the manuscript proofs.

17. International agreements follow the mood of nation-states and this is why sometimes, like the cavalry, they arrive too late to have a specific impact (e.g. the International Labour Office Convention of 1975, which

only gave general guide-lines for equality of treatment while many states had already gone a long way in this direction).

18. Without enumerating all the international conventions calling for the recognition and respect of the universal character of fundamental rights, one should mention, under United Nations aegis, the International Covenant on Civil and Political Rights (1966) and the International Covenant on Economic, Social, and Cultural Rights (1966); on the initiative of the Council of Europe, the European Convention on Human Rights (1950); as well as a number of ILO conventions.

19. Conventions are actually often criticized for resembling laundry lists because their catalogue of rights often reiterates old ones but omits important aspects (see *International Migration Review*, 25/4, Special Issue).

20. One should except the European treaties, which recognize equality of treatment for EU citizens.

21. See the 1958 International Labour Office Convention 111.

22. Germany and the Netherlands have yet to ratify this Protocol.

23. One of the cases before the ECHR (*Lüdicke, Belkacem, and Koc*) regarded the right to a free interpreter during a legal procedure for a non-German speaker. After Germany was condemned, the German Parliament amended the relevant legislation.

24. This is what should be influencing political decisions, according to scholars such as Rogers Brubaker (1992) and Gérard Noiriel (1991), who stress the importance of national self-understanding in policy towards migrants.

25. Although this was not the case everywhere and all the times, which implies that, instead of trying to generalize as he sets out to do, these variations will be taken into account and explained.

26. He defines 'client politics' as 'a form of bilateral influence in which small and well-organized groups intensely interested in a policy develop close working relationships with those officials responsible for it' (Freeman 1995: 386).

27. The question whether this assessment of the social impact of immigration is accurate is still subject to debate, depending on which economist's reading of the consequences of foreign labour on industrial restructuring, wage costs, growth, welfare state contributions, housing, and infrastructures (etc.) one agrees with. It is in any case a complex equation. Perhaps the key is to concentrate on the *perception* of the costs and benefits by different social groups, whether they were justified or not.

28. The politicization of alien rights is no longer a simple cost–benefit problem, nor can we deduce the level of conflict and participation on these issues by their character issue (as Theodore Lowi did when he distinguished between distributive, redistributive, and regulatory measures (1964). It seems in this case that redistributive measures, such as aliens' access to social services, have not been so much the object of public controversy as regulatory ones, such as, let us say, their right to participate politically.

29. See Polsby (1984) for a discussion of this type of agenda-setting.

30. When a law covers both citizens and foreigners or is vague about its recipients, there is no reason to believe that there will be a 'backlash' in public opinion. This applies to foreigner-specific measures.

31. See Melich (1995) for a presentation of the 1988–92 data and *Eurobaro-meter*, 42 (1994), 223, for an update up until winter 1994. See Mayer (1994) for an analysis of cross-national variations in attitudes revealed in the 1989 poll.

32. In contrast, organizations such as unions or professional associations can have their voices heard by the central executive even in a closed debate and human rights associations and pro-migrant groups can voice their arguments in courts through a litigation strategy in ways that is easier to achieve than mass mobilization.

33. Major elections here mean national elections in which the governing coalition's survival is at stake.

34. The SPD was aware of this pressure: its General Secretary, Peter Glotz, stated in 1982 that his party was in danger of losing votes to 'populist' groups and called for measures to stop the growth of the alien population (*Frankfurter Rundschau*, 24 May 1982).

35. Interior Ministry circular issued on 29 May 1981.

36. Interior Ministry circular dated 11 Aug. 1981.

37. Poll published in *Paris Match*, no. 1863 (1981).

38. The Secretary of State in charge of immigrants, François Autain, in a letter to the Prime Minister, boasted that, for his part, he had never made declarations to the press: 'Je n'ai jamais quant à moi, parlé de cette question dans aucune déclaration que j'ai pu faire aux journalistes' (Classeur Patrick Weil, Fond d'Archives d'Histoire Contemporaine, FNSP, Paris). It was he who ended what he viewed as a deleterious press campaign by denying that voting rights were on the government's agenda.

39. For instance, in her study, she points to referendums in Switzerland which provide an opportunity to override legislation.

40. The constitutional courts of all three countries have deemed that changing the definition of the electoral and eligible body requires constitutional revision. The French Constitutional Council had the opportunity to state its views on this matter when it ruled on 9 Apr. 1992 that the clause of the Maastricht Treaty which granted EU citizens voting rights in local and European elections was incompatible with Article 3 of the Constitution. In France, local voting rights for foreigners would require that a modification of Article 3 of the Constitution be approved by three-fifths of members of the Senate and National Assembly assembled together, as well as the passing of a *loi organique* to change the electoral code. In Germany on 30 Oct. 1990 the Constitutional Court in Karlsruhe voided two state laws which respectively granted voting rights in the election of neighbourhood assemblies in Hamburg and in municipal elections in Schleswig-Holstein. The Court considered that both laws were unconstitutional. In the Netherlands, there was a constitutional revision approved by two-thirds of parliamentarians in 1985.

41. Especially in the 1980s the FDP and CDU–CSU, who were government partners, voiced their disagreements over *Ausländerpolitik* in Parliament, in the press and in the electoral sphere.

42. The lack of unified policy of this issue is no omission but a way of not acknowledging the permanency of immigration as well as of not having

to build a consensus around an issue which divides the governing coalition. The Director of the Frankfurt Multicultural Affairs Bureau quipped: 'organized as we Germans are supposed to be . . . if we don't have a coherent policy, it's because we don't want to!' (interview, Rosi Wolf-Allmanasreh, City of Frankfurt Bureau for Multicultural Affairs, Frankfurt am Main, 1995).

43. They are funded by the state, yet not bound by government discipline, i.e. not bound to agree with the federal government's stance on foreigner-related issues.

44. In this respect, Peter Katzenstein found that foreigners' policy was almost an exception to his vision of Germany as a centralized society–decentralized state (1987). In other ways however, we find features that fit his vision of Germany such as large parapublic institutions providing services for migrants (the 'centralized society' part of his model).

45 There have been instances when ministerial conflicts on immigration issues have not been fully contained and have erupted in Parliament, yet, as the following example shows, they do not undermine the fact that, in France, executive rule dominates in such a way as to be able to mask internal bureaucratic conflict. In 1981 divergence arose between the Ministry of the Interior, headed by Gaston Deferre, and the State Secretariat in Charge of Immigrants, headed by François Autain. The latter wanted to improve the legal protection of foreigners against expulsions, which had been a discretionary power of the Interior Ministry. Gaston Deferre was not willing to relinquish his prerogative. This was a very 'Schattschneiderian' situation. The Minister of the Interior, because of both his position and his personality, had much more clout, and an interministerial arbitrage let him have his way, so Autain needed to expand the number of participants in the debate. He sought allies in another institution, Parliament, and found sympathetic Socialist MPs who were willing to present amendments reflecting his plans to a bill submitted by the Interior Minister. The spill-over of the debate in the legislative arena was nevertheless nipped in the bud. Deferre, having heard about the tactics to be used, took advantage of the fact that he controlled the legislative order of the day and took the bill off the agenda until the parliamentarians agreed to withdraw their amendment (Weil 1991: 145–6). In other words, rules ensuring the ascendancy of the executive prevented Parliament from acting as a 'veto point'.

46. Clearly, a judicial decision cannot be equated with the passage of a law. Rather, it functions as panacea, a way of delaying a process of reform (in the case of constitutional courts) or a means of altering practices (in the case of administrative tribunals), an argument in the hands of pro-migrant reformers. Still, it does affect policy outcomes. It also leads to 'self-censorship' on the part of the bureaucrats or politicians writing bills and circulars who do not wish to be condemned by the courts by submitting a legally loose text.

47. See the section on rule-bound expansion of debate, above.

48. Jim Hollifield emphasized that 'most battles by special interests in France about the use of foreign labor have taken place not in the National Assembly but behind close doors in the ministries' (1992a: 188).

49. Interview with the Secretary-General of the Council of State, Bernard Stirn, French Council of State, Paris, Jan. 1995.

310 *Virginie Guiraudon*

50. The benefit was 'l'allocation municipale de congé parental d'éducation pour le troisième enfant' (see *Plein droit*, Feb. 1989, Nov. 1990).
51. The current German government recognizes these facts. In a recent report, the 1991 Aliens Act is described in such a way as to constitute a confession of past arbitrariness: 'The wide scope of discretion of aliens authorities has given way to clearly formulated legal conditions' (Federal Ministry of the Interior 1993: 8).
52. Important Federal Constitutional Court decisions: 26 Sept. 1978 and 7 Jan. 1979 (*Entscheidungen des Bundesverfassungsgerichts*, 49: 168, 185; 51: 166, 175).
53. See, in particular, a 1979 deportation case: Decision of 18 July 1979 in *Entscheidungen des Bundesverfassungsgerichts*, 51: 386.
54. Decision of 20 Mar. 1979, in *Entscheidungen des Bundesverfassungsgerichts*, 51: 1.
55. Interview, Kees Groenendijk, Faculty of Law, University of Nijmegen, June 1995.
56. The fact that there is evidence supporting a distinct proposition which is consistent (and follows from) the main thesis should strengthen the core argument. For details on this technique which consists in generating further observable implications in a study, see King *et al.* (1994) on scientific inference in qualitative research.
57. I am indebted for this term to Gallya Lahav and David Kyle, who are currently conducting research on this issue.
58. The demands of states like California in the United States also show that demands for more local power concur with plans for restrictions of foreigners' rights (in this case preventing undocumented aliens from attending schools and receiving welfare benefits).
59. An example of another area where a closed debate would heighten the chances of reform is welfare state retrenchment in Europe.

# REFERENCES

Ansay, Tugrul (1992), 'The New UN Convention in Light of the German and Turkish Experience', *International Migration Review*, 25/4: 831–45.
Arnold, Douglas (1990), *The Logic of Congressional Action* (New Haven: Yale University Press).
Battegay, Alain, and Ahmed Boubeker (1993), *Les Images publiques de l'immigration* (Paris: L'Harmattan/CIEMI).
Bauböck, Rainer (1994a), *Transnational Citizenship: Membership and Rights in International Migration* (Aldershot: Edward Elgar).
—— (ed.) (1994b), *From Aliens to Citizens: Redefining the Legal Status of Immigrants* (Aldershot: Avebury).
—— (1995), *Transnational Citizenship: Membership and Rights in International Migration* (Aldershot: Edward Elgar).

Baumgartner, Frank (1989), *Conflict and Rhetoric in French Policy-Making* (Pittsburgh: University of Pittsburgh Press).

—— and Bryan Jones (1993), *Agendas and Instability in American Politics* (Chicago: Chicago University Press).

Beaud, Olivier (1993), 'Asile et politique générale de l'État', *Les petites affiches*, no. 123.

Bendix, Reinhard (1977), *Nation-Building and Citizenship*, 2nd edn. (Berkeley: University of California Press).

Berger, Vincent (1994), *Jurisprudence de la Cour européenne des Droits de l'Homme*, 4th edn. (Paris: Sirey).

Blanke, Bernhard (ed.) (1993), *Zuwanderung und Asyl in der Konkurrenzgesellschaft* (Opladen: Leske & Budrich).

Body-Gendrot, Sophie (1993), *Ville et violence* (Paris: Presses universitaires françaises).

Bonnafous, Simone (1991), *L'Immigration prise aux mots: Les immigrés dans la presse au tournant des années 1980* (Paris: Kimé).

Brubaker, Rogers (ed.) (1989), *Immigration and Politics of Citizenship in Europe and North America* (Washington: German Marshall Fund and University Press of America).

—— (1992), *Citizenship and Nationhood in France and Germany* (Cambridge: Harvard University Press).

—— (1995), 'Comments on Modes of Immigration Politics in Liberal Democratic States', *International Migration Review*, 29/4.

Campbell, John (1995), 'Institutional Analysis and the Role of Ideas in Political Economy', paper presented at the State and Capitalism since 1800 Seminar, Center for European Studies, Harvard University, 13 Oct.

Castles, Stephen (1984), *Here for Good: Western Europe's New Ethnic Minorities* (London: Pluto Press).

—— and Godula Kosack (1985), *Immigrant Workers and Class Structure in Western Europe*, 2nd edn. (New York: Oxford University Press).

Checkel, Jeff (1995), 'International Norms and Domestic Institutions: Identity Politics in Post-Cold-War Europe', paper presented at the American Political Science Association annual meeting, 30 Aug.–3 Sept., Chicago.

Cobb, Roger, and Charles Elder (1983), *Participation in American Politics: The Dynamics of Agenda-Building* (Baltimore: Johns Hopkins University Press).

Costa, Jean-Paul (1993), *Le Conseil d'État dans la société contemporaine* (Paris: Economica).

Costa-Lascoux, Jacqueline, and Patrick Weil (eds.) (1992), *Logiques d'états et immigrations* (Paris: Kimé).

Czada, Roland, and Manfred Schmidt (eds.) (1993), *Verhandlungsdemokratie, Interessenvermittlung, Regierbarkeit* (Opladen: Westdeutcher Verlag).

Dohse, Knuth (1981), *Ausländische Arbeiter und bürgerlicher Staat* (Königstein: Verlag Anton Main).

Eichengreen, Barry, and T. J. Hatton (1988), *Interwar Unemployment in International Perspective* (Dordrecht: Kluwer).

Eurobarometer (1989), *L'Opinion publique dans la Communauté européenne: Racisme et xénophobie* (Brussels: Commission of the European Communities).

Faist, Thomas (1994a), 'How to Define a Foreigner? The Symbolic Politics of Immigration in German Partisan Discourse 1978–1992', *West European Politics*, 17/2: 50–72.

—— (1994b), *A Medieval City: Transnationalizing Labor Markets and Social Rights in Europe*, ZeS Working Paper no. 9 (Bremen: Universität Bremen Zentrum für Sozialpolitik).

Federal Ministry of the Interior (1993), *Survey of the Policy and Law concerning Foreigners in the Federal Republic in Germany* (Bonn: Federal Ministry of Interior).

Finnemore, Martha (1993), 'Norms, Culture and World Politics: Insights from Sociology's Institutionalism', in *International Organization*.

Franz, Fritz (1975), 'The Legal Status of Foreign Workers in the Federal Republic of Germany', in R. D. Krane (ed.), *Manpower Mobility across Cultural Boundaries* (Leiden: Brill).

Freeman, Gary (1986), 'Migration and the Political Economy of the Welfare State', *Annals of the American Academy of Political and Social Sciences*, 485: 51–63.

—— (1995), 'Modes of Immigration Politics in Liberal Democratic States', *International Migration Review*, 29/4: 881–903.

Goldstein, Judith, and Robert Keohane (eds.) (1993), *Ideas and Foreign Policy* (New York: Cornell University Press).

Groenendijk, Kees (1980), 'The Working Group on Legal Aid for Immigrants: A Public Interest Law Organization in the Netherlands', in E. Blankenburg (ed.), *Innovations in the Legal Services* (Cambridge, Mass.: Anton Main).

Guiraudon, Virginie (1994), 'Atavisms and New Challenges: (Re)Naming the Enemy in Contemporary French Political Discourse', *History of European Ideas*, 19/1–3: 71–8.

—— (1996), 'Reaffirming the French Model of Integration', *French Politics and Society*, 14/2: 71–8.

Habermas, Jürgen (1994), 'Citizenship and National Identity', in Van Steenbergen (1994a).

Hailbronner, Kay (1989), *Ausländerrecht*, 2nd edn. (Heidelberg: C. F. Müller Juristischer Verlag).

Hall, Peter (ed.) (1989), *The Political Power of Economic Ideas: Keynesianism across Nations* (Cambridge: Cambridge University Press).

Hammar, Tomas (ed.) (1985), *European Immigration Policy* (Cambridge: Cambridge University Press).

—— (1990), *Democracy and the Nation-State: Aliens, Denizens and Citizens in a World of International Migration* (Aldershot: Avebury).

Heclo, Hugh (1974), *Modern Social Politics in Britain and Sweden* (New Haven: Yale University Press).

Herbert, Ulrich (1990), *A History of Foreign Labor in Germany* (Ann Arbor: University of Michigan Press).

Hirschman, Albert (1970), *Exit, Voice and Loyalty* (Cambridge: Harvard University Press).

Hollifield, James (1992*a*), *Immigrants, Markets, and States: The Political Economy of Postwar Europe* (Cambridge: Harvard University Press).

—— (1992*b*), 'Migration and International Relations: Cooperation and Control in the European Community', *International Migration Review*, 26/2: 568–95.

Horowitz, Donald (1977), *The Courts and Social Policy* (Washington: Brookings Institution).

Husbands, Christopher (1994), 'Crises of National Identity as the "New Moral Panics": Political Agenda-Setting about Definitions of Nationhood', *New Community*, 20/2: 191–206.

Immergut, Ellen (1992), 'The Rules of the Game: The Logic of Health Policy-Making in France, Switzerland, and Sweden', in Sven Steinmo, Kathleen Thelen and Frank Longstreth (eds.), *Structuring Politics: Historical Institutionalism in Comparative Perspective* (New York: Cambridge University Press).

Ireland, Patrick (1994), *The Policy Challenge of Ethnic Diversity: Immigrant Politics in France and Switzerland* (Cambridge, Mass.: Harvard University Press).

—— (1995), 'Migration, Free Movement and Immigrant Integration in the EU: A Bifurcated Policy Response', in Stephan Liebfried and Paul Pierson (eds.), *European Social Policy* (Washington: Brookings Institution).

—— (1996), '*Vive le jacobinisme: Les étrangers* and the Durability of the Assimilationist Model in France', *French Politics and Society*, 14/2: 33–46.

Jones, Bryan (1994), *Reconceiving Decision-Making in Democratic Politics: Attention, Choice and Public Policy* (Chicago: Chicago University Press).

Kastoryano, Riva (1994), 'Mobilisations des migrants en Europe: Du national au transnational', *Revue européenne des migrations internationales*, 10/1: 169–81.

Katzenstein, Peter (1987), *Policy and Politics in West Germany* (Philadelphia: Temple University Press).

—— (ed.) (1996), *Norms and National Security* (New York: Columbia University Press).

Kepel, Gilles (1987), *Les banlieues de l'Islam* (Paris: Éditions du Seuil).

King, Gary, Robert Keohane, and Sydney Verba (1994), *Designing Social Inquiry: Scientific Inference in Qualitative Research* (Princeton: Princeton University Press).

Kingdon, John (1984), *Agendas, Alternatives and Public Policies* (Boston: Little Brown).

Krüger, Hans, and Wolfgang Strasser (1994), 'Combating Racial Discrimination: The European Convention on the Protection of Human Rights and Fundamental Freedoms', in Julie Cator and Jan Niessen (eds.), *The Use of International Conventions to Protect the Right of Migrants and Ethnic Communities* (Strasbourg: Churches' Commission for Migrants in Europe).

Layton-Henry, Zig (1990), *The Political Rights of Migrant Workers in Western Europe* (London: Sage).

Lijphart, Arend (1975), *The Politics of Accommodation: Pluralism and Democracy in the Netherlands*, 2nd end. rev. (Berkeley: University of California Press).

Lipset, Seymour Martin, and Rokkan Stein (eds.) (1967), *Party Systems and Voter Alignments* (New York: Free Press).

Lochak, Danièle (1985), *Étrangers: De quel droit?* (Paris: Presses universitaires françaises).

Lowi, Theodore (1964), 'American Business, Public Policy, Case Studies and Political Theory', *World Politics*, 16: 677–93.

McClain, Paula (ed.) (1993), *Minority Group Influence: Agenda-Setting, Formulation and Public Policy* (Westport, Conn.: Greenwood Press).

Marsh, David, and R. A. W. Rhodes (eds.) (1992), *Policy Networks in British Government* (Oxford: Clarendon Press).

Marshall, T. H. (1965), *Class, Citizenship and Social Development* (New York: Doubleday).

Mayer, Nonna (1994), 'Racisme et xénophobie dans l'Europe des Douze', in *1993: La lutte contre le racisme et la xénophobie* (Paris: La Documentation française).

Meier-Braun, Karl-Heinz (1987), 'Einwanderungsland Europa: Die Ausländerpolitik der EG-Mitgliedstaaten am Beispiel der Bundesrepublik Deutschland', in Manfred Zuleeg (ed.), *Ausländerrecht und Ausländerpolitik in Europa* (Baden-Baden: Nomos Verlag).

Melich, Anna (1995), *Comparative European Trend Survey Data on Racism and Xenophobia* (Brussels: Directorate General X).

Messina, Anthony (1989), *Race and Party Competition in Britain* (Oxford: Clarendon Press).

Meyer, John (1980), 'The World Polity and the Authority of the Nation-State', in A. Beressen (ed.), *Studies of the Modern World System* (New York: Academic Press).

Moravcsik, Andrew (1994), 'Lessons from the European Human Rights Regime in Inter-American Dialogue', in *Advancing Democracy and Human Rights in the Americas: What Role for the OAS?* (Washington: Inter-American Dialogue).

Murray, Laura (1994), '*Einwanderundgsland Bundesrepublik Deutschland?* Explaining the Evolving Positions of German Political Parties on Citizenship Policy', *German Politics and Society*, 33.

Netherlands Scientific Council for Government Policy (1990), *Immigrant Policy*, 36th Report (The Hague: Netherlands Scientific Council for Government Policy).

Neuman, Gerald (1990), 'Immigration and Judicial Review in the Federal Republic of Germany', *New York University Journal of International Law and Politics*, 23/1: 35–85.

Noiriel, Gérard (1991), *La Tyrannie du national: Le droit d'asile en Europe 1793–1993* (Paris: Calmann-Lévy).

Nordhaus, William (1975), 'The Political Business Cycle', *Review of Economic Studies*, 42: 169–90.

Penninx, Rinus, Jeannette Schoorl, and Carlo van Praag (1994), *The Impact of International Migration on Receiving Countries: The Case of the Netherlands* (Amsterdam: Swets & Zeitlinger).

Pierson, Paul (1993), 'When Effect Becomes Cause: Policy Feedback and Political Change', *World Politics*, 45 (July), 595–628.

—— (1994), *Dismantling the Welfare State: Reagan, Thatcher, and the Politics of Retrenchment* (New York: Cambridge University Press).

Piore, Michael (1979), *Birds of Passage: Migrant Labor and Industrial Societies* (Cambridge: Cambridge University Press).

Polsby, Nelson (1984), *Policy Innovation in America: The Politics of Policy Initiation* (New Haven: Yale University Press).

Powell, Walter (1990), 'The Transformation of Organizational Forms: How Useful is Organization Theory in Accounting for Social Change?', in Roger Friedland and A. F. Robertson, *Beyond the Marketplace* (New York: Aldine de Gruyter).

Quillian, Lincoln (1995), 'Prejudice as a Response to Perceived Group Threat: Population Composition and Anti-Immigrant and Racial Prejudice in Europe', *American Sociological Review*, 60: 586–611.

Rath, Jan (1983), 'The Enfranchisement of Immigrants in Practice: Turkish and Moroccan Islands in the Fairway of Dutch Politics', *Netherlands Journal of Sociology*, 19/2: 151–80.

—— (1988), 'Political Action of Immigrants in the Netherlands: Class or Ethnicity?', *European Journal of Political Research*, 16: 623–44.

—— (1991), *Minorisering: De Sociale Constructie van 'Ethnische Minderheden'* (Amsterdam: Sua).

—— (1993), 'Les Immigrés aux Pays-Bas', in Wihtol de Wenden *et al.* (1993).

—— Kees Groenendijk, and Rinus Penninx (1991), 'The Recognition and Institutionalization of Islam in Belgium, Great Britain and the Netherlands', *New Community*, 18/1: 101–14.

Riker, William (1986), *The Art of Political Manipulation* (New Haven: Yale University Press).

Ruggie, John (1982), 'International Regimes, Transactions and Change: Embedded Liberalism in the Postwar Economic Order', *International Organization*, 36: 379–415.

Ruhrmann, Georg, and Jochem Kollmer (1987), *Ausländerberichterstattung in der Kommune: Inhaltanalyse Bielefelder tageszeitungen unter Berücksichtigung 'ausländerfeindlicher' Alltagstheorien* (Opladen: Westdeutscher Verlag).

Saggar, Shamit (1992), *Race and Politics in Britain* (London: Harvester-Wheatsheaf).

Sassen, Saskia (1996), *Losing Control? Sovereignty in an Age of Globalization* (New York: Columbia University Press).

Schain, Martin (1994), 'Ordinary Politics: Immigrants, Direct Action and the Political Process in France', *French Politics and Society*, 12/2–3: 65–83.

Schattschneider, Eric (1960), *The Semisovereign People: A Realist's View of Democracy in America* (New York: Holt, Rhinehart, Winston).

Shepsle, Kenneth (1986), 'Institutional Equilibrium and Equilibrium Institutions', in Herbert Weisberg (ed.), *Political Science: The Science of Politics* (New York: Agathon).

Schermers, Henry (ed.) (1993), *Free Movement of Persons in Europe: Legal Problems and Experiences* (Dordrecht: Martinus Nijhoff).

Schmidt, Manfred (1992), *Regieren in der Bundesrepublik Deutschland* (Opladen: Leske & Budrich).

Schuck, Peter (1984), 'The Transformation of Immigration Law', *Columbia Law Review*, 84 (Jan.), 1–90.

—— (1993), 'Public Law Litigation and Social Reform', *Yale Law Journal*, 102: 1763–86.

Schwerdtfeger, G. (1980), 'Welche rechtlichen Vorkehrungen empfehlen sich, um die Rechtsstellung von Ausländern in der Bundesrepublik Deutschland angemessen zu gestalten?', in *Verhandlungen des dreiundfünfzigsten deutschen Juristentages Berlin 1980*, (Munich: Beck'sche Verlagsbuchhandlung).

Scott, James (1985), *Weapons of the Weak* (New Haven: Yale University Press).

Scott, Richard, and John Meyer (1994), *Institutional Environments and Organizations* (Newbury Park, Calif.: Sage).

Skocpol, Theda (1985), 'Bringing the State back In: Strategies of Analysis in Current Research', in Peter Evans, Dietrich Rueschemeyer, and Theda Skocpol (eds.), *Bringing the State back In* (New York: Cambridge University Press).

Soysal, Yasemin (1994), *Limits of Citizenship* (Chicago: Chicago University Press).

Spreng, David, and John Meyer (1993), 'Institutional Conditions for Diffusion', *Theory and Society*, 22: 487–511.

Steinberger, Helmut (1985), 'Reference to the Case-Law of the Organs of the European Convention of Human Rights before National Courts: Communication on the Courts of the Federal Republic of Germany', *Proceedings of the Sixth International Colloquy about the European Convention on Human Rights* (Boston: Martinus Nijhoff).

Steinmann, Gunter, and Ralf Ulrich (1994), *The Economic Consequences of Immigration to Germany* (Heidelberg: Springer Verlag).

Stone, Alec (1992), *The Birth of Judicial Politics in France: The Constitutional Council in Comparative Perspective* (New York: Oxford University Press).

Stone, Deborah (1989), 'Causal Stories and the Formation of Policy Agendas', *Political Science Quarterly*, 104: 281–300.

Swindler, Ann (1986), 'Culture in Action: Symbols and Strategies', *American Sociological Review*, 51: 273–86.

Taguieff, Pierre-André (1987), *La Force du préjugé: Essai sur le racisme et ses doubles* (Paris: La Découverte).

Thomas, George *et al.* (1987), *Institutional Structure: Constituting State, Society, and the Individual* (Newbury Park, Calif.: Sage).

Thränhardt, Dietrich (1994), 'The Political Uses of Xenophobia in England, France and Germany', MS.

Turner, Bryan (1986), *Citizenship and Capitalism* (London: Allen & Unwin).

Turpin, Dominique (ed.) (1989), *Immigrés et réfugiés dans les démocraties occidentales: Défis et solutions* (Marseille: Presses universitaires d'Aix-Marseille).

Van Dijk, Teun (1988), 'The Tamil Panic in the Press', in *News Analysis* (Hillsdale, NJ: Erlbaum).

—— (1993), *Élite Discourse and Racism* (Newbury Park, Calif.: Sage).

Van Steenbergen, Bart (1994a), 'Four Conceptions of Citizenship', in Van Steenbergen (1994b).

—— (ed.) (1994), *The Condition of Citizenship* (London: Sage).

Verba, Sydney, Jae-On Kim, and Norman Nie (1978), *Participation and Political Equality* (Cambridge: Cambridge University Press).

Vogel, Ursula, and Michael Moran (eds.) (1991), *The Frontiers of Citizenship* (New York: St Martin's Press).

Wapner, Paul (1995), 'Politics beyond the State: Environmental Activism and World Civic Politics', *World Politics*, 47: 311–41.

Weaver, Kent (1986), 'The Politics of Blame Avoidance', *Journal of Public Policy*, 6/4: 371–98.

Weides, Peter (1989), 'Les Réponses de la législation et de la jurisprudence aux questions urgentes du droit des immigrés et des réfugiés en république fédérale d'Allemagne', in Turpin (1989).

Weil, Patrick (1991), *La France et ses étrangers: L'aventure d'une politique de l'immigration 1938–1991* (Paris: Calmann-Lévy).

Weimann, Gabriel, and Hans-Bernd Brosius (1994), 'Is there a Two-Step Model of Agenda-Setting?', *International Journal of Public Opinion Research*, 6/4: 323–41.

Wihtol de Wenden, Catherine (1988), *Les Immigrés et la politique* (Paris: FNSP).

—— (1993), 'Migrations et droits de l'homme en Europe', in *Études internationales*, 24/1: 163–76.

—— *et al.* (1993), *Les Étrangers dans la cité* (Paris: La Découverte).

Wilson, James (ed.) (1980), *The Politics of Regulation* (New York: Harper).

Zincone, Giovanna (1992), *Da sudditi a cittadini* (Bologna: Il Mulino).

# 9

# Multicultural Race Relations in Britain: Problems of Interpretation and Explanation

ADRIAN FAVELL

## INTRODUCTION

It is widely accepted both in Britain and on the Continent that Britain is, politically speaking, a special case in Europe. Such political exceptionalism has become a familiar and self-serving British strategy in Europe in recent years, and the field of immigration and integration policies is no exception. Yet Britain clearly is a difficult case for the emerging academic field that this volume reflects: a systematic *comparative* politics of immigration and citizenship that is able to connect disparate national cases in western Europe and North America in terms of macro-processes of social change and the transformation of the nation-state, and locate each in relation to common dynamics of political debate and policy evolution. Britain's peculiar institutional formula of race relations and multiculturalism fits badly with other cases across the Western world, in particular emerging institutions at the European level. Its post-colonial history, and the problems faced by its distinct and now established ethnic minorities, are not the same as those of newer migrants and refugees across Europe. And the relative lack of salience of race or xenophobia in mainstream politics in Britain belies the rising tide of ethnic dilemmas in liberal democratic societies elsewhere. How then do we go about fitting Britain into a wider comparative scheme and make sense of its peculiarities and apparent divergence from other cases?

The lack of any genuinely comparative dimension is perhaps the most important deficiency in the copious home-grown British literature on immigration and ethnic minorities. Indigenous conservative, liberal, and radical commentaries resemble each other at least in the lack of any serious effort to translate the peculiar language and logic of the British institutional solution of multicultural race relations into terms that might read Britain as but one in a group of other west

European case-studies.[1] This in part may be because the often-told
story of the emergence of British race relations legislation appeared to
take place so much in advance to the rest of Europe. In response to
the dangerous heating up of racial issues as long ago as the 1960s, the
mainstream British political parties appeared to have fashioned by
the mid-1970s a durable compromise of tight immigration control and
self-styled 'progressive' legislation that pre-empted the emergence of
the kinds of racial and ethnic conflict seen across Europe in recent
years. Within this framework an apparently benign but peculiarly eso-
teric form of British multiculturalism has evolved in the last twenty-
five years that is often taken to be wholly particular: a translation of
British colonial practices, which took the specificities of Commonwealth
immigration and its island status and tailored them to British legal and
parliamentary structures. These particularities have restricted British
commentators to relate Britain to Europe only in terms which underline its distinctiveness or originality. Some set it up as a more advanced
'model' that might offer instruction to policy-makers on the continent
(Forbes and Mead 1992). Others use their critique of British institutions as the starting-point for an exposure of the racism and exclusion
similarly inherent in other European countries (Miles 1993; Solomos
and Wrench 1993). All of these works wrongly assume that the eso-
teric language of the British sociology of race and ethnicity—a lexicon
profoundly structured by the institutions that it grew up around—can
be meaningfully transposed to other European cases without any loss
in understanding.

New opportunities for locating the British case in relation to European ones have, however, been opened by the North-American-led
growth in study of immigration and citizenship in Europe. Following
in the wake of Rogers Brubaker's work, especially *Citizenship and
Nationhood in France and Germany* (1992), there has been an explosion in explicitly comparative attempts to fit other cases into a similar
general theoretical frame that draws on mainstream theoretical debates
in the social sciences (Brubaker 1992, 1989; Soysal 1993, 1994; Freeman
1992, 1995; Hollifield 1992; Messina *et al.* 1992; Cornelius *et al.* 1994;
Baldwin-Edwards and Schain 1994; Ireland 1991, 1994; Geddes 1995).
Brubaker's work suggests there might be mileage in looking to see if
a similar account of deeply held historical ideas about citizenship and
nationhood in Britain might explain the tendencies and development of
recent internal British politics and policies on immigration and ethnic
minority integration. However, the immediate problem of this kind of

approach—signalled by other rival comparatists in the field—is that it seems to only re-emphasize nationally bounded and nation-state-sustaining views of the politics of immigration and citizenship over other accounts that emphasize the convergence of European practices and the breaking down of nation-state control over policy-making on the subject. This is an issue that needs to be sorted out by distinguishing between the influence of apparently fixed national political cultural 'legacies' on the politics of the present, and the more mundane dynamics of contemporary party-political interaction and policy development within an evolving political context. In theoretical terms, this is a debate between a historical institutionalist approach and a version of new institutionalism that attempts to downplay the determining force of national tradition, and show rather how such ideas are continually reworked and transformed by political actors for self-interested reasons at contingent points in time. I shall argue that the latter type of explanation offers a better view of the dynamics of national politics in this field, a theoretical frame which opens the way to a fully comparative perspective of Britain in relation to other European cases.

The superficial peculiarity of the British case still presents an initial barrier to this kind of comparative framework. To get to questions of comparative *explanation*—and illustrate the relevance of new institutionalism to this field of study—it is thus necessary first to do a good deal of preliminary *interpretative* work to make sense of some of the distinctive peculiarities of the British case. My strategy in this chapter therefore is to foreground the dual methodological need for interpretation and explanation in comparative work, by raising problems at the interpretative level in the first half that I shall fully answer at the explanatory level in the second. In the first half, I take two distinctive and puzzling features of the contemporary British case—issues concerning the place of Muslims in Britain, and British behaviour towards policy developments at the European level—and indicate the pitfalls connected with getting the interpretation of these phenomena right. Only then do I move to the explanatory level in which Britain is fitted into a wider theoretical scheme of immigration and citizenship politics in Europe. In the latter half of the chapter, I thus first discuss the theoretical issues thrown up by applying the theoretical terms of Brubaker and his critics to the British case. I then go on to use this perspective in order to retell the familiar British story of the invention and evolution of multicultural race relations in more general and comparative terms.

## INTERPRETING A PECULIAR CASE 1: MUSLIMS AND MULTICULTURALISM IN BRITAIN

One of the hottest issues thrown up by multiculturalism in Britain has been the growing significance of political and social issues involving Muslims. Since the mid-1980s, issues involving Muslims in Western liberal democracies have come to prominence right across Europe. This 'discovery' of Islam among otherwise integrated ethnic groups—often now full citizens of their host countries—and their apparently militant Islamic tendencies in some cases, has raised a great deal of general political and academic debate (Gerholm and Lithman 1988; Rex and Drury 1994). Britain has provided much of the more spectacular case material: the Rushdie affair, in which a death threat was pronounced on the author of a blasphemous novel; the controversial creation of a parallel 'Muslim parliament' by a radical group financed by Iran; the recent Muslim rioting in Bradford, a northern city with a large Asian population; and troubles with radical fundamentalist groups in universities. Such examples are often cited to show that there is something culturally specific about Islam that makes it inherently a problem for Western society, and which would explain Muslims' behaviour. They are also read more generally as generic dilemmas of 'cultural pluralism' that can be found everywhere in Western liberal democracy. These problems are often framed as 'philosophical' dilemmas: in terms of the limits of tolerance or as the threat to the political unity—the universal rights and duties—of citizenship, that certain distinctive elements of Muslim 'culture' are typically seen to threaten (see Gellner 1992; Lukes 1993).

Many of the attempts by outside observers to cast these questions into fully fledged academic comparative studies have been crude and have failed to pay attention to the peculiarities of the distinct institutional framework within which British Muslims operate *politically*, and which thereby explains their behaviour in perfectly comprehensible, self-interested terms. A number of the more strongly critical studies have come from French writers anxious to use the British case as a negative looking-glass for the virtues of republican citizenship in France, and a tough anti-Islamic line in French politics. This is a kind of typological approach in which Britain represents the archetypal 'multicultural' society. Integration is pictured to take place through a kind of 'communautarisme' in which distinct, racially classified ethnic groups are allowed political concessions to their communal forms. Over time, this has been said to lead to a growing wave of ethnic politics and cultural intolerance, urban ghettos and politically marginalized minorities, a generally racially divided apartheid in society, and an expedient, unprincipled flexibility about the rights and duties of citizens in politics (Schnapper 1992; Todd 1994; Kepel 1994). Britain and America in fact are usually meaninglessly lumped together as the 'modèle anglo-saxon' (a classic francophone intellectual stereotype). Weaker versions of this critique tend rather to see Britain as one in a series of 'multicultural' countries which generally display certain pathological 'paradoxes of multiculturalism' (others being Sweden, the Netherlands, Canada, and Australia, for example) (Lapeyronnie 1993; Joppke 1996; Alund and Schierup 1991). Such studies often derive their root insights from recent neo-conservative and neo-liberal worries about multiculturalism in the United States—rough-house urban ethnic politics, shrill campus debates about political correctness, the threat of 'balkanization' and the disintegration of American citizenship (e.g. Schlesinger 1992). Suitably focused on a select part of the evidence available, the British case then indeed yields many examples of ethnic politics and conflict rampant at local levels (e.g. the 'loony left' politics of the 1980s), and the apparent disregard shown in separatist claims raised by Muslim communities (in Bradford and elsewhere) of the liberal principles of the British education and legal systems.[2]

Without doubt, such studies do put their finger on some of the more problematic consequences of British multicultural race relations, but they are far from providing a complete or sensitive comparative picture. The alarmist concern with the threat of Islam, and the search for fundamental millenarian 'cultural' conflicts, masks the fact that the behaviour of a minority of militant British Muslims is predominantly an exception to the way multiculturalism has generally functioned in Britain. Concentrating on this group thereby gives a false picture of the essence of the British institutional framework. What we find rather is that the particular issues associated with Muslims in Britain have to be set in the context of twenty-five years of generally successful functioning of these institutions, a framework designed to deal with dilemmas associated with race relations and multiculturalism and lay a path towards integration. In this context, it has to be noted that during the last decade ethnic minority issues have remained localized away from mainstream politics in Britain and are currently, in relative terms, remarkably unimportant compared with almost anywhere else in Europe (measured in social attitudes or the emergence of powerful right-wing or nationalist movements) (see Baumgartl and Favell 1995).

This leads to the conclusion that the narrow emergence of Muslims as a focal issue in Britain has more to do with the structuring institutional conditions specific to British political and social circumstances than any wider millenarian geopolitical tide.

The emergence of British Muslims as a distinct political group and voice can thus be traced to certain peculiarities of the British institutional framework of multicultural race relations. To begin with, British race relations legislation is a framework which does not provide minority rights as such, but rather allows—via the incremental extension of anti-discrimination claims to different groups through individual test cases—recognition to groups able to identify themselves as a publicly identified 'racial' group. This works as a kind of symbolic 'safety-valve' that offers a channel for ethnic minority claims and frustrations that would otherwise boil over into public demonstrations. Beyond the obvious allowances for 'Blacks' or 'Asians', the framework has allowed for certain 'visible' groups such as Sikhs and Jews to gain recognition, but crucially not Muslims, who are classified as a non-racial religious group. Although the Commission for Racial Equality (CRE) has identified this as a problem, there is little chance of this situation changing because the maintenance and coherence of the whole 'race relations' framework depends on the legal recognition—spelt out in the famous *Mandla* v. *Dowell Lee* case about Sikhs—that ethnic groups be seen to have a 'racial flavour'.[3] In other words, this block to anti-discrimination provisions for Muslim interests represents the limits of the adaptive properties that the self-styled 'evolutionary' race relations legal framework has depended on for securing successful integration.

Despite this, the framework has elsewhere at the same time encouraged the promotion of specifically cultural issues. Such issues are often channelled by offering representation for ethnic minority interests through specifically religious and ecumenical groups that are provided finances and concessions for building mosques and 'spreading the word', courted by local politicians, and strongly involved as 'religious' representatives in local civic affairs (Rex 1991; Lewis 1994; Joly 1995). An example is the Inner Cities Religious Council, a forum funded by the Department of Environment which liaises closely with the UK Action Committee on Islamic Affairs on questions of education, health, housing, and social services. A motive has thus been created and encouraged for 'Asian' groups to fight for distinction from the generic category of 'Black' in order to better pursue their political interests (Modood 1992; Gilroy

1990). One of the consequences of this split in ethnic minority interests has been the sidelining in social policy of inner-city issues about poverty and welfare in favour of cultural interests concerning education and language provision. This shift was reflected most notably in the controversial changes in focus of successive versions of the eventual Swann Report of 1985, *Education for All*, the report of a special commission set up to reflect on education provisions for Britain's ethnic minorities. After several resignations and attacks by Tory ministers and the press, the radically worded inner-city poverty concerns of the interim Rampton Report were abandoned in favour of a more conservative, consensual position that represented the balance of power held by Asian members of the committee (Swann 1985; Verma 1989; Modgil *et al.* 1986).

However, there are serious divisions within the Asian community along race, class, and urban lines. While middle-class Hindi or Tamil groups have prospered and thrived over the last twenty years—and often escaped entirely the damaging effects of racial prejudice and barriers to advancement—Pakistani or Bangladeshi groups have often not been so fortunate. They come from poorer rural backgrounds, have had greater problems with language and cultural adaptation, and—most crucially—have endured the same kinds of inner-city concentration and deprivations that West Indian blacks have faced: high unemployment, low achievement (see Samad 1992; *The Economist* 1995). Although religious identity has provided a focus for frustrations, the cultural concessions won by religious representation have often been at the expense of more targeted, interventionist social policies for these inner-city problems.

The intersection of three factors has thus pushed the creation of a distinct Muslim group: a group fuelled by grievances about institutional non-recognition and a poor, disfranchised social status, and encouraged by the promotion of religious and cultural forums as the place to raise these issues. The 'problems' specifically associated with Muslims in Britain are therefore the *side-effects* of an institutional structure that can be said to have had beneficial effects *overall* for ethnic minorities globally conceived (and the idea of a multicultural Britain generally). The reason Islam has in more recent years become a salient point of local political conflict in Britain—e.g. riots and political militancy in Bradford—is because the general framework of multicultural race relations has provided a structure of opportunities for such groups to use cultural issues to solder collective action in this way (Saggar 1991). It is absurd then to use the specific example of Muslims in Britain as fuel for crude rhetorical or normative conclusions about 'multicultural politics' generally conceived: that multiculturalism is therefore wrong and always leads to such so-called disintegrative, balkanized effects. 'Multiculturalism' in fact should be avoided as the frame of comparison for Britain in relation to other national cases, because it simply does not mean the same thing in different countries. Sensitivity to the rules of comparative research should underline the fact that the differences between national cases lie in the different ways they illustrate the institutionalizing of ethnic dilemmas into politically tractable terms: the way they are constructed and focused as issues of public policy (Gusfield 1981; Majone 1989). Across different national cases, we will find distinct constitutional frameworks for minority issues, differing legal mechanisms and categories for dealing with discrimination or protection, and different political forums as the sites for bringing problems into the open. Within these institutional frameworks, we will also find ethnic minorities behaving as we would expect any political actors to: in a rational, self-interested fashion, tailoring their interests to the structural opportunities on offer.

The Rushdie case of spring 1989 was the mainspring of the emergence of Muslim politics in Britain. As such, it has also been the perfect source of many poorly contextualized false interpretations that have failed to respect these comparative rules. The basic political and legal issue at stake was overlaid with a *fin de siècle* 'clash of civilizations' plot line, which orientalized the genuine anger and offence taken by Muslims—and their right to protest and affirm certain beliefs —into a series of grand ethical dilemmas about free speech, the limits of toleration and cultural flexibility, and the starting-line requirements of citizenship in the public sphere.[4] None of these frames for the issues involved is typical of the way ethnic dilemmas are usually dealt with by the institutions of race relations and multiculturalism in Britain. Cultural and anthropological east–west 'differences' were suddenly claimed to be the source of an impasse that reversed overnight the fairly benign and well institutionalized way Islam has established itself in Britain, free of the excesses of fundamentalism. Superficial links were made with the threat of fundamentalism in France, where the issues are very different because of the troubled French relations with its former colonies and the closeness of their political struggles.

This way of picturing the issues at stake thus actually denatured the specific form that the problem took in terms of Britain's institutions, and what might be learned about British multicultural race relations from the episode.[5] What should have been noted was the way the case revealed the lack of institutional recourse for Muslim groups to pursue a claim of discrimination through legal institutional channels, which was enough to mobilize even the most moderate groups to articulate their frustration angrily out in the streets. The lack of any clear legal distinctions between the public and private sphere on the question of a writer's right to blaspheme or ridicule—and hence the crude way in which questions of public morality get decided in populist moral major-ity terms—revealed weaknesses in the British legal system, grounded in a common law that offers no formal constitutional protection to minor-ity groups. The only available legal grounds for the Muslims was an inappropriate and archaic anti-blasphemy law protecting Christian texts that had last been used to prosecute a homosexual magazine in the 1970s. Moreover, the lack of institutional channels available for main-stream Muslim groups highlighted the over-representation in the media given to radical groups, particularly the 'Muslim parliament' group led by Kalim Siddiqui, a media-wise ex-journalist. Their prominence quickly died away, when starved of the oxygen of publicity given to them by paranoid Western fears about the imminent Islamic insurrection.

Muslim groups' behaviour should again, therefore, be explained as typical political action structured by the British institutional context, showing how much the issue was a dilemma about institutional recog-nition and representation. Perhaps at its widest it questioned the viabil-ity of the British idea of subjecthood and loyalty to the crown, when a minority has no constitutional guarantees or rights with which to voice its claims. The Muslims' cardinal sin was to question the sovereignty of British law, and apparently listen to the voice of a foreign leader. It is interesting, however, that, despite the media and public outcry, the behaviour of mainstream politicians most involved in the issue on both the left and right actually followed more closely the contours of the political institutional dilemma. They were listening no doubt to the underlying, longer-term political pressures involved in representing con-stituencies with significant Muslim populations, and the need to uphold the dominant institutional framework of race relations. Condemning the Ayatollah on the grounds of international law, they nevertheless were at pains to sympathize with the Muslim community, reaffirm religious

toleration and the multi-denominational idea of British multiculturalism, and generally seek to defuse and play down the issue rather than
use it for political capital.

However, the well-publicized and somewhat hysterical intellectual
interpretation of these events did certainly have a wider effect, and
contributed to the growing tension felt between 'Islam and the West'
that has significantly set back the integration of Muslim immigrants in
western Europe in recent years. It is an interpretation which reinforces
the thought that such ethnic dilemmas are somehow different from
other political dilemmas: in virtue of 'exotic' cultural differences or
some property of the minority themselves. This in turn makes the political problem harder to see through or diagnose. A political problem
can be created and heated up, or conversely played down and dissip-
ated, according to the way that actors and commentators picture it.
One has only to look at how much more political capital was made of
the Rushdie affair in France in the heated run-up to the *affaire du
foulard*, and the crucial role that this event played in cementing the
rejection of multiculturalism in France in favour of a new, revamped
republicanism.[6] To characterize another nation's politics falsely in
order to sustain a political position in one's own country is one of the
crudest forms of political argument. Yet, it is a strategy that has often
proved very effective in the field of ethnic politics. Academic comparative work surely must get beyond this interpretative pitfall, by the
careful differentiation of the way apparently common issues get translated into different institutional contexts.

## INTERPRETING A PECULIAR CASE 2:
## BRITISH EUROPHOBIA

> When you travel in Europe you are not protected by the Race
> Relations Act. Travel in Europe can often be a traumatic experi-
> ence for Britain's ethnic minorities—even when they have British
> passports. You could be hassled by an immigration officer, the
> police or racists in the country you are visiting. Unfortunately
> there's not a lot that can be done to help you from here . . .
>
> (Commission for Racial Equality/BBC Radio One,
> *Race Through the 90s*, 1994)

Our enquiry can be broadened by considering another of the curios-
ities of the British case: its negative behaviour in the last few years in

the face of European efforts to harmonize European anti-discriminatory measures and immigration policies, and the push to create citizenship rights or guarantees for minorities and non-nationals within the framework of the nascent European political system. Perhaps, on the face of it, this comes as no surprise, given the Conservative Party's well-known scepticism about Europe. Yet if we take a closer look at the reasons given by the right-wing Conservative former Home Secretary Michael Howard, for his rejection of new plans to harmonize anti-racist anti-discrimination laws at a European level, a more surprising fact emerges.

Many of the proposed measures are unnecessary and others would be counter-productive. The UK already has effective legislation. It would mean changing our laws in a very significant way for reasons that do not have much to do with the circumstances we encounter in Britain. We have a longer history of laws affecting race relations than almost any other country in the EU, more comprehensive legislation than any other country and better race relations than almost any other country. (*The Financial Times*, 25–6 November 1995)

Stirring words indeed, as are those quoted from the CRE publication above, advising young members of ethnic minorities about the hazards of travel in Europe. Right or left, they share the same conviction: a deep Europhobia, justified by the proud, almost whiggish belief in the progressive superiority of British anti-discrimination provisions and multicultural tolerance. What is remarkable about them is their similarity: how the Home Office and the left-wing race relations lobby in Britain have always put forward the same arguments for why the government must not dilute or weaken the familiar structure of race-based legislation, in order to harmonize with European efforts to reframe positive legislation in egalitarian or rights-based terms. Notably, it was lobby groups on behalf of new migrants and refugees and the Jewish community who reacted against Howard's statement, not the mainstream CRE. Indeed, prominent radical anti-racist activists went so far as to set up a rival organization in Brussels, the Standing Conference on Racial Equality in Europe (SCORE), to campaign *against* the main organization pushing for measures at the European level, the Forum for Migrants. British ethnic minority leaders refuse all association of their problems with the problems of new migrants, refugees, and immigrants on the Continent. The CRE has been hamstrung at a European level, and unable to endorse openly or participate in the formulation of much-needed new measures. The Labour Party had little to say on the subject, despite the obvious constitutional ramifications such legislation would have. Now, with New Labour in power, they uphold the race relations lobby's prejudice about the superiority of British legislation. There seems, in short, to be a curious consensus across the board on the content of Howard's argument. Indeed, the new Labour government immediately underlined its support for the existing institutional status quo, by asserting the sovereignty of British border and immigration control. Nobody, it seems, wants to start dismantling parts of this framework. There is hardly any space on the political agenda in Britain for challenging or questioning this consensus. Why is this? What is going on here?

The standard sort of explanation offered by British commentators might attempt to account for this in ideological terms. British resistance to European co-operation is the fault of certain residual insular ideas across the political spectrum that are historically anti-European and which only a more pronounced public shift towards a pro-European position could change: the self-serving British 'exceptionalism' again (Miles 1993). Yet this does not explain the fact that the resistance to change is on all sides justified in 'progressive' terms, in defence of the open, inclusive idea of British multiculturalism against what it sees as a downgrading effect that Europe would have (similar to Scandinavian worries about welfare and workers' rights). A similar weakness afflicts what is one of the most common litanies among British race relations writers: that it was just another example of the Tories 'playing the race card' again.[7] In fact, it is difficult to argue—particularly when viewed in comparative terms—that any real political capital has been made of populist racist or anti-ethnic feelings in elections since 1979, or that it is even a latent issue waiting to be tapped by a government passing some even more strict immigration controls (see Saggar 1996). The Conservative Party officially has spared no effort in portraying itself in politically correct terms on racial and ethnic issues, while feeling far less inclined to curb open outbursts of anti-European xenophobia. The anti-race relations right made a lot of noise in the late 1980s without effecting any significant policy changes. None of this goes to deny the prevalent existence of prejudiced and racist views among the public at large, but it is surely an enormously significant fact that, beyond a very small right-wing extreme, no significant political use is made of racist or anti-ethnic arguments in open political debate. This is something that cannot be said about France, Belgium, Germany, or Italy, or even countries widely recognized to be more open and accommodating than Britain, such as the Netherlands or Denmark (Baumgartl and Favell 1995). What explains this strange coalition that holds back the left from seriously challenging draconian immigration laws or pushing for more extensive Euro-legislation (indeed which finds the most vocal activists sounding like good 'one nation' patriots), and the Conservative Party from revoking race relations legislation, eliminating multiculturalism, or using racial and ethnic tension for easy political capital?

What we find is that, under the perpetual everyday conflict of rhetoric that sees both sides permanently seeking to distance themselves and compete over the issues, there is in fact a strong and broad underlying consensus across the mainstream left and right on the basic ideas, concepts, and terms of the institutional structure that has been put in place in Britain to deal with its particular ethnic dilemmas.[8] An open, inclusive idea of integration and the implementation of anti-discrimination commitments has been accepted by all sides as dependent on overtly strict immigration and nationality controls. These are said to have both created stable and relatively fixed ethnic minority groupings with the time and geographical concentration to establish themselves, and forestalled the threat of a hostile majority population reaction. The strategy has always been to allow integration to happen through civil and social processes, not through the channel of full political representation. This strategy has several key components: to keep the issues out of mainstream politics; to regulate problems paternalistically through a limited race relations framework that allows incremental symbolic recognition to publicly defined groups; to localize the representation of ethnic minority interests in religious and cultural groups; and to keep the issues well away from substantive questions about constitutional minority rights, citizenship, or welfare. It is thus, despite the forward-looking rhetoric of 'equal opportunities' and 'multiculturalism', an institutional structure built on profoundly conservative political ideas of nationalist subjecthood, common law, *laissez-faire*, and a traditional 'corporation and guilds'-based localized pluralism.

Moreover, it is axiomatic that the various elements of this structure stand together as a whole, such that a challenge to one part of it would threaten another part elsewhere. For example, associating new European migrants and asylum-seekers—whose claims are framed in terms of international human rights and refugee conventions—with existing British ethnic minorities might see their special anti-discrimination protection wound up in favour of a general bill of rights and equality for minorities. Or rethinking Britain's rationale for refusing the benefits of certain classes of economic migrants might threaten the special status that British 'Commonwealth' Asian groups currently enjoy. The unfortunate Hong Kong Chinese, for example, have fallen foul recently of this inflexibility. British passport-holders, they have found because of distinctions in the nationality law that their passports in fact offer no access to or right of abode in Britain, and so have instead taken their immigration applications (and often substantial personal capital) to countries such as Canada or Australia. Such inflexibility is typical of an institutional framework that has held firm for around twenty-five years, despite all the political change going on around it. Not least, it survived the enormous fundamental changes of the Thatcher decade, in which nearly every other institutional bedrock of the post-war political consensus was dismantled. And, characteristically, it has always been where the framework has struggled to adapt to new circumstances, or seen new emerging groups unhappy with the place it allows them, that the major problems in British race and ethnic relations have always surfaced.

If read in a certain way, the institutional structure of British multicultural race relations is by no means as *ad hoc* or unprincipled as it is often claimed. In many ways, its underlying 'philosophy' was mirrored in the widely discussed all-party reflection *Encouraging Citizenship* (Commission on Citizenship 1990), the report of an official commission of academics and public servants which spelt out the post-Thatcher consensus on the conditions and sources of British social ties and civility.[9] Although this report cited Marshall as an inspiration, it defended a profoundly un-Marshallian idea of citizenship: given that it does not contain a substantial idea of welfare rights or the exercise of political rights and participation in the public sphere as advancing the cause of social integration (although it does endorse private local voluntary and communal activism). These ideas do express a coherent, if idiosyncratic, philosophy: the rather communitarian combination of traditional English pluralism and cultural and religious toleration, perhaps best stated in the recent writings of several well-known 'English'— albeit some by adoption—philosophers (Raz 1986; Dahrendorf 1988; Dunn 1990; Gray 1993; Selbourne 1994; Nicholls 1994). That is, we can make much more sense of the peculiarities of the British case than either foreign observers or Britain's own writers on ethnic and racial studies have managed, by reading its home-grown idea of multicultural race relations as a curiously anachronistic version of classic conservative English liberalism: a political philosophy, in other words, in the tradition of Hobbes, Locke, and Mill.

If our question is one of understanding the distinctive shape of the institutional structure and the rationale that sustains the political consensus which underlies it, these guiding ideas should be our interpretative key. A sensitivity to such internal peculiarities is certainly the first step to understanding another country's politics and policies in a comparative manner. However, the accent on peculiarities still appears to put a barrier between inter-case comparison. Given this, a wider question must be asked: how can the understanding thus far reached of the respective political and institutional dimensions of the British case, be set in more general theoretical terms that enable a comparative explanation of it in relation to other European cases?

## EXPLAINING BRITISH AND EUROPEAN IMMIGRATION POLITICS

Thus far, my account of two distinctive peculiarities of the British case has concentrated solely on getting the interpretation of certain visible contemporary elements of the case-study right. I have put the emphasis on specifying the interaction of the recognizably political behaviour of actors and groups with the nationally specific institutional structure that the British framework of multicultural race relations represents. This naturally raises the explanatory question of how such an institutional structure for dealing with the new public policy problems of immigration and integration got there in the first place. Such a question is indeed the obvious way of broadening out our perspective on the British case into a fully comparative one, and can be posed as a general theoretical one: how and when a given set of political conditions and balance of political forces is able to respond to new social needs and circumstances with the innovative creation of new institutions.[10]

The most obvious suggestion would be to answer this question in the manner of Rogers Brubaker's (1992) now seminal comparison of France and Germany. That is, by reading the institutional 'philosophy' I have identified behind British multicultural race relations as the expression of a deep historical 'legacy': a national political culture of citizenship that can explain the emergence and evolution of the recent politics of immigration in Britain. It is here, however, that certain important distinctions need to be made between the historical 'cultural idioms'-based form of new institutionalism practised in this work by Brubaker, and a version of new institutionalism based on charting the

dynamics of more contemporary political forces.[11] An interpretation of
present-day politics in terms of a reworking of classical ideas from
British political philosophy is not yet an explanation of any kind. To
make this step would be to claim that these culturally rooted ideas
directly *cause* institutions and political behaviour within these institutions to take the shape they do. The historical effort of Brubaker's
work about France and Germany is to reconstruct the emergence of
this political culture during the nation-building of the nineteenth century in order to explain the politics of the present. Yet there is a deep
problem with this new-found fondness for political cultural explanations. Given his argument that the same nation-building is going on in
post-colonial France that went on during the Third Republic, Brubaker's
conclusion unsurprisingly is that Euro-resistant nation-state nationalism is doing fine. His work thereby underlines and reinforces many of
the Third Republic myths that have been assiduously reconstructed in
1980s France to justify a new nationalist republican version of citizenship, in the face of new currents of multicultural pluralism, regional
devolution, and supranational co-operation.[12] In other words, a political
cultural argument about nation-building ('we have always done things
differently here') is a perfect way of bolstering nationalism as a political option. It is the perfect self-serving 'neo-nationalist' strategy to
mask the political and institutional room for manœuvre that is always
there—particularly the new dimensions opened up by the European
question—in vague, obfuscating talk of national identities or cultural
idioms (see Feldblum, Chapter 7 in this volume). It also suggests that
fundamental institutional change is less possible than it really is: as
evidenced by Brubaker's bad call about reform to the 'sacred' idea of
*jus solis* in France, which did in fact come in 1993. All of which leaves
open the possibility that Brubaker might actually be right about the
resistance of the nation-state form, but be wrong in identifying the
causes as deep cultural or historical reasons rather than more contingent recent political factors.

The historical, political culture-based study of the origin of key political concepts and ideas may then be essential to the interpretative background of the subject (the palette of ideas that exist as reference-points
in political debates and justifications), but it is insufficient on its own
for explanatory questions raised about the political dynamics involved
in the emergence and evolution of new institutions. It is not enough,
for example, to claim that British race relations institutions simply
translated the traditional cultural pluralism of colonial practice into

home territory. This tells us nothing about the timing of their introduction, or the conditions that were required for it to come about: the
balance of political forces, the entrepreneurship that was needed, the
bargaining or trade-offs that took place, or indeed how ideas were used
to solder political agreement at a particular point in time (Hall 1989,
1993; Majone 1989, 1996; Goldstein and Keohane 1993). Nor, more
importantly, does it offer a great deal of insight into why those institutions have encountered difficulties over time, what new political forces
have developed within the tracks it provides, and the changes or break-
downs that may take place because of new conditions or external factors.[13] It misses crucially the key dimension of social change that has
occurred: why the Britain of today is a multicultural and multiracial
society profoundly transformed from the one that ruled over an empire
fifty years ago. 'Political cultural' exceptionalism is therefore no excuse:
British behaviour towards Europe is governed primarily by mundane
local political reasons, not by any impossible cultural or geographical
barriers or the weight of history.

An alternative kind of theory for explaining the emergence of new
citizenship institutions is put forward by Yasemin Soysal. Her case is
the emerging common European framework for dealing with immigration and citizenship questions, a 'post-national' institutional framework of citizenship policies that, she argues, is shifting the emphasis
of national politics away from neo-nationalist barrier-building, and working to break down national cultural particularities in practice (Soysal
1993, 1994). The European question of harmonizing legal and political
provisions indeed offers a test site of new institution-building in progress, which may reveal the mechanisms by which new institutions and
policy frameworks are able to emerge, as well as indicate the factors
or conditions which might be needed for an intransigent member state
such as Britain to change its behaviour over new proposals.

Soysal's argument for the convergence of national policies of immigration and integration in a single supranational framework of post-
national citizenship is one gratefully echoed by the arguments of
leading policy groups pushing for this at the European level. It is,
she argues, being pulled by a rational policy convergence and co-
ordination among the élite civil servants and policy-makers who have
to respond directly to the problems of new migration, refugees, and the
status of non-nationals; and pushed from below by the success of ethnic
groups and other lobby groups tailoring their actions to the given institutional structures, first at national levels and now increasingly at the

emerging international ones, such as the European courts and European social policy funding. In short, the emergence of new institutions is created by a mix of lobbying and activist partisanship, which responds rationally to objective needs and circumstances. And the language in which this process is argued for is the set of ideas associated with 'new citizenship' predominantly focused on the idea of formal legal guarantees. In practical terms this has been translated into the starting-line project for Euro-citizenship and the attempt to get minority guarantees into a revised version of the Treaty on European Union discussed at the Intergovernmental Conference of 1996–7. Other proposals seek to extend the developing immigration co-operation within the European Union's 'third pillar' of justice and home affairs on the back of the Schengen Agreement signed in the mid-1980s (Hix 1995).

The example of Britain, however, poses an anomaly for Soysal's perspective; as, on the face of it, does Brubaker's France. Although there is widespread evidence of emergent 'new citizenship' talk, and no shortage of 'behind-closed-doors' contact between responsible national civil servants and policy-makers at the European level, there are plenty of counter-currents in the mainstream 'open' politics (e.g. public democratic debate and electoral behaviour) in these two countries and others to suggest that national forms of dealing with the problems are likely to remain resistant and particular to the nations concerned. This is evidenced as much by the political potency of xenophobia or right-wing nationalist parties as by the open hostility of countries such as France and Britain to the new European proposals, consistently rejected on 'progressive' grounds—in defence of the benefits of their 'particular' national philosophies of integration. The nationally bounded models of citizenship and integration that sustain the distinct institutions that France and Britain have developed to deal with their dilemmas of immigration and ethnic conflict, are still far stronger unifying frames of reference for the issues and political perception of the public—what might be called 'policy paradigms' (Hall 1993)—than the vague promise of European new citizenship. As long as these national philosophies provide the grounding for the political responses to the problem, political forces are likely to hold back politicians from openly endorsing a European framework, no matter how strong the rational appeal of behind-closed-doors formulations. In essence, this is the classic dilemma of legitimacy spoken of as the 'democratic deficit' in Europe, where rational policy directives and formulations fail to seek or gain the public democratic recognition needed to establish their currency as a paradigmatic political framework. This is perhaps why, even where co-operation is achieved—such as the Schengen Agreement—it tends to reinforce the powers of the national governments rather than locating the powers elsewhere, and invariably falls short of its 'post-national' potential.

In short, a publicly recognized conceptual framework—on a par with the national philosophies of integration that ground French and British institutions—must be put together before the élite formulations of policy ideas and directives can become established new institutions. Such a framework has yet to be established at a European level, and the balance therefore still favours nationally bounded solutions. Soysal is right to build arguments with a mechanistic political institutional theory that seeks to downplay the longer-term historical, political culture-based explanations that Brubaker uses. However, her arguments are difficult to sustain empirically, at least for the French and British cases. The weakness in her theory does, however, reveal what is needed for the mechanisms to work: the critical element in establishing new institutions is the political dynamic which pushes policy-making out of the behind-closed-doors technocratic circles into a wider public democratic sphere.[14] In effect, this involves the political recognition of the issue as a distinct public problem and the creation of a whole new niche or policy focus. In the case of immigration, this entails creating a new policy language of categories that these groups can be fitted into, and conceptual ideals that spell out the goals of the integration process. There will indeed be much conflict and confusion politically and socially until this is achieved; the search is given urgency by the extreme reactions against the immigrants who are identified as causing the confusion. The expansion of the issue out of technocratic circles into wider democratic ones is thus a potentially dangerous process. In creating an open political issue out of the status and accommodation of immigrants–foreigners and so on, it opens up a large political space for reaction and xenophobia, and opportunities for populist politicians. Yet it is this opening up and heating up of the issue that provides the crucible for innovative ideas. My position is thus rather different to the one defended in this volume by Virginie Guiraudon (Chapter 8). Her case-studies find that the opening of the issue to the public democratic forum is in fact dangerous, and that advances in the building of new institutions can be made only by keeping the policy process behind closed doors or in the élite legal arena. As we will see, the British case in the 1960s and 1970s certainly contradicts this, and the current fears over the democratic deficit in European institutions certainly suggest that the public democratic forum can only be ignored at peril.

## RETELLING THE HISTORY OF MULTICULTURAL RACE RELATIONS IN BRITAIN

With these thoughts in place, it may now finally be possible to give a full account of the British case—tracing the emergence and evolution of its distinctive institutions (the path of institutional change) and diagnosing where it currently stands as regards Europe—in genuinely translatable comparative terms. In doing so, I hope also to vindicate the theoretical form of new institutionalism based on contemporary political dynamics that I have advocated throughout. In Britain new policy institutions did indeed emerge out of period in the late 1960s and early 1970s in which the issue of immigrants and the place of ethnic minorities in Britain became a heated, salient issue of party-political debate and conflict. And an open, socially inclusive conceptual frame of 'integration'—qualified by a set of inflexible, complex, institutional trade-offs—did become the one around which the mainstream parties found a consensual focus. However, the actual mechanisms by which this took place demonstrate a very un-whiggish sort of story, very different from the classic kind of Marshallian explanation for the emergence of the British welfare state: the happy evolutionary tale in which left-wing partisanship and campaigning from below achieved the incremental, expansive creation of new sets of legal, political, and social rights, and the transcending of class conflict in a nationally unifying idea of citizenship (Marshall 1950; Rose *et al.* 1969).

It was indeed a paternalist liberal lobby—led by Roy Jenkins in a brief spell as Home Secretary in the mid-1960s—that put forward the ideas that were to found the new British race relations institutions. These were inspired rhetorically by American civil rights language, but were transformed beyond recognition for the British institutional framework of common law and localized pluralism. But the power of the ideas themselves and the objective needs they responded to—violence in the streets and the growing intolerance of the white indigenous population—would have been insufficient to pull through any kind of reforms had it not been for the political dimension behind their development. Firstly, their very possibility was conditional on the Wilson government of 1964—and all successive Labour leaderships—immediately going back on its internationalist commitments and accepting that strict immigration restriction was an unavoidable necessity. Secondly, Jenkins's ideas were going nowhere until the dramatic intercession of Enoch Powell, a prominent right-wing Conservative, with his infamous 'rivers of blood' speech (April 1968), which thrust the political question of integration into the centre of British political life at the end of the 1960s. Powell's speech threatened to split the right over the issue of English nationalism and the stability of the British 'Union'.

It was thus the aligning of the main body of the Conservative Party with the need for a new institutional framework—focused on an idea of national integration able to incorporate the new ethnic minorities 'here to stay'—that proved the key. The threat of continued majority population reaction against these groups, and the destabilizing of the national political order, pushed the Conservative Party to join Labour in seeking to depoliticize the issue and take it off the mainstream political agenda (see Katznelson 1973: 123–51; Freeman 1979; Banton 1985; Messina 1989). Cast in the right way, reformist ideas on race relations and a multicultural Great Britain could be found to ring true with traditionally conservative principles about managing public order and devolving citizenship to localized, communitarian representation: something that has historically been the dominant practice of the élite English centre towards the various national peripheries of the 'United Kingdom'. The path of integration for the designated post-colonial immigrants— within strictly closed doors to further immigration or British nationality —was thus chosen as the best consensual point between left and right views on the subject, expressing a loose core of traditional British liberal ideas that all could agree on. The triumph of the 'liberal hour', then, was not down to any public ideological swing to 'progressive' ideas; but rather the outcome of a contingent political situation and wider political pressures on the 'Union' that favoured consensus across the mainstream political spectrum on creating a new open and inclusive framework around an idea of multicultural, 'multinational' Britain. For the main part, this consensus has held remarkably firm for twenty-five years, and provided a stable structure within which a new idea of Britain as a multicultural society has been able to evolve.

The left–right political dynamics of this story—incorporating the key role of 'ideas' in consensual policy framework building—suggests a more general explanatory model of policy-making in this field that could equally be found to apply to other cases such as France. The conditions for new institutions to emerge hinge therefore on the opening up of reformist ideas and policy formulations to the forces of public democratic debate and party political positioning. *If*, under pressure from extreme figures articulating 'exclusive' ideas of the nation, the issues become centralized in the open political mainstream and debated in publicly recognized terms across the political spectrum, and *if* the right finds an instrumental need to identify with the nationally inclusive frame being offered, *then* new institutions are able to emerge. What is of course characteristic of the framework of integration converged on in Britain—and other 'experienced' immigration societies such as France—is that it is a strictly bounded 'national' solution. This is typical of the post-colonial or the guestworker situation, where immigration is delimited by a special national 'responsibility' for strictly defined groups of immigrants, and where integration is predicated on tight border control and closed doors to new immigrants. Moreover, we have here the reason why national integration (or assimilation) policies *appear* deceptively to be one more instance of classical nineteenth-century nation-building, despite the paradoxical fact that the new immigration simultaneously undermines the fixed classical notions of nationhood and boundaries based on distinct cultures or peoples.

The problems associated with new migratory movements, refugees, and non-nationals, however, call for rather different institutional responses from those contained in the idea of integration for post-colonial immigrants or guestworkers. They call less for social and political assimilation into the host country culture than a devolution of responsibilities for rights and protection to agencies other than the traditional nation-state: whether local, federal, or supranational. Issues such as freedom of movement, welfare benefits, work rights, and legal protection for 'non-members'—the kinds of things being considered in European citizenship proposals for third-country nationals and so on—become more important than access to the full symbolic status of membership in the 'British' or 'French' nation. And, in an era of political deregulation and rolling back the state, it should come as no surprise that the state has lost powers over the rights, benefits, and freedoms it used to control and redistribute. Yet, to a greater or lesser degree, all of the west European countries with immigrants of the original kind tried to create a nationally bounded, nation-state-focused solution of integration. Those seeking to promote the expansion of rights and inclusionary measures thus find themselves hamstrung between the two different models of dealing with this family of 'ethnic dilemmas': national integration or post-national devolution. This is what might be called

Europe's 'British' problem, since it certainly is not limited to Britain's own 'European' problem.

Some of the conditions that might be expected to encourage new European institutions to emerge are to be found in certain European countries. In Germany, for example, where issues concerning ethnic minorities and immigrants have also become politically heated in recent years, the right has come to endorse a version of the 'post-national' multicultural solution. German politicians have sought a European institutional solution for the citizenship problems of resident ethnic minorities, because of the constitutional problem Germany has with its blood-based idea of nationality, and the large numbers of east Europeans returning to claim full German citizenship. Smaller countries such as Belgium endorse a European solution, both because they have failed to put together a coherent national-based solution, and because classic questions of boundary-drawing and nation-building are meaningless in an already heavily federalized political state. Britain's island status has protected it from the far greater impact of new migration felt in continental Europe, but it too will have to look for new solutions to the question of refugees, new economic migrants, and the presence and status of non-nationals. All of these raise questions that fit very badly within the existing nationally bounded framework of multicultural race relations.

The German example confirms that it is something irresolvable in the problematic issue of national identity and unity that is most likely to push a country away from national integration policies towards new forms of devolution. It is likely, then, that the increasing problematization of the British Union and the constitutional upheaval this would involve might be the background against which the current institutional framework for integrating ethnic minorities is forced to shift its focus to the European level. What is clear is that, if the British constitutional framework is challenged, many of the foundations on which British multiculturalism has been built will be threatened. British ethnic minorities are particularly vulnerable when their 'citizenship' is based on increasingly archaic ideas of subjecthood, and where they do not enjoy formal full political rights or representation as minorities, or any kind of minority status in a written constitution. The Thatcher years also helped destroy many of the traditional decentralized and local pluralist corporate structures that facilitated their integration through civil society. A European path of minority status and rights within a framework of Euro-citizenship might offer better security in the long run, but the short-term effect would be to deprive them of the special status they have enjoyed in the twenty-five years of British multiculturalism. Little wonder, then, that British ethnic minorities are so hostile to European proposals. In new institutionalist terms, this is a textbook example of suboptimal 'path-dependent' behaviour: a phenomenon increasingly characteristic of the inability of British institutions to evolve within the new European political context (see North 1990: 92–104).

## CONCLUSION

In this chapter, I have sought to break with the dominant indigenous and foreign interpretations of multicultural race relations in Britain, and instead locate the British case fully within the new emerging field studying the comparative politics of immigration and citizenship in western Europe. As I have emphasized throughout, fitting Britain into the scheme raises complex theoretical problems of interpretation and explanation. It is precisely the awkwardness of fitting Britain into any European and North American comparisons that makes it an interesting and important case. Such an approach offers a new way of reading British multicultural race relations and unlocks the paradox of why such a self-styled 'progressive' and advanced legislative framework has begun to have such seriously stagnant effects in recent years.

Most of the growing problems with British multiculturalism—associated with the European question and the increasingly undesirable side-effects that are emerging as it struggles to adapt to new conditions and demands—come from the fact that it embodies a curious idea of 'multiculturalism in one nation'. This is a brand of multiculturalism that is not in any way internationalist, as the idea of multiculturalism is generally understood to be. In the end, this makes the British institutional solution to its ethnic dilemmas an unstable one in an increasingly international and globalized field. In the final analysis, the functioning of British multiculturalism depends on the shaky idea of British national unity. As the Union creaks and crumbles, 'British' blacks and Asians might find themselves excluded from a re-emerging English nationalism. Their diasporic tendencies might get used against them, to delegitimize the place that they have found through integration into a multicultural Britain. Everyone remembers Thatcherite minister Norman Tebbit's famous cricket 'test', when he suggested that West Indian or Asian claims to be British could be assessed by asking who they supported in Test matches. The quietness and apparent success of racial and ethnic politics in Britain may prove an illusion in the near future, if the 25-year-old institutional solution—unable to adapt to new needs and conditions—proves to now be a set of ideas whose time is over.

## NOTES

This chapter is based on arguments spelt out in a full-length comparative study of Britain and France, from Macmillan, London, and St Martin's Press, New York (Favell 1997). I would like to thank the Leverhulme Trust, London for their financial assistance, the Chaire Hoover d'éthique économique et sociale, Université catholique de Louvain for nominating me Hoover Fellow 1995–6, and CEVIPOF for hosting me in Paris.

1. The respective 'standard' accounts are: the new right critique of Honeyford (1988); the orthodox liberal reading of e.g. Layton-Henry (1992), or Hiro (1991); and the radical critique inspired by the new field of 'cultural studies', e.g. Centre for Contemporary Cultural Studies (1982) or Gilroy (1987). The majority of the literature thus offers either the technical and descriptive policy-orientated approach characteristic of writers associated with the government quango the CRE, the influential non-governmental organization the Runnymede Trust, and the ESRC Centre for Research in Ethnic Relations at Warwick University; or it offers the thoroughly disenchanted vision of endemic 'institutionalized racism' in Britain, exposed by radical academics who combine post-Marxist and post-modern theorizing with openly polemical anti-racist activism. There are notable exceptions to this division of labour, works which I cite in the course of this chapter.

2. Arguments that have also been made much of by new right critics of British race relations: e.g. Honeyford (1988). For more sensitive discussions of the issues involved, see Poulter (1990), or CRE (1990*a*).

3. *Mandla* v. *Dowell Lee* (1983) HL 2 AC 548; see Bourne and Whitmore (1993) or CRE (1990*b*).

4. Such as in the well-publicized 'Counterblast' pamphlet by Fay Weldon (1989); see also press and other articles collected in Appignanesi and Maitland (1989). For a French perspective of this kind, see Kepel (1994, 'Les Versets britanniques').

5. Much more sensitive interpretations of the affair can be found in various writings by Parekh (1989, 1990*b*), and with Bhabha (1989). See also Mendus (1990) and Asad (1990). For important Muslim perspectives on the affair, see Ahsan and Kidwai (1991) and Akhtar (1989).

6. For example, the way false interpretations of the British case are used in Schnapper (1992), Todd (1994), and Kepel (1994) to bolster their 'high republican' arguments for immigration politics in France.

7. This is a rather lazy, 'taken for granted' explanation used by radical and liberal commentators on British race relations alike: e.g. in Gilroy (1987) or Layton-Henry (1992).

8. My argument here is spelt out in greater length in my reading of Britain in Favell (1997). It is essentially based on a close textual analysis of key official public documents in which the terms and language of the British 'philosophy of integration' have been defined and developed. Crucially, it is also the need to make sense of Britain in *comparison* with another national philosophy that enables this kind of reading. Among the principal documents I use are: Rose *et al.* (1969); jurisprudence of the Race Relations Act 1976; Scarman (1981); Swann (1985); reports by the CRE (e.g. CRE 1985); Commission on Citizenship (1990); and Commission on Urban Priority Areas (1985, 1990). Among indigenous British commentators, it is necessary to be highly selective. I find most helpful the kind of readings put forward by Parekh (e.g. 1990*b*); the work of Rex (e.g. 1991, 1996); Dummett and Nicol (1990); Modood (1992); Saggar (1991); Spencer (1994); and various writings by Crowley (e.g. 1993).

9. See Hurd (1988, 1989); numerous recent statements by the 'New' Labour Party; and, as a general statement of the post-Thatcher concerns, John Keane's interview with Ralf Dahrendorf (Keane 1990). For a critical view of these developments, see Crouch (1992), Phillips (1993, ch. 4).

10. This starting-point is, in effect, the theoretical starting-point of many other contributions to this field. Besides the work of Brubaker and Soysal which I discuss, see also Guiraudon's contribution to this volume (Ch. 8); and numerous essays by Freeman (e.g. 1992, 1995). Hall (1993) is the best theoretical attempt to formulate an answer in general terms; and for an application of the approach to the politics of immigration in the United States, see Schuck (1992).

11. For the distinction between the form of new institutionalism I defend and others, see the comprehensive literature survey by Hall and Taylor (1996). Mine is closest to what they call 'rational choice institutionalism', most clearly exposed by North (1990). Other uses of 'historical institutionalism' include Steinmo *et al.* (1992) and Putnam (1993).

12. See esp. the highly influential official reports on the subject: Commission de la Nationalité (1988), Haut Conseil à l'Intégration (1993).

13. My account is informed by theoretical ideas and terms of analysis in the work of North (1990) ('institutional performance; 'path dependency') and Hirschman (1991) ('pathologies'; 'effets pervers').

14. A model, adopted from Schattschneider (1961), that was revived by Baumgartner (1989). Schain (1988) and Guiraudon (Ch. 8 in this volume) also make use of this model.

# REFERENCES

Ahsan, M. M., and A. R. Kidwai (eds.) (1991), *Sacrilege versus Civility: Muslim Perspectives on 'The Satanic Verses Affair'* (Leicester: Islamic Foundation).
Akhtar, Shabbir (1989), *Be Careful with Muhammad!* (London: Bellew).

Alund, A., and C. U. Schierup (1991), *Paradoxes of Multiculturalism* (Aldershot: Avebury).

Appignanesi, Lisa, and Sarah Maitland (eds.) (1989), *The Rushdie File* (London: Fourth Estate).

Asad, T. (1990), 'Multiculturalism and British Identity in the Wake of the Rushdie Affair', *Politics and Society*, no. 18: 455–80.

Baldwin-Edwards, Martin, and Martin Schain (eds.) (1994), *The Politics of Immigration in Western Europe* (London: Sage).

Banton, Michael (1985), *Promoting Racial Harmony* (Cambridge: Cambridge University Press).

Baumgartl, Bernd, and Adrian Favell (eds.) (1995), *New Xenophobia in Europe* (The Hague: Kluwer Law International).

Baumgartner, Frank (1989), *Conflict and Rhetoric in French Policy Making* (Pittsburgh: University of Pittsburgh Press).

Bourne, Colin, and John Whitmore (1993), *Race and Sex Discrimination*, 2nd edn. (London: Sweet & Maxwell).

Brubaker, Rogers (ed.) (1989), *Immigration and the Politics of Citizenship in Western Europe* (New York: University Press of America).

—— (1992), *Citizenship and Nationhood in France and Germany* (Cambridge, Mass.: Harvard University Press).

Centre for Contemporary Cultural Studies (1982), *The Empire Strikes Back* (London: Hutchinson).

Commission de la Nationalité (1988), *Être français aujourd' hui et demain* (Paris: La documentation française).

Commission on Citizenship (1990), *Encouraging Citizenship* (London: HMSO).

Commission on Urban Priority Areas (1985), *Faith in the City: A Call for Action by Church and Nation* (London: Church House).

—— (1990), *Living Faith in the City: A Progress Report* (London: Church House).

Cornelius, Wayne, Philip Martin, and James Hollifield (eds.) (1994), *Controlling Immigration* (Stanford, Calif.: Stanford University Press).

CRE (Commission for Racial Equality) (1985), *Immigration Control Procedures* (London: CRE).

—— (1990), *Schools of Faith: Religious Schools in a Multicultural Society* (London: CRE).

—— (1994), *Second Review of the Race Relations Act 1976* (London: CRE).

Crouch, Colin (1992), 'Citizenship and Community in British Political Debate', in C. Crouch and A. Heath (eds.), *Social Research and Social Reform* (Oxford: Clarendon Press).

Crowley, John (1993), 'Paradoxes in the Politicisation of Race: A Comparison of the UK and France', *New Community*, 19/4: 627–43.

Dahrendorf, Ralf (1988), *The Modern Social Conflict: An Essay on the Politics of Liberty* (London: Weidenfeld & Nicolson).

Dummett, Ann, and Andrew Nicol (1990), *Subjects, Citizens, Aliens and Others: Nationality and Immigration Law* (London: Wiedenfeld & Nicolson).

Dunn, John (1990), *Interpreting Political Responsibility* (Oxford: Polity Press).

*Economist, The* (1995), 'Why Bradford Burned', 17 June.

Favell, Adrian (1997), *Philosophies of Integration: Immigration and the Idea of Citizenship in France and Britain* (London: Macmillan; New York: St Martin's Press).

Forbes, Ian, and Geoffrey Mead (1992), *Measure for Measure: A Comparative Analysis of Measure to Combat Racial Discrimination in the Member Countries of the European Community* (Sheffield: Employment Department).

Freeman, Gary (1979), *Immigrant Labour and Racial Conflict in Industrial Societies: The French and British Experience 1945–1975* (Princeton: Princeton University Press).

—— (1992), 'Migration Policy and Politics in the Receiving States', *International Migration Review*, 26/4: 1144–67.

—— (1995), 'Modes of Immigration Politics in Liberal Democratic Societies', *International Migration Review*, 29/4: 881–902.

Geddes, Andrew (1995), 'Immigrant and Ethnic Minorities and the EU's Democratic Deficit', *Journal of Common Market Studies*, 33/2 (June), 197–212.

Gellner, Ernest (1992), *Postmodernism, Reason and Religion* (London: Routledge).

Gerholm, Tomas, and Yngve Georg Lithman (eds.) (1988), *The New Islamic Presence in Western Europe* (London: Mansell).

Gilroy, Paul (1987), *There Ain't no Black in the Union Jack* (London: Hutchinson).

—— (1990), 'The End of Anti-Racism', *New Community*, 17/1: 71–83.

Goldstein, Judith, and Bob Keohane (eds.) (1993), *Ideas and Foreign Policy* (New York: Cornell University Press).

Gray, John (1993), *Beyond the New Right: Markets, Government and the Common Environment* (London: Routledge).

Gusfield, Joseph (1981), *The Culture of Public Problems* (Chicago: University of Chicago Press).

Hall, Peter (ed.) (1989), *The Political Power of Economic Ideas: Keynesianism across Nations* (Princeton: Princeton University Press).

—— (1993), 'Policy Paradigms, Social Learning and the State: The Case of Economic Policy Making in Britain', *Comparative Politics*, 25/3: 275–96.

—— and Rosemary Taylor (1996), 'Political Science and the Three New Institutionalisms', *Political Studies*, 25/4.

Haut Conseil à l'Intégration (1993), *L'intégration à la française* (Paris: La Documentation française).

Hiro, Dilip (1991), *Black British, White British: A History of Race Relations in Britain* (London: Grafton).

Hirschman, Albert O. (1991), *The Rhetoric of Reaction* (Cambridge, Mass: Harvard University Press).

Hix, Simon (1995), *The Intergovernmental Conference and the Future of the Third Pillar*, Briefing Paper no. 20 (Brussels: Churches Commission for Migrants in Europe).

Hollifield, James (1992), *Immigrants, Markets and States: The Political Economy of Western Europe* (Cambridge, Mass.: Harvard University Press).

Honeyford, Ray (1988), *Integration or Disintegration? Towards a Non-Racist Society* (London: Claridge Press).

Hurd, Douglas (1988), 'Citizenship in the Tory Democracy', *New Statesman*, 27 Apr.

—— (1989), 'Freedom will Flourish where Citizens Accept Responsibility', *Independent*, 13 Sept.

Ireland, Patrick (1991), 'Facing the True Fortress Europe: Immigrants and Politics in the EU', *Journal of Common Market Studies*, 29/5: 451–80.

—— (1994), *The Policy Challenge of Ethnic Diversity: Immigrant Politics in France and Switzerland* (Cambridge, Mass.: Harvard University Press).

Joly, Danièle (1995), *Britannia's Crescent: Making a Place for Muslims in British Society* (Aldershot: Avebury).

Joppke, Christian (1996), 'Immigration and Multiculturalism: A Comparison of the US, Germany and Britain', *Theory and Society*, 25/4: 449–500.

Katznelson, Ira (1973), *Black Men, White Cities* (Oxford: Oxford University Press).

Keane, John (1990), 'Decade of the Citizen', interview with Ralf Dahrendorf, *Guardian*, 1 Aug.

Kepel, Gilles (1994), *A l'ouest d'Allah* (Paris: Éditions du Seuil).

Lapeyronnie, Didier (1993), *L'Individu et les minorités: La France et la Grande Brétagne face à ses minorités* (Paris: Presses universitaires françaises).

Layton-Henry, Zig (1992), *The Politics of Immigration* (Oxford: Blackwell).

Lewis, Philip (1994), *Islamic Britain: Religion, Politics and Identity among British Muslims: Bradford in the 1990s* (London: Tavistock).

Lukes, Steven (1993), 'Five Fables about Liberty', in Stephen Shute and Susan Hurley (eds.), *On Human Rights* (New York: Basic Books).

Majone, Giandomenico (1989), *Evidence, Argument and Persuasion in the Policy Process* (New Haven: Yale University Press).

—— (1996), 'Public Policy: Ideas, Interests and Institutions', in Robert Goodin and Dieter Klingemann (eds.), *New Handbook of Political Science* (Oxford: Oxford University Press).

Marshall, Thomas H. (1950/1992), 'Citizenship and Social Class', in T. H. Marshall and Tom Bottomore, *Citizenship and Social Class* (London: Pluto).

Mendus, Susan (1990), 'The Tigers of Wrath and the Horses of Instruction', in Bhikhu Parekh *et al.*, *Free Speech* (London: CRE).

Messina, Anthony (1989), *Race and Party Competition* (Oxford: Oxford University Press).

—— *et al.* (1992), *Ethnic and Racial Minorities in Advanced Industrial Democracies* (London: Greenwood Press).

Miles, Robert (1993), *Racism after 'Race Relations'* (London: Routledge).

Modgil, Sohan, *et al.* (1986), *Multiculturalism: The Interminable Debate* (London: Falmer).

Modood, Tariq (1992), *Not Easy Being British: Colour, Culture and Citizenship* (London: Runnymede Trust and Trentham).

Nicholls, David (1994), *The Pluralist State*, 2nd edn. (London: Macmillan).

North, Douglass (1990), *Institutions, Institutional Change and Economic Performance* (Cambridge: Cambridge University Press).

Parekh, Bhikhu (1989), 'Between Holy Text and Moral Void', *New Statesman*, 24 Mar.

—— (1990*a*), 'The Rushdie Affair: Research Agenda for Political Philosophy', *Political Studies*, 38: 695–709.

—— (1990*b*), 'The Social Logic of Pluralism', in B. Parekh *et al.*, *Britain: A Plural Society* (London: CRE).

—— and Homi Bhabha (1989), 'Identities on Parade: A Conversation', *Marxism Today* (June).

Phillips, Anne (1993), *Democracy and Difference* (Oxford: Polity Press).

Poulter, Sebastian (1990), *Asian Traditions and English Law* (London: Runnymede and Trentham).

Putnam, Robert (1993), *Making Democracy Work: Civic Traditions in Modern Italy* (Princeton: Princeton University Press).

Raz, Joseph (1986), *The Morality of Freedom* (Oxford: Clarendon Press).

Rex, John (1991), *Ethnic Identity and Ethnic Mobilisation*, Monographs in Ethnic Relations no. 5 (Warwick: CRER).

—— (1996), *Ethnic Minorities in the Modern Nation State* (London: Macmillan).

—— and Beatrice Drury (eds.) (1994), *Ethnic Mobilisation in a Multi-Cultural Europe* (Aldershot: Avebury).

Rose, E. J. B., *et al.* (1969), *Colour and Citizenship: A Report on British Race Relations* (London: Oxford University Press).

Saggar, Shamit (1991), *Race and Public Policy: A Study of Local Politics and Government* (Aldershot: Avebury).

—— (ed.) (1996), *Race and British Electoral Politics* (London: Prentice-Hall).

Samad, Yunas (1992), 'Book Burning and Race Relations: Political Mobilisation of Bradford Muslims', *New Community*, 18/4: 507–19.

Scarman, Lord Leslie (1981), *The Brixton Disorders 10–12 April 1981: Report of an Enquiry* (London: Penguin).

Schain, Martin (1988), 'Immigration and Changes in the French Party System', *European Journal of Political Research*, 16: 597–621.

Schattschneider, E. E. (1961), *The Semi-Sovereign People: A Realist's View of Democracy in America* (New York: Free Press).

Schlesinger, Arthur D. (1992), *The Disuniting of America: Reflections on a Multicultural Society* (New York: Norton).

Schnapper, Dominique (1992), *L'Europe des immigrés: essais sur les politiques de l'immigration* (Paris: Bonnin).

Schuck, Peter (1992), 'The Politics of Rapid Legal Change: Immigration Policy in the 1980s', *Studies in American Political Development*, no. 6: 37–92.

Selbourne, David (1994), *The Principle of Duty: An Essay on the Foundations of Civic Order* (London: Sinclair-Stevenson).

Solomos, John, and John Wrench (eds.) (1993), *Racism and Migration in Western Europe* (Oxford: Berg).

Soysal, Yasemin Nuhoglu (1993), 'Immigration and the Emerging European Polity', in S. S. Anderson and R. A. Eliassen, *Making Policy in Europe: The Europification of National Policy* (London: Sage).

—— (1994), *Limits of Citizenship: Migrants and Postnational Membership in Europe* (Chicago: University of Chicago Press).

Spencer, Sarah (ed.) (1994), *Strangers and Citizens: A Positive Approach to Migrants and Refugees* (London: IPPR and River Oram Press).

Steinmo, Sven, K. Thelen, and F. Longstreth (eds.) (1992), *Structuring Politics: Historical Institutionalism in Comparative Perspective* (New York: Cambridge University Press).

Swann, Lord (1985), *Education for All*, House of Commons, Cmnd. 9453.

Todd, Emmanuel (1994), *Le destin des immigrés: assimilation et ségrégation dans les démocraties occidentales* (Paris: Éditions du Seuil).

Verma, G. K. (ed.) (1989), *Education for All: A Landmark in Pluralism* (London: Falmer).

Weldon, Fay (1989), *Sacred Cows*, Counterblast pamphlet (London: Chatto & Windus).

# INDEX